BUSINESS DATA COMMUNICATIONS

David A. Stamper

University of Northern Colorado
Greeley, Colorado

The Benjamin/Cummings Publishing Company, Inc.

Menlo Park, California • Reading, Massachusetts • Don Mills, Ontario
Wokingham, U.K. • Amsterdam • Sydney • Singapore
Tokyo • Mexico City • Bogota • Santiago • San Juan

To Virginia

Sponsoring Editor: **Susan Nelle**
Production Supervisor: **Wendy Earl**
Cover and Consulting Designer: **Gary Head**
Copy Editor: **Elliot Simon**
Composition: **Vera Allen Composition**

The basic text of this book was designed using the Modular Design System, as developed by Wendy Earl and Design Office Bruce Kortebein. The art was produced by Vera Allen Composition on ViewTech, a CAP system.

ENCOMPASS,™ Pathway,™ and Non-Stop™ are registered trademarks of Tandem Computers Incorporated.

Library of Congress Cataloging in Publication Data

Stamper, David A.
  Business data communications.

  Includes bibliographies and index.
  1. Data transmission systems.   2. Computer networks.
I. Title.
TK5105.S734 1986   004.6   85-15803
ISBN 0-8053-9104-5

CDEFGHIJ-HA-89876

The Benjamin/Cummings Publishing Company, Inc.
2727 Sand Hill Road
Menlo Park, California 94025

Contents in Brief

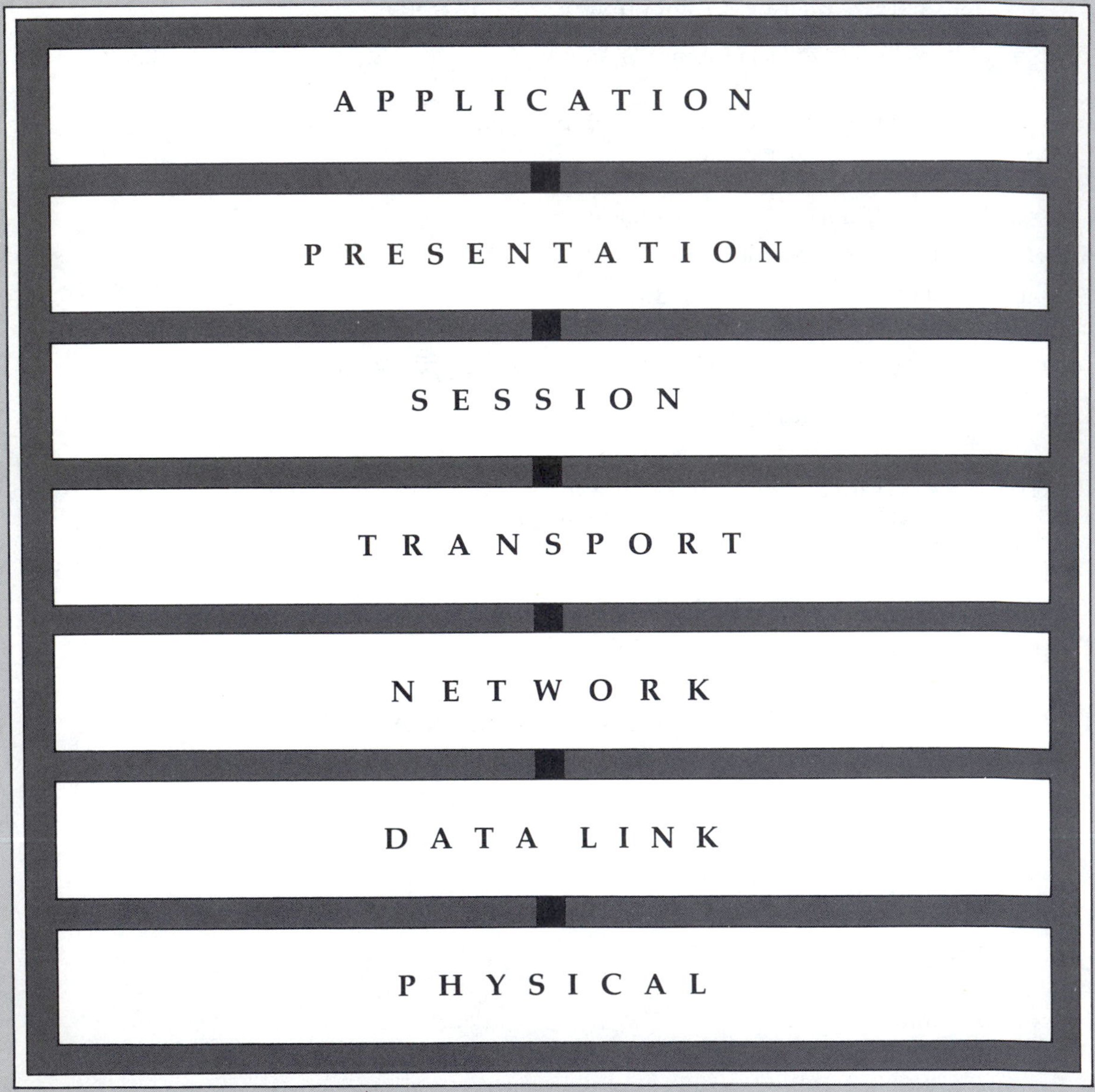
APPLICATION
PRESENTATION
SESSION
TRANSPORT
NETWORK
DATA LINK
PHYSICAL

Preface

This text is designed for an introductory course in data communications. An increasing number of business schools require or recommend such a course as part of the information systems curriculum.

Scope of the Book

Business Data Communications was written to meet an unfulfilled need. A sizable number of texts are available, but they are either too technical or they lack the breadth of coverage required in an information systems curriculum.

This textbook provides a balance between the technical aspects of data communications and related managerial issues. A number of features distinguish this text from others on data communications.

Organization of the Text

The chapter organization follows the seven layers for Open Systems Interconnection from the bottom up. These seven layers, established by the International Standards Organization, are shown in the flowchart on the facing page and are reflected in the part opener titles.

Supplemental Sections

Chapters 6, 7, and 9 each contain a supplement that provides additional, in-depth details about the chapter and its business implementation. For example, the chapter supplement on data link protocols discusses the requirements of a data link protocol and includes brief descriptions of asynchronous, character synchronous, and bit synchronous protocols. It explores the advantages and disadvantages of each protocol and describes "typical" implementations. The supplement also includes session examples, control information, and a discussion of how character messages are formed. Let the level of the curriculum determine whether to assign the supplement as review reading, as new material, or not to assign it all. The existence of the supplements as separate units makes this book suitable for short overview courses as well as detailed presentations of introductory data communications.

International Aspects

Data communications is not restricted to national boundaries. Wherever possible, differences between U.S. and international standards and usage, and their associated unique problems, are covered.

Learning Aids

Each chapter begins with an *introduction* highlighting the major topics within the chapter. A *chapter summary* concludes every chapter and is followed by *review questions* and a *chapter bibliography. Key terms* are indicated in italics throughout each chapter.

 A realistic *case study* illustrating data communications applications appears in many chapters. The case examples are identified by the symbol shown at the left.

Acknowledgments

I am grateful to the numerous individuals who contributed to the preparation of this textbook. First, thank yous go to the reviewers who gave us many excellent suggestions for improving the text. Those who reviewed the text were Herbert Bomzer, Central Michigan University; John Crane, TymShare Integrated Systems; Ralph Duffy, North Seattle Community College; John Gotwals, Purdue University; Mary Loomis, University of Arizona; Doug May, Appalachian State University; and Mary Newton, Austin Community College.

Much appreciation goes to the editorial and production departments at Benjamin/Cummings. In particular, I wish to thank Susan Nelle (Editor) and Wendy Earl (Production Supervisor) for their ideas, encouragement, and support.

David Stamper
Greeley, Colorado

Contents

PART IV   NETWORKS AND SYSTEM SOFTWARE: THE NETWORK, TRANSPORT, AND SESSION LAYERS

APPLICATION

PRESENTATION

SESSION

TRANSPORT

NETWORK

DATA LINK

PHYSICAL

I

INTRODUCTION: OVERVIEW AND HISTORY

Chapter 1: Introduction to Data Communications

1

Introduction to Data Communications

INTRODUCTION

This book provides an overview of *data communications*, a field so extensive that there are entire books devoted to each chapter topic presented here. You will find in this text sufficient detail to familiarize you with the terminology and capabilities of data communications systems, and your mastery of this material will enable you to participate in decisions regarding alternative configurations of data communications components.

A data-processing system may be viewed as an integration of subsystems that aid in solving business or scientific problems. Common subsystems include the operating system, database management system, languages, applications, and data communications. Each of these subsystems is implemented as a combination of software, hardware, and/or firmware. This text will discuss each data communications subsystem along with its *interfaces* with the other subsystems. These relationships are depicted in Figure 1-1 on page 2.

What is meant in this text by the term *data communications*? Although the terms *telecommunications* and *data communications* have become almost synonymous in some circles, there is a distinction between them.

Figure 1-1
An Applications
Environment

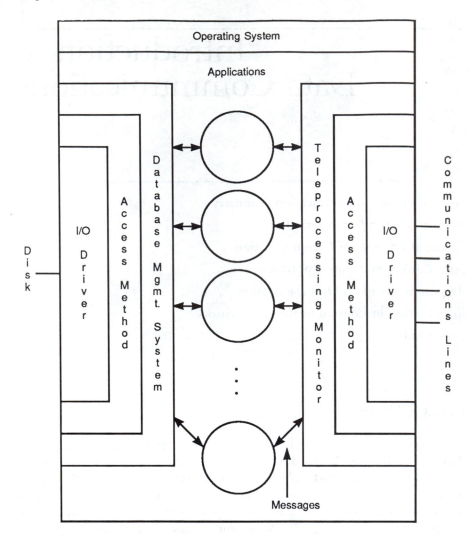

Telecommunications vs. Data Communications

James Martin (1972, p. 654) gives a broad definition of *telecommunications*:

> Any process that permits the passage from a sender to one or more
> receivers of information of any nature delivered in any usable form
> (printed copy, fixed or moving pictures, visible or audible signals, etc.)
> by means of any electromagnetic system (electrical transmission by
> wire, radio, optical transmission, guided waves, etc.). Includes teleg-
> raphy, telephony, video-telephony, data transmission, etc.

This definition is too broad for the scope of this book, which will
present only that portion of telecommunications involving the transmis-

sion of data to and from computers and components of computer systems. Data communications thus can be defined as that part of telecommunications that relates to computer systems, or the electronic transmission of computer data. This definition excludes the transmission of data to local peripherals such as disk, tape, and printers.

System Complexity

Data communications systems may be simple or complex. A simple system might be composed of a processor and a number of terminals, all located within a single building. Figure 1-2 illustrates the hardware components of such a system, that is, the terminals, processor, and user-provided wiring. A more elaborate system might consist of numerous processors and terminals in multiple locations, all connected via communications lines leased from a common carrier (such as a telephone company) and via microwave and satellite transmission. Figure 1-3 on page 4 depicts a system that meets this description. These two figures should provide insight into the variety and complexity of communications systems. The illustrated components will be discussed in later chapters.

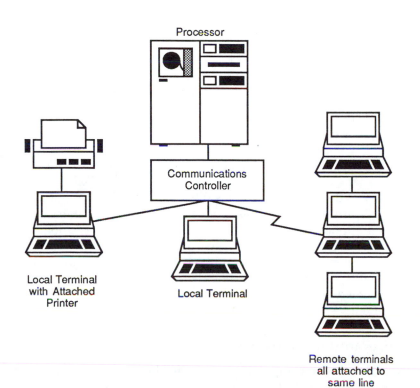

Figure 1-2
A Simple Data Communications System

Figure 1-3
An Expanded Data
Communications
System

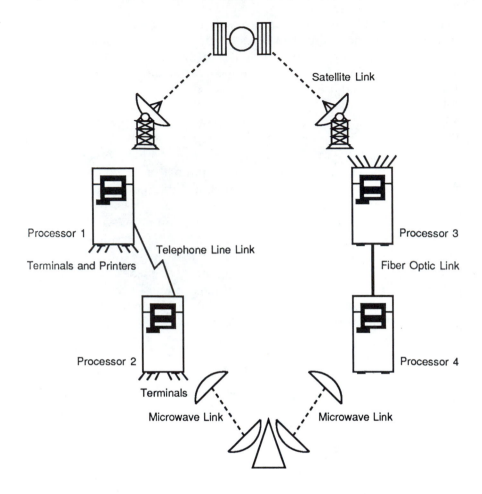

HISTORY OF THE COMMUNICATIONS INDUSTRY

The history of data communications differs significantly from that of other computer technologies, such as languages, hardware, database management, and applications. Because data communications is a joint venture between the communications industry and the computer industry, development has been a combined effort. And because the telephone companies have been the primary source of long-distance communication circuits, this history begins with the state of telephone companies at the advent of the computer era.

Early Communications Networks

By the dawn of the computer era in 1940, the communications industry was already well established. Telephone and telegraph companies had developed a network of communications facilities throughout the industrialized world. In the United States and numerous other countries, telephone companies had been given exclusive rights to install lines and to provide services in specific geographical areas, with government agencies exercising control over tariffs and the services provided. This situation benefitted both the telephone companies and consumers. The objective of the system was to provide service at an affordable rate. However, some users paid less than the actual cost of service while others paid more. Essentially the pricing structure worked as follows.

Every individual was to have access to telephone service at a reasonable cost. Service was to be provided to all geographical areas, irrespective of remoteness or population density. That is, small, remote towns were to have the same type of service as large metropolitan communities, and at approximately the same rates. If the total cost of installing lines and switching equipment in a small town had actually been borne entirely by users in that town, the cost of service would have been prohibitive to most residents. Therefore, loss incurred in such a town was offset by profits from other geographical areas. There were three major sources of profit in the United States: the major metropolitan areas, businesses, and long-distance service. The large metropolitan areas were profitable because of economies of scale and density of installations. Business rates were much higher than rates for individuals because the value received was ostensibly greater (since the telephone was being used to generate income) and because the businesses could afford to pay more. Finally, long-distance tariffs were set high so as to subsidize those portions of the system operating at a loss. The service thus provided was generally good, and prices reasonable for each class of user. (Note that two of these profitable segments— business and long distance—also pertain to data communications.)

In addition to having exclusive rights to transmission facilities, the telephone companies in the United States and numerous other countries had exclusive rights to attach any equipment to the telephone networks. This means they had a monopoly on the equipment needed to transmit and receive data, such as modems (devices for changing a computer's signal from digital to analog format for transmission along a *medium* such as telephone lines, and then converting the signal back to digital format at the receiving end. See Chapter 2 for more on modems.) With such exclusive rights, phone companies also could turn the sale or lease of such equipment to profit, which is exactly what U.S. telephone companies did.

System Growth

Partly because of this monopoly on equipment, as well as the special status given providers of data transmission facilities, the growth of data communications was somewhat slower than that of other computer-related technologies. The development of databases, languages, operating systems, and hardware components was strong from the 1950s through the early 1970s, but large-scale expansion of data communications systems really did not occur until the 1970s. The growth experienced then was primarily the result of three developments:

1. Large-scale integration of circuits, with the attendant reduction in the cost and size of terminals and communications equipment

2. Development of software systems that made the establishment of data communications *networks* relatively easy

3. Competition among providers of transmission facilities with an associated cost reduction for data circuits.

Without these developments, data communications systems would have been financially unfeasible for many computer users.

This last point may be illustrated by comparing transmission costs in 1968 and 1973, just before and after competition appeared. In 1968, American Telephone and Telegraph Company (AT&T) charged an average of $315 for 100 miles of leased telephone line. In 1973, the average cost of the same line was as low as $85. Furthermore, a simple teletypewriter terminal (TTY) that sold for $2595 in 1971 could be replaced in 1975 for $750, and the 1975 terminal had more features than the older model. In July 1971, an IBM model 3270 terminal cost $71,000 (with a lease price of $1900 per month). In early 1985, the equivalent terminal listed for $6035!

HISTORY OF DATA COMMUNICATIONS

The development of the first electronic computer is variously attributed to Howard Aiken, IBM, and Harvard University—for the MARK I; to John Atanasoff and Clifford Berry at Iowa State—for the ABC (Atanasoff, Berry Computer); or to John Mauchly and J. Presper Eckert at the University of Pennsylvania—for the ENIAC (Electronic Numerical Integrator and Calculator). Work on each of these machines started prior to 1940 and the machines were fully operational by the early to mid-1940s. Other computer and sophisticated calculator projects were undertaken in parallel with these efforts, and some were actually operational sooner.

The Role of Computers

Data communications was present at the beginning of the computer era—long before there were any operating systems, high-level languages, assemblers, or databases. In 1940, data was transmitted remotely from three sites to a Bell Laboratory computer in New York City. This computer, called the COMPLEX computer, had been developed to perform complex calculations for the U.S. military. Later that year, Bell Lab publicly demonstrated this communications capability by transmitting data via a modified tele-typewriter circuit from Dartmouth University in Hanover, New Hampshire, to a computer in New York City.

In 1948, there was a court case not specifically related to the data communications industry that eventually had a significant impact on it: the *Hush-a-Phone case*. Recall that telephone companies in the United States had a legal monopoly over all equipment attached to their networks, to keep anyone from attaching devices that might interfere with or destroy signals and equipment in the network. When the Hush-a-Phone Company developed and marketed a passive device (no electrical or magnetic components) to be installed over the transmitting telephone handset so as to block out background noise and provide more privacy, AT&T threatened to suspend service for users and distributors of the device. Hush-a-Phone appealed to the Federal Communications Commission (FCC). After numerous hearings, the FCC decided in favor of AT&T. In 1956, however, an appeals court overturned the FCC ruling and decided in favor of the Hush-a-Phone Company, holding that no harm to the AT&T network would result from use of such a device. This precedent opened the door for other companies to attach equipment to the telephone networks. The tariff as modified by this decision stated that "[the telephone company would not] prohibit a customer from using a device that served his convenience so long as the devices did not injure the telephone system, involve direct electrical connection to the system, provide a recording device on the line, or connect the telephone company line with any other communication device." [Kleinfield, 1981]

In 1951 the first commercial computer, a UNIVAC I, was sold to the U.S. Bureau of the Census; the first private commercial computer was installed in 1953 at the General Electric Research Park in Louisville, Kentucky. Just one year later, IBM introduced *Remote Job Entry (RJE)* communications. RJE involves input from a remote location, and optional remote output, via a data transceiver, a device that transmits and receives card images remotely. One RJE application is depicted in Figure 1-4.

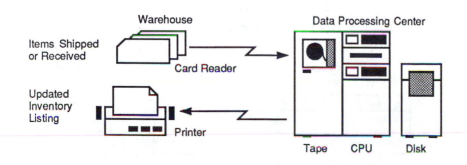

Figure 1-4
Remote Job Entry

Satellites and Microwave Transmission

The National Aeronautics and Space Administration (NASA) launched the first U.S. communications satellite in 1958. It was used to broadcast President Eisenhower's Christmas message. That year also saw the advent of one of the first major data communications networks, the *Semi-Automatic Ground Environment (SAGE)* radar early warning system, installed by the U.S. Department of Defense to provide early warning and fire control in the event of nuclear attack. Work continued on the SAGE project until 1961, by which date it consisted of more than 1.5 million miles of communication lines. The SAGE configuration is given in Figures 1-5 and 1-6.

The door to greater competition for communications circuits opened further when the FCC approved private microwave communications networks in 1959. That is, a business could establish its own microwave transmission network if the network was used only for that company's data. The owner of such a network was prohibited from selling or leasing transmission facilities to other companies or to individuals. Having much the same impact as the Hush-a-Phone case, this decision helped set the stage for competition in areas previously the exclusive domain of the telephone and telegraph companies.

The first *geosynchronous* orbiting satellite, SYNCOM II, was launched in 1963. In geosynchronous orbit, which requires an altitude of approximately 22,300 miles, a satellite maintains a fixed position relative to the earth. A geosynchronous orbit ensures that a satellite will be permanently stationed over one point on the planet and hence be continuously available for communication between all points in its range, for instance, between North America and Europe.

Figure 1-5
The SAGE Early
Warning System

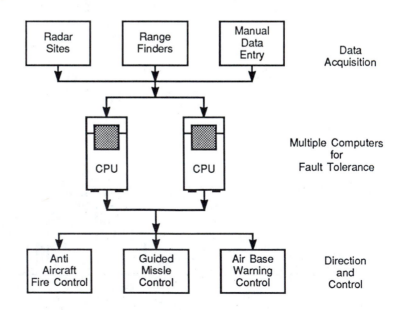

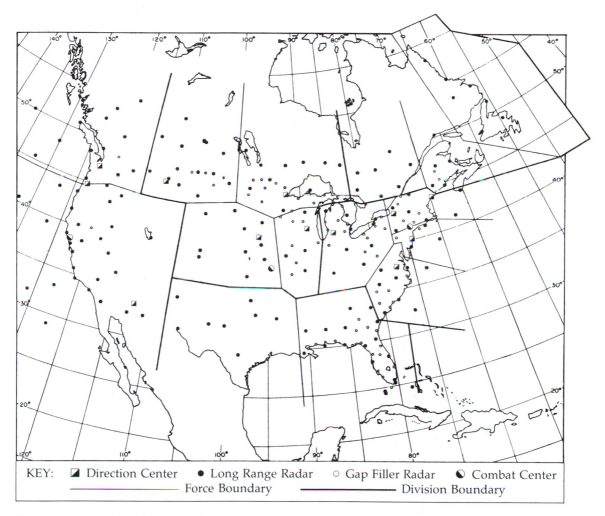

Figure 1-6 The SAGE Radar Environment

Also in 1963, Microwave Communications Incorporated (MCI) filed with the FCC to provide microwave communications services between Chicago and St. Louis, their objective being to sell data transmission circuits to private industry. AT&T objected to MCI's petition on the grounds that MCI could operate at much lower overhead than AT&T, since MCI—unlike AT&T—would not have to serve the lower-volume markets, such as Montana, Wyoming, Idaho, and Kansas. Despite AT&T's objections, MCI received approval for the communications link in 1970. Since then, MCI has expanded into other major metropolitan areas. It added an individual telephone service (Execunet) in 1975, by which date MCI had service to 24 cities. This start of heavy competition for data transmission circuits in the United States has led to lower rates for data communications users.

Transaction Networks

Two major data communications events occurred in 1964. The first was the completion of the ten-year development of the *Semi-Automatic Business Research Environment (SABRE)* network, a joint venture of IBM and American Airlines. The SABRE system, depicted in Figure 1-7, handles airline reservations. It was one of the first major *on-line transaction processing* systems. With on-line transaction processing, a business transaction such as reserving a seat on an airplane, placing an order for goods, or withdrawing money from a bank account is recorded in the business database at the time the transaction occurs, rather than being recorded at a later time (a *batch* system). There has been considerable growth in on-line transaction processing since the introduction of SABRE.

Figure 1-7
An Airline
Reservation System

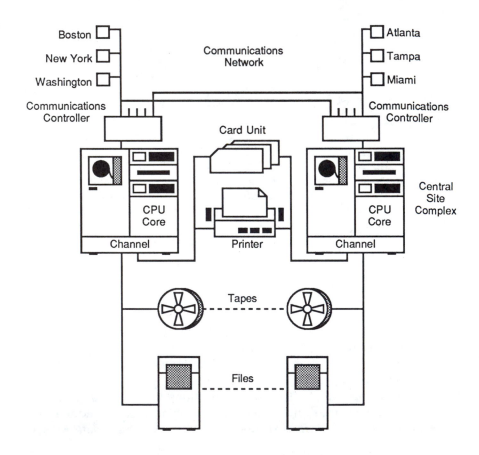

The second milestone of 1964 was not a new system but a new concept. The Rand Corporation introduced the idea of a packet switching network, or *packet distribution network (PDN)*. A PDN divides a user's message into specific-sized packets, or units of transmission. These message packets are reassembled at the receiving end. In 1969, the Advanced Research Projects Agency (ARPA) of the U.S. Department of Defense established the first two links in a packet switching network known as ARPANET, which has since been expanded to over 100 sites. Other packet switching networks as well have been developed throughout the world. PDNs are discussed in more detail in Chapter 7.

Another court case important in opening data communications to competition occurred in 1966: the *Carterphone case* (also spelled Carterfone). Carter Electronics Company had been marketing a radio telephone system that allowed for communication between a moving vehicle and a base station via radio wave transmission. Since the original Carterphone was unable to forward a call to another location, the company introduced a device that could pass on the radio transmission through a telephone network. AT&T objected to attaching the Carterphone to its network on the grounds of potential harm to the network and violation of the FCC prohibition against connecting an outsider's communications device to AT&T's telephone line. The 1968 ruling was in favor of Carter Electronics. As an outgrowth of the decision, it became legal for any device to be attached to the telephone network provided the telephone companies were allowed to install a protective device between the "foreign" equipment and the network. This provision later was changed to allow connection of FCC-approved equipment without any protective devices. This made it legal to attach other manufacturers' communications equipment to the network, and led to improved products, at lower prices. As another side effect of the Carterphone decision, individuals were allowed to purchase and install their own telephone sets.

Local Area Networks

A *local area network (LAN)* is a communications network all of whose components are located within several kilometers of each other. Major uses of LANs include (1) exchange of data at high speed between computers within a local area, (2) factory or production control, and (3) *office automation*. The original specifications for ETHERNET, one of the most publicized LANs, were published by the XEROX Corporation in 1972. Later, Digital Equipment Corporation (DEC) and Intel joined XEROX in developing ETHERNET further. LANs and ETHERNET are discussed in greater detail in Chapter 8.

Data Link Protocols

A *data link protocol* governs the flow of data between sending and receiving stations. The original data communications *protocols* were borrowed from the telegraph and telephone industries. In 1967, IBM introduced the binary synchronous (BISYNC or BSC) protocol for use in RJE applications, later expanded for wide use in other applications. In 1972, IBM introduced the synchronous data link control (SDLC) protocol, which has become the prototype for many contemporary data link protocols. Data link protocols are discussed in more detail in Chapter 6.

System Network Architecture

In 1974, IBM introduced its System Network Architecture (SNA). Its significance is twofold. First, since IBM has long dominated the computer industry, SNA will probably set the industry standard. Second, since all communications networks on IBM systems are meant eventually to conform to SNA, other manufacturers participating in networks utilizing IBM equipment will probably have to provide some type of interconnection to SNA.

In 1975, General Telephone and Electronics TELENET system became operational. TELENET is a packet distribution network that provides transmission circuits the charges for which are based on the number of packets transmitted rather than on connect time. This provides a cost effective mechanism for many data transmission applications. An additional benefit is that the circuits provided reach many locations. Figure 1-8 shows the cities connected by TELENET as of early 1985.

Divestiture

The final historical event we shall mention is the AT&T *divestiture*. As of early 1985, the total impact of this breakup of AT&T was still being determined. Changing prices for transmission services and new entrants into both the data communications marketplace and the computer marketplace are already obvious. AT&T had been prohibited from entering the computer market, and other companies, including computer manufacturers, had been prohibited from entering the communications arena. Now that these restrictions are gone, AT&T is selling its own line of computers. And IBM, MCI, Southern Pacific Communications, and other companies have entered the data transmission business.

There is little doubt that data communications technology will continue to expand at a rapid rate, effecting a marked change in the manner in which businesses are run and by which individuals communicate and work. The combination of low-cost computational power and efficient, economical data transmission has the potential for social change equal to that created by the automobile and the telephone.

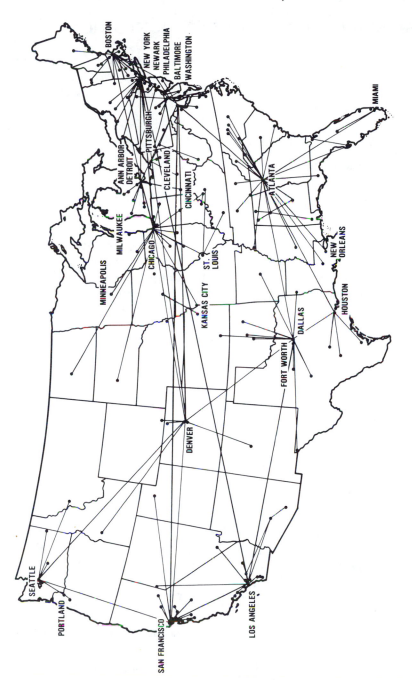

Figure 1-8   Cities Connected by TELENET

ESSENTIAL FEATURES OF COMMUNICATION

Communication has several essential features. In order for communication of any type to occur, there must be a *message*, a *sender*, a *receiver*, and a *medium*. In addition, the message must be *understandable* and there must be some means of *error detection*.

Message

For two entities to communicate, there must be a message, which can assume a number of forms and be of varying length. Data communications message types include a file, a request, a response, status, control, and correspondence. These are illustrated in Figure 1-9.

A File.   With Remote Job Entry (RJE), one of the first applications of data communications, messages were transmitted from a remote location to a processor. The message there was the entire card file. In computer networks where several processors are connected together, it is not unusual for complete or partial files to be transferred between processing units.

A Request.   In on-line transaction processing, one may request that the computer processor(s) take some type of action, such as display information, update the database, or "logon" or "logoff."

A Response.   A request ordinarily receives a return message, or response. In the case of an inquiry for information, the response is either the information requested or an error message indicating why the data was not returned (for instance, *security* violation, information not on file, or hard-

Figure 1-9
Types of Messages

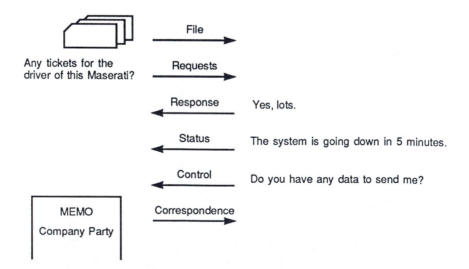

ware failure). For a database update transaction, the response could be either an explicit message that the action was performed, an error message, or an implicit acknowledgment that the transaction has been performed successfully such as a progression to the next transaction.

Status. A status message, which can be sent to all users or only selected users, reveals the functional status of the system. For example, if the system must be halted for scheduled maintenance, then a status message might be broadcast to all users to enable them to bring their work to an orderly halt.

Control. Control messages are transmitted between system components. For instance, an automatic teller machine (ATM) might indicate to the controlling computer that it is out of cash; a printer might indicate that its buffer (information storage area) is full and cannot receive additional data; or the message that a new processor has been added to the network might be routed to all other processors, thus updating routing tables.

Correspondence. Correspondence involves messages sent from user to user. Such messages include electronic mail systems, where memos and correspondence may be routed between employees of a company. There are also systems that transmit document images, provide bulletin board message posting, or enable telephone-like *interactive* communication.

Sender

The sender is the transmitter of the message—either a person or a machine. Frequently the sender is a computer or terminal with enough intelligence to originate a message or response without human intervention. The sender can also be a system user, sensor, badge reader, or other input device.

Receiver

Receivers include computers, terminals, remote printers, people, and devices such as drill presses, furnaces, and air conditioners. There can be a message and a sender without there being a receiver; however, without a receiver, there is no communication. Thus, signals have been beamed into outer space in an attempt to contact other intelligent life forms; until these signals are received, no communication has taken place. In a computer system, a message could be sent to all terminals indicating that a new system feature is available; if all terminals happen to be turned off at that time, no communication will have occurred.

Medium

Messages are carried from sender to receiver through some medium of communication. For instance, in oral communication, sound waves are transmitted through air (the medium). Data communications uses a number of media to transmit data, including wires, radio waves, and light pulses. Media are discussed in the next chapter. Figure 1-10 illustrates the sender, receiver, medium, and message in a telephone connection.

Understandability

Even if all the components just discussed are present, if the message is not understood, then communication has not taken place. In human communication the most obvious obstacle is language differences, for which a translator or interpreter may be necessary. Computer systems have similar obstacles to communication. For instance, data can be represented by any of several different codes, the two most common being the American Standard Code for Information Interchange (ASCII) and Extended Binary Coded Decimal Interchange Code (EBCDIC). Sometimes it is necessary to translate from one code to another to ensure that data are interpreted correctly.

Error Detection

In human communication, we as receivers can frequently detect errors because we are able to reason and interpret. Grammatical errors, misspellings, and even some misstatements can usually be corrected by a human receiver. (For example, if a teacher mistakenly gives the distance between the earth and the sun as 93 million *light years* rather than 93 million *miles*, we would probably realize the error and presumably even

Figure 1-10
The Essential
Features of
Communication

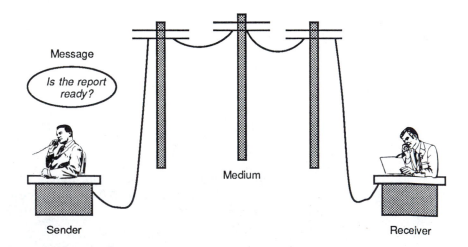

correct it.) But computer networks generally don't reason. And even when a human computer operator realizes that a received message is erroneous, that operator may be unable to correct the error. When the receiver is a piece of hardware, incapable of reasoning and unable to detect or correct errors, it becomes necessary to employ special schemes for determining if an original message has been distorted during transmission. All such schemes involve transmitting additional information along with the data, to increase the chances of detecting errors without eliminating the possibility that the received data actually may be erroneous. Error detection is discussed in Chapter 3.

DATA COMMUNICATIONS APPLICATIONS

The myriad applications of data communications can be grouped into several broad categories: *inquiry/response, interactive, batch, data entry, distributed*, and *sensor-based*. Note that the categories are not mutually exclusive; that is, some transactions may fall into more than one category.

Inquiry/Response Applications

In this type of application, inputs generally have only a few characters and output responses have many. Inquiry/response applications typically involve requests to display information. For example, a police inquiry might consist of a drivers license number and the response could be several thousand characters of information, detailing the driver's name, address, driving record, etc. In a hospital application, a nurse might input the nurse's station number (consisting of relatively few characters) and the output would likely consist of several thousand characters giving each patient's name, status, medicial requirements, and so on.

Interactive Applications

The interactive type of application is characterized by relatively short inputs and outputs. The computer system would generally prompt the user for an input, eliciting a relatively short response. Since the sender and receiver are essentially conversing with each other, this application is sometimes referred to as *conversational*. This type of application is frequently used for on-line transaction processing with terminals that do not allow the entering of an entire screenful of information and for applications in which the user's response dictates the next prompt, such as certain computerized games. Figure 1-11 on page 18 gives an example of an interactive session used to add a name and address to a file. Prompts are italicized; responses are not.

ENTER LAST NAME:	JOHNSON
ENTER FIRST NAME:	RALPH
ENTER MIDDLE INITIAL:	F
ENTER STREET ADDRESS:	123 MAIN STREET
ENTER CITY:	SYDNEY
ENTER STATE:	COLORADO
ENTER ZIP CODE:	80201

Batch Applications

Batch applications, including RJE, are characterized by large data transfers in two directions. For instance, information from a batch of inventory cards might be transferred from a warehouse to a remote computer center, and in return the warehouse would receive an updated inventory list. In some batch applications, large amounts of data flow in one direction only (which actually resembles data entry—see next section). When a sales representative records sales on a portable computer terminal, but waits until the end of the workday to transmit the entire day's orders, this results in a large amount of data flow in one direction and little or no data flow in the other direction.

Data Entry Applications

Data entry applications consist of lengthy inputs with short responses. For example, there is a credit card authorization system in Australia in which input for a "batch" of receipts consists of credit card number, merchant number, and charge amount, plus the batch total. The system then calculates its own batch total and compares it with the input total; if the figures agree, the only response is a prompt to continue entering the next batch.

Distributed Applications

Distributed applications are characterized not so much by input and output size as by whether the data or the processing or both are distributed among a number of processing units. Thus, requests as well as data will flow between a number of system components, with possibly some parallelism in data access and processing. Order entry is an example of this type of processing. When an order for an item is entered, the system tries to determine if the item is in stock in any of its several regionally located warehouses. Since each warehouse will have its own computer system and will maintain its own local inventory, the system will likely inquire into these remote databases to find a location with sufficient stock to fill the order. The system will then update the inventory at the location(s) from which the order is to be filled, update the invoicing and accounts receivable at the accounting location, and supply the ordering location with a shipment date and other relevant data.

Office automation systems are a special case of distributed systems, one in which both data and processing are distributed among several different components. Applications include word processing, communications between members of the corporation via electronic mail, spread sheet analysis, graphics, and facsimile generation for presentations, reports, and contracts.

Sensor-Based Applications

Sensor-based applications involve special data-collection devices for such uses as controlling temperature in buildings, monitoring and maintaining patient condition in hospitals, and controlling a manufacturing process. The processor receives data from the sensors, and if necessary takes control action.

REQUIREMENTS OF AN ON-LINE SYSTEM

Although data communications applications are quite diverse, almost all of them have certain basic requirements that must be met. These are: *performance, consistency, flexibility, availability, reliability, recovery,* and *security.*

Performance

System performance can be measured in a number of ways. Two very common measures are response time and transaction rate (or throughput). Response time refers to the amount of time a user must wait between entering data and receiving a reply. Transaction rate, or throughput, is the amount of work performed by the system per unit of time.

Response Time Versus Throughput.   At first it may appear that fast response time and high throughput are equivalent. Actually the opposite is sometimes true. For example, banking transactions in which customers are involved might be deemed deserving of quick response time. Optimizing the speed of such transactions might slow down other processing activity, such as batch reporting. Thus, although response time in customer transactions might be reduced, the total amount of banking work accomplished declines. In a truly successful system, both response time and throughput are optimal.

Transaction Rates.   Transaction rates (for example, processing 100 transactions per second) are often quoted as a measure of system performance. However, this type of performance measure is meaningless without more information, because all transactions are not alike, and even similar transactions may have a wide variance in the amount of processing required. For transaction rates to be a meaningful measure of performance, one must ascertain first what work is being accomplished and then the techniques used to perform the work. Let's consider a simple hospital transaction: assigning a patient to a room.

One hospital might implement this function as transaction A, whereas another might implement it as transaction B. The time required for each of these transactions is considerably different.

Transaction A.   Find a vacant room for the patient and remove the room from the list of vacant rooms. A total of two data reads and two data writes are required. For this exercise we ignore other time-consuming activities, such as searching index tables within the database management system. A profile of the transaction is given in Figure 1-12.

Figure 1-12
Activities for
Transaction A

Obtain vacant room list header from memory location

Read vacant room record

Read patient record

Update vacant room list header in memory from room record

Rewrite room record linked to patient record

Rewrite patient record

Transaction B.   In this transaction it takes more work to assign a patient to a room. But it also includes building a room charge record and issuing patient supplies. The activities are outlined in Figure 1-13.

Figure 1-13
Activities for
Transaction B

Obtain vacant room header from memory

Read vacant room record

Read patient record

Update vacant room header from room record

Rewrite room record linked to patient record

Read related charge record for room

Write charge record for patient

Read standard patient issue record

Write patient charge record for issue of supplies

Rewrite patient record

The second transaction does twice as much work as the first, yet both are patient admission transactions. Thus, whenever transaction rates are quoted as a measure of system performance, it is necessary to gather additional information not only about what is being measured, but also about transaction response times.

Response Time.   Response time is the time interval between entering a message and obtaining the response. Some define the measurement interval as being from the end of the entry to the appearance of the first response character; others define it as the interval from the end of the entry to receipt of the final response character. The difference between the two can be significant. For example, if the speed of the communications circuit is 30 characters per second and the response consists of 1200 characters, then the response time by the first definition is 40 seconds less than that by the second definition.

Response time has two major components, the time required for data transmission and the time required for processing. (Each of these components has subcomponents.) This text deals only with data transmission time.

Consistency

A consistent system is one that works in a predictable manner, both with respect to the people who use the system and with respect to response times. If, for example, the system has a HELP function that provides operational information to the user, there should be a consistent transaction code to invoke the HELP function and to display the HELP data.

Inconsistent response time is extremely annoying to system users, and in fact is sometimes worse than a slow but consistent response time. Of course, complete consistency is difficult to achieve (because of occasional periods of heavy processing). Frequently, one system design objective is for the response time of most transactions of a given type—say, 95%—to be lower than a certain threshold—say, 3 seconds. It would be quite disconcerting if 50% of these transactions took 3 seconds, 20% took 10 seconds, 15% took 30 seconds, 10% took 1 minute, and 5% took over a minute. Such inconsistency is not only frustrating, but it limits the effectiveness of the system.

Flexibility

One thing typical of on-line systems is that they change. For instance, users might want to alter the types of transactions available, change the data format, expand an application, or add new applications. This means that both growth and change must be accommodated, and with minimal impact on existing applications and users. The ability to increase processing power, terminals, communication circuits, and database capacity is critical to the long-term success of a system.

Expandable Modular Systems. Since the ability for growth in an on-line system is extremely important, users of a product line that lacks a wide span of equipment will have a limited growth path; and if the business and application grow, they will need to acquire systems from another manufacturer. This almost always means a time-consuming and difficult conversion. If a manufacturer does have a wide range of products that offers the user a long growth path, the growth may nonetheless require exchanging processing equipment. That is, when the applications have grown to a certain point then the user must acquire the next larger processor in the product line. Another option, that of acquiring the larger system at the outset, in anticipation of growth, may be unduly costly because users are paying for more than they actually need. To solve this problem of growth, several companies have designed computing systems especially for the on-line transaction marketplace. These systems allow for modular growth, in modest increments, to protect the user's investment in software (no conversion) as well as cash flow.

Another important feature of these expandable on-line processing systems is *fault tolerance*, that is, the ability to continue processing despite component failure. Figure 1-14 shows a Tandem Computer NonStop™ TXP transaction processing system that offers fault-tolerant operations and modular expansion. A fault-tolerant system is one in which single points of failure will not cause system failure. A graphic of the Tandem system is presented in Figure 1-15. It illustrates a system composed of multiple processors and peripherals, which can be configured so that no single point of failure will disable the system. Thus, if a processor fails, its workload will be assumed by one or more of the remaining processors; if a disk drive fails, its mirror drive will continue to provide the required information. Thus, every component in the system has a backup component that takes over in the event of a failure. Furthermore, the components are not passively awaiting failure; all are active and contribute to the overall throughput of the system. More specifically, every processor is active in the processing of transactions. If one processor should fail, the remaining processors absorb its activities. If these processors had already been at peak capacity, then response times will likely be degraded, but the applications continue and users will probably be unaware that a processor failure has occurred.

In addition to protecting against hardware failures, fault-tolerant systems also provide backup for continuous processing in the event of software failure.

Availability

An on-line system must be continuously available to the user community during the workday. In some cases this means 24 hours a day, every day of the year. In some applications the unavailability of the on-line system can result in significant financial loss to a business. For example, an airline might be unable to sell seats on a flight if the reservation system is down, or it may overbook a flight, which will necessitate extra work for the employees and possible penalty payments to travelers for their inconvenience. Availability is discussed in more detail in Chapter 9.

Reliability

Reliability is an important system attribute that should not be overlooked. It is a measure of the frequency of system failure, and in some ways com-

Figure 1-14   Tandem Computer's NonStop™ TXP/TPS
Tandem Computers Incorporated

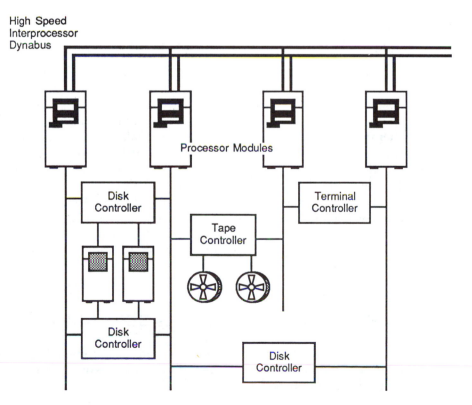

High **Speed**
Interprocessor
Dynabus

Processor Modules

Disk
Controller

Disk
Controller

Tape
Controller

Terminal
Controller

Disk
Controller

Figure 1-15
The Basic Architecture of the Tandem NonStop™ System

bines consistency and availability. A system failure may be described as any event that prohibits users from processing transactions. This includes a breakdown in hardware, such as a processor failure in a system that is not fault tolerant, as well as an application or system software failure, or the failure of the medium (such as a faulty data communications line). *Mean time between failure* (MTBF) is a measure of the average time a given component may be expected to fail, and *mean time to repair* (MTTR) is the average time required to fix a failed component. Both figures are important in determining the frequency of failure and the time required to return the system to successful operation. Reliability is discussed in more detail in Chapter 9.

Recovery

All systems, even those built for continuous operation, are subject to failure. In some cases it may not be the system that fails, but the people who operate it or the source of power. Regardless of the cause, the system must be able to recover to a consistent point—that is, the point where the database has no partially updated transactions, no transactions have been processed twice, and no transactions have been lost. System users should also be advised of the state of all work they had in progress at the time of failure, to keep them from submitting a duplicate transaction or from failing to reenter a transaction not received prior to failure.

Security

Security has become increasingly important in data communications applications now that the personal computer has made computer networks accessible to almost everyone (as is evident from the recent reports about computer hobbyists "invading" computer systems across the country). Furthermore, now that more businesses are making use of data communications, the number of accessible computer systems is greater than ever before, thus making a vast amount of sensitive information available, including financial data and classified military information. Unfortunately, security has not always received a high priority in system and network design, so making up for these deficiencies will be a necessity in the development of future systems and in enhancing existing ones. Systems security is discussed in more detail in Chapter 10.

INTRODUCTION TO COMMUNICATIONS NETWORKS

This section discusses two definitions of computer networks and some functions common to them. The functions described will become the basis on which subsequent chapters are developed.

Computer Networks

What exactly is a computer network? First, a computer network can be defined as a single computer, called a *host*, together with communications circuits, communications equipment, and terminals (see Figure 1-2 on page 3). A computer network can also be defined as two or more computers connected via a communications medium, together with associated communications links, terminals, and communications equipment (see Figure 1-3 on page 4). In this definition the host computers are referred to as *nodes*. In Figures 1-2 and 1-3, the communications links are depicted by lines attached to nodes. These are sample configurations only, actually, there is a wide variety of configurations in use, and for one application there may be several viable configurations.

The only difference between these two definitions is the number of computers involved; the second definition can be thought of as referring to a network of computers or systems. In general, the term *computer network* refers to such a network of computers. This definition also includes such major data communications networks as an airlines reservation system with miles of communication lines, a large central processor, and over 1000 terminals, many of which contain some degree of processing power and are able to participate in the processing of transactions.

Computer Applications and Configurations

Ignoring for now the distinction between the two definitions, several different applications and configurations of computer equipment will be presented.

Company X.   This company provides a service to trucking companies that enables their drivers to cash script at truck stops throughout the country. This has the advantages that drivers do not need to carry large amounts of cash for long trips, truck stop owners are guaranteed against losses from bad checks, and the trucking companies need not provide significant cash advances to their drivers. The communications network consists of approximately 50 terminals located in the same building as the host computer in Company X's office. Truck stop employees can telephone data entry personnel on a toll free number to receive authorization to pay the driver (or call the police). The total amount of money allocated to the driver then is updated on the computer files. All links between computer and terminals are local and controlled by Company X, that is, not leased or purchased from a common carrier such as a telephone company. The Company X configuration is depicted in Figure 1-16 on page 26.

Company Y.   This service company is involved in the automated preparation of tax returns. Its clients are accounting firms who contract to use Company Y's computer facilities and software. Depending on the size of the accounting firm, clients may elect to have a private, dedicated communications link to the host computer, or they can share a communications link with other users. Clients who share a telephone link will compete with each other for access to the telephone lines available. For example, if these are 50 lines shared by 150 clients, each client would typically use the connection fewer than 3 hours per day. Ordinarily, then, there will not be much competition for these shared lines. But just before the April 15th income tax filing deadline, clients may dramatically increase their use of the system, so availability of the communications links will become a problem. If a client needs a line more than 3 hours a day, it would likely be more economical to use a dedicated line. The Company Y configuration is depicted in Figure 1-17.

Company Z. This multinational company manufactures and markets computer systems. Every large sales office has a demonstration computer, and all of these computers as well as computers in the software development facility, home office, and manufacturing plants are linked in one large network, consisting of over 100 nodes and approximately 3000 terminals. Company Z is forward-thinking and uses in addition to long-distance telephone lines and local, private lines, a number of newer transmission facilities: fiber optics, to link computers located within 1 kilometer of each other; satellite communications for long-distance high-volume transmission between manufacturing plants and divisional offices; and packet switching networks (these types of media are all discussed in Chapter 2). A drawing of the Company Z configuration is represented in Figure 1-3 on page 4.

These three companies have greatly different network configurations, yet each network is ideal in that it solves its business's problem in an effective, cost-efficient manner. Both Company X and Company Y could have installed a network similar to that of Company Z, with terminals at client locations and computers in the larger clients' offices; unfortunately,

Figure 1-16
The Company X
Configuration

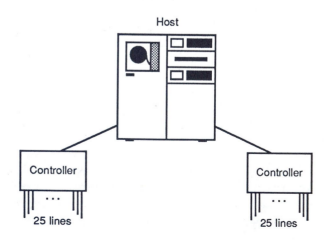

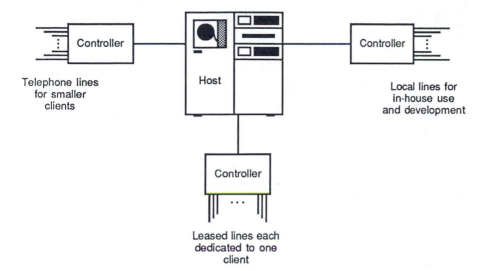

Figure 1-17
The Company Y
Configuration

Telephone lines
for smaller
clients

Host

Controller

Local lines for
in-house use
and development

Leased lines each
dedicated to one
client

doing so would also probably mean they would have to charge considerably more for their services and thus lose their competitive edge.

Comparing these three dissimilar installations illustrates that there are a number of different alternatives available to a system designer and that any of numerous configurations can probably solve the communications requirements. A few such alternatives might be highly cost effective, a number may be only mediocre, and a few might actually drive the company into bankruptcy. It is important to realize that there are usually several "right" approaches, not just one.

Hierarchy of Functions

Fortunately, a description for a hierarchical or layered set of functions that every network must fulfill has been provided by the *International Standards Organization (ISO)*.

To contend with the growing number of different computer networks being developed, and in the belief that these diverse systems would eventually need to be connected, the ISO has identified and stratified the functions that every network must fulfill. With such a definition it becomes less difficult to develop interfaces between these different networks.

The recommendation of the ISO is called the *reference model for open systems interconnection (OSI)*, or the ISO OSI recommendation. Most of the details of this reference model are found in the chapters on networks (Part 4), but since the OSI model is used as a road map for the development of this text, a brief description is provided here. This discussion also provides an overview of communications systems in general.

OSI Functional Layers

The OSI recommendation identifies seven functional layers, as shown in Figure 1-18: application, presentation, session, transport, network, data link, and physical. The objective of any data communications network is to exchange data between applications or between users. To do this, the information to be transferred must be formatted, packaged, routed, and delivered. The receiver must then unpackage and possibly reformat this information. These are essentially the functions performed by the seven layers.

Figure 1-19 depicts the layers in two different processors. The information from the *application layer* in processor 1 moves down through the lower layers in its node until it reaches the *physical layer*, which physically transmits the data to the physical layer in processor 2. The data then work their way up through the layers in processor 2 until they reach the application layer of that processor.

Each layer in the sending processor performs work for, or acts on behalf of, its peer layer in the receiving processor. Thus, *presentation layers* support

Figure 1-18
The Seven OSI
Layers

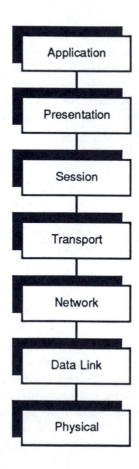

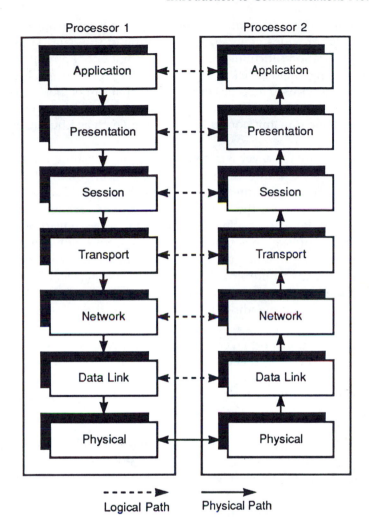

Figure 1-19
OSI Peer Layer
Communication

presentation layers, *session layers* support other session layers, etc. Between the different layers are interfaces through which the data pass. The following sections describe briefly the function of each layer.

Application.   The application layer is functionally defined by the user. Data known to or generated by one application may be needed by another application or system user. The content and format of this information is dictated by the business problem being addressed. The application determines the data to be sent, the message or record layout for the data, and the function or activity codes that identify the data to the receiving application.

Presentation.   The presentation layer accepts the data from the application layer and provides generalized formatting of the data. Thus, if there are data preparation functions common to a number of applications, rather than embedding them in each application, they can be resolved by the presentation services. The types of functions that can be performed at this level are encryption, compression, terminal screen formatting, and conversion from one transmission code to another (such as EBCDIC to ASCII).

Session.   The session layer is responsible for establishing the connection between applications, enforcing the rules for carrying on the dialogue, and attempting to reestablish the connection in the event of failure. The dialogue rules specify both the order in which the applications are allowed to communicate and the pacing of information so as not to overload the recipient. If an application is sending data to a printer with a limited buffer size, the agreed-upon dialogue may be to send a buffer-size block to the printer, wait for the printer to signal that its buffer has been emptied, and then send the next block of data. The session layer is responsible for controlling this flow and avoiding buffer overflow at the printer.

Transport.   The transport layer is the first layer concerned with the world external to its processor. It is responsible for generating the address of the end user and ensuring that all blocks or packets of data have been received, that there are no duplicate blocks, and that blocks have not been lost in transmission.

Network.   The network layer is responsible for end-to-end routing of packets or blocks of information, collection of billing and accounting information, and message routing.

Data Link.   The data link layer must establish and control the physical path of communication to the next node. This includes error detection and correction, definition of the beginning and ending of the data field, resolution of competing requests for a shared communications link (that is, who can use the circuit, and when), and ensuring that all forms of data can be sent across the circuit. The last point may sound trivial, but as Chapter 6 will illustrate, some data link transmission systems were not designed for transmission of binary fields, and sometimes must accomplish this in a rather awkward way. The conventions used to accomplish these data link functions are usually referred to as protocols.

Physical.   The physical layer specifies the electrical connections between the transmission medium and the computer system. It describes how many wires or pins will be used to carry the signals, which wires are used to carry specific signals, the size and shape of the connectors or adaptors between the transmission medium and the communications circuit, the speed at which data will be transmitted, and whether data (represented by voltages on a line, modification of radio waves, or light pulses) are allowed to flow in both directions and, if so, whether in both directions simultaneously.

Our discussion in subsequent chapters will start from the bottom up, beginning with the physical layer (together with hardware components used in configuring a data communications network).

CASE STUDY

To help make the material more understandable and relevant, numerous examples will be cited throughout the book. In addition, there will be a common case study carried from chapter to chapter, where applicable. This case study is adapted from actual situations, although some details have been changed to protect the anonymity of those involved.

Syncrasy Corporation is a startup company located in Puma Flats, Kansas. The president and two founders have decided to capitalize on the boom in the personal computer marketplace by becoming a mail order discount outlet for personal computer hardware, software, and supplies. They have just opened their offices and warehouse, and have begun taking orders. All their data processing requirements are met by a personal computer and there is no need for data communications. As subsequent chapters will illustrate, Syncrasy becomes a high-growth company whose needs for computing power and data communications begin to change rapidly as they grow and extend the enterprise.

SUMMARY

The data communications industry, somewhat dormant through the 1960s, has experienced tremendous expansion in the 1970s and 1980s, largely the result of lower prices for both equipment and transmission media. In the 1970s, competition emerged for the provision of data communications circuits and for hardware components that attach to these circuits. The number of applications making use of data communications facilities has continued to grow, with on-line data processing forming one of the most rapidly growing segments of the industry. This demand for on-line data processing has given rise to computer systems designed to meet the needs for high performance, expansion, and reliability.

Key Terms

Application layer	Network
Availability	Node
Batch	Office automation
Carterphone case	Open Systems Interconnection (OSI)
Consistency	On-line
Conversational	Packet distribution network (PDN)
Data communications	Performance
Data entry	Physical layer
Data link protocol	Presentation layer
Distributed	Protocol
Divestiture	Receiver
Fault tolerance	Recovery
Flexibility	Reliability
Geosynchronous	Remote Job Entry (RJE)
Hush-a-Phone case	SABRE
Inquiry/response	SAGE
Interactive	Security
Interface	Sender
International Standards Organization (ISO)	Sensor-based
	Session layer
Local area network (LAN)	Telecommunications
Medium	Transaction processing
Message	Transport layer

Questions and Exercises

1. What is the distinction between telecommunications and data communications?

2. Why has the data communications industry grown so rapidly in the 1970s and 1980s?

3. Explain the significance to the data processing industry of each of the following: (a) the Hush-a-Phone decision; (b) the Carterphone decision; and (c) MCI.

4. How does the history of data communications differ from that of database development?

5. Investigate in detail two data communications applications. Note specifically the hardware used. Determine the categories of data communications into which the applications fall.

6. Select a specific application of data communications, and identify the functions that would be required in the application, presentation, and session layers of the OSI recommendation.

7. Discuss the history of telephone companies in the United States as it relates to the data communications industry.

8. How do U.S. telephone companies differ from their counterparts in Great Britain, France, West Germany, Japan, and Australia? In what respects are they the same?

9. How might data communications systems be used in the home?

References

Bell Laboratories. *A History of Engineering and Science in the Bell System, National Service in War and Peace (1925–1975)*. Murray Hill, NJ: Bell Laboratories, 1982.

Brock, Gerald W. *The Telecommunications Industry*. Cambridge, MA: Harvard University Press, 1981.

Kleinfield, Sonny. *The Biggest Company on Earth*. New York: Holt, Rinehart & Winston, 1981.

Martin, James. *Introduction to Teleprocessing*. Englewood Cliffs, NJ: Prentice-Hall, 1972.

Metropolis, N., Howlett, H., and Rota, Gian-Carlo, eds. *A History of Computing in the Twentieth Century*. New York: Academic Press, 1980.

Tanenbaum, Andrew S. *Computer Networks*. Englewood Cliffs, NJ: Prentice-Hall, 1981.

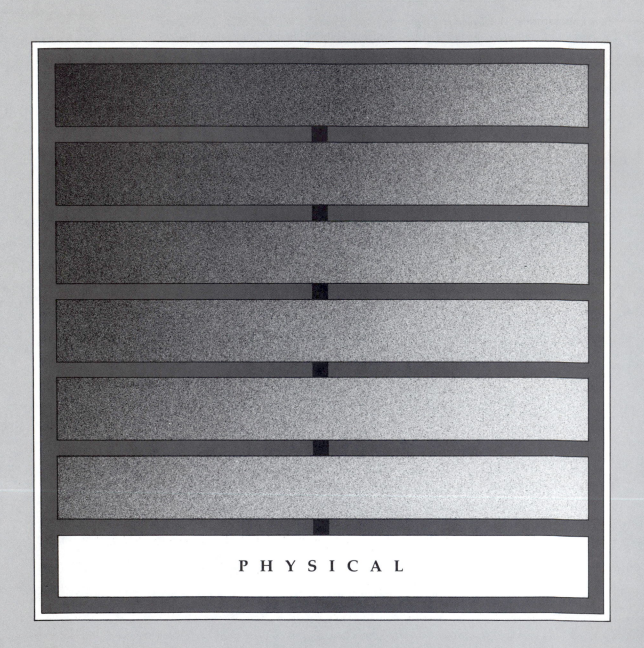

PHYSICAL

II

MEDIA AND HARDWARE: THE PHYSICAL LAYER

2

Physical Aspects of Data Communications

INTRODUCTION

The first chapter examined the essential features of communication, one of which was a medium. It also briefly discussed the ISO OSI reference model, including the physical layer. This chapter will acquaint you with the various media available for transporting information, the strengths and weaknesses of each medium, and the ways to represent data during its transmission.

The transmission media in common use in today's data communications networks can be broken down into two major categories, conducted and radiated. *Conducted media* include telephone and telegraph wires, private wires, coaxial cables, and fiber optics. *Radiated media* include radio broadcast, microwave radio transmission, infrared transmission, and satellite transmission. These options are listed in Figure 2-1 on page 38. The frequency ranges for each type of radiated medium are given in Figure 2-15 on page 50. Each medium, together with its necessary transmission facilities, is discussed below. The discussion focuses on those characteristics that make each medium desirable or undesirable in different situations, including speed, security, distance, susceptibility to error, and cost. These attributes form the basis of the selection criteria discussed later in the chapter.

Figure 2-1
Transmission Media

Conducted Media	Radiated Media
Electrical Conductors	Radio Frequency
Wires	Broadcast
Coaxial cable	Microwave
Light Conductors	Satellite
Fiber optics	Light Frequency
	Infrared

CONDUCTED MEDIA

Wires

Wires, today's most commonly used data transmission medium, are also the earliest. Much of the terminology and technology regarding this communications medium derives from telephony and telegraphy because, in setting up its own data communications networks, the computer industry had utilized the already existing vast network of telephone and telegraph lines.

The advantages of wires are their availability and relatively low cost. Their disadvantages include susceptibility to signal distortion or error, and the relatively low transmission rates they provide for long-distance links.

Private vs. Public Lines.   Wires employed in data communications are either private or public. *Private lines* are those deployed by the user and *public lines* are those provided by a *common carrier* like a telephone company. In general, public lines are in use where distances are great or the terrain or other environmental factors prohibit the use of private wires.

Transmission Speed and Frequency Range.   Theoretically, the maximum transmission speed along wire links is over 1 million bits of information per second (bps). In actuality, this speed is seldom attained, being limited by the distance spanned, the diameter of the wire, and—in the case of twisted wire pairs used by the telephone companies—the mutual capacitance of the wires in the pair. For example, Freeman (1981) pointed out that "in the early days of telephony in the United States it was noted that a telephone connection including as much as 30 mi (48 km) of 19-gauge nonloaded cable was at about the limit of useful transmission."

A twisted wire pair can handle frequencies up to and in excess of 1 million cycles per second (Hertz) [Hewlett-Packard, 1977], which provides a potential carrying capacity of more than 2 million bps. Local or private connections typically operate at speeds up to 80,000 bps, and long-distance connections up to 9600 bps.

Cable Cost, Gauge, and Types.   Private cable ranges in cost from 16¢ per foot to over $1 per foot, depending on the shielding, gauge, and number of conducting wires in the cable. The type of wire most commonly used for private lines is stranded copper, of American Wire Gauges 19, 22, 24, 26, and 28. Figure 2-2(a) shows a single conductor wire. Private wires are usually bundled, providing multiple conductors in one insulating sheath. The number of conducting strands in such a cable varies, with 4, 7, 8, 10, 12, 15, and 25 conductors being the most common. Figure 2.2(c) shows a wire bundle with multiple conductors.

Ordinary telephone wire consists of a twisted pair of wires. Bundles of these wire pairs from telephones in a given area are sheathed together. Each pair of wires is twisted together to minimize signal distortion from adjacent wire pairs in the sheath. Figure 2.2(b) depicts an individual twisted wire pair.

Switched Connections vs. Leased Lines. Data communications applications use either switched connections or leased lines. *Switched connections* are established when a communications station dials a telephone number with which it needs to communicate. Such a communications link uses the same wires as voice transmission. Since the telephone company cannot guarantee exactly which path or switching equipment such a connection will use, the speed and quality of the switched connection is limited. Most switched connections operate at speeds of 300, 1200, 2400, or 4800 bps. Higher speeds are possible, but their potential for error and the cost of the necessary extra equipment currently make them cost prohibitive for most users. This limit on speed is being increased in certain areas as telephone companies implement the new digital data transmission technology. This technique will allow speeds of up to 56,000 bps with switched connections.

Being relatively more expensive than leased lines, switched lines are used when the amount of transmitted data is small or when many locations must be contacted for relatively short periods of time, such as when a team of salespersons enters information on their portable terminals or when a central host computer for a retail organization contacts its retail outlets at the close of the business day to collect sales and inventory information.

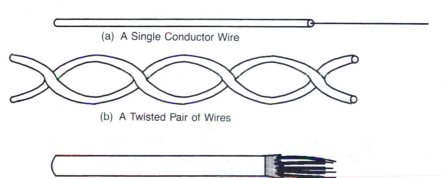

(a) A Single Conductor Wire

(b) A Twisted Pair of Wires

(c) A Shielded Multi-Conductor Wire Bundle

Figure 2-2
Types of Wires

In both these situations the amount of the information to be transferred is small, and the number of locations may be large or changeable. Switched lines become more expensive as their connection time increases, and their cost effectiveness may depend on their location, the hour of transmission, and the number of required connections. Chapter 7, on networking, discusses an alternative to switched lines—packet distribution networks.

Leased lines are used when the connection time between locations is long enough to cover the cost of leasing or if speeds higher than those available with switched lines must be attained. The cost of a leased line is a function of the distance covered, the transmission speed of the line, in some cases, and the susceptibility to error.

Common carriers provide a wide variety of options to satisfy diverse needs. For example, a leased line would enable terminals in a sales office in Seattle to communicate with a host computer in San Francisco. For this application the data volume is relatively low, but the connection is required throughout the day, making the leased line cost effective. In this application the transmission speed required is not high. An application in which a leased line would be used for both economy *and* speed is when two distant computers—say, in Chicago and Los Angeles—must exchange high volumes of information in a timely manner. (For now, only the medium of wires is being considered, and other alternatives are being ignored.)

Leased telephone lines can be *conditioned* by the telephone companies so as to provide lower error rates and increased transmission speeds. There are five levels of conditioning, C1 through C5, with level C3 not commercially available. Conditioned leased lines typically operate at speeds of up to 9600 bps. Again, digital data transmission will be considerably faster.

Very-high-speed connections are also available. Although such high-speed links may utilize other media, such as fiber optics and microwave, they are included in this discussion of wires because of their association with telephone lines. These high-speed services are designated T1, T2, T3, and T4 and offer transmission rates of 1.5, 6.3, 46, and 281 million bits per second (Mbps), respectively. The initial offering of T1 service, in 1962, used 24 voice-grade lines, for circuits up to 50 miles in length. In many situations today, these high-speed lines are divided into subchannels of lower transmission speed, in which case the sum of the bit rates on the several lower-speed lines is less than that of the aggregate rate quoted for the service. This is so because part of the carrying capacity is used to separate the multiple channels. For example, a T1 line with an aggregate bit rate of 1.5 Mbps can be divided into twenty-four 56,000-bps lines, giving a data carrying capacity of 1.3 Mbps. This technique—called *multiplexing*—is discussed in Chapter 5.

The cost of leased lines has been continually changing as a result of new technologies as well as industry competition. Divestiture of AT&T in 1984 has brought a period of tariff fluctuations. The cost of leasing digital lines from AT&T in Denver, Colorado, in September 1983, for instance, is given in Figure 2-3.

Line Speed	Monthly Flat Rate	Monthly Rate Per Mile
2,400 bps	$128.15	$1.03
4,800	160.19	1.28
9,600	221.26	2.56
56,000	416.48	8.97

Figure 2-3
AT&T Digital Line
Charges, Denver,
Colorado, September
1983

Coaxial Cable

Coaxial cable is primarily utilized in local area networks or over relatively short distances, generally less than 10 miles (except for uses by common carriers). (A local area network (LAN) typically is privately owned and restricted to a relatively small geograpahical area such as an office building or complex of buildings. LANs are discussed in more detail in Chapter 8.) Coaxial cable is also used to connect terminals with terminal controller units. Data transmission rates of up to 50 Mbps are not uncommon and the theoretical bit rate is in excess of 400 Mbps.

Coaxial Cable Technology.   Coaxial cable comes packaged in a variety of ways, but essentially it consists of one or two central data transmission wires surrounded by an insulating layer, a shielding layer, and an outer jacket, as depicted in Figure 2-4.

Coaxial cable transmission involves two basic techniques, baseband and broadband. In *broadband transmission* the data are carried on high-frequency carrier waves; thus, several channels may be transmitted over a single cable. Frequency separation, referred to as *guardbands*, help to avoid one signal's interfering with another. Broadband technology allows one medium to be used for a variety of transmission needs. For example, there could be voice, video, and multiple data channels of varying trans-mission speeds all on one broadband cable. *Baseband transmission*, on the other hand, does not use a carrier wave but sends the data along the channel by means of voltage fluctuations. Baseband technology cannot transmit multiple channels on one cable. Baseband transmission is also somewhat less expensive than broadband because it can use less expensive cable and connectors. There is also a coaxial cable that can transmit either baseband or broadband. The advantages and disadvantages of baseband

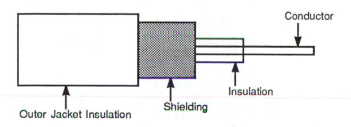

Figure 2-4
A Single Conductor
Coaxial Cable

versus broadband technologies are discussed in Chapter 8 in conjunction with local area networks. Baseband and broadband transmission are illustrated in Figure 2-5.

Cost.   The cost of coaxial cable ranges from approximately 65 cents per foot to several dollars per foot. Other major cost items in a coaxial network are the adaptors, controllers, and transceivers that transmit and receive data at high speeds.

Advantages and Disadvantages of Coaxial Cable.   The television industry has helped develop coaxial cable technology, including the capabilities to add stations or tap into a line without interruption of existing service. In an automated office environment where work stations are regularly added, moved, or deleted, the ability to alter the equipment configuration without disruption to existing users is significant. However, this same ability to tap into the cable without disrupting service is a disadvantage in situations where a high degree of security is required.

The triple shielding of coaxial cable provides a high degree of immunity to externally caused signal distortion. In local area networks of less than a mile's range, signal loss (attenuation) is generally not a concern; for longer distances, however, repeaters that enhance the signals are necessary.

Coaxial cable has several disadvantages, although one disadvantage might also be considered an advantage—that is, security: If a very secure medium is required, with taps being difficult to make and easy to detect, coaxial cable presents a serious problem. Whenever distances are great, attenuation becomes a problem. So does cost—the cost of the greater

Figure 2-5
Baseband and
Broadband
Transmission

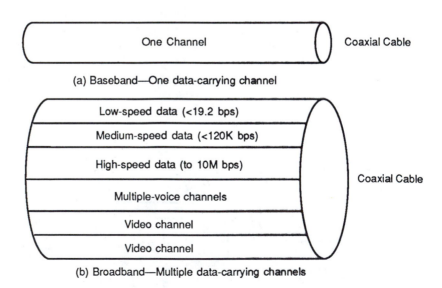

(a) Baseband—One data-carrying channel

(b) Broadband—Multiple data-carrying channels

amount of cable as well as the cost of repeaters that must be installed to enhance the signals over long distances.

The advantages of coaxial cable include its high data transmission rates, its immunity to noise or signal distortion, the capability it brings to add additional stations, and its reasonable cost over short distances.

Fiber Optics

Fiber optics is a fairly new communications medium. It is used by telephone companies in place of long-distance wires as well as by private companies in implementing local data communications networks.

Fiber Optics Technology.   Although fiber optic cables come in three varieties, each with a different way of guiding the light pulses from source to destination, they all have the same general form and characteristics. One or more glass or plastic fibers are woven together to form the core of the cable. This core is surrounded by a glass or plastic layer called the cladding. The cladding in turn is covered with plastic or other material for protection. Figure 2-6 shows a cross-section of a fiber optic cable. All three cable varieties require a light source, with laser and light-emitting diodes (LED) being those most commonly used.

The oldest of the three fiber optic technologies uses *multimode step-index fiber,* in which the reflective walls of the fiber move the light pulses to the receiver. Figure 2-7 illustrates multimode step-index transmission. *Multi-*

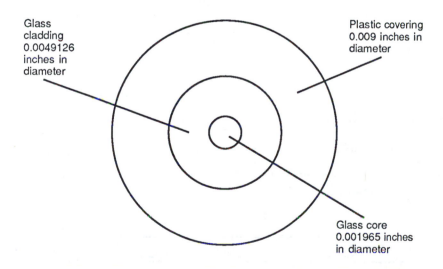

Glass cladding 0.0049126 inches in diameter

Plastic covering 0.009 inches in diameter

Glass core 0.001965 inches in diameter

Figure 2-6
An End View of a Fiber Optic Cable

Light

Figure 2-7
Fiber Optic Multi-mode Step-Index

mode graded-index fiber acts to refract (bend) the light toward the center of the fiber by means of variations in the density of the core. Figure 2-8 depicts the movement of light in a multimode graded-index fiber. The third—and potentially the fastest—of the fiber optic techniques is *single mode transmission*, a technique still being developed, whose potential has yet to be reached. With single mode transmission, light is guided down the center of an extremely narrow core. Single mode transmission is depicted in Figure 2-9.

Transmission rates currently available range up to approximately 500 Mbps, with speeds over 1 billion bps (Gbps) possible.

Benefits and Cost.   Because current technology makes it difficult to tap into a fiber optic cable and add new stations, its most significant role to date has been in static environments in which stations are not frequently added or deleted from the cable. Continuing research in this area may make fiber optics an attractive medium for local area networks, which also require the ad hoc addition of nodes. Whereas the capability to tap into a channel is a disadvantage with respect to local area networks, it becomes advantageous in areas where security is a significant consideration.

Fiber optic links for very short distances cost more than wires; but as distance or required transmission rate increases, fiber optics becomes cost effective. The breakeven point generally occurs when the distance is so great that coaxial cable or wires would require expensive signal enhancing equipment. A significant advantage that fiber optics has over copper wires is its reduced size and weight—approximately 20 times lighter and five times smaller than equivalent copper wire (either coaxial or twisted pair). Very low error rates and immunity to electrical or magnetic interference are additional benefits.

RADIATED MEDIA

Microwave Radio

Microwave radio technology no doubt has a place in any U.S. data communications hall of fame. It was MCI's proposal for a microwave linkage

Figure 2-8
Fiber Optic Multi-mode Graded-Index

Light

Figure 2-9
Fiber Optic Single Mode

Light

between Chicago and St. Louis that first stimulated competition for long-distance telephone service. The first commercially implemented digital microwave radio system was installed in Japan by Nippon Electric Co. in 1968.

Microwave Technology.   Microwave transmission rates range up to 45 Mbps. Because microwave signals travel in a straight line, transmitter and receiver must be in each other's line of sight (that is, no obstructions between them). The curvature of the earth therefore necessitates that microwave stations be no more than approximately 30 miles apart. The total *bandwidth* of a microwave channel is subdivided into numerous subchannels, which are used for either voice-grade transmission or high-speed data links or both. Bandwidth, one measure of the carrying capacity of a medium, and other measures of carrying capacity are discussed later in this chapter.

Advantages and Disadvantages.   Microwave transmission offers speed, cost effectiveness, and ease of implementation, however it has the unfortunate potential for interference from other radio waves. It also is limited by line-of-sight considerations. Furthermore, commercial transmissions are relatively insecure, since they can be intercepted by anyone with a receiver in the line of transmission. The advantages of microwave transmission include speed, cost effectiveness, and ease of implementation. Figure 2-10 on page 46 shows a picture of a microwave relay station.

Broadcast Radio

Broadcast radio employs not only the radio frequencies typical of AM and FM stations, but short-wave or short-distance radio frequencies as well, with total frequency range from 500,000 to 108 million cycles per second. Broadcast radio's primary application is in paging terminals, the devices carried by people (such as doctors) who are on call. It has not found wide use in data communications networks, although one exception was the ALOHANet at the University of Hawaii. Broadcast radio was chosen there to overcome the difficulty of establishing wire links in the islands, and it proved quite effective when the number of stations was relatively small. As more stations were added, however, contention between broadcasting stations increased, collisions or interference became more frequent, and effective utilization dropped. Furthermore, the medium proved to be susceptible to interference from other radio broadcast sources. The ALOHANet transmission rate was 9600 bps.

One area in which radio waves may prove effective is Videotex, the transmission of data for display on television monitors or home computers.

Figure 2-10   A microwave relay station
Courtesy of David Stamper

Satellite Radio

Satellite radio transmission, like microwave radio transmission, transmits data via very-high-frequency radio waves; both media also require line-of-sight transmission between stations. The primary differences between the two media are station location and signal transmission method: Microwave makes use of land-based stations only, whereas satellite uses both land-based stations and orbiting stations. Microwave transmitters may use just one frequency to send and receive a message, whereas satellites transmit from ground to satellite via one frequency and from satellite to ground via a different frequency.

Commercial satellites are placed in a 22,300-mile-high geosynchronous earth orbit, which as discussed in Chapter 1 means that the satellites remain stationary relative to a given position on the earth as illustrated in Figure 2-11. At this altitude, only three satellites are required to have all points on the earth in range. This is portrayed in Figure 2-12.

Satellite Transmission Technology. The basic components of satellite transmission are the earth stations, for sending and receiving, and the satellite component called a *transponder*. The transponder functions to

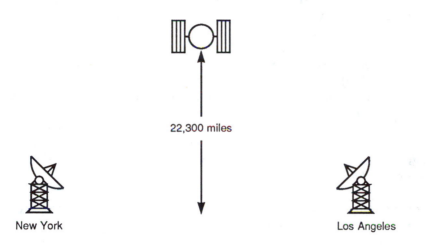

Figure 2-11
A Geosynchronous
Satellite Orbit

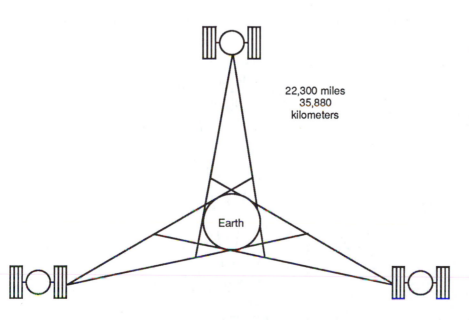

Figure 2-12
Satellite Positioning

receive the transmission from earth (up-link), amplify the signal, change the frequency, and retransmit the data to a receiving earth station (down-link). The up-link frequency differs from the down-link frequency in order that the weaker incoming signals are not interfered with by the stronger outgoing signals. Thus, satellite frequencies are spoken of in pairs, such as 12/14 gigahertz. The first number represents the down-link frequency and the second the up-link frequency. *Giga* means one billion, and one *hertz* is one cycle per second. Thus, 12/14 gigahertz means a down-link transmission frequency of 12 billion cycles per second and an up-link transmission frequency of 14 billion cycles per second.

Communication satellites in space must be separated to avoid interference, generally by an arc of at least 4°, as depicted in Figure 2-13. (This has led to concern, especially among countries presently incapable of launching satellites, that there is only a limited amount of space available for these satellites and that the space will be allocated without their obtaining a slot.)

Each transponder has a transmission rate of approximately 50 Mbps, which can be divided into 16 1.5-Mbps channels, 400 64-Kbps channels (*Kbps* means kilobits per second, or 1000 bits per second), or 600 40-Kbps channels. Although this transmission rate is relatively high, there still is a significant delay, since the signals, must travel such a long distance from source to destination.

Propagation Delay.   The amount of time it takes for a signal to travel from its source to its destination is called *propagation delay*. Since almost all data communications signals travel at nearly the speed of light, propagation delay on earth is insignificant (approximately 16 milliseconds for a 3000-mile transcontinental journey). Across the extremely long distances of space, however, propagation delay can be significant. In addition to travel

Figure 2-13
Satellite Separation

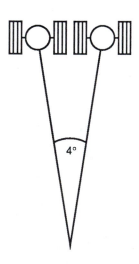

time, the delay includes the time required to accept, enhance, and retransmit the signal. Propagation delay becomes significant for applications that have sending times of less than a quarter-second or response times of a half-second or less. Although propagation delay is ordinarily ignored for terrestrial links, satellite transmission system designers must be cognizant of this factor. Figure 2-14 gives an example of how propagation delay is computed for a transaction in which a remote terminal sends a message to a host computer and receives a reply from it.

Remote–satellite input up-link	22,300 miles
Satellite–host input down-link	22,300
Host–satellite response up-link	22,300
Satellite–remote response down-link	22,300
Total distance	89,200 miles

$$\text{Travel time} = \frac{89{,}200 \text{ miles}}{186{,}000 \text{ miles/second}} = 0.48 \text{ seconds}$$

Figure 2-14
Satellite Propagation Delay

Satellite Providers. There are numerous providers of transponders for communication, including RCA, Satellite Business Systems (a joint venture started by IBM, Comsat, and Aetna), American Satellite, AT&T, GTE, Western Union, and NASA, as well as broadcast agencies in Canada, Japan, Europe, and Russia. The number of transponders per satellite is typically between 12 and 24. Providers of satellite time usually lease a whole transponder, but it is also possible to sublease transponder subchannels from another user.

Satellites make expansion of a data communications network relatively easy. All that is required is to add earth stations. This can present security problems, however, since transmission can be intercepted by anyone with proper receiving equipment.

Infrared Transmission

Infrared transmission uses electromagnetic radiation of wavelengths between visible light and radio waves (which is very near that of lasers). Like microwaves, infrared transmission is a line-of-sight technology, principally to provide local area connections between buildings. Data transmission rates are typically on the order of 100 Kbps. This technology, like that of broadcast radio, is not used much in the data communications industry.

Radiated Media Frequencies

The frequencies of various radiated media are given in Figure 2-15 on page 50.

Figure 2-15
Frequency Spectrum
Classification

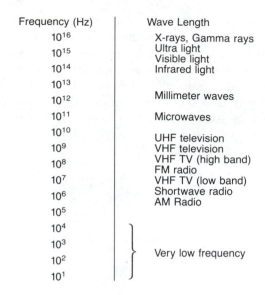

Frequency (Hz)	Wave Length
10^{16}	X-rays, Gamma rays
10^{15}	Ultra light
	Visible light
10^{14}	Infrared light
10^{13}	
10^{12}	Millimeter waves
10^{11}	Microwaves
10^{10}	
	UHF television
10^9	VHF television
10^8	VHF TV (high band)
	FM radio
10^7	VHF TV (low band)
10^6	Shortwave radio
	AM Radio
10^5	
10^4	
10^3	
10^2	Very low frequency
10^1	

MEDIA SELECTION CRITERIA

There are a number of factors that influence the choice of a medium when configuring a data communications network. These factors are given in Figure 2-16. Since every configuration has its own set of constraints, not all factors apply in every situation; in some situations, there may even be only a single viable alternative. However, system designers must consider every criterion, either implicitly or explicitly. In most situations, the factors may influence one another. For example, there is often a strong correlation between a medium's application and its required speed, so much so that the application usually dictates a minimum acceptable transmission speed (although other factors such as cost and expandability can also pertain).

Figure 2-16
Media Selection
Criteria

Cost	Security
Speed or capacity	Distance
Availability	Environment
Expandability	Application
Error rates	Maintenance

Cost

A dramatic expansion in the application of data communications began in the 1970s, influenced strongly by improvements in technology and a lowering of costs. The cost reductions were the result of the improved technology and the competition among the common carriers providing transmission services. The technological advances included communications equipment capable of supporting higher data transmission rates at lower costs, as well as the commercial availability of fiber optics and satellite transmission.

The costs associated with a given transmission medium include not only the costs of the medium, but also ancillary costs, such as for additional hardware and software that might be required. A deferred ancillary cost that is important to consider when making an initial selection, is the cost of expansion. For example, an emerging marketing organization located in, say, Houston, Texas, might intially select specific market areas, each with its own large market, say, New York City, Chicago, Houston, and Los Angeles. The logical choice for connecting the remote offices to the host computer in Houston is to lease a line from a common carrier. As the corporation expands into other cities, however, a satellite link might become more economical because the expense of adding new locations might be less than for leasing more land lines.

Speed

There is a tremendous range of transmission speeds available. Low-speed circuits transmit at rates under 100 bps, and high-speed circuits at over 100 Mbps. Within a given medium, higher speeds mean higher costs (see Figure 2-3 on page 41), not necessarily attributable to the medium itself. Higher data transmission rates require more sophisticated (read, expensive) communications equipment.

Two factors dictate the speed of a medium: response time and aggregate data rate. Design objectives for an on-line application should include the anticipated *response time* for each type of transaction. *Aggregate data rate* refers to the amount of information that can be transmitted per unit of time.

Response Time.   Response time has two components, transmission time and processing time, and each of these can be broken down into subcomponents. Say the design objective is for 95% of a certain type of transaction to have a response time of 3 seconds. If *processing* takes 1 second, then *transmission* must take 2 seconds or less. If the transaction involves the exchange of 500 characters of information, then the speed of the medium must be at least 250 characters per second (500 characters divided by 2 seconds), which represents approximately 2400 bps. (This assumes that there is no sharing of the communications link. If the line is shared, then allowances must be made for the time in which the line might be unavailable to a specific user. Chapters 4 and 5 discuss several ways in which one communications line can be shared among several users.)

Aggregate Data Rate.   In other applications, such as bulk data transfers, aggregate data rate may be the factor dictating line speed. Suppose the application just discussed required the line to be used by office personnel during the day to make inquiries and updates, and within an hour of closing time at the conclusion of the business day to transmit a file of 2 million characters to a host computer. The business day requirements for response time could be satisfied with a 2400-bps channel, but the file transfer would require an aggregate data rate of approximately 555 characters per second (2 million characters per hour divided by 3600 seconds per hour), that is, a 7200–9600-bps channel.

Media speeds are summarized in Figure 2-17.

Figure 2-17
Media and Their Common Transmission Speeds

Medium	Common Transfer Rates (bps)
Private line	300, 1200, 2400, 4800, 9600, 19200, 38400, 56000, 64000, 80000
Switched connection	300, 1200, 2400, 4800
Leased line	2400, 4800, 9600
T1, T2, T3, T4	1.5M, 6.3M, 46M, 281M
Coaxial cable	1M, 2M, 10M, 50M (over 400M potential)
Fiber optics	to 275M
Microwave	to 45M
Broadcast radio	9600 (in ALOHANet)
Satellite	to 50M

Availability

Availability here has two meanings: (1) Is the medium available when it is needed? (2) Is there sufficient carrying capacity to handle the volume of data? An operation that uses a switched telephone line would be at a disadvantage when phone lines are busy, as on certain holidays. For instance, imagine a fast-food chain with stores throughout the United States that maintains a central file of sales and inventory information. Each store's terminals record the daily receipts and foods dispensed. At the end of the business day, the central location dials the phone number of each store, transfers and processes the data collected during the day, and then orders supplies for each restaurant. On Mother's Day, the phone circuits are extremely busy, thus interfering with the chain's ability to contact all of its locations. This lack of availability would not be catastrophic for this application, but for a process control or factory control application lack of availability could produce disastrous results. In the income tax application discussed in Chapter 1 there is also a potential lack of available lines during the heavy tax season.

Shared Lines.   Shared lines also can create problems of availability, for when multiple users share a line (see Chapters 4 and 5), then one user can monopolize the line, thus making it unavailable to others. Suppose, for example, that there are two terminals sharing a line, and one user is attempting interactive queries into a database while the other attempts to copy a lengthy file to an attached printer. The line's capacity might well be fully taken up with the file transfer, essentially making the line un-available to the other user.

Control Messages.   Some of a line's full capacity must be reserved for control messages. For instance, to detect errors in data requires additional bits of information to be appended to the data. A long message that must be broken down into segments for transmission requires extra information to delimit the message's beginning, end, and segments. Acknowledging receipt of transmitted data creates additional line congestion. When erroneous messages are received, then the last message, and perhaps several previous messages, must be retransmitted. Multiple devices per line require addresses to be appended to messages; in many instances, control sequences need to be transmitted to establish when each device can use the medium and receive data. Finally, there may be idle time on the circuit because there are no data to be sent or because the state of the circuit is being changed (such as the transition from sending data to receiving, known as "turnaround"). These types of control functions can take up a considerable amount of the carrying capacity of a circuit—as much as 30%, excluding idle time. Figure 2-18 illustrates some of the extra fields appended to a message for transmission and for segmenting a long message.

Expandability

Frequently it becomes necessary to expand the scope of a data communications configuration, either by adding more devices at a given location or by adding new locations. Some media—such as coaxial cable and satellites—make expansion into new locations relatively easy, whereas others—such as leased telephone lines—make expansion more difficult or more

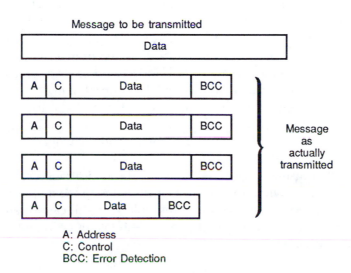

Figure 2-18
Message
Transmission

costly. It is important that communications networks be designed for the future as well as for immediate needs. For example, imagine a rapidly growing computer company that used private wires to attach terminals for some employees in the head office. The initial applications were extremely successful, and new applications and employees were quickly added. This created a need for more terminals, which then required additional communications circuits. The company had to go through the time-consuming and somewhat expensive process of stringing additional wires throughout the facility. Had they anticipated their growth correctly, the additional wires could have been installed along with the initial set.

Several other alternatives are also available in situations such as the one just described. Instead of supplying additional circuits, the company could have added new hardware, such as concentrators, multiplexers, or addressable terminals. Such solutions are the subject of Chapters 4 and 5.

Expandability is a problem not just of media availability, but also of hardware. When a system has reached its maximum capacity with respect to available number of devices and communications circuits, then a larger machine or additional machines must be added. The airline industry's reservations systems have faced this problem several times, as more subscribers were added to the network.

Errors

All transmission media are subject to signal distortion, which can produce errors in the data. The propensity for error influences not only the quality of transmission but also its speed. For example, switched telephone lines are highly subject to noise from switching equipment as well as other sources, limiting the speed to 4800 bps or less. Such errors pose no problem in voice communication because humans are adept at detecting errors and recovering from them—either a person does not understand what is being said, or the context is incorrect. And recovery is simple because a person can usually ask that a message be repeated from a particular point. Computers, on the other hand, do not understand context, and therefore are unable to detect a corrupted data bit. The impact of even one inverted bit can be highly significant. Suppose, for instance, that a bank must use data communications to transfer several million dollars to another bank. If just one of the high-order bits in the money field is changed, a difference of several million dollars can result.

To detect transmission errors in data communications environments requires that redundant information be included with the transferred data. This acts to reduce the efficiency of the link, and still cannot ensure absolute accuracy of the data. The common methods for detecting errors are discussed in Chapter 3.

Security

The lack of security in certain data communications networks was made very evident when "hackers" managed to penetrate several major systems. Personal computers have spread widely the capability of entering other systems, and competition among the providers of communications networks and value-added carriers has reduced the cost of long-distance connections. Providing complete security, like providing an error-free medium, is impossible. However, some media—like fiber optics—are considerably more difficult to penetrate, whereas others—like coaxial cable, microwave, and satellite—are relatively easy to tap. The medium most vulnerable to the average hacker is switched lines.

Distance

Distance includes not only transmission distance, but also the number of locations served. If the distances are short (say, within one building or complex of buildings), private media such as wires, coaxial cable, or fiber optics may be feasible. With greater distance or number of locations, it usually becomes necessary to obtain media from a common carrier. And as the number of locations to be reached becomes very great, or when it is necessary to communicate with relatively remote locations, a broadcast medium such as satellite may be the only viable solution.

Environment

The constraints of environment can eliminate certain types of media from consideration. For instance, even when the distance between two buildings to be connected in a data communications network is small enough to make private lines feasible, local ordinances may prohibit the user from installing them. Or where a locale prohibits the stringing of wire over or under a public street, the user might have to pick a medium other than the optimum one. Or direct satellite links in leased office facilities might be made impossible because the lease prohibits installing earth stations on the premises. Or private lines that must be strung through areas with considerable electrical or magnetic interference might be impractical because of the potential for inducing error in transmission. These are but a few of the examples in which the environment plays a critical role in the selection of a transmission medium.

Application

Certain applications (such as environmental monitoring) employ devices designed to connect to a system in a very specific way and at specific speeds. In such applications, the characteristics of the required equipment may dictate the type of medium and interfaces to be used. Furthermore, as noted above, the particulars of an application help determine other required characteristics of the medium, such as speed, security, and availability. For instance, the most obvious media for a high-speed local area network are coaxial cable, fiber optics, and perhaps the private automated branch exchange (PABX) telephone system. If one also wants to be able to easily add and delete stations, then fiber optics becomes a less viable solution. Implementing the PABX using twisted wire pairs limits the transmission rates and makes impossible the support of video and 10-Mbps data channels. The best choice to satisfy all of these requirements is coaxial cable.

Maintenance

Just as all media are subject to error, all are subject to failure, which means that the medium must be repaired or replaced. In some cases this is simple—a telephone cable severed in an excavation accident can usually be repaired within several days; and while repairs are being made, an alternate path might be made available. Repair or replacement of a defective satellite, however, is usually a lengthy process, which is why communications companies frequently have a backup transponder available. Because such failures are not all that frequent, maintenance concerns do not have a high priority. Nonetheless, system designers usually must consider the impact of medium failures and their probable duration, and prepare a backup or contingency plan so communications can continue while any repairs are being made. As an example, there is the case of a major bank in Australia that depended heavily on its computer center. The bank established multiple computer centers, each serviced by different telecommunications trunk lines. It also made provisions for switching lines from one center to another should the communications links to one of the centers be severed. As a result, no failure at a single point was able to disrupt their ability to process data.

A comparison of all of the media is provided in Figure 2-19. In some instances it is difficult to separate one criterion from another. For example, consider the expandability of a network that uses wires. Some of the options available involve hardware; one option adds additional lines. If this last alternative is chosen, there is usually no problem in obtaining the circuit; unfortunately, the cost may be quite high; which is why this cell in the chart is assigned a rating of *fair*. (This chart should be used in conjunction with Figure 2-17, on transmission speeds, p. 52). If an application requires high speed and a secure link, then fiber optics would be the first choice.

SIGNAL REPRESENTATION AND MODULATION

Having discussed the various transmission media, it is now time to explore how data are stored and the manner in which data are transmitted.

	Wires	Coaxial Cable	Fiber Optics	Microwave	Broadcast Radio	Satellite
Availability	Good	Good	Good	Good	Possible contention	Fair to good
Expandability	Fair	Good in local area	Fair	Good	Good	Good
Errors	Fair	Good	Good	Fair	Fair	Fair
Security	Fair	Fair	Good	Poor	Poor	Poor
Distance	Good	Poor	Good	Good	Good	Good
Environment	Fair	Good	Good	Fair	Fair	Fair

Figure 2-19   Media Comparison Chart

Digital vs. Analog Representation

All the computers we are considering store data in digital form and transmit these data in analog or digital form. In *digital* form, data are represented by a series of distinct entities. In data communications equipment this is almost always a binary digit, or bit—either 0 or 1. *Analog* refers to measurable physical quantities, which in data communications take the form of voltages and variations in the properties of waves. Data are represented in analog form by varying the amplitude, frequency and/or phase of a wave.

Modems

Translation from digital format to analog format and back to digital format is accomplished by a device known as a *data set* or *modem* (an acronym for *mo*dulator—*dem*odulator). A modem functions to accept digital data (a string of bits), transform it into an analog signal, and pass the signal along a medium to another modem. The receiving modem translates the analog signal back into digital data (presumably exactly the same as that transmitted by the sender). Since most of the telephone companies' communications systems transmit information in analog form, these systems must change the data to analog form to meet the requirements of data communications transmission facilities.

Carrier Signals

Figure 2-20 on page 58 depicts a simple sine wave, which has the potential for carrying information. If the wave continues without any change, as depicted, then no information can be discerned. Such an unmodulated signal is called a *carrier signal*. The object of a modem is to change (mod-

Figure 2-20
A Simple Sine Wave

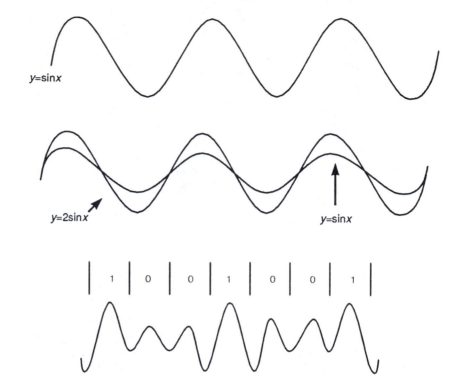

$y=\sin x$

Figure 2-21
Superimposed Sine
Waves

$y=2\sin x$ $y=\sin x$

Figure 2-22
Amplitude
Modulation

| 1 | 0 | 0 | 1 | 0 | 0 | 1 |

ulate) the characteristics of the carrier wave so that a receiver can interpret information. The simple sine wave has several properties that can be altered in order to represent data: it has amplitude (height), it has frequency (period), and it has phase (relative starting point). Modems alter one or more of these characteristics in order to represent data.

Amplitude Modulation

The simplest characteristic to visualize is *amplitude modulation (AM)*. Figure 2-21 represents two sine waves superimposed on one another. One curve represents sin *wt* and the other represents 2 sin *wt*. Note that the 2 sin *wt* curve has twice the amplitude of the sin *wt* curve. (Varying the amplitude of a curve is analogous to changing the voltage on a line.) Now, how is this variation used to convey information? Suppose the bit pattern 1001001 is to be transmitted. If a 1 bit is represented by the curve of 2 sin *x* and the 0 bit by the curve traced by sin *x*, then the bit pattern would be represented by the modulated sine curve depicted in Figure 2-22.

Frequency Modulation

The period or frequency of a sine curve is the interval required for the curve to complete one entire cycle. In the simple sine curve the period is

2π, where π is approximately 3.1416. In data transmission, such intervals usually last only a matter of seconds, so the period is the number of seconds required for the wave to complete one cycle. The mathematical function that will alter the period is sin wt. Figure 2-23 shows the curve of sin $2x$. When the horizontal axis represents time, the period is frequency (oscillations) per unit of time. Hertz (Hz) is the term used to denote frequency; one hertz is one cycle per second. The human ear can detect sound waves with frequencies between 20 and 20,000 Hz. Telephone systems use the much smaller frequency range between 300 and 3400 Hz, which is satisfactory for voice transmission.

To convey information by *frequency modulation* (FM) is to vary the frequency of the transmission. To transmit the binary pattern 1001001 by frequency modulation on a voice-grade line a frequency of 1300 Hz can represent the 1 bit and a frequency of 2100 Hz can represent the 0 bit (one of the actual values used for transmission between 0 and 1200 bps). The signal received must be within 10 Hz of these values to be acceptable; that is, the range for a 1 bit is 1290–1310 Hz. These frequency values must be different enough to minimize the possibility of signal distortion altering the values transmitted. Thus, if the 1 bit were represented by 1500 Hz and the 0 bit by 1510 Hz, then a decrease of only 10 Hz would change a 0 bit into a 1 bit. Figure 2-24 on page 60 shows an example of frequency modulation for our selected bit pattern 1001001.

Phase Modulation

A third modulation technique is *phase modulation* (phase shifting). If the simple sine curve is represented by sin wt, then a change of phase is represented by sin($wt + n$). Figure 2-25 on page 60 shows the curve of sin wt, Figure 2-26 on page 60 the curve of sin($wt + \pi$), and Figure 2-27 on page 61 the two curves superimposed on one another. Transmitting the bit pattern of 1001001 using phase modulation, where a 1 bit is represented

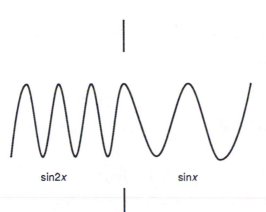

sin2x sin$x$

Figure 2-23
The Curve Sine 2x

Figure 2-24
Frequency
Modulation

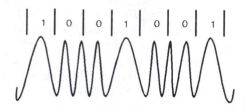

Figure 2-25
The Curve of Sin *wt*

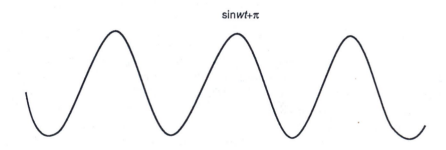

Figure 2-26
The Curve of
Sin *wt* + π

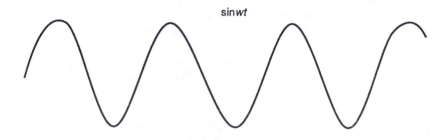

by no phase change and a 0 bit by a change in phase of π radians, yields the curve in Figure 2-28.

The most common modulation techniques in data communications are frequency modulation, also known as *frequency shift keying (FSK)*, and phase modulation, also known as *phase shift keying (PSK)*. There is also a variation known as *differential phase shift keying (DPSK)*, and a combination of phase and amplitude modulation known as *quadrature amplitude modulation (QAM)*.

Bit Rates, Baud Rates, and Bandwidth

Up to this point, data transmission speed has been discussed exclusively in terms of bits per second. This *bit rate* is the most appropriate unit for

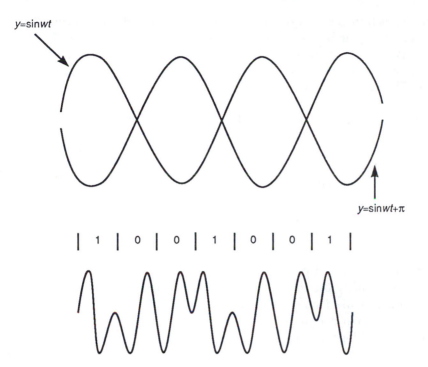

$y=\sin wt$

$y=\sin wt+\pi$

Figure 2-27
Superimposed Sine
Waves

| 1 | 0 | 0 | 1 | 0 | 0 | 1 |

Figure 2-28
Phase Modulation

systems analysis. However, two other terms also are in common usage: baud and bandwidth. The *bandwidth* of a channel is the difference between the minimum and maximum frequencies allowed. Thus, a voice-grade channel that can transmit frequencies between 300 and 3400 Hz has a bandwidth of 3100 Hz. Bandwidth is a measure of the amount of data that can be transmitted per unit of time and is directly proportional to the maximum data transmission speed of a medium.

Nyquist's Theorem. In 1933 Harry Nyquist developed a theorem stating that the maximum amount of binary data that can be transmitted by a channel is twice the bandwidth. This theory refers to a simple binary signal (only two amplitudes or two frequencies can represent data) and specifies that the amount of data which can be transmitted is twice the bandwidth. (Additional data can be transmitted using some of the modulation techniques already discussed.) Thus, for a bandwidth of 3100 Hz and binary data representation, the maximum amount of data that can be transmitted is 6200 bps.

Shannon's Formula. A second important theory is that of C. E. Shannon. Shannon's formula relates transmission speed to signal power and error rates. The speed of the circuit is given by

$$S = B \log_2 (1 + (W/N))$$

where S is transmission speed (in bps), B is bandwidth (in hertz), W is the power of the signal (in watts), and N is Gaussian noise (in watts). The term W/N is the signal-to-noise ratio. A typical telecommunications line has a signal-to-noise ratio of 15 and a bandwidth of 3100 Hz. In such a case, Shannon's formula yields

$$S = 3100 \log_2(1 + 15) = 3100 \log_2(16) = 3100(4) = 12{,}400 \text{ bps}$$

There is a slight discrepancy between Nyquist's theorem and Shannon's formula. This is because Shannon did not consider the fact that signals do not die off immediately, and there is some amount of intersignal interference that slows down the transmission rate. The Nyquist theorem, being more conservative, is closer to what has been achieved in actual practice.

Baud Rate.   The *baud rate* is a measure of the number of discrete signals that can be observed per unit of time. Only in the binary situation is the baud rate exactly the same as the bit rate. Unfortunately, the two terms are frequently used synonymously. But the bit rate is higher than the baud rate when a baud represents more than one bit of information. For example, in the binary amplitude modulation situation, two different signal levels can represent the bits 0 and 1 (as discussed earlier). If the signal changed 1200 times a second, then the baud rate would be 1200 and the bit rate would be 1200 bps. Suppose instead that four different amplitudes were represented—say, 1, 2, 3, and 4 per unit of time, as in Figure 2-29. Each level could then be used to represent two bits. This technique is referred to as *dibits*. One possible representation is given in Figure 2-30.

Figure 2-29
Dibits Using
Amplitude
Modulation

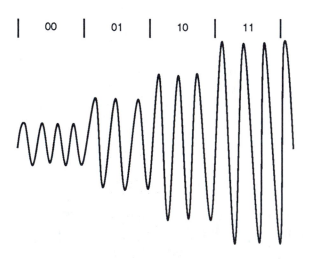

Bit Pattern	Amplitude
00	1
01	2
10	3
11	4

Figure 2-30
One Possible Dibit
Representation

Suppose further that a signaling rate of 1200 changes per second is maintained. The baud rate remains at 1200, but the bit rate has now doubled to 2400 bps because each signal represents two bits. Figure 2-31 shows the transmission of the bit pattern 1001001 using dibits (with one bit added to make the number of bits even). Similarly, eight signal levels could represent three bits with each signal, a technique referred to as *tribits*. If 16 different signaling levels were used, then four bits per signal could be represented, a technique referred to as *quadbits*. Hence, with current technology the bit rate equals the baud rate or a multiple thereof (two, three, or four times the baud rate). PSK or a derivative is the most common method of achieving dibit and tribit transfer; QAM is the most common for quadbit.

Modem Capabilities

When modems are needed to transmit data over communications links, they are always used in pairs. Furthermore, the modems in each such pair must be configured exactly alike. Most modems have a variety of available options; setting these options is sometimes referred to as strapping, a term held over from times when the options were set by wiring, as opposed to switches or computer control. Figure 2-32 on page 64 shows a modem. A number of modem capabilities are presented in Figure 2-33 on page 64.

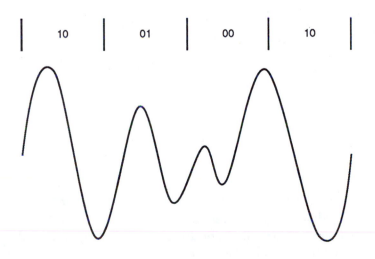

10   01   00   10

Figure 2-31
Dibits Using
Amplitude
Modulation

Figure 2-32
A Codex 2660 High-
Speed Modem

Photo courtesy of Codex Corporation, world leader in data communications systems and equipment, including wide area and local networking products, statistical multiplexers, nodal processors, T1 multiplexers, modems for dial and leased lines, network management and control systems and electronic matrix switches.

Figure 2-33
Some Modem
Capabilities

Speed and variable speed

Auto-answer

Manual answer

Auto-dial

Manual dial

Auto-disconnect

Manual disconnect

Programmable control (e.g., computer-controlled dialing and setting of data rate)

Automatic redial

Keyboard dial

Speaker (to monitor dialing and connection)

Synchronous or asynchronous

Full or half duplex

Reverse channel

Secondary channel

Multiport

Line conditioning capabilities (equalization)

Self-testing mode

Voice-over data

Compatibility with:

　Bell modems

　Consultative Committees on International Telegraphy and Telephony (CCITT) standards

Continued

Electronic Industries Association (EIA) standards

U.S. Government standards

Most modems on the market do not offer all of these capabilities. Some of these options are explained here; the remainder are discussed in Chapters 3, 5, and 6.

Speed. All modems are designed to operate at a specific speed or range of discrete speeds. The speed of a variable-speed modem can be set via switch(es) on the modem, via program control, or by automatic adjustment to the transmission speed.

Telephone Options. Auto-answer, manual answer, auto-dial, auto-disconnect, automatic redialing, and keyboard dialing all refer to use of switched telephone lines. Most newer modems can react to the ring indicator on the line and automatically answer a call. For a *manual answer* modem, someone must assist in making the connection. This "inconvenience" actually promotes better security. *Auto-dialing* means the modem can dial a number itself. Many modems can remember certain frequently called numbers. Each memory location can usually be associated with a code name, making dialing even easier. With *auto-disconnect* a modem will terminate a call automatically whenever the other party hangs up or a disconnect message is received. *Automatic redialing* modems will automatically redial a call that resulted in a busy signal or no connection. Finally, *keyboard or programmable dialing* means that the number can be dialed using the keyboard of a terminal or via program control.

Self-Testing. Almost all new modems, and many older models, have some type of self-testing mode. These include a loop-back test, in which the modem's outgoing signal is looped back to itself; memory diagnostic checks; and modem-to-modem test transmissions. These self-tests are quite valuable in isolating problems in the communications equipment.

Voice-Over. Voice-over data capability allows voice communication over the same circuit as the data, either as voice or data, or voice and data simultaneously. This type of arrangement is beneficial when the data transmission requirements require a dedicated circuit to a remote location. For example, suppose a company requires a lot of personal telephone communication between offices already linked by leased lines. Every such call can be dialed, incurring a toll for each, or voice-over data modems can be used, occupying a portion of the line capacity already leased. The only additional costs of voice transmission, then, are the price of the modems and the reduced data capacity on the line.

Multiport modems are discussed in Chapter 5; reverse and secondary channels, full and half duplex operations, and conditioning are covered in

Chapter 3; synchronous and asynchronous transmission are addressed in Chapter 6.

Cost.   The price of modems is much like that of media—constantly changing and, in general, dropping as a result of new technology and competition. The price also varies according to the capabilities offered, with speed being the most influential factor. The following chart provides the reader with a rough idea of modem costs. The costs presented are for very basic models; actual costs might be somewhat lower, or considerably higher (for additional capabilities).

Speed (bps)	Cost
300	$ 150
1200	400
300/1200	600
2400	1000
4800	2000
9600	3400

Bell Modems.   The modems developed by the telephone companies have become standards of reference for other modem manufacturers. Since it is fairly typical to have a manufacturer of modems cite compatibility with a particular Bell modem, the characteristics of the more common Bell modems are presented in Figure 2-34. Despite manufacturers' claims regarding compatibility with certain modem types, it is safest to pair modems from the same rather than different manufacturers, if for no other reason than to make support, maintenance, and problem resolution simpler. Figure 2-35 shows a pair of modems used to attach a terminal to a computer.

Figure 2-34
BELL Modems—
Basic Description

Modem Number	Speed (bps)	Timing	Channel Mode	Modulation
103	300	Async	HDX or FDX	FSK
108	300	Async	FDX	FSK
113	300	Async	HDX or FDX	FSK
201A	2000	Sync	HDX or FDX	PSK
201B, C	2400	Sync	HDX or FDX	PSK
202C, D, E, R, T	1200 1800	Async	HDX or FDX	FSK
202S	1200	Async	HDX	FSK
208A	4800	Sync	HDX or FDX	PSK
208B	4800	Sync	HDX	PSK

Continued

Modem Number	Speed (bps)	Timing	Channel Mode	Modulation
209	9600*	Sync	HDX or FDX	FSK
212	1200 300	Sync or Async	FDX	PSK
2024	2400	Sync	HDX or FDX	PSK
2048	4800	Sync	HDX or FDX	PSK
2096	9600	Sync	HDX or FDX	QAM

HDX = half duplex mode
FDX = full duplex mode
*May be subdivided into several slower channels, e.g., two 4800 bps lines.

Short-Haul Modems. When distances are relatively short, short-haul modems can be used. These allow for transmission distances up to approximately 20 miles, at varying speeds. In general, as distance increases, speed decreases. Figure 2-36 on page 68 presents the relationship between distance and speed with short-haul modems. Strictly speaking, distance is a function of the resistance of the conductor, and speed a function of the capacitance and resistance of the conductor. For practical purposes, distance and speed are a function of the thickness or gauge of the conductor. Figure 2-36 holds for 22-gauge wire; greater speeds or distances are possible with 19-gauge wire; and lower speeds or distances would result from the use of 26-gauge wire. The advantage of short-haul modems is a significant reduction in cost; 10-fold savings or better are possible.

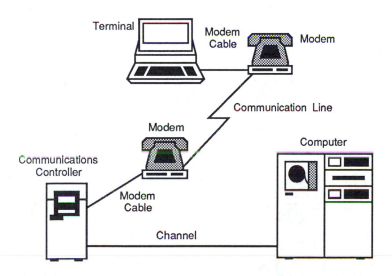

Figure 2-35
Terminal–Computer Connection Using Modems

Figure 2-36
Short-Haul Modems,
Speed vs Distance

Distance miles	Maximum Speed bps
17	2,400
15	4,800
12	9,600
7	19,200

Modem Eliminators.   For very short distances, *modem eliminators* exist that provide additional savings and very high data transmission rates. Modem eliminators, also referred to as line drivers or null modems, can connect two devices that are in close proximity. Although distances of 2000 feet or less are most common, some modem eliminators can span distances up to 25 miles. A modem eliminator provides clocking and interface functions between two devices. One modem eliminator can replace two modems, as illustrated in Figure 2-37. The spanable distances are covered by interface specifications such as RS-232-C, which specifies a maximum distance of 50 feet, or RS-449, which specifies 200 feet maximum. Although manufacturers usually certify their modem eliminators at these standard distances, longer distances are possible. One of the uses of modem eliminators is high-speed computer-to-computer communications links. Data transmission rates up to 1 million bps can be supported by modem eliminators.

The previously described modems are ones connected directly to communications wires. An *acoustic coupler* such as shown in Figure 2-38 allows for data transmission across telephone lines, using the telephone handset to pass the data. Acoustic couplers have a send-and-receive receptacle into which the handset is set. Transmission rates for acoustic couplers are usually either 300 or 1200 bps. They cost less than most modems. Acoustic couplers are widely used with portable terminals, some of which even incorporate the acoustic coupler as an integral part of the terminal.

Current Loops.   For distances up to 1500 feet, current loop technology allows for data transmission speeds up to 19,200 bps without any type of modem. The common model is a *20-milliampere current loop*. To transmit data by this technology, the current on the line is switched on and off or

Figure 2-37
A Modem Eliminator

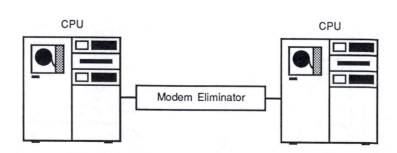

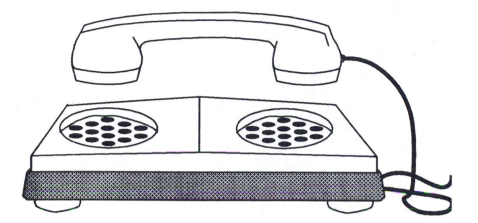

Figure 2-38
An Acoustic Coupler

the direction of the current is changed. In the first method, the presence of current represents a 1 bit and the absence of current denotes a 0 bit. This technique is referred to as *neutral working*. When current direction is switched, current flowing in one direction represents a 1 bit and current in the opposite direction is a 0 bit. This technique is termed *polar working*.

Fiber Optic Modems.   Modems are also used for fiber optic transmission at speeds ranging from 1200 bps up to 50 Mbps, with popular intermediate speeds of 56 Kbps, 100 Kbps, 250 Kbps, 1.544 Mbps, 5 Mbps, and 10 Mbps.

CASE STUDY

Business at the Syncrasy Corporation has been progressing. President Ima Overseer and the other two founders report that business has been excellent and expansion is in order. The first phase of expansion will include a larger computer system and two new locations, New York City and Los Angeles. The remote offices will each have ten terminals connected to the host computer in the Puma Flats office, where all inventory, pricing, and customer information is stored. It is anticipated that sales activity will occur throughout the day in both remote locations. The average order consists of 500 input characters and 100 response characters. The company's objective is to provide 5-second response time for each order; it has been determined that processing time per order averages 2.5 seconds. Thus far, each terminal operator enters 20 orders per hour on the average, with peak loads of 30 transactions per hour.

Given this information, Ms. Overseer wants to know which medium will best serve Syncrasy's immediate needs. To respond requires some basic calculations, the first of which is to determine the necessary speed of the lines.

Line Speed

Usually a system is configured to meet the peak transaction load; if it can handle the peaks, it can definitely handle the valleys. Although configuring for peak loads is not absolutely necessary, it would be rather disconcerting to have the system bog down when needed the most. Configuring to the peak work load also provides some latitude for expanding work during off-peak periods, including development activities like program compiling and batch operations such as payroll and periodic reports.

At this point it is assumed that two or more terminals might share a communications path (Chapters 4 and 5 discuss how this is done). First the needs of a single terminal are considered. Five hundred input characters and 100 output characters total to 600 characters transmitted per average transaction. The expected response time is 5 seconds, of which 2.5 seconds is probably communication time (estimated processing time was 2.5 seconds). Thus, one terminal will require a path with a speed of $600/2.5 = 240$ characters per second. Assuming 10 bits per character, a line speed of 2400 bps will be required. Since it is inconceivable that a line can operate at 100% capacity, a 4800 bps line is preferable.

Number of Terminals per Line

To determine how many terminals could effectively share a line demands some intuition: a peak rate of 30 transactions per hour per terminal equates to 300 transactions per hour or 5 transactions per minute. This rate is not excessive, and all ten terminals could conceivably use the same 2400-bps line. The only problem would be if two terminals were to enter data at exactly the same time; one response time would be the expected 5 seconds, whereas the other would be approximately 7 seconds. The logic behind this is provided in Figure 2-39, in which T represents transmission time, P represents processing time, and ш represents wait time. Terminal 2 sees a slower response time because it must hold off transmitting until Terminal 1 has sent its data. If the line speed were twice as fast (4800 bps), two concurrent terminals could be handled within the 5-second response time. If three of the terminals enter information at exactly the same time, one of them, of course, will have a lower response time. However, the chances of that happening with ten terminals on a line is slight. Assuming a random arrival rate, the probability of three transactions occurring in a 2-second interval is less than one in a hundred (0.0005); hence, a 4800-bps line should be satisfactory for all ten terminals.

Figure 2-39
Transaction Activity

```
Terminal 1    TTTTTTTTTTPPPPPPPPPPPPPPPTT
Terminal 2    ШШШШШШШШШШTTTTTTTTTTPPPPPPPPPPPPPPPTT
              ----1----2----3----4----5----6----7----8
              Time in Seconds
```

Other Criteria

There are no special environmental, security, expansion, maintenance, or error rate concerns to resolve in this system, and the application issues have already been addressed. The calculations indicate that a high-speed path is not necessary. Distance is definitely a factor in the remote connections, and transmission facilities should therefore be acquired from a common carrier such as a telephone company, MCI, or another circuit provider.

Private wires are best for the local terminals in the Puma Flats offices because the offices are free of environmental disturbances and there are no distance problems to overcome. Besides, private wires are far more cost effective than other solutions. Their speed can be greater than that of leased lines. Fiber optics and coaxial cable are definite possibilities, but they would be more costly if privately implemented, and such high data transmission rates are not required at this time.

SUMMARY

A wide variety of transmission media are available to the network designer, and many networks employ several of them. In fact, if the telephone companies' use of fiber optics, microwave, and satellite channels is considered, most long-distance networks are a combination of media. Numerous factors influence the selection of transmission media.

Each medium has information-carrying capacity, which varies from a few characters per second to millions of characters per second. The terms bit rate, baud rate, and bandwidth are used to describe a medium's carrying capacity, and these measures are interrelated.

In transmitting information between devices in a computer network, it is frequently necessary to convert a device's digital signals to analog format for transmission. There are several ways to do this; frequency modulation, phase modulation, and phase modulation plus amplitude modulation are the most common. The device that translates digital signals to analog signals and then back again is known as a modem or data set. Modems differ greatly in the bit rate provided as well as in the options available.

Key Terms

Acoustic coupler	Frequency modulation (FM)
Amplitude modulation (AM)	Frequency shift keying (FSK)
Analog representation	Leased line
Bandwidth	Microwave radio
Baseband transmission	Modem
Baud rate	Modem eliminator
Bit rate	Phase modulation
Broadband transmission	Phase shift keying (PSK)
Carrier signal	Private line
Coaxial cable	Propagation delay
Common carrier	Public line
Conducted media	Quadbit
Conditioned lines	Quadrature amplitude modulation
Data set	(QAM)
Dibit	Radiated media
Differential phase shift keying	Response time
(DPSK)	Satellite radio
Digital representation	Switched connection
Fiber optics	Tribit
	20-milliampere current loop

Questions and Exercises

1. What are the advantages and disadvantages of private lines?

Given the different modes of communication—private lines, switched lines, leased lines, coaxial cable, fiber optics, microwave, and satellite—which would be the most suitable for the following applications (2–8)? Why?

2. A large U.S. marketing organization must transmit large amounts of product information, sales data, facsimiles, and electronic mail to 40 cities. The 40 locations each have computers and send volumes of sales data, facsimiles, and electronic mail. Response time is not critical.

3. A manufacturing plant has multiple computers, data processing work stations, and terminals, all spread throughout six buildings. All facilities are located within 1 kilometer's distance of each other and all rights of way are controlled by the company. The data being transmitted include small files, memos, electronic mail, and on-line transactions. Response time is critical for the on-line transactions.

4. A hospital has automated its patient care system. Terminals have been placed in all administrative offices, laboratory facilities, doctors' and nurses' offices, and nursing work stations. The on-line transactions include data entry, inquiries, and short reports. Rapid response time is important.

5. A research corporation is engaged in evaluating solar energy systems. It has data collection devices attached to a number of experimental wind and solar collectors. The computer center to which the data must be transmitted is 10 miles from the test grounds. There is a large, continuous volume of data transmitted to the computer center. The computer center can be seen from the testing grounds.

6. A major fast-food chain has chosen to centralize its inventory and sales data. Each restaurant maintains its sales and inventory data on a small computer located in the store. This computer is attached to point-of-sale terminals that serve as data entry devices. Every time an item is sold, the inventory and sales data on the local computer are updated. Every evening the central office must retrieve the information from each store. The amount of information to be transmitted is approximately 10,000 characters per restaurant.

7. A major car rental agency has decided to regionalize their inventory and reservations system. Approximately 75% of the reservation requests are resolved by the regional center, and the remaining 25% must be forwarded to another regional processing center. The peak amount of data to be transmitted to another center is approximately 10,000 characters per minute. This also means that each regional center will receive approximately 10,000 characters per minute.

8. A research corporation must exchange data between three computers located in different departments within one building. The data are highly sensitive, so security is a major concern. The data consist of text, research results, graphics, and electronic mail. Response time is not critical. A communication speed of 9600 bps would be adequate. The optimum path for private wires would require the wires to pass through research areas with a considerable amount of electrical or magnetic activity.

References

Bellamy, John. *Digital Telephony.* New York: Wiley, 1982.

Digital Equipment Corp. *Introduction to Local Area Networks.* Digital Equipment Corporation, 1982.

Douglass, Jack L., and Zupko, Bill. *More About Modems.* Huntsville, AL: Universal Data Systems, 1983.

Farmer, Robin. "Cost Benefits of Fibre-Optic Systems." *Telecommunications,* July 1983.

Frank, Howard. "Broadband Versus Baseband Local Area Networks." *Telecommunications,* March 1983.

Freeman, Roger L. *Telecommunication Transmission Handbook.* New York: Wiley, 1981.

Held, Gilbert. *Data Communication Components.* Rochelle Park, N.J.: Hayden Book Co., 1979.

Hewlett-Packard Corp. *Guidebook to Data Communications.* Santa Clara, CA: Hewlett-Packard, 1977.

Jurenko, John A. *All About Modems.* Huntsville, AL: Universal Data Systems, 1981.

Loomis, Mary E. S. *Data Communications.* Englewood Cliffs, NJ: Prentice-Hall, 1983.

Lowndes, Jay C. "Optical Fiber Threatens Satellite Role in Voice Links." *Aviation Week & Space Technology,* January 31, 1983.

Martin, James. *Telecommunications and the Computer.* Englewood Cliffs, NJ: Prentice-Hall, 1976.

Redmond, Donald L., and Beveridge, Gregory J. *Fiber Optics, Believe It—Or Not.* Mountain Bell Network Engineering.

Schmidt, Wolfgang. "Field Trial of Fiber-Optic BIGFON LAN." *Telecommunications,* July 1983.

More Physical Aspects of Data Communication

Data Flow

Data Codes

Error Sources

Error Prevention

Error Detection

Error Correction

Digital Data Transmission

Interface

INTRODUCTION

This chapter, an extension of Chapter 2, continues the discussion of physical transmission of data. You will learn about the different sources of data transmission errors and how they are detected and corrected. You will also learn the advantages of digital transmission of data and the various standards for interfacing transmission media and data processing equipment.

DATA FLOW

Every data communications network must have some mechanism of control over the flow of data. There are two levels at which this is accomplished. The first level provides for *contention control*, which determines which stations may transmit, the conditions under which transmission of data is allowed, and the pacing of data transmission. Contention control is discussed in subsequent chapters. The other, more fundamental level of data flow relates to the transmission equipment used—lines, modems, and devices. There are three elementary types of data flow: simplex, half duplex, and full duplex.

Simplex Transmission

Simplex transmissions are those in which the data may flow in only one direction, like traffic on a one-way street. Radio and television transmissions, which are illustrated in Figure 3-1(a), are examples. In simplex transmission one station assumes the role of transmitter while the other station is the receiver; these roles may not be reversed.

Although this may seem rather limiting, simplex transmission still has numerous applications. Receive-only devices such as printers and paper tape punches, involve simplex communication. Although communications with the many printers that are capable of transmitting status information back to the host are not classified as simplex, the many data collection devices serving as input devices only do use simplex communication. For instance, in solar energy research installations, heat sensors, insolation monitors, and flow meters have been used to monitor the environment and transmit samples of data via a simplex line. A building environmental monitoring system would also operate in this mode by sending temperature and humidity readings to a computer that controls the heating and cooling of the building.

Simplex lines are uncommon in business applications; they are used primarily for certain printers and for monitoring devices in environment and process-control applications.

Figure 3-1
Examples of Data
Flow

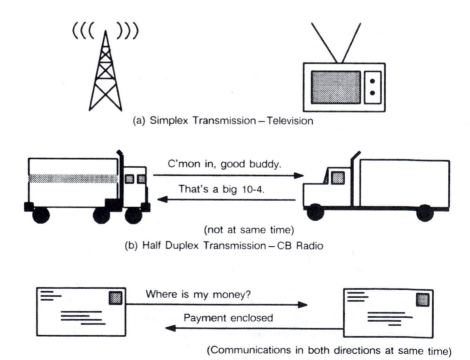

(a) Simplex Transmission – Television

C'mon in, good buddy.

That's a big 10-4.

(not at same time)
(b) Half Duplex Transmission – CB Radio

Where is my money?

Payment enclosed

(Communications in both directions at same time)

(c) Full Duplex Transmission – Mail System

Half Duplex Transmission

In *half duplex transmission*, data may travel in both directions, although only in one direction at a time, like traffic on a one-lane bridge where vehicles may traverse in either direction but only one vehicle at a time. An example, illustrated in Figure 3-1(b), is citizens band (CB) radio, where radio operators on the same frequency may be either sender or receiver but not both at the same time.

Continuous vs. Noncontinuous Carriers.   When data flow is controlled by a modem, there are two half duplex options available—continuous carrier and noncontinuous carrier. A carrier signal, which involves a continuous frequency, is the signal that is modulated to represent data. In *continuous carrier* mode, even though data may only pass in one direction at a time, the carrier signal on which the data is imposed is passed in both directions, as indicated in Figure 3-2. *Noncontinuous carrier* mode allows a carrier signal to be passed in either direction, but only one direction at a time, as shown in Figure 3-3.

Modem Turnaround Time.   In noncontinuous carrier mode there is an additional delay in transmitting the data. This delay, referred to as *modem turnaround time* and illustrated in Figure 3-4 on page 78, is the period required for the old sender to drop the carrier signal, for the new sender to recognize that the carrier signal has been dropped, and for the new sender to raise the carrier signal that must be detected by the new receiver.

Because modem turnaround time can exceed 100 milliseconds, it has an important impact on total transmission time. For example, suppose a banking transaction at an automatic teller machine (ATM) requires the following transmissions on a half duplex line with noncontinuous carrier and a transmission speed of 4800 bps.

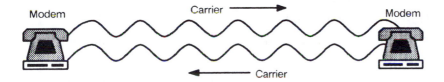

Figure 3-2
Continuous Carrier

Figure 3-3
Non-Continuous Carrier

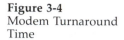
Figure 3-4
Modem Turnaround
Time

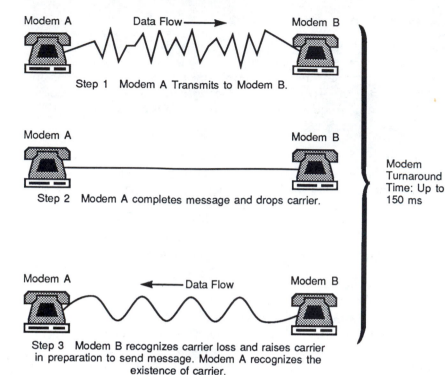

ATM transmits 20 characters to host computer.

Host computer transmits 40 characters to ATM.

ATM transmits 20 characters to host computer to acknowledge the transaction.

Host computer transmits 10 characters to ATM to ready it for the next transaction.

In all, 90 characters are transmitted, with four modem turnarounds. Assuming 10 bits per character and a modem turnaround time of 50 milliseconds, this gives: 10 bits per character × 90 characters = 900 bits transmitted, requiring 900/4800 = 0.19 seconds transmission time; and 4 modem turnarounds × 50 milliseconds per turnaround = 0.20 seconds modem turnaround time. Although transactions involving transfer of such small amounts of data are atypical, this shows that modem turnaround time can be a significant part of total data transmission time.

Reverse Channel Capability.   In order to minimize the effect of modem turnaround time, some half duplex modems provide a reverse channel. For example; certain communications systems require the receiver to briefly (a few characters) acknowledge receipt of each data transmission before another can be sent. In other situations, printers pass back brief status signals to indicate their readiness to receive more data. One set of conventions is known as XON and XOFF: When a terminal or printer wants the host to send more data, it transmits an XON signal, and when it does not want more data transmitted it sends an XOFF signal. If modem turnaround were required for each of these short sequences, then overall turnaround time would be significant. A reverse channel provides a very slow circuit that allows the receiver to send these short messages without forcing a line turnaround. Thus, reverse channel capability is a subcase of continuous carrier mode. That is, there is a carrier in both directions, but the reverse channel has a lower transmission rate than the forward channel. Bell series 202 modems provide such a reverse channel capability with a 50 bps carrying capacity, as illustrated in Figure 3-5.

Full Duplex Transmission

In *full duplex mode*, data can be transmitted in both directions simultaneously, like traffic on a two-way street. An example of data transmission using full duplex capabilities is the postal service: Letters can be transmitted in both directions simultaneously, as illustrated in Figure 3-1(c) on page 76. Figure 3-6 on page 80 shows full duplex communication. In full duplex transmission there is no modem turnaround time to consider.

Two Wire Pairs vs. Four-Wire Connections.   There has been some terminological confusion regarding the number of wire pairs involved in full duplex transmission. This is because telephone companies utilize wire pairs (also referred to as two-wire connections) to transmit voice and data, since a wire pair is less error-prone than a single wire. Two-wire connec-

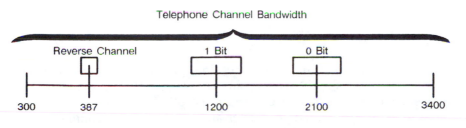

Figure 3-5
A Reverse Channel
Bell 202 Modem

Figure 3-6
Data Flow
Alternatives

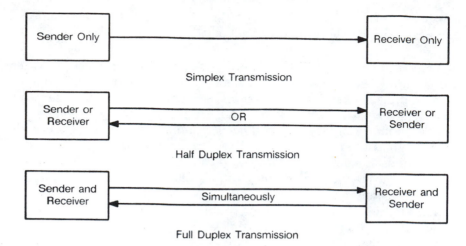

tions are essentially half duplex; thus, long-distance telephone conversations, especially overseas, can lead to signal distortion when the two parties attempt to talk at the same time and only one wire pair has been used to make the connection. As a result, long-distance calls employ either 2 wire pairs or a four-wire connection and thus provide a full duplex connection. Most local connections use only one wire pair. The confusion arises from the use of four-wire connections as full duplex and two-wire connections as half duplex. Four-wire connections will support full duplex but can operate in half duplex mode with or without continuous carrier, depending on the modem. It is *not* true; as is frequently heard, that a four-wire connection is required for full duplex operations; two-wire connections can allow full duplex operations by dividing the bandwidth of the wire pair, thereby creating a pseudo-four-wire connection out of a two-wire link. Thus, the statement that full duplex operations require a four-wire connection really means that a "logical" four-wire connection is necessary.

Full duplex operations are effected in radio wave transmissions by using two different frequencies, one for each direction. With coaxial cable, full duplex operations require broadband transmission.

DATA CODES

As already mentioned, data are stored in digital computers as sequences of binary digits (bits), each with a value of either 0 or 1. To provide meaning to a sequence of bits, it is necessary to establish the number of bits that are grouped to form a data character and to create an encoding scheme, or translation table, by which the system translates each group of bits into a character. In the encoding scheme of telegraphy—Morse code—each character is represented as a combination of dots and dashes. Although these could be also interpreted as bits, Morse code is not suitable for data communications, because characters are represented by a different number of bits (for example, the letter *A* is represented by dot-dash and the letter *S* by dot-dot-dot). Telegraphers distinguish one letter grouping from another by the time delay between characters. Such a scheme is impractical for computer-based systems. As a result, virtually all computer codes use a fixed number of bits per character.

The number of bits that make up the characters also determines the number of distinct characters that can be represented. Figure 3-7 lists several data encoding schemes as well as the number of bits per character and the number of characters that can be represented by those codes.

Coding Scheme	Number of Bits	Characters Representable
BCD	4	16
BAUDOT	5	32 (62 using shift key)
BCD	6	64
SBT	6	64
Standard ASCII	7	128
Extended ASCII	8	256
EBCDIC	8	256
Touchtone telephone		12 frequencies

Figure 3-7
Some Common Data Codes

BCD

BCD is an acronym for *binary coded decimal* and exists in both 4-bit and 6-bit versions. The 4-bit code is used for economy in transmission of numeric data. With 4 bits, at most 16 different entities can be represented, so 4-bit BCD is not at all suited to the transmission of alphabetic or punctuation characters. However, for transmitting strings of numeric data, 4-bit BCD uses 3 bits fewer than ASCII and 4 bits fewer than EBCDIC or Extended ASCII, thus increasing the effective line utilization. When used in this manner, 4-bit BCD is normally transmitted in mixed mode with another code, making it the responsibility of the application to determine the context of the data. The 4-bit BCD code is given in Figure 3-8.

Bit Pattern	Numeric Equivalent
0000	0
0001	1
0010	2
0011	3
0100	4
0101	5

Figure 3-8
The 4-bit BCD Code

Continued

Bit Pattern	Numeric Equivalent
0110	6
0111	7
1000	8
1001	9

As an example of the efficiency to be gained from using 4-bit BCD, consider the transmission of a payroll file from one computer to another, one possible record layout of which is given in Figure 3-9. Suppose that there are 50,000 records in the file and that each character is represented by 8 bits. Without BCD, the total number of bits transferred would be $50,000 \times 100 \times 8 = 40,000,000$ bits. With BCD, the first nine digits would be transmitted in nine 4-bit groups. In this example, 4 bits would be added to "pad" the group so that the *employee name* field would begin at an 8-bit boundary. Thus, 40 bits (5 characters) would be required for *employee ID*. BCD would *not* be used on the *employee name* field. The remaining numeric fields could each be translated into BCD. These 61 characters would require 61 4-bit entities; again, there would be 4 bits of padding to round up to a character boundary. Rather than transmitting 61 8-bit characters, 31 8-bit entities would suffice. The number of bits required for transfer is thus $50,000 \times (5 + 30 + 31) \times 8 = 50,000 \times 66 \times 8 = 26,4000,000$ bits, representing a savings of 13,600,000 bits, or 34%. With a line speed of 4800 bps, this would save approximately 47 minutes of transmission time. In actuality, the savings could be even greater, since error rates and the characters necessary to provide control of the communication link (see Chapter 6) have been excluded.

Figure 3-9
A Payroll History
Record

Field	Contents	Size
Employee ID	Numeric	9
Employee name	Alphabetic	30
Department	Numeric	4
Hours worked	Numeric	6
Pay rate	Numeric	6
Exempt code	Numeric	1
Year to date (YTD), gross	Numeric	8
YTD, FICA	Numeric	8
YTD, federal tax	Numeric	8
YTD, local tax	Numeric	8
YTD, other	Numeric	8
Dependents	Numeric	2
Status code	Numeric	2
		100

The 6-bit BCD code is not used extensively because it can represent only 64 different symbols, a rather limited number. For example, one could represent only 26 letters (uppercase or lowercase but not both), 10 numeric digits, and 28 other symbols for punctuation and control. A standard typewriter has 24 special punctuation or use symbols alone.

BAUDOT

BAUDOT is a code derived from the telegraph industry and so its primary use in data communications is with telegraph lines or equipment originally designed for telegraphy. Its biggest limitation is in the number of representable characters: With only 5 bits per character, BAUDOT can represent at most 32 distinct characters, which is inadequate for all 26 letters of the Roman alphabet and the ten numeric digits, let alone uppercase and lowercase and punctuation.

A technique is needed to extend the limited character set. One additional bit, for instance, would allow a total of 64 characters to be represented. But since BAUDOT cannot physically be extended to 6 bits, obtaining this additional bit requires up-shift and down-shift modes, like on a typewriter (up-shift produces capital letters and punctuation, down-shift produces lowercase letters and numbers, and in this way, 47 typewriter keys create 94 characters). In the Baudot code, the 5 bits transmitted must be interpreted according to whether they are up-shifted (uppercase) or down-shifted (lowercase). For instance, the bit pattern *11111* represents down-shift characters and the bit pattern *11011* represents up-shift characters. And all characters transmitted after the sequence *11111* but before the shifted sequence of *11011* are treated as down-shift characters. Similarly, all characters transmitted after the sequence *11011* are treated as up-shift (uppercase) characters until the pattern *11111* is recognized. Since two bit patterns are reserved to indicate the shift mode and therefore may not be used to represent transmitted characters, the total number of characters that can be represented is reduced to 62. Figure 3-10 gives the Baudot code.

Bit Pattern	Down-Shift Character	Up-Shift Character
00000	Blank	Blank
00001	T	5
00010	Carriage return	Carriage return
00011	O	9
00100	Space	Space
00101	H	English currency
00110	N	,
00111	M	.
01000	Line feed	
01001	L	)
01010	R	4
01011	G	&
01100	I	8
01101	P	0
01110	C	:
01111	V	;
10000	E	3
10001	Z	"
10010	D	$
10011	B	?

Figure 3-10
The Baudot Code

Continued

Bit Pattern	Down-Shift Character	Up-Shift Character
10100	S	Bell
10101	Y	6
10110	F	!
10111	X	/
11000	A	-
11001	W	2
11010	J	'
11011	Shift down	Shift down
11100	U	7
11101	Q	1
11110	K	(
11111	Shift up	Shift up

As an example of the up-shift and down-shift requirements of the Baudot code, suppose the message *FLIGHT 10* is to be transmitted. This would necessitate the sequence given the Figure 3-11.

Figure 3-11
An Example of
Baudot Transmission

11111	10110	01001	01100	01011	00101	00001	00100	11011	11101	0110
Down-shift	F	L	I	G	H	T	Space	Up-shift	1	0

Baudot code has an additional shortcoming: it does not follow the standard collating sequence for letters and numbers. Thus, for instance, the bit pattern 11101, which represents the number *1*, is numerically higher than the pattern for the number *9*—00011; and 11000, the pattern for the letter *A*, is higher than 10001, the pattern for *Z*. Although this is not a problem from a purely data communications point of view, it does require additional expense when used for comparing data field values.

SBT

SBT, an abbreviation for *six-bit transcode*, was created by IBM primarily for remote job entry communications. It is not used extensively.

ASCII

ASCII is an acronym for *American standard code for information interchange*. ASCII and EBCDIC (see next section) are the codes most commonly used. ASCII (also known as USASCII) is implemented primarily as a 7-bit code, although an extended 8-bit version also exists. With 7 bits, 128 characters can be represented: with 8 bits there are 256 characters available. As an alternative to the 8-bit code, the 7-bit form can be extended in much the same manner as the Baudot code (using the special characters *shift out* and *shift in*, with bit patterns of 0001110 and 0001111, respectively). Extending the number of characters provides for additional character sets for graphics and foreign languages such as Katakana. The 7-bit ASCII code is presented in Figure 3-12.

High Order Bits

	000	001	010	011	100	101	110	111
0000	NUL	DLE	SPACE	0	@	P	`	p
0001	SOH	DC1	!	1	A	Q	a	q
0010	STX	DC2	"	2	B	R	b	r
0011	ETX	DC3	#	3	C	S	c	s
0100	EOT	DC4	$	4	D	T	d	t
0101	ENQ	NAK	%	5	E	U	e	u
0110	ACK	SYN	&	6	F	V	f	v
0111	BEL	ETB	'	7	G	W	g	w
1000	BS	CAN	(	8	H	X	h	x
1001	HT	EM	)	9	I	Y	i	y
1010	LF	SUB	*	:	J	Z	j	z
1011	VT	ESC	+	;	K	[	k	{
1100	FF	FS	,	<	L	\	l	|
1101	CR	GS	-	=	M	]	m	}
1110	SO	RS	.	>	N	^	n	~
1111	SI	US	/	?	O	_	o	DEL

Low Order Bits

Figure 3-12
The USASCII Bit
Code

To read this chart, combine the bits in the columns with those in the rows, with the column bits first in the high order position. That is, the bit pattern which represents the letter A is 1000001 and the bit pattern which represents the number 9 is 0111001.

EBCDIC

EBCDIC stands for *extended binary-coded decimal interchange code*. It utilizes 8 bits to form a character, and thus, 256 different characters can be represented. The EBCDIC code is presented in Figures 3-13(a) and 3-13(b) on pages 86 and 87.

As Figures 3-12 and 3-13 show, both ASCII and EBCDIC have some codes (for example, ASCII 0000000 and 0000011) with mnemonic names such as NUL and ETX. These special characters, which are discussed in more detail in Chapter 5, are used to provide control information to nodes on the network as well as to represent binary data.

Figure 3-13(a)
The EBCDIC 8-Bit
Code

High Order Bits

Low Order Bits	1000	1001	1010	1011	1100	1101	1110	1111
0000					{	}	\	0
0001	a	j	~		A	J		1
0010	b	k	s		B	K	S	2
0011	c	l	t		C	L	T	3
0100	d	m	u		D	M	U	4
0101	e	n	v		E	N	V	5
0110	f	o	w		F	O	W	6
0111	g	p	x		G	P	X	7
1000	h	q	y		H	Q	Y	8
1001	i	r	z		I	R	Z	9
1010								
1011								
1100								
1101								
1110								
1111								

Touch-tone™ Telephone

The Touch-tone™ telephone code turns a touch tone telephone into a data communications terminal. Some banks, for instance, allow customers to pay bills and transfer money between accounts using their touchtone telephone in this way. Each telephone key transmits a signal at a unique frequency that is acceptable to voice-grade lines. Telephone sets have 12 keys, so 12 different frequencies can be transmitted. This rather limited code set also limits the communications applications of the telephone instrument.

Data Code Size

The transition from 5-bit and 6-bit codes to 7-bit and 8-bit codes became necessary to increase the number of unique code sequences that could be

High Order Bits

<table>
<tr><th>Low Order Bits</th><th>0000</th><th>0001</th><th>0010</th><th>0011</th><th>0100</th><th>0101</th><th>0110</th><th>0111</th></tr>
<tr><td>0000</td><td>NUL</td><td>DLE</td><td>DS</td><td></td><td>SPACE</td><td>@</td><td>-</td><td></td></tr>
<tr><td>0001</td><td>SOH</td><td>DC1</td><td>SOS</td><td></td><td></td><td></td><td></td><td></td></tr>
<tr><td>0010</td><td>STX</td><td>DC2</td><td>FS</td><td>SYN</td><td></td><td></td><td></td><td></td></tr>
<tr><td>0011</td><td>ETX</td><td>DC3</td><td></td><td></td><td></td><td></td><td></td><td></td></tr>
<tr><td>0100</td><td>PF</td><td>RES</td><td>BYP</td><td>PN</td><td></td><td></td><td></td><td></td></tr>
<tr><td>0101</td><td>HT</td><td>NL</td><td>LF</td><td>RS</td><td></td><td></td><td></td><td></td></tr>
<tr><td>0110</td><td>LC</td><td>BS</td><td>ETB</td><td>UC</td><td></td><td></td><td></td><td></td></tr>
<tr><td>0111</td><td>DEL</td><td>IL</td><td>ESC</td><td>EOT</td><td></td><td></td><td></td><td></td></tr>
<tr><td>1000</td><td></td><td>CAN</td><td></td><td></td><td></td><td></td><td></td><td></td></tr>
<tr><td>1001</td><td>RLF</td><td>EM</td><td></td><td></td><td></td><td></td><td></td><td>\</td></tr>
<tr><td>1010</td><td>SMN</td><td>CC</td><td>SM</td><td></td><td>¢</td><td>!</td><td>|</td><td>:</td></tr>
<tr><td>1011</td><td></td><td></td><td></td><td></td><td>.</td><td>$</td><td>,</td><td>#</td></tr>
<tr><td>1100</td><td>FF</td><td>IFS</td><td></td><td>DC4</td><td><</td><td>*</td><td>%</td><td>@</td></tr>
<tr><td>1101</td><td>CR</td><td>IGS</td><td>ENQ</td><td>NAK</td><td>(</td><td>)</td><td>-</td><td>'</td></tr>
<tr><td>1110</td><td>SO</td><td>IRS</td><td>ACK</td><td></td><td>+</td><td>;</td><td>></td><td>=</td></tr>
<tr><td>1111</td><td>SI</td><td>IUS</td><td>BEL</td><td>SUB</td><td>|</td><td></td><td>?</td><td>"</td></tr>
</table>

Figure 3-13(b) The EBCDIC 8-Bit Code

To read this chart, combine the bits in the columns with those in the rows, with the column bits first in the high order position. That is, the bit pattern which represents the letter A is 11000001 and the bit pattern which represents the number 9 is 11111001.

represented. The two most common data communications codes are 7-bit and 8-bit codes and are able to represent 128 and 256 unique symbols, respectively. Is this a sufficient number of symbols? An 8-bit code can represent the 26-letter Roman alphabet, (both uppercase and lowercase), the ten Arabic numerals (0 through 9), and punctuation, totaling approximately 100 characters and symbols. Additional bit patterns may be required for line control, so perhaps up to 128 characters can be used. What are the rest used for?

Alphabets and Graphics. For one thing, there may be a need to accommodate other alphabets, such as Greek and Cyrillic (Russian), and their accompanying diacritical marks, such as the tilde, umlaut, and accents. Still, 256 bits can accommodate the Roman alphabet and one other alphabet, with characters left over—that is, until we look at Asian and Mid-East languages. The Kanji character set used for written communication in Japan and China, for instance, contains over 30,000 ideograms and symbols. Thus, 256 unique symbols does not really go very far.

In addition to accommodating various alphabets, a data code may need to transmit, store, manipulate, and display graphics information, thus requiring additional characters consisting of line drawing characters that can easily exceed 100 different symbols. It is also likely that some of the newer technologies, such as videotex (in which text and images are transmitted together) will require a large number of characters. The data communications codes in current use have proved to be inadequate to meet the demands of increased communication between different cultures and languages, as well as the anticipated demands for extended services such as videotex. Now that the limitations of 8-bit codes are apparent, perhaps an international code using 16 bits will emerge. In Japan this has already been addressed in a number of standards.

ERROR SOURCES

All data transmissions are subject to error, although there is variation among media regarding their susceptibility to error. Contextual recognition of errors is almost never possible in data communications systems. If the data transmitter and receiver are computers, it is virtually impossible for editing routines to determine if one or more bits have been changed; even if data are displayed on a terminal, the operator may be unable to discern all the errors. For example, if a bank teller interrogates a customer's account balance as illustrated in Figure 3-14, the teller would be unlikely to recognize that a 1-bit error had altered the balance from $100 to $228. There are a number of ways in which errors can be induced during data transmission. The most common are: white noise, impulse noise, crosstalk, echo, phase jitter, envelope delay distortion, and attenuation.

White Noise

White noise, also referred to as thermal noise and *Gaussian noise*, results from the normal movements of electrons and is present in all transmission media at temperatures above absolute zero. The amount of white noise is directly proportional to the temperature of the medium (hence, the term *thermal*). White noise also is distributed randomly throughout a medium (hence the term *Gaussian*). White noise in telephone circuits is sometimes heard as a static or hissing on the line. Usually, the magnitude of white noise is not sufficient to create data loss in wire circuits, but it can become

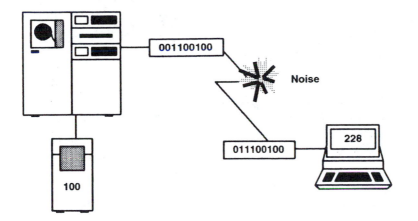

Figure 3-14
A Transmission Error

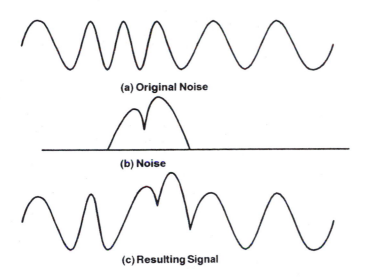

Figure 3-15
The Impact of Noise
on a Data Signal

significant in radio frequency links such as microwave and satellite. Because white noise is proportional to bandwidth as well as temperature, improperly focused antennas (e.g., directed toward the sun) can create enough disturbance to produce errors. Figure 3-15 illustrates the impact of noise on a data communications signal.

Impulse Noise

Impulse noise is characterized by signal "spikes." In telephone circuits it can be caused by switching equipment or by lightning strikes, and in other situations by transient electrical impulses such as those occurring on a shop floor. Impulse noise, the primary cause of data errors in telephone circuits, is heard as a clicking or crackling sound. It is usually of relatively short duration (several milliseconds), with varying levels of magnitude.

Crosstalk

Crosstalk occurs when signals from one channel distort or interfere with the signals of a different channel. In telephone connections, crosstalk sometimes appears in the form of another party's conversation heard in the background. Crosstalk is also present in radio frequency and multiplexed transmissions (see Chapter 5) when the frequency ranges are too close together. Crosstalk in wire-pair transmission occurs when wire pairs interfere with each other as a result of strong signals or improper shielding or both. Another common cause of crosstalk is interference between receivers and transmitters when a strong outgoing signal interferes with a weaker incoming signal. Crosstalk is directly proportional to distance, bandwidth, signal strength, and proximity to other transmission channels; it is inversely proportional to shielding or channel separation. Crosstalk is not usually a significant factor in data communications errors.

Intermodulation Noise.   One special form of crosstalk is intermodulation noise, which is the result of two or more signals combining to produce a signal outside the limits of the communications channel. For example, given that one mode of FSK modulation represents a one bit as a frequency of 1300 Hz and a zero bit as a frequency of 2100 Hz, with a variance of 10 Hz, if crosstalk were to combine signals of 1350 and 2150 Hz, then the resultant signal (1350 + 2150 = 3500 Hz) would be out of the accepted frequency range of voice communication over telephone lines (300–3400 Hz).

Echo

Echo is essentially the reflection or reversal of the signal being transmitted. This is most likely to occur at junctions in the transmission where wires are interconnected, or at the end of a line in a local area network. On a telephone line, a listener hears the echo of his/her voice several seconds after speaking.

Echo Suppressors.   To minimize this echo effect telephone companies have installed *echo suppressors* on their networks. The echo suppressor works by essentially allowing the signal to pass in one direction only. In voice transmission, the suppressor continually reverses itself to match the direction of conversation. Obviously this would impede data transmissibility in full duplex mode. To over come this problem, suppressers can be disengaged when full duplex transmission is required.

Phase Jitter

Phase jitter is a variation in the phase of a continuous signal from cycle to cycle; it is especially significant when the modulation mode involves phase shifting.

Attenuation

Attenuation is weakening of a signal as a result of distance and characteristics of the medium, and can produce a significant number of data errors. For a given gauge of wire and bit rate, a signal can be carried for a certain distance without enhancement. Beyond that distance, however, a signal repeater or amplifier would have to be included to ensure that the receiving station can properly recognize the data.

Envelope Delay Distortion

Envelope delay distortion occurs when signals that have been weakened or subjected to outside interference by transmission over long distances are enhanced by passing them through filters. Passing the signals through a filter delays them a certain amount, depending on the frequency of the signal.

Impact of Data Errors

Figure 3-16 shows the possible effects of impulse noise of various durations, for different line speeds. It is significant that fewer bits are subject to error when transmission is at lower rather than higher speeds. Although the figure applies to any type of noise for the same durations, impulse noise has been chosen because it is one of the most common types of noise affecting telephone wires.

Line Speed (bps)	Impulse Noise Duration (milliseconds)				
	0.2	0.4	0.6	0.8	1.0
300	0.06	0.12	0.18	0.24	0.30
1,200	0.24	0.48	0.72	0.96	1.20
2,400	0.48	0.96	1.44	1.92	2.40
4,800	0.96	1.92	2.88	3.94	4.80
9,600	1.92	3.94	5.76	7.88	9.60
19,200	3.94	7.88	11.52	15.76	19.20

Figure 3-16
Potential Number of Corrupted Data Bits

The most significant thing shown by Figure 3-16 is that the potential number of bit errors increases with both duration of the noise and line speed. While the ideal is to eliminate all errors in data, for practical purposes a goal of fewer than one error per 100,000 bits is considered satisfactory. (Most line media and radio wave transmission systems are designed for fewer than one error per 1 million bits transmitted.)

ERROR PREVENTION

The best method to guard against data errors is to correct their source. Eliminating all noise is impossible, but error prevention techniques can reduce the probability of error corruption in the data.

Telephone Line Conditioning

When a line is leased from a telephone company, *conditioning*—sometimes referred to as *equalization*—can optionally be included, for an additional charge. There are two classes of conditioning available, Class C and Class D, with four commercial levels of Class C conditioning: C1, C2, C4, and C5 conditioning, each of which provides increasingly stringent constraints on the amplitude and phase distortion permitted on the line. For instance, a line with C5 conditioning should be more error-free than a line with C1 conditioning or no conditioning at all. One useful aspect of Class D conditioning—a relatively new service—is that the telephone company will inspect the circuits available between the desired communication points to select the one with the least amount of noise. The user can obtain equipment, for instance certain modems, that aid in the conditioning of lines.

Lower Transmission Speed

As was just seen, a bit error is much less likely to occur at lower transmission speeds. Some modems can perform this function automatically or via program control. For example, with a high-quality line such a modem will operate at 2400 bps; if the quality of the line deteriorates, it has the capability of switching to a lower speed, say, 1200 bps.

Shielding

Although additional shielding of leased telephone cables is not a user option, shielding can be provided for private lines to reduce the amount of crosstalk and impulse noise from the environment.

Line Drivers (Repeaters)

Line drivers, or repeaters, can be placed at intervals along a communications line to amplify and forward the signal. Digital signal noise can usually be eliminated, because the signal is being regenerated. For analog signals, however, it is difficult to separate most noise from the signal. Thus, noise that is picked up will also be amplified by the repeaters. The function of repeaters is to restore signals to their full strength.

Better Equipment

Since some older mechanical switching equipment and some older transformers and power supplies are more likely to produce noise than are newer equipment (such as electronic switches), replacing these components with better equipment can reduce the amount of noise.

ERROR DETECTION

Generally, the remedies just cited to minimize the number of errors are impractical from either a cost or feasibility standpoint. Since error elimination is impossible, it becomes necessary to determine if an error has occurred and then to return the data to proper form.

Error detection algorithms in data communications networks are based on the transmission of redundant information. In telegraphy, one way to ensure correctness of data is to transmit each character twice. Since even this is not entirely error-proof, it could be taken one or more steps further by sending each character three or more times. Although this might increase the reliability of the transmission somewhat, line utilization drops dramatically. That is, as the error rate approaches zero, so does the effective utilization of the medium. Obviously, some middle-ground approach is required. It is necessary to detect almost all errors without significantly reducing the data-carrying capacity of the medium.

Parity Check

One of the simplest and most widely used forms of error detection is known as a *parity check* or *vertical redundancy check (VRC)*. A parity check involves adding a bit—known as the *parity bit*—to each character when transmitted, to bring the total number of one bits in the code representation of each character up to either an even number (*even parity*) or an odd number (*odd parity*). Each character when received is then checked to see if the number of bits is even or odd, as transmitted. For example, consider the string of characters "DATA COMM" as coded in 7-bit ASCII with odd parity. The representation of these characters plus the parity bit for odd parity are given in Figure 3-17 on page 94. It can be seen that the number of one bits in each 8-bit sequence (octet) is always odd (either 1, 3, 5, or 7); it is the parity bit that ensures this. If even parity were chosen, the number of one bits would always be an even number because of the parity bit chosen.

If there is no parity bit or if the parity bit is not checked (called *no parity check*), then the ability to detect errors using this method is lost (although there are other methods, to be described later, that could be utilized).

Figure 3-17
Parity Bit Generation

Letter	ASCII	Parity Bit	Transmitted Bits
D	1000100	1	10001001
A	1000001	1	10000011
T	1010100	0	10101000
A	1000001	1	10000011
space	0100000	0	01000000
C	1000011	0	10000110
O	1001111	0	10011110
M	1001101	1	10011011
M	1001101	1	10011011

Parity Check Effectiveness.   In the odd-parity example in Figure 3-17 each character transmitted consists of 8 bits—seven for data and one for parity. Odd parity enables the user to detect whether 1, 3, 5, or 7 bits have been altered in transmission, but it will not catch whether an even number (2, 4, 6, or 8 bits) has been altered. One common error situation involves *burst errors*, or a grouping of errors (recall the possible effect of impulse noise during high transmission rates). Thus, the likelihood of detecting errors of this nature with a parity check is approximately 50%. At higher transmission speeds this limitation becomes significant. (Note: A burst error for the duration of two bits does not necessarily result in two bit errors. None, one, or two bits could be affected.)

Longitudinal Redundancy Check (LRC)

We can increase the probability of error detection beyond that provided by parity by making, in addition, a *longitudinal redundancy check (LRC)*. With LRC, which is similar to VRC, an additional, redundant character called the *block check character (BCC)* is appended to a block of transmitted characters, typically at the end of the block. The *first* bit in the BCC serves as a parity check for all of the *first* bits of the characters in the block; the *second* bit of the BCC serves as parity for all of the *second* bits in the block; and so on. An example of LRC is provided in Figure 3-18. Since an odd parity scheme has been chosen to perform the redundancy check, each column has an odd number of one bits.

Figure 3-18
Longitudinal Redundancy Check (LRC) Generation

Letter	ASCII	Parity Bit	Transmitted Bits
D	1000100	1	10001001
A	1000001	1	10000011
T	1010100	0	10101000
A	1000001	1	10000011
space	0100000	0	01000000
C	1000011	0	10000110
O	1001111	0	10011110
M	1001101	1	10011011
M	1001101	1	10011011
BCC	1000011	0	10000110

LRC Effectiveness.   LRC combined with VRC is still not sufficient to detect *all* errors (indeed, no scheme is completely dependable). For instance, Figure 3-19 presents the same "DATA COMM" message transmission, with errors introduced in rows and columns marked by an asterisk. It shows that although both LRC and VRC appear correct, the data recieved are not the same as those transmitted. Again what we have accomplished by adding LRC to VRC is a *greater probability* of detecting errors in transmission.

Letter	ASCII	Parity Bit	Transmitted Bits
D	**1000100	1	10001001
A	1000001	1	10000011
T	*1100100	0	10101000
A	*1110001	1	10000011
space	0100000	0	01000000
C	1000011	0	10000110
O	1001111	0	10011110
M	1001101	1	10011011
M	1001101	1	10011011
BCC	1000011	0	10000110

Figure 3-19
LRC Transmission Errors

Cyclic Redundancy Check (CRC)

A *cyclic redundancy check (CRC)* can detect bit errors better than either VRC or LRC or both. The mathematics behind CRC is beyond the scope of this book, but the application is essentially as follows.

A CRC is computed for a block of transmitted data. The bits in the block are used to form a polynomial function. If the number of bits in the block is k, then the degree of the polynomial is $k - 1$ and there are k coefficients a. That is, the polynomial is of the form

$$a_{k-1}x^{k-1} + a_{k-2}x^{k-2} + \cdots + a_1x + a_0$$

A generator polynomial of degree p is chosen to divide into the data polynomial, yielding a quotient and a remainder of degree $p - 1$. The p coefficients of this remainder polynomial become the block check character(s).

The transmitting station calculates the BCC and transmits it with the data. The receiving station computes the BCC for the data as received and compares it to the received BCC; if the two are equal then the block is assumed to be error-free.

CRC Effectiveness.   If the generator polynomial is chosen with care and is of high enough degree, then over 99% of multiple bit errors can be detected with CRC. Several standards exist—CRC-12, CRC-16, and CRC-CCITT—that define both the degree of the generating polynomial and the generating polynomial itself. Since CRC-12 specifies a polynomial of degree 12, and the latter two standards specify a polynomial of degree 16, the BCC will have 12 or 16 bits. CRC-16 and CRC-CCITT can:

(a) Detect all single-bit and double-bit errors

(b) Detect all errors in cases in which an odd number of bits are erroneous

(c) Detect two pairs of adjacent errors

(d) Detect all burst errors of 16 bits or fewer

(e) Detect over 99.998% of all burst errors greater than 16 bits

Because of its reliability, CRC is becoming the standard method of error detection for block data transmission (as opposed to one character at a time). Chapter 6 discusses different data transmission methods and their associated error detection schemes.

Sequence Checks

When a data communications network is simple enough so that sending and receiving nodes are connected directly, the receiving station will receive all transmissions without the intercession of other nodes. However, large communications networks may have one or more intermediate nodes responsible for forwarding a message to its final destination, and one complete message may be divided into a number of transmission blocks. Furthermore, these blocks may not all be routed along the same path and hence could be received out of order. In such a case, it is important to assign sequence numbers to each block so that the ultimate receiver can be assured that all blocks have indeed arrived and that the blocks can be put back into proper sequence.

Message Sequence Numbers.　One sequencing technique appends a message sequence number to each data block transmitted between two stations. If a processor is communicating with two different stations, each link would have its own sequence number. Every time a message is transmitted, the sequence number is sent along with the message. The receiving station compares the received sequence number with a number maintained in its memory. If the message numbers agree, it means that no messages have been lost; if the received message number disagrees with the expected message number, an error condition is created and the receiver would request the sender to retransmit the missing messages.

Packet Sequence Numbers.　In some networks, messages are segmented into smaller transmission groups, or packets. If there are multiple communication paths between sender and receiver, the packet routing strategy may use several of the paths simultaneously to speed delivery of the entire message, in which case the packets could arrive out of order. To ensure that such a message can be reassembled in proper sequence, packet sequence numbers are appended to each packet. These sequence numbers also allow for error control.

In any of the situations just discussed, if a data block arrives and an error is detected, or if not all of the blocks in a sequence have been received, the recovery method is to ask the sending station to retransmit the erroneous or lost data. Usually, an acknowledgment is sent for all blocks received correctly; if a block is not positively acknowledged, the transmitter must resend it. This imposes an obligation on the transmitting node to retain all transmitted blocks until they have been acknowledged. Several recovery methods are discussed in more detail in Chapter 6.

Error Correction Codes

Some error detecting schemes allow the receiving station to not only detect errors, but also to correct some of them. Such codes are called *forward error correcting codes*, the most common of which are called *Hamming codes*. As with straight error detection codes, additional, redundant information is transmitted with the data.

Error correcting codes are convenient for situations in which single bit errors occur, but for multiple bit errors, the amount of redundant information that must be sent is cumbersomely large. Since the effectiveness of forward error correcting codes is reduced by transmission noise that frequently creates bursts of errors, these codes are not used as commonly as are error detection schemes. Hamming codes have good applications in other areas, however, such as memory error detection and correction, where the probability of single bit errors is higher. Some semiconductor memories use a 6-bit Hamming code for each 16 bits of data to allow for single bit error correction and double bit error detection.

Miscellaneous Error Detection Techniques

There are several other methods for increasing the probability of detecting data errors.

Check Digits.   *Check digits* or *check numbers* are one or more characters (often simply the sum of fields being checked) that are appended to the data being transmitted, usually generated by the sending application or device and checked by the receiving application or device. The block check characters previously discussed are excluded in this context.

Hash Totals.   One technique that functions to validate operator input as well as augment an error detection scheme involves appending a hash total, which is the sum of a group of items. For example, for a batch of credit card authorizations, the sum of all charges can be computed separately or by the input device. When computed separately prior to operator input it provides an accuracy check of data entry as well as transmission. The receiving computer sums the number of fields transmitted and compares its total with the transmitted hash total. If the totals agree, it means that there are no errors; if the hash totals do not agree, then the data must be retransmitted.

Byte Counts.   A byte count field can be added to a message. When an entire block of data is sent at one time (*synchronous transmission*), the loss of a character would ordinarily be detected by either LRC with VRC, or CRC. When every character is transmitted individually with its own error detection—usually VRC—scheme (*asynchronous transmission*), if a character is lost, it could go undetected. Thus, transmitting one or more characters that indicate the total number of characters in the message helps detect transmission errors in which entire characters may be lost.

Character Echoing.   In some systems, especially with asynchronous transmission, the characters transmitted are echoed back to the user as a check. Because of the additional line time required, this technique is less frequently used in synchronous transmissions. As an example of character echoing, consider an operator at an asynchronous terminal: When a key is struck the character is transmitted to the host computer, which echoes back (resends) the received character to the terminal. If the character displayed at the originating terminal is incorrect, the operator will back up the cursor to the character position and re-enter the character. With a high-speed communications line it appears to the operator as if the character is locally displayed as well as being transmitted to the host; with low-speed communications links, or when communicating with a busy processor, the echoing may become somewhat apparent. The same technique can be used with synchronous transmissions.

Echoing has the disadvantage of doubling the chances of obtaining an error, since the message must be transmitted twice. That is, the original message may be received correctly, but if the echoed message has been corrupted, the original sender will detect an error.

ERROR CORRECTION

Whenever an error is detected, it must be corrected. If an error correcting code is used, the transmitted data can be corrected by the receiver. However, this is usually not the case in data communications. The most common error correction mechanism is to retransmit the data. In asynchronous transmission, individual characters are retransmitted, whereas in synchronous transmissions, one or more blocks may need to be retransmitted. This type of correction is known as ARQ, which stands for *automatic request for retransmission* or *automatic request for repetition*.

Message Acknowledgment

The mechanism used to effect retransmission is the positive or negative acknowledgment of message receipt, often referred to as ACK and NAK, respectively. When a station receives a message, it computes the number of error detection bit(s) or characters and compares the result with the check number received. If the two are equal, then the message is assumed to be error-free and the receiver returns a positive acknowledgment to the sender; if the two are unequal a negative acknowledgment is returned and the sending station retransmits the message. Of course, the sending station must retain the message(s) until they have been positively acknowledged.

Retry Limit

In some instances the second message will also be received in error, perhaps due to an error-prone communications link or faulty hardware or software. In order to cut down on continual retransmission of messages, a retry limit—typically between 3 and 100—can be set, usually by the user. Thus, a retry limit of five means that a message received in error will be retransmitted five times; if it is not successfully received by the fifth try, then the receiving station usually will disable the link or will disable the sending station itself. The objective of a retry limit is to avoid the unproductive work of continually processing corrupted messages. Once the cause of the problem has been corrected, the communications path will be reinstated.

DIGITAL DATA TRANSMISSION

Although all communications media are capable of transmitting information in either digital or analog form, and despite the fact that computer data are represented in digital form, computer data have been transmitted mostly in analog form. The primary reason for this is that the providers of communications transmission facilities had established analog facilities for voice transmission. However, advances in digital technology and lower prices for digital transmission electronics are bringing about a change from analog transmission to *digital transmission*. Within several decades most major metropolitan areas probably will have made the transition. And were it not for the considerable existing investment in analog transmission facilities, the changeover might be even sooner. In other words, if telephone companies were to begin today, all their transmission facilities would likely be digital rather than analog.

Advantages of Digital Transmission

The advantages of digital transmission for data communications are lower error rates, higher transmission rates, and no need to convert from digital format to analog and back to digital.

Lower Error Rates.   Current telephone networks transmit signals over wires or via radio broadcast, continually amplifying the signals in order to overcome the weakening from attenuation. Long-distance transmission demands that the signals be amplified multiple times to overcome attenuation. And since any frequency within the bandwidth is acceptable, it is difficult to filter out any introduced noise or distortion, so both are amplified and propagated along with the original signals.

Like analog signals, digital signals also lose strength due to attenuation, as Figure 3-20(b) illustrates. Since a digital signal represents only two discrete values, however, it is possible to regenerate the signal. Restored to its original state and strength, the bit can be forwarded to the next regeneration point or the final destination without any associated noise. This is accomplished by a digital regenerator. Figure 3-20(c) shows a regenerated signal.

Higher Transmission Rates.   Another benefit to be derived from digital transmission is increased transmission speed, attributable to the fact that a wider bandwidth is required. With digital transmission, switched connections will be able to operate at speeds up to 56 Kbps, where currently the limit is 4.8 Kbps for switched circuits and 9.6 Kbps for leased lines.

Figure 3-20
Digital Signal
Regeneration

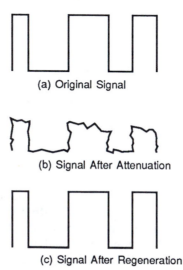

(a) Original Signal

(b) Signal After Attenuation

(c) Signal After Regeneration

No Digital–Analog Conversion. Theoretically, digital transmission avoids the need for conversion between formats. Unfortunately, not all locations are serviced by digital networks, whose implementation has been restricted thus far to the more highly populated urban centers. Furthermore, the connection from a given location to the digital transmission and switching equipment is, in many cases, still an analog link. In such instances it is necessary to convert a signal from digital to analog and back to digital for transmission to the message's destination. The device that converts the analog signal to digital is known as a *codec*, an acronym for *coder-decoder*.

Pulse Code Modulation. The primary method for transmitting digital data is *pulse code modulation (PCM)*. On a communications wire, PCM is represented as pulses of current. For example, a pulse of 3 volts could represent the digit 1, and 0 voltage could represent the digit 0. In some schemes a 1 would be represented by a voltage of $+1.5$, and the 0 by a voltage of -1.5. The first technique is referred to as *unipolar signaling*; the latter is termed *polar signaling*. Both techniques are illustrated in Figures 3-21(a) and 3-21(b), respectively.

INTERFACE

Once a medium has been selected, it is necessary to connect it to the computer equipment. There are two classes of equipment in data communications: data communications equipment (DCE) (modems, media, and media-support facilities such as telephone switching equipment, microwave relay stations, and transponders) and data terminal (or terminat-

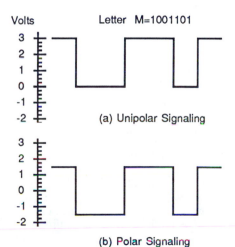

Figure 3-21
Pulse Code
Modulation

ing) equipment (DTE) (including terminals, computers, concentrators, and multiplexers, all of which are covered in Chapters 4 and 5). The physical interface is the manner in which these two classes of equipment are joined together. Figure 3-22 depicts a data communications linkage with the DCE and DTE components identified.

The interface between DCE and DTE can be divided into four aspects: mechanical, electrical, functional, and procedural. The *mechanical* portion includes the type of connectors to be used, the number of pin connections in the connectors, and the maximum allowable cable lengths. The *electrical* characteristics include the allowable line voltages and the representations for the various voltage levels.

The *functional* interface specifies which signals—timing, control, data, or ground leads—are to be carried by each pin in the connector. Figure 3-23 lists the signals assigned to each of the 25 pins in an RS-232-C interface (see below).

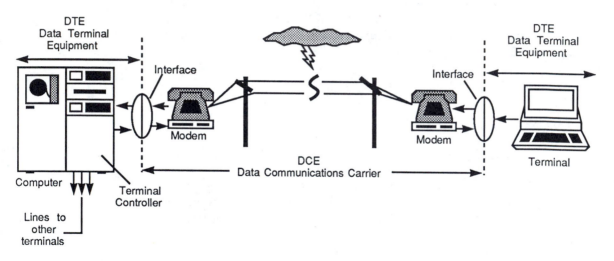

Figure 3-22   DTE and DCE Components

	Pin Number	Circuit	Description
Figure 3-23 Interface Connector Pin Assignments	1	AA	Protective Ground
	2	BA	Transmitted Data
	3	BB	Received Data
	4	CA	Request to Send
	5	CB·	Clear to Send
	6	CC	Data Set Ready
	7	AB	Signal Ground (Common Return)
	8	CF	Received Line Signal Detector
	9	—	(Reserved for Modem Testing)

Continued

Pin Number	Circuit	Description
10	—	(Reserved for Modem Testing)
11		Unassigned
12	SCF	Secondary for Pin 8
13	SCB	Secondary Clear to Send
14	SBA	Secondary Transmitted Data
15	DB	Transmission Signal Timing
16	SBB	Secondary Received Data
17	DD	Receiver Signal Timing
18		Unassigned
19	SCA	Secondary Request to Send
20	CD	Data Terminal Ready
21	CG	Signal Quality Detector
22	CE	Ring Indicator
23	CH/CI	Data Signal Rate Selector
24	DA	Transmit Signal Element Timing
25		Unassigned

Procedural characteristics define how signals are exchanged and delineate the environment necessary to transmit and receive data. For example, one pin or conducting wire in the connector might represent the ability of a terminal to accept a transmission; when the terminal is ready to receive data, a signal will be raised on that lead. When no signal is raised on that circuit, transmission to the terminal is not valid.

Interface Standards

There are numerous standards adhered to in establishing an interface between DCE and DTE. The following brief descriptions should familiarize you with these standards and what they generally cover.

RS-232-C Standard.   Currently in the United States the predominant interface standard is the Electronic Industries Association (EIA) *RS-232-C standard*, established in October 1969 and reaffirmed in June 1981. RS-232-C encompasses serial binary data interchange at rates up to 20,000 bps and distances up to 50 feet; because of the speed limitations, RS-232-C has its greatest application in interfacing to wire media, where this bit transmission rate is most common. It covers private, switched, and leased connections, with provisions for auto-answer switched connections.

Serial binary transmission (or *bit serial transmission*) is a mode wherein bits are transmitted in single file. This is contrasted with *bit parallel transmission*, wherein bits are transmitted in parallel. Figure 3-24 illustrates the difference between these two techniques.

Figure 3-24
Serial vs. Parallel
Transmission

Message to be Transmitted: LINE
Representation: ASCII

L   1001100
I   1001001
N   1001110
E   1000101

1001100 1001001 1001110 1000101
L   I   N   E

(a) Bit Serial Transmission

1 1 1 1
0 0 0 0
0 0 0 0
1 1 1 0
1 0 1 1
0 0 1 0
0 1 0 1
L I N E

(b) Bit Parallel Transmission

The RS-232-C standard does not specify size or type of connectors to be used in the interface, although it does define 25 signal leads, three of them unassigned, two reserved for testing, and the remaining 20 used for grounding, data, control, and timing. In the absence of a standard, one connector—a 25-pin connector—has become extremely common in implementing RS-232-C connections. Figure 3-25(a) depicts this type of connector. Despite the fact that 25 signal leads have been specified, actual transmissions typically use fewer. A simple modem interface, for example, can

Figure 3-25
Cable Connectors

(a)

(a) 25-pin connector for RS-232-C or CCITT V.24 Interface

(b)

(b) 15-pin connector for RS-232-C or CCITT V.24 Interface

(c)
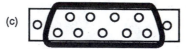

(c) 9-pin connector for RS-232-C, RS449, or CCITT V.24 Interface

require that only seven pins be active; yet on occasion, connectors supporting 15, 9, and 7 pins are used to interface with these devices. A 15-pin connector and 9-pin connector are illustrated in Figures 3-25(b) and 3-25(c).

The RS-232-C standard covers all four aspects of the interface, mechanical, electrical, functional, and procedural. This is significant because other interface specifications treat them separately, and thus, two or three standards may be cited that together form the equivalent of what is specified by RS-232-C.

RS-449 Standard.   Because of the speed and distance constraints of RS-232-C standard, EIA *RS-449 standard* was adopted. It provides for a 37-pin connection, for cable lengths up to 200 feet, and data transmission rates up to 2 million bps. RS-449 equates with the functional and procedural portions of RS-232-C (the electrical and mechanical specifications are covered by RS-422 and RS-423). Because of RS-449's enhanced capabilities over RS-232-C, it should eventually replace RS-232-C as the predominant interface within the United States.

RS-366 Standard.   EIA has also adopted an *RS-366 standard*, which is a 25-pin connection with enhanced capabilities for automatic calling equipment. (The electrical portion of the interface is covered by the RS-423 standard.)

The International Standards Organization (ISO) and the Consultative Committees on International Telegraphy and Telephony (CCITT) have also adopted standards that are widely adhered to. The most significant of these international standards for interfaces are briefly described below; other international standards for data communications are discussed in Chapter 7.

ISO-2110 Standard.   *ISO-2110* is a functional interface standard similar to the functional portion of RS-232-C. It describes which signals will be carried on specific pins.

CCITT V.10 and V.11.   *CCITT V.10 and V.11* are electrical interfaces similar to those specified by RS-422 and RS-423.

CCITT V.24.   The *CCITT V.24 standard* covers both the functional and the procedural aspects of a 25-pin interface similar to that specified by RS-232-C.

CCITT V.25.   The *CCITT V.25 standard* covers the procedural aspects of establishing and terminating automatic calling unit connections over switched lines.

CCITT V.28.   The *CCITT V.28 standard* covers the electrical interface in a manner similar to that of RS-232-C.

CCITT V.35.   The *CCITT V.35 standard* defines a 34-pin connection for interfaces with speeds of 48,000 bps.

CCITT X.20 and X.21.   The *CCITT X.20 and X.21 standards* cover the interface between DCE and DTE for packet distribution networks (PDN). (PDNs are discussed in detail in Chapter 7.)

CCITT X.24.   The *CCITT X.24 standard* covers the functional aspects of interface for PDNs.

Other Standards.   The U. S. Government and U. S. military have their own interface standards. Specifically, MIL-STD-188-114 and U. S. Government standards 1020 and 1030 provide for electrical interfaces similar to those of RS-422 and RS-423.

SUMMARY

There are three basic types of data flow: simplex, half duplex, and full duplex. Most business data communications systems use either full or half duplex. In half duplex mode, modem turnaround time may adversely affect terminal response time. Several different communications codes are used in data communications, the most common being ASCII and EBCDIC.

All media are subject to error. Detecting errors requires that redundant information be transmitted with the data. The three most common error detection schemes in data communications are vertical redundancy check (VRC), longitudinal redundancy check (LRC), and cyclic redundancy check (CRC). The most effective is CRC. In some protocols sequence checking is also used to improve the reliability of transmission.

Digital data transmission provides both higher transmission speeds and fewer errors. The common carriers are gradually making the conversion from analog transmission equipment to digital equipment.

Interface standards exist regarding connecting data terminal equipment (DTE) to data communications equipment (DCE). There are both domestic and international standards regarding mechanical, functional, procedural, and electrical interfaces; unfortunately they do not always agree.

Key Terms

ASCII

Attenuation

Baudot

BCD

Bit parallel transmission

Bit serial transmission

Block check character (BCC)

CCITT V.24, V.25, V.28, V.35,
   X.20, X.21, and X.24 standards

Conditioning

Crosstalk

Cyclic redundancy check (CRC)

Digital transmission

EBCDIC

Echo

Echo suppresser

Full duplex transmission

Gaussian noise

Half duplex transmission

Impulse noise

Longitudinal redundancy
   check (LRC)

Modem turnaround time

Parity check

Phase jitter

Pulse code modulation (PCM)

RS-232-C standard

RS-366 standard

RS-449 standard

SBT

Simplex transmission

Vertical redundancy check (VRC)

White noise

Questions and Exercises

1. Label each of the following items as simplex, half duplex, or full duplex in nature.
   (a)   commercial radio
   (b)   CB radio
   (c)   television
   (d)   smoke signals
   (e)   classroom discussion
   (f)   family arguments
   (g)   ocean tides
   (h)   shortwave radio communications

2. Calculate the line time and modem turnaround time required for the following transaction. Assume a modem turnaround time of 20 milliseconds, a line speed of 2400 bps, and 10 bits per character.
   (a)   Operator enters 10-character employee ID.
   (b)   System returns 500-character employee record.
   (c)   Operator changes zip code and retransmits only the 5-character zip code back to the system.
   (d)   System acknowledges receipt and positive action by sending operator 20-character message.

3. Identify instances other than those mentioned in the chapter in which a code with 256 different characters may be insufficient.

4. Obtain and examine the Japanese Industrial Standard (JIS) for data codes that contain a portion of the Kanji character set. What other characters are allowed? How many bits are required to support this standard? What, if any, special features are included?

5. Why is Morse code not a viable alternative for computers?

6. If the speed of transmission is 7200 bps on a line that is hit by lightning that causes an impulse distortion of 3.5 milliseconds, what is the maximum number of bits that could be in error?

7. Assuming the worst case in Problem 6, what percentage of the errors incurred would be caught by VRC? by VRC and LRC in combination?

8. Explain how digital data transmission can obtain higher speeds than analog and at the same time have fewer errors.

9. Why are interface standards important?

References

Bellamy, John. *Digital Telephony*. New York: Wiley, 1982.

Cypser, R. J. *Communications Architecture for Distributed Systems*. Reading, MA: Addison-Wesley, 1978.

Electronic Industries Association. *Interface Between Data Terminal Equipment and Data Communications Equipment Employing Serial Binary Data Interchange*. RS-232-C Standards Document. Washington, DC: Electronics Industries Assoc., 1969, 1981.

Freeman, Roger L. *Telecommunications Transmission Handbook*. New York: Wiley, 1981.

Harper, William L., and Pollard, Robert C. *Data Communications Desk Book: A Systems Analysis Approach*. Englewood Cliffs, NJ: Prentice-Hall, 1982.

Kuo, Franklin F. *Protocols and Techniques for Data Communications Networks*. Englewood Cliffs, NJ: Prentice-Hall, 1981.

4

Terminal
Equipment

Terminals

Terminal Capabilities

Terminal Attributes

Terminal Configuration

Specific Terminal Devices

Case Study

INTRODUCTION

The previous two chapters discussed transmission media; the two methods used to represent data—analog and digital; how errors are introduced, detected, and corrected; various data codes; and one piece of hardware, the modem. Chapters 4 and 5 continue the discussion of the physical components of data communications systems—specifically, hardware, starting with the extremities of the system, the terminal equipment. The discussion then moves toward the primary processors of a system, host computers, examining along the way line-sharing devices that make the use of a medium more efficient, more cost effective, or both. Chapter 5 goes on to examine the equipment used in conjunction with the host processors—front end processors, message switchers, and communications controllers. One configuration of such equipment is illustrated in Figure 4-1 on page 110. Chapter 5 concludes with a brief discussion of miscellaneous though important equipment such as line monitors, breakout boxes, protocol converters, and power surge protectors.

This entire chapter is devoted to terminals. There are three reasons for giving so much space to this subject: the overall increase in the cost of the terminal component of a system, the growing variety of equipment, and the expansion of personal use. The cost of individual terminals has been dropping, in general, while their numbers in a given system have been increasing, making the cost of terminal components a growing percentage of total system costs. It is not unusual for the cost of a system's terminals to equal or exceed that of other hardware. The variety of terminals, ter-

Figure 4-1
A Hardware
Configuration

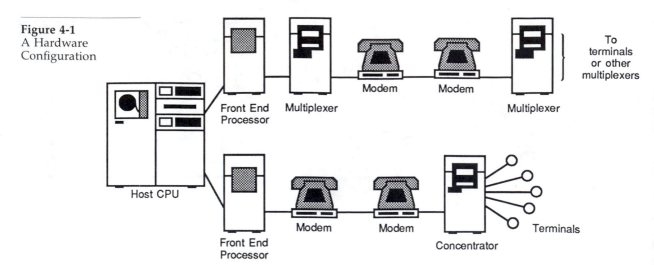

minal capabilities, and cost is immense. This variety, coupled with the fact that you are more likely to be involved in selecting a terminal than in selecting any other component of a system, makes knowledge of terminals important. Finally, since more and more people are spending a significant portion of their work and leisure time at computer terminals, it is essential to select equipment that is easy to use and that lends itself well to a particular application.

TERMINALS

Definition

What is a *terminal*? Here is Webster's *New World Dictionary* definition:

> *terminal (noun).* 1. a terminating part; end; extremity; limit. 2. a connective device or point on an electric circuit or conductor. 3. either end of a transportation line.

Since this definition is too general for data communications, here is how terminal is defined for this book:

> *terminal (noun).* An input and/or output device that may be connected to a local or remote computer, called a *host computer*. The terminal is at certain times dependent on the host for either computation or data access or both.

The phrase "may be connected" allows for switched connections and devices that have some degree of processing power and are connected to a host on a periodic basis. Even this definition is not quite as rigorous as is desirable, but further qualifications would make the definition unusable. There are some environments, particularly distributed processing systems, in which data and/or processing functions are distributed among a number of host systems; to comply with this definition, each host would be classified as a terminal as well as a host. This text does not consider such systems to be within the main category of terminals.

Typical Uses of Terminals

A variety of terminal devices meet this book's definition, and they can be used in numerous ways.

Microcomputer Work Stations.   Much of the work required at a microcomputer work station can be satisfied locally, but on occasion a host computer is required to provide additional data or to perform time-consuming calculations. For instance, if the microcomputer is involved in data entry applications, then prompting for information, editing data, and storing transactions could be handled locally, the data thus collected eventually being forwarded to a host system for inclusion in the main database. Or in a scientific or design application, for example, the microcomputer could be used to enter data and perhaps to perform initial, simple calculations, then being forwarded to a larger, more powerful host system for extensive, detailed design calculations. Or one large project could be distributed among a number of work stations, with the final results assembled and processed on a host computer. Finally, work stations can be used for electronic mail systems, perhaps relying on a host system to accept and forward messages to the proper destinations. A microcomputer is shown in Figure 4-2 on page 112.

Remote Job Entry Stations.   A terminal can be used to forward record images to a host system and to possibly receive updated reports back from the host. Historically, input from such terminals has been card images and the resulting output has been printed reports or punched cards. In some instances tape has also served as an input or output medium. This type of operation is sometimes referred to as *remote batch processing*.

Data Entry and Display.   A *video display unit (VDU)* or a hard-copy device such as a *teletypewriter* can serve for data entry or data display or both. Such devices can carry on a dialogue with the host(s) and obtain data from and provide data to the business's applications. A VDU is also sometimes referred to as a *video display terminal* (*VDT*) or as a *cathode ray tube (CRT)*. Several VDU terminals are shown in Figure 4-3 on page 113.

Sensor Devices.   Sensor devices are used in laboratory, hospital, or data collection applications, frequently for input only. For example, many of

Figure 4-2
A Microcomputer

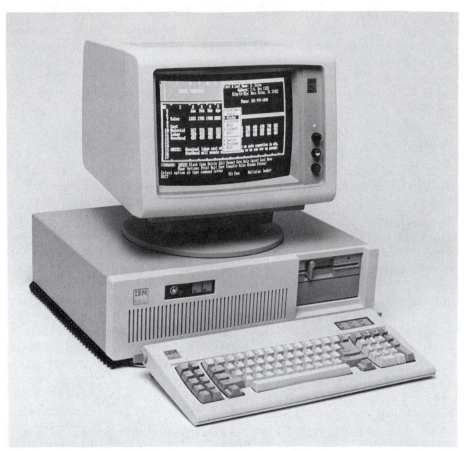

Courtesy of IBM

the newer, large office buildings have a computer-controlled environmental monitoring system. Sensors located throughout the building alert the system to areas in which temperature is outside the comfort zone. The host responds by sending a message to an output-only terminal device that switches on either heating or cooling. When the temperature once again is within the comfort zone, the host sends a message to the thermal controller to discontinue its function. Sensor devices are also used in automobile testing to monitor engine performance and emissions, periodically transmitting data samples to a host for later analysis. In hospital and clinical laboratories, data collection devices and special terminals attached to host systems help in the classification, categorization, and processing of clinical samples.

Display-only Devices.   A display-only device frequently serves as a receiver of data. For example, the display monitors in stock market applications are display-only devices. Remote printers also fit in this category, although some also have the ability to transmit control information such as "out of paper" or "not ready to receive."

Figure 4-3   VDU Terminals
Courtesy of Lear Siegler, Inc., Data Products Division

Point-of-Sale Terminals.   Point-of-sale (POS) terminals are used to help maintain inventory, gross receipts, and—in some instances—participate in money transfers from a buyer's account to a merchant's account. The capabilities of POS terminals vary significantly. Many of these functions are described in the following example.

A customer brings several items to a checkout counter in a department store that uses POS terminals. An *optical character recognition (OCR)* reader attached to the terminal reads the sales tags for the item numbers, which are printed in a special OCR type font, and enters them into the system. Alternatives to OCR input include the *universal product code (UPC)* reader, which reads the bar codes on items, and manual entry by the store clerk. Once the product has been identified, the computer sends the items' current prices from the database to the terminal for totaling the sale, including tax, and for accumulating the terminal's daily sales. If the customer wishes to pay with a credit card or check, the terminal will ask the user to enter a personal identification number (PIN) and authorize the sale. If a debit card is used, the funds are transferred from the customer's account to the store's account. At the completion of the transaction, the database inventory records are adjusted for the items sold.

Portable Terminal Devices.   One application for portable terminals is in direct sales. Some marketing agencies provide their salesforce with portable terminals capable of storing information in memory. The salesperson

Figure 4-4
A Portable Terminal

Courtesy of Hewlett-Packard Company

records customer orders during the day and can use a telephone link to transmit them to the home office for processing. Figure 4-4 pictures a portable terminal.

Touch-tone™ Telephones.   Touch-tone™ telephones can be used in bill paying and account inquiry or transfer applications. Although not employed extensively because of their limited input and output capabilities, they lend themselves well to certain applications. For example, a California bank piloted a project that allowed its customers to pay some credit card, utility, and department store bills using a touchtone telephone.

Automatic Teller Machines (ATM).   Most banks now have networks of teller machines that enable the customer to handle simple banking transactions without the assistance of a human teller, and that also allow the customer to make withdrawals and deposits during non-banking hours.

Credit Card Gas Pumps.   In California, Atlantic Richfield Co. and the Bank of America have joined forces so customers can use their ATM cards in microcomputer-controlled gasoline pumps. The customer enters the dollar amount of the sale, the pump dispenses that amount of gas, and the sales amount is transferred from the customer's account to that of Atlantic Richfield.

TERMINAL CAPABILITIES

Rather than discuss the wide variety of terminal types, this text focuses on terminal capabilities, and then goes on to present a list of attributes to be considered in selecting the proper terminal for a given application.

In studying the following terminal categories, the applications of the Syncrasy Corporation are used to see how different kinds of terminals participate in order processing. The Syncrasy Corporation remote sales office enters orders into the system. Its customers are mostly repeat customers for whom there is an existing customer profile. The order processing transaction requires that you verify the customer record, check the credit limit, enter the order information, compute the amount of the order, and submit the order (if the customer's credit limit has not been exceeded). The data processing center is located in Puma Flats, Kansas, and the sales offices are located in Los Angeles and New York City.

Terminals can be categorized as dumb, smart, or intelligent, although the lines separating these categories are indistinct. For instance, there is some overlap between smart and intelligent terminals, and thus one type of terminal might be considered smart by one individual yet dumb by another.

Dumb Terminal Capabilities

A *dumb terminal* does not participate—that is, it passively serves for input and/or output but does no more processing. Since dumb terminals usually have no memory to store entered data, each entered character must immediately be transmitted to the host, unsolicited, and the host must be ready at all times to accept data from the terminal. Of course, data entry errors are sent to the host, as well, so an additional load is placed on the communications medium. Transmission a character at a time, termed *asynchronous transmission*, is discussed in detail in Chapter 6. Because the dumb terminal rather than the host determines when data are transmitted, there is usually only one dumb terminal per line. Chapter 5 discusses some devices that allow several dumb terminals to share a line.

Dumb Terminal Applications: An Example

The many dumb terminals in use serve especially well in applications that are *conversational* in nature. In fact, they are limited to conversational-type data entry, as described in Chapter 1. The host prompts the terminal operator to enter the first field, and the operator responds with the data for the first field. Then the host edits the received data to determine if it conforms to predefined standards—that is, are the data numeric, alphabetic, or what? Have sufficient characters been supplied—for example, is there a minimum of five characters allotted for zip code? Are all required fields present? Are only acceptable values entered—for example, does the sex field contain only an F or an M? If the first field fails the *data editing*, then the operator is asked to re-enter the entire field; if the edit test is passed, the operator is prompted for the second data field. When the operator recognizes a keystroke error, the entry must be backspaced the proper number of characters and all subsequent characters—not just the one in error—resubmitted. Every backspace is sent to the host, which adjusts the position for storing the next character received. This process continues until all necessary data fields have been entered.

There is a high degree of interaction between the dumb terminal and the host. With low-speed lines, operator efficiency may be impaired because of having to wait for the next prompt before data entry can begin again. Usually this means that data entry is somewhat slower than with smart or intelligent terminals. Should the operator realize that an input error has not been detected by the editing function, the operator must be able to request that the field be re-entered, and this must be accommodated for by the application which is usually a more complex task than that required by more intelligent terminals.

Smart Terminal Capabilities

Memory, Adressability, and Host Control.   Unlike dumb terminals, *smart terminals* have a certain amount of memory, meaning they can receive, store, and display data and entry formats or *screen templates* from the host. Data entered by the operator can be saved in the terminal's memory until the entire record or some number of screens of data have been entered. The terminal can then transmit the entire data record in one or more blocks. This type of block transmission, called *synchronous transmission*, is covered in more detail in Chapter 6. *Block (page) mode* functions include the following.

Page mode editing. The cursor can be moved to any position in the displayed text to make corrections or alterations. Words and blocks of text can be moved around, and blocks of information, rather than just individual characters, can be received or transmitted.

Data entry. An input template is displayed on the terminal screen and the entire screen of data is entered before being transmitted to the host. The operator can move the cursor to any input field on the screen. The data transmitted may consist of multiple screens of data.

Windowing. The screen can be divided into multiple "windows," with each window portion of the screen representing a different object set. For example, one window could represent the text being written, one could contain notes relating to the text being composed, another could contain a graphic image of an item being described in the text, while a fourth could contain a menu of tasks or commands that are valid in the current window. Figure 4-5 shows a screen with windows.

Conversational mode can also be used with smart terminals. Thus, a smart terminal can handle applications designed for a dumb terminal, whereas the opposite is not necessarily true.

Almost all smart terminals are *addressable*; that is, they can be given a

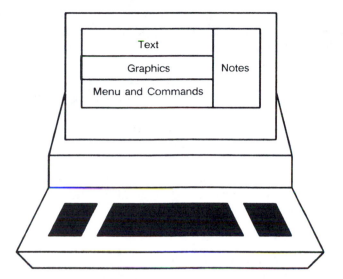

Figure 4-5
A Terminal Screen
with Windows

name that both they and the host recognize. Thus, the host can transmit data addressed to that terminal, and the terminal will recognize that the data is intended for it, and store it in its memory. Smart terminals also are subject to *host control*, meaning that the host can specify when the terminal is allowed to send or receive data, can position the cursor on the display, can designate certain *protected fields*—such as an employee's salary—to be protected from alteration, can control the *keyboard* and disallow any data entry, can specify the display attributes of fields such as *blink* and *half intensity*, and can read from or write to selected portions of the display. Addressability, memory, and host control capabilities enable several terminals to share the same medium, and thereby reduce transmission costs.

Auxiliary Data Entry Devices and Function Keys.   Some smart terminals support auxiliary data entry devices such as light pens, mice, and touch screens. Many can have a *printer* attached, for printing a displayed page and for automatic logging of data received by the terminal. Many smart terminals have additional keys known as *function keys* or program attention keys, which transmit specific character sequences to the host. Typically they allow the operator to indicate to the application what function is to be performed on the data provided. Figures 4-6, 4-7, and 4-8 illustrate three data entry screen templates. The instructions at the bottom of the screen indicate actions that can be triggered by pressing the function keys F1, F2, etc. The number of function keys per terminal usually varies from 4 to 32. Some special-purpose terminals have up to 50 keys or more.

Smart Terminal Applications: An Example

Since a smart terminal's memory can store multiple pages, the screen formats could be transferred into the terminal from the host. Assuming host control, the host transmits an initial menu screen, as depicted in Figure 4-6. The operator selects the *order entry* application by pressing the F2 function key. The host then transmits the first of the order entry screens, the customer data screen shown in Figure 4-7. The *date* will have been transmitted with the screen format by the host system. The operator enters *customer number* or *customer name* and presses the F2 function key, which instructs the host to read the data in the terminal's buffer. The host searches the database for particulars on that customer and displays the information. The operator then alters the information displayed if necessary and enters the information with the F1 key. The host reads the data from the terminal and edits the data. If edit errors are encountered, the host transmits an error message and identifies the erroneous field by changing the display attributes of the field, for instance, causing the field to blink, or reversing the video. The operator corrects the flagged data and then retransmits either the entire screen or just the field that had to be changed. (The latter option is not supported by all smart terminals.) If the data are without detectable errors, the host transmits the next screen template, as shown in Figure 4-8 on page 120.

On receiving the screen shown in Figure 4-8, the operator continues with data entry, entering the *part number* and the *quantity ordered*. On completion, the data are transmitted to the host for editing, for determining the unit prices and discount rate, and for calculating the line item, page, and order totals. The host then sends the screen of calculations back to the operator so the operator can inform the customer of the total amount. If the terminal has an attached printer, the sales data can be printed for the office or customer.

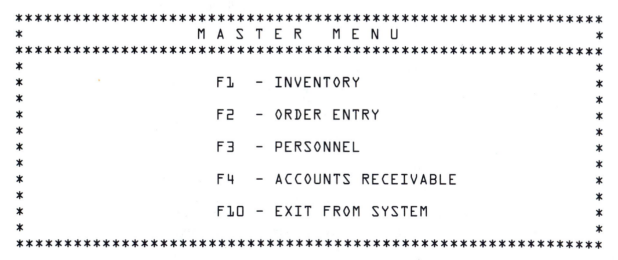

Figure 4-6   Master Menu Screen

```
*********************************************************************
*            C U S T O M E R   D A T A   S C R E E N            *
*********************************************************************
*                                                                  *
*   DATE [            ]     PURCHASE ORDER NUMBER [           ]   *
*                                                                  *
*   CUSTOMER NAME [                                          ]   *
*                                                                  *
*   CUSTOMER NUMBER [                  ]                         *
*                                                                  *
*   ORDER PLACED BY [                                        ]   *
*                                                                  *
*   CONTACT TELEPHONE [                          ]              *
*                                                                  *
*   SHIP TO ADDRESS   [                                      ]   *
*                     [                                      ]   *
*                     [                                      ]   *
*                     [                                      ]   *
*   SHIP TO CONTACT NAME [                                   ]   *
*                                                                  *
*   SHIP TO TELEPHONE    [                                   ]   *
*                                                                  *
*   INVOICE ADDRESS   [                                      ]   *
*                     [                                      ]   *
*                     [                                      ]   *
*                     [                                      ]   *
*   INVOICE CONTACT NAME [                                   ]   *
*                                                                  *
*   INVOICE TELEPHONE    [                                   ]   *
*                                                                  *
*   SPECIAL SHIPPING INSTRUCTIONS                               *
*   [                                                        ]   *
*   [                                                        ]   *
*   [                                                        ]   *
*   [                                                        ]   *
*   [                                                        ]   *
*   [                                                        ]   *
*                                                                  *
*********************************************************************
*   F1 - ENTER INFORMATION          F2 - GET CUSTOMER RECORD   *
*   F3 - CREATE NEW CUSTOMER RECORD F4 - DELETE CUSTOMER       *
*   F9 - DISPLAY HELP SCREEN        F10- EXIT TO MAIN MENU     *
*********************************************************************
```

Figure 4-7 Customer Data Entry Screen

```
**************************************************************************
*                O R D E R   E N T R Y   L I N E   I T E M S          *
**************************************************************************
*                                                                      *
*   DATE [          ]              CUSTOMER NUMBER [              ]     *
*                                                                      *
*                                                                      *
*      PART          QUANTITY        UNIT        DISCOUNT       TOTAL   *
*      NUMBER        ORDERED         PRICE        PERCENT       PRICE   *
*      ------        --------        -----       --------       -----   *
*   [          ]   [          ]   [          ]  [        ]  [          ] *
*   [          ]   [          ]   [          ]  [        ]  [          ] *
*   [          ]   [          ]   [          ]  [        ]  [          ] *
*   [          ]   [          ]   [          ]  [        ]  [          ] *
*   [          ]   [          ]   [          ]  [        ]  [          ] *
*   [          ]   [          ]   [          ]  [        ]  [          ] *
*   [          ]   [          ]   [          ]  [        ]  [          ] *
*   [          ]   [          ]   [          ]  [        ]  [          ] *
*   [          ]   [          ]   [          ]  [        ]  [          ] *
*   [          ]   [          ]   [          ]  [        ]  [          ] *
*   [          ]   [          ]   [          ]  [        ]  [          ] *
*   [          ]   [          ]   [          ]  [        ]  [          ] *
*   [          ]   [          ]   [          ]  [        ]  [          ] *
*   [          ]   [          ]   [          ]  [        ]  [          ] *
*   [          ]   [          ]   [          ]  [        ]  [          ] *
*   [          ]   [          ]   [          ]  [        ]  [          ] *
*   [          ]   [          ]   [          ]  [        ]  [          ] *
*   [          ]   [          ]   [          ]  [        ]  [          ] *
*                                                                      *
*   PAGE TOTAL  [              ]                  [              ]      *
*                                                                      *
*   ORDER TOTAL [              ]                  [              ]      *
*                                                                      *
**************************************************************************
*   F1 - ENTER INFORMATION        F2  - CLEAR SCREEN                   *
*                                                                      *
*   F9 - DISPLAY HELP SCREEN      F10 - RETURN TO FIRST PAGE           *
**************************************************************************
```

Figure 4-8   Order Entry Line Items Screen

The operator will signal the host of the completion of the order by hitting the F10 key, which brings up the first data entry screen to start the cycle over again.

Advantages of Smart vs. Dumb Terminals

The advantage of smart terminals over dumb terminals is a certain amount of independence between operator and host. Once a template is displayed, the operator is free to enter data at his or her own pace, unrestricted by the transmission speed of the line. Any errors made by the operator can be corrected without the host's being involved. The cursor can be moved by the operator to any field on the record, and entry or corrections made prior to transmission to the host. The host can control the terminal and solicit inputs and outputs according to its priorities rather than being periodically interrupted by unsolicited inputs, as required by the dumb terminals. The operator can use function keys to indicate which actions are to be performed on the data entered, thus increasing operator efficiency.

Intelligent Terminals

An *intelligent terminal*, the most obvious example of which is a microcomputer, has all or most of the capabilities of a smart terminal, but in addition it can participate in the data processing requirements of the system. In some situations the intelligent terminal is completely independent of the host; however, to satisfy the definition of terminal given earlier, at some point the intelligent terminal must be connected to a host processor for processing or data access. It is also possible for an intelligent terminal to act as host for another terminal. An intelligent terminal is *programmable*.

Special Features.   Intelligent terminals generally have more memory than smart terminals, part of it devoted to program code and program data storage. Some may also have secondary storage in the form of disk, tape, or magnetic bubble. An attached printer is a common option. If there is no *auxiliary storage*, the programs can be down-loaded to the terminal from the host computer. *Down-loading*, or down-line loading, is the act of transferring programs or data from a host to a terminal. *Up-loading* happens when the terminal sends data or programs to the host. Like smart terminals, intelligent terminals can also be controlled from the host and can operate in both conversational and block mode.

Some of the processing functions available on intelligent terminals include storage and display of screen formats, *data editing, data formatting, compression/decompression*, and possibly some local database access and validation. In addition, intelligent terminals can allow local data entry in case the communications link is disrupted.

Intelligent Terminal Applications: An Example

Assume that the intelligent terminal is a microcomputer with disk drives and printer. The disk contains the data entry screen templates, together with the data entry program for sequencing logic for the screens and data editing. There are two major components of the order entry form, the customer portion and the product or order portion. Two or more screens of information are required to complete the order entry, as represented in Figures 4-7 and 4-8 on pages 119 and 120.

The data entry function of intelligent terminals is simplified; they can use the same menu and entry screens as for smart terminals, although with the intelligent terminal they can be stored and displayed locally, thus reducing the amount of data transmitted over the communications link. The *date* of the order is filled in by the terminal from its date register. On entering either the *customer name* or *customer number*, the default customer information can be accessed and entered from a file on the local disk drive. The person taking the order can, of course, alter any of the default entries or bypass local access altogether. Hitting the F2 function key is a prompt to obtain local customer information. Other terminals might make the selection via transaction codes embedded in the data, or by mouse, light pen, touch screen, or similar data entry device.

On completing data entry for the first screen, the operator hits function key F1, causing, first, the second screen of data to appear, and second, editing the entered data for consistency and then storing the edited data in a buffer in the terminal's memory. The operator enters the *part numbers* and *quantities* only. The *unit price, customer discount,* and *total price* will be extracted from a local database. *Page* and *order totals* are computed by the terminal. After editing the data and making the necessary calculations, the terminal performs compression on the data to be transmitted to the host. For example, repeating groups of characters such as blanks at the end of a *name* field are compressed into a repeat count and one-character sequence. This makes more effective use of the line. If the host uses a code different from that of the terminal, for example, an EBCDIC host and an ASCII terminal, then the terminal also performs the code conversion.

The final step is to transmit the data to the host and await the reply. The data in this example will be transmitted in one or more blocks, depending on the length of the order. Any required blocking and deblocking of data are performed by the terminal.

Advantages of Intelligent vs. Smart Terminals

The advantages of the intelligent terminal over the smart terminal stem from the fact that control and processing are local. Customer information is maintained locally, where it is frequently used, and line time is not required for obtaining customer information, transmitting screen templates, or correcting edit errors.

TERMINAL ATTRIBUTES

A number of terminal attributes are listed in Figure 4-9. These attributes are among the things to consider in selecting a terminal for a given application.

Cost	Synchronous	Auxiliary storage	EBCDIC
Conversational	Batch	Protected fields	Protocol support
Block mode	Point-to-point	Graphics	Attached devices
TTY-compatible	Multi-point	Formatting	Duplex
Dumb	Function keys	Character sets	Screen size
Smart	Editing	Keyboard	Character size
Intelligent	Cursor control	Blink	Modified data tags
Printer	Host control	Half intensity	CPU
Speed	Color	Reverse video	Interface
Asynchronous	Programmable	ASCII	Portability

Figure 4-9
Some Terminal Attributes

Output

Essentially there are two different types of terminal output, hard copy and volatile. Hard-copy output leaves a permanent record of the data sent to the terminals, whereas volatile display units leave no copy of the inputs or outputs. Hard copy uses some type of printed or punched output, and volatile format uses a display monitor such as a VDU or plasma display.

Hard Copy. Being mechanical, hard-copy devices generally have a much slower output rate than CRT devices. In addition to the interactive class of terminals, hard-copy devices include output-only equipment such as printers and plotters. Having a hard copy of the dialogue between host and terminal is sometimes extremely important, and dictates either a hard-copy terminal or a VDU with attached printer. Instances where hard copy may be especially desirable include computer consoles where error and operator messages are displayed and funds transfer applications where the auditors require an audit trail of all transactions.

Volatile Display. Volatile display devices come in several variations, including VDU, plasma display units, and light emitting diode (LED) display units. VDU technology is similar to television. A phosphor-coated screen is bombarded with directed electron beams, causing the phosphor to glow and thereby producing an image. Because the screen image fades in the absence of the electron beam, it must be constantly refreshed by repeating the electron beams. The refresh rate varies with the phosphor coating, but 60 repeats per second is quite common. Slow refresh rates can result in flickering screens and washed-out images.

VDU technology is by far the most common one in business data processing systems. Plasma terminals, being capable of higher resolution, are more commonly found in *graphics* applications. The images in plasma terminals are created by arrays of neon lights that can be individually illuminated. The bulbs themselves are not separate lights, but are integrated into a panel composed of several layers of glass, providing a continuous image on the terminal screen. In LED display units, light emitting diodes are used to form figure or character images much like a dot matrix printer forms images. In a variation of this technique, neon tubes or wires are used to form the character images. Liquid crystal display (LCD) panels similar to those found in digital watches and pocket games are also used for terminals. LCD display units are most commonly found in portable terminals.

Input

The most common input mechanism is the *keyboard*, in a variety of types. Other input devices include various types of readers—badge readers, OCR readers, paper tape readers—and light pens, mice, trackball, touch screens, sensors, voice recognition and generation equipment, and image processing devices such as digitizers that scan graphic images and create digital images of them.

Keyboards.   The standard keyboard has its keys arranged like those of a typewriter. This type of keyboard is sometimes referred to as a QWERTY keyboard because the letters on the left half of the third row spell QWERTY. The keyboard can be augmented with additional keys—such as function keys, numeric key pads, and control keys.

Function keys serve to indicate the functions to be performed on the entered data, or as interrupt keys. When used to interrupt, striking the key interrupts the process being run from the terminal and allows the operator to perform other functions such as stopping the process, starting a new process, or debugging the program. In general each function key has an associated character sequence. When a function key is struck, its unique character sequence is transmitted to the host, which then infers the action to be taken.

Numeric key pads are extremely convenient when a lot of the data to be entered are numeric. **Control keys** are used to transmit bit sequences that can be acted on by the program directly controlling the terminal, operating system, or application. Terminal control programs are discussed in Chapter 9.

Specialized keyboards also exist. In the Asian countries where the Kanji or Chinese character sets are used, the total number of allowable character symbols exceeds 30,000; usually only a subset consisting of approximately 10,000 characters is selectable. Special expanded keyboards with multiple characters per key are used in these situations. Some keyboards are specially designed for certain applications—for example, specific medical laboratory applications, such as serology and urology, with the number of keys and keyboard layout designed to enable the lab technician to characterize specimens with a minimum number of keystrokes. The urology keyboard, for instance, might have a number of keys for describing specimen color, another group to describe clarity, and so on, with only one keystroke per attribute required.

Light Pens.   Light pens are used to select from a number of options displayed on a VDU. The pen is essentially like a small, high-intensity flashlight. When aimed at a place on the VDU screen, the light image can be read and the coordinates of the point are determined. The data are translated into a selection displayed on the VDU screen. The process is similar to pointing to the object being selected.

Readers.   Reader devices read images that have been encoded in various ways. One such device with which most of you will be familiar is the automatic teller machine (ATM), which reads a magnetic tape strip or holographic image to determine the identity of the user.

Touch Screens.   Touch screens vary in how they discern input. Some use a matrix of infrared light beams emanating from two sides, say, the top and the left side, with photosensors on the opposite sides of the screen. Touching the screen interrupts these beams, and the coordinates of the area touched are read. Another method utilizes a resistance technique wherein two conductive layers are separated by a small distance; the touching causes a connection between the two at the point of the touch. A third technique uses a conductive surface on the screen: When the screen's surface is touched, the electrical characteristics of the screen are disrupted, allowing the position of the finger to be discerned. Advantages of touch screens include their ease of use and of training. They are especially effective in applications for people unfamiliar with data processing. For example, a number of hotels have touch screen information boards that allow patrons to inquire about news, events, and services.

Mice, Joy Sticks, and Trackballs.   The mouse, joy stick, and trackball input devices have found application in both computerized games and business. They are involved in *cursor control*. The *mouse* allows the user to move the cursor position on the screen by moving the mouse on a table surface: moving the mouse to the right causes the cursor also to move to the right. A *trackball* is similar to a mouse except that the cursor is moved not by moving a mouse, but by rotating a ball mounted in a fixed holder, the cursor moving in the direction that the ball is rotated. *A joy stick* moves the cursor by moving the stick in the desired direction. Most of these devices also contain additional input capabilities such as a button for selecting options. A mouse attached to a microcomputer is pictured in Figure 4-10 on page 126.

Figure 4-10
A Mouse Attached to
a Microcomputer

Courtesy of Apple Computer, Inc.

Graphics Imagers.   Graphics imaging equipment can scan images and translate those images into digital formats that can be stored and later modified or reproduced by a computer system. This technique, called digitizing or image scanning, can produce picture images as well as text images. One computerized business application of image scanning is facsimile acquisition, storage, transmission, and reproduction. This technique allows contracts bearing signatures and documents containing graphics images to be acquired, stored, reproduced, and distributed to remote locations electronically. This application of data communications and database technology is destined to expand in the near future.

Voice Synthesis and Recognition.   Voice synthesis is an output technology and voice recognition an input technology. While more research is needed in this area its future looks promising; numerous applications are making use of what has already been developed. In one such application, telephone companies have implemented directory assistance in some areas with voice generation hardware and software. In shop floor applications, all workers can enter voice commands, leaving their hands free to operate equipment. Voice store and forward systems allow users to enter data via a telephone, store a digitized image of the message, and later forward it to a recipient. Currently the technology and the costs prohibit voice as a cost-effective input or output device for most business applications.

Cost of Terminals

There is a dramatic range in the cost of terminals, varying from several hundred dollars for a dumb terminal to tens of thousands of dollars for special terminals such as RJE or very-high-resolution graphics terminals with imaging devices. Cost analysis is difficult, since cost factors like line utilization, operator acceptance, efficiency, and local processing ability are not always easy to quantify. In selecting a terminal for a given application, each of these factors must be considered in addition to the purchase and maintenance prices. Figure 4-11 represents a cross-section of terminal prices in 1983.

Terminal Type	Compatibility	Price Low	Price High	Typical
Dumb	TTY	$,250	$ 3,500	$ 500–1,500
Smart	IBM 3270	1,500	12,000	1,500–4,000
Smart	TTY	250	5,000	500–2,500
Intelligent	IBM 3270	2,000	50,000	2,500–5,000
Intelligent	TTY	1,500	40,000	2,500–4,500

Figure 4-11
Representative Terminal Prices, 1983 (From "Computerworld Buyer's Guide," 1983)

Speed

The *speed* at which a terminal accepts and transmits data is dependent on the terminal hardware, the type of line to which it is attached, and the types of modems used (if any). For a given terminal, there is also a discrete set of rates at which it may receive and transmit information. An unbuffered hard-copy terminal may have a maximum receive speed of 1200 bps because its print capacity is 120 characters per second. A CRT device, on the other hand, may be capable of receiving data at 19.2 Kbps or more. In addition to the maximum available speed, the intermediate speeds available should be considered. Some terminals have one or two settings for speeds, whereas others support numerous common speeds, such as 75, 300, 600, 1200, 2400, 4800, 9600, and 19,200 bps.

Maintenance and Support

Some computer manufacturers sell with their system terminals manufactured by other companies. They usually also provide support for the terminals they sell. Many manufacturers also build terminals designed to complement their own computer system. If acquired on this basis, the terminals can receive support consistent with the support for the rest of the system. An advantage of such vendor support is having only one organization to contact regardless of the problem. In some cases, for instance, what appears to be a terminal problem is actually an error in the software or hardware communicating with that terminal. Single vendor support tends to eliminate the question of who is responsible for errors. In multiple vendor installations, determining which vendor is responsible for a problem can become a difficult issue.

But single vendor support has a disadvantage, for both terminals and computer equipment: Computer manufacturers sometimes charge more for their terminals than manufacturers who specialize in terminal equipment. For these companies to survive they must offer better prices, equipment, or support than the computer supplier. Thus, you can frequently save a considerable sum of money by obtaining terminals from an outside source, especially when the number of terminals is large. A note of caution when acquiring terminals from other than the computer vendor: Be sure to have the terminal demonstrated on your system. Some terminals may not be supported by the vendor's software and hardware, and what appears an excellent purchase may turn into a colossal blunder. Furthermore, terminals advertised as being compatible with the computer vendor's terminals may have small areas of incompatibility that can adversely impact the application.

Memory

Not all terminals have memory available. Those that do may allow for different sizes of memory, some of which may not be available to a particular application. This is because, for intelligent terminals, a portion of the memory is needed to store programs run at the terminal. For example, an intelligent terminal with 128K bytes of memory may not have the entire memory space available for data. Typically, part of the space is for the operating system, for input/output routines that interface with the communications links and peripherals, and for the application. If the application involves a spreadsheet, the program code would restrict the amount of data that can be stored in the terminal's memory.

Some smart terminals may reserve a portion of available memory for the teminal's use. For example, suppose a terminal has sufficient memory to store the data for six screens of information, and it also supports field attributes such as *color*, protection, and modified data tags. This terminal will allow only three pages of data to be stored, and the other three pages are used to store the field attributes. *Modified data tags* are used by the terminal to detect which fields on the screen have changed, allowing the terminal to transmit only those fields altered since the previous time the data were sent. They make efficient use of the medium, especially when correcting input errors. In order to support these capabilities, a portion of the memory is reserved to record the attributes of each character or field to be displayed. Half of the memory in the terminal could be reserved for these purposes, with every character defined by an attribute character.

Display Attributes

Hard-copy devices have very few display attributes to select, with the possible exception of colored pens for plotters, graphics, italics, underline, type fonts, or overprint. However, with video display units, many possibilities exist, including multiple colors, shading, and highlighting such as blinking fields. Also to be considered are *screen size* and the *character size*. That is, the number of characters per line and the number of lines per screen can vary significantly.

Color Display. *Color* display units vary from two colors to 4096 colors, typically 4, 8, 16, 32, 64, or 256 different colors. Some also allow shading of colors or black and white. For example, if a display unit has 16 colors, then the number of combinations of foreground or symbol colors and background colors is $16 \times 15 = 240$ different display capabilities. If each color has two intensities then the number of combinations increases to 960, although some of these combinations may be rather difficult to read due to lack of contrast—for instance, white letters on a yellow background.

Monochrome Display. The users of monochrome displays, that is those having only one foreground and one background color, also may have several options. *Half intensity* displays the characters with half the intensity of full-intensity characters. That is, the contrast between half intensity and the background is less than that of full intensity. In the screens defined in Figures 4-7 and 4-8 on pages 119 and 120, the prompts would probably be at half intensity and the data at full intensity; the operator's attention would then be drawn to the data entered, not to the prompts.

Reverse video exchanges foreground and background colors: Instead of white characters on a black background, there would be black characters on a white background. Half intensity can also be used in combination with reverse video to provide four different display modes. Reverse video is very effective in highlighting fields that are in error, error messages, and format headings. Another method for drawing attention to fields is to cause the field or a portion thereof to blink.

Ergonomics

Ergonomics is the study of how people adjust to their work environment. Currently, a very important consideration in terminal selection is the unit's human engineering. A number of physical problems have been attributed to poor terminal design, including radiation side effects, headaches, eyestrain, muscle and tendon problems, and arthritic conditions.

Perhaps the major side effect of VDU terminals is their emission of radiation. Some companies have noted a higher incidence of birth defects from women working at their VDUs, and a number of law suits have been filed in this regard. By U.S. law, radiation emitted from a terminal must be less than 0.0005 rem per hour at a distance of two inches from the screen. This is usually achieved by filtering the radiation with a glass screen.

Ideal Display Characteristics. The ideal display should be easy on the eyes, with a nonglare surface. Green phosphor or amber characters on a black background are preferred to white characters on a black background. The display should tilt and swivel for ease of reading. The keyboard should be detachable and should be at a convenient height. Keys should be sculpted and arranged for easy access. The displayed characters should be well formed and easy to read. The screen image should be refreshed at a sufficient rate to avoid flicker. The contrast should be adjustable to ease eyestrain. The keyboard should emit a click to reinforce each key stroke, and the loudness of the click should be controllable, from inaudible to somewhat loud.

The ergonomics of terminals should not be taken lightly. Several law suits are currently in progress regarding excess emissions and debilitation of the fingers as a result of prolonged use of terminals. For international organizations the inclusion of ergonomic features is critical, since the laws in some countries require the features mentioned above. At least one corporation has found itself unable to use its terminals in some European countries because they lacked the desired human engineering features.

Interface

The manner in which terminals *interface* with devices varies widely. In the United States, RS-232-C is currently the most common interface, with RS-449 gaining in popularity. In many other countries, CCITT standards are used. Some terminals are attached to devices other than modems. For instance, most of the *IBM 3270* terminals can be attached directly to a cluster controller rather than to a modem, in which case coaxial cable is used for the interface, and terminals on a local area network attach to the medium using a transceiver and controller. This interface is usually different from an RS-232-C or RS-449 connection. The type of interface is dependent on the terminal and the environment in which it is to be used.

Terminals also have interfaces to other devices, such as light pens, printers, and other input or output systems. For printers, the more common interfaces are either serial or parallel. These ports may also be used for attaching other types of equipment.

Protocol

Terminals communicate by a convention that transmits either a character at a time or a block at a time. These conventions, called protocols, are discussed in more detail in Chapter 6. *Protocol support* is generally one of the primary concerns when purchasing a terminal. Many terminals communicate via only one of these conventions. Some terminals may have an option of being either asynchronous or synchronous. In addition to supporting a particular protocol, there also is usually a price difference between an asynchronous terminal and a synchronous one; an asynchronous terminal usually being less expensive than a synchronous terminal.

The average price for a simple asynchronous terminal is less than one-third the price for a synchronous one, with monthly maintenance charges for asynchronous terminals being perhaps one-fourth the price for synchronous terminals.

Miscellaneous Attributes

There are many other terminal characteristics to be considered, including alternate character sets, addressability, codes, central processing units, and portability.

Alternate Character Sets. Alternate *character sets* are available on some terminals. The alternate set may be a foreign language, a graphics character set, or possibly both.

Addressability. Some transmission techniques work on the principle that terminals have an address (see the section on "polling" later in this chapter). If this transmission technique is used, then the terminal must be addressable. This characteristic is usually found in both smart and intelligent terminals.

Codes. The code used by a terminal is important. Most terminals use either *ASCII* or *EBCDIC* data coding, but some 6-bit and 5-bit codes are still used. The terminal must either be compatible with the code used by the host or a code translation must be made. If implemented in host software, the translation can consume a significant portion of the processing power of the CPU.

Central Processing Units. Most of the smart terminals and all of the intelligent ones have some type of *microprocessor* to control the terminal functions. The type of *CPU* used can be important, particularly with intelligent devices. The terminal's processor is a significant factor in the speed with which instructions are executed and with respect to expansion capabilities. Many of the newer intelligent terminals are based on a 16-bit or 32-bit CPU.

Portability. At one time, terminal *portability* was confined mostly to dumb devices. Portable personal computers have made intelligent terminals portable as well. In those applications where the terminal operator may need to move from location to location, portability is beneficial. For instance, the traveling salesperson who enters orders on a portable computer during the day can quickly transmit those orders from a telephone to the data processing center at the end of the day.

TERMINAL CONFIGURATION

On any given communications channel, there are two options for attaching terminals, point-to-point and multi-point.

Point-to-Point Connections

Point-to-point connections have one terminal at the end of a communications link from a host. There is little contention for the use of the channel in a point-to-point configuration, since only the host and the terminal are candidates for transmission. Point-to-point connections are very common in computer-to-computer communications, local connections, and remote connections with only one terminal. In communicating with several terminals over a long distance, true point-to-point communications would be quite expensive, since each terminal would require a separate line with a pair of modems. As is discussed in the next chapter, there are hardware components that allow terminals to share a communications channel while logically operating in a point-to-point manner.

The methodology for controlling the station that is allowed to use the communications link is sometimes referred to as a *line discipline*. Point-to-point configuration has several ways in which the data flow can be managed: contention, pure contention, and supervisor-tributaries.

Contention.   One mechanism for managing data flow is known as *contention*. In the contention mode the host and the terminal contend for control of the medium. Each is considered to have an equal right to transmit to the other. In order to transmit, one station generally issues a bid for the channel, that is, asks the other party for control. If the other is ready to receive the data, then control is granted to the requester. Upon completing the transfer, control is then relinquished, and the link goes into an idle state, awaiting the next bid for control. A collision can occur on occasions when both stations simultaneously bid for the line. If this occurs, either one station is granted the request based on some predetermined priority scheme, or each station waits a while and then reattempts the bid. With the latter approach, the time-out intervals must not be the same, for having the same time-out intervals is likely to cause another collision.

Pure Contention.   A second method of point-to-point communication is also a contention method, but without line bids. This technique, known as pure contention, allows either of the two devices to transmit data whenever it is ready, the assumption being that the other station is ready to receive the data when it arrives. The sending station is made aware that the message was received correctly via a positive acknowledgment message from the recipient. In the absence of a positive acknowledgment, and after a designated time-out interval, the sending station must assume the message was not received correctly and resend it. Collisions can also occur with this technique. Pure contention is advantageous in situations where modem turnaround times make line bids costly.

Supervisor-Tributaries.   A third line discipline requires that one station be designated as the supervisor of the link and the other station as a tributary or *secondary station*. In this configuration the supervisor has absolute control over the link, and the secondary station may send data only when given permission by the supervisor. The host computer almost always assumes the role of supervisor. This form of control is more commonly used in the multi-point environment.

Multi-point Connections

A *multi-point connection* is one in which multiple terminals share the same communications channel. The number of terminals allowed to share the medium is a function of channel capacity and the workload at the terminals themselves, and sometimes of other hardware employed. Chapter 2 discussed the calculations required to determine the optimum number of terminals on such a line: As the number of terminals on the link increases, the average time each terminal has access to the link decreases.

A contention-type line discipline would work in a multi-point configuration. In fact, contention is one of the popular methods used in local area networks consisting of hundreds of stations. However, studies have shown that as the number of stations communicating in this manner increases, so does the number of collisions on the channel. When the number of collisions is high, the effective rate of data transfer declines because of the time required to resolve the collisions.

Polling.   The most common method of establishing line discipline in multi-point terminal networks is referred to as *poll/select*, or simply *polling*. In the polled configuration, one station is designated as the supervisor or *primary station*. This role is almost always assumed by the host computer, although other pieces of equipment such as controllers or concentrators may be used instead (see Chapter 5). There is only one primary per multi-point link; all other stations are referred to as *secondary* or tributary *stations*. The discussion that follows assumes that the host computer is the primary.

The primary station is in complete control of the link. Secondary stations may transmit data only when given permission by the primary station. It is this process of asking terminals whether they have data to transmit that is referred to as polling. Each tributary station is given a unique address, and each terminal must be able to recognize its own address. Although there are several distinct methods of polling, essentially the process is as follows.

The primary is provided a list of addresses for terminals on a particular link. There may be several multi-point lines controlled by one primary, although addresses on a given link are unique. The primary picks an address from the list and sends a poll message across the link using that address. The poll message is very short, consisting of the poll address and a string of characters that have been designated as a poll message. All secondary stations receive the poll message, but only the addressee responds. The poll message is an inquiry to the secondary station as to whether it has any data to transmit to the primary. If it has data to transmit, the secondary responds with either the data or a positive acknowledgment and then the data. If the secondary station has no data to send, then it responds with a negative acknowledgment. Upon receipt of either the data or the negative acknowledgment, the primary selects another station's polling address, and repeats the process. For a terminal to operate in this manner it must have memory to buffer data until it is asked to transmit.

Selection.   When the primary has data to send to one or more secondary stations, it selects the station in much the same manner used for polling. Some terminals have two addresses, one for polling and one for selecting. In the selection process, the primary sends a selection message to the terminal. Essentially a selection message consists of the terminal's selection address and an inquiry to determine whether the terminal is ready to accept data. The terminal may respond to the selection positively or negatively. For instance, if the terminal's buffer is full, it cannot accept additional data and so responds negatively. After a positive acknowledgment to the selection message, the primary transmits the data to the terminal. In some multi-point networks the primary is able to send a message to all stations simultaneously via a broadcast address; that is, one address that all terminals recognize as theirs. Other addressing schemes allow terminals to be divided into broadcast groups by using a common prefix for their addresses.

Fast Select.   A variation of selection is a method known as a fast select. With fast select, the data accompanies the select message. This is effective when the receiving stations are usually able to accept the data being transmitted. If a station is not ready to receive data, the message is lost and must be retransmitted. In this situation the primary could revert to the previous selection method for that terminal.

Types of Polling.   There are three basic types of polling: roll call, hub polling, and token passing.

In *roll call polling* the primary obtains a list of addresses for terminals on the line and then proceeds sequentially down the list, polling each terminal in turn. If one or more stations on the link are of higher priority or are more likely to have data to send, their address could be included in the list multiple times so they can be polled more frequently. Roll call polling is illustrated in Figure 4-12.

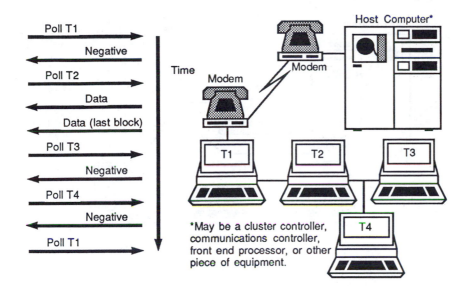

Figure 4-12
Roll Call Polling

Hub polling requires the terminals to become involved in the polling process. The primary sends a poll message to one station on the link. If that station has data to transmit, it does so. After transmitting its data or if it had no data to transmit, the terminal passes the poll to an adjacent terminal. This process is repeated until all terminals have had the opportunity to transmit. The primary then starts the process all over again. In this discipline, the primary relinquishes some of its control of the link to the terminals. Hub polling is more efficient than roll call polling because less of the line capacity is devoted to polling and acknowledgment messages. It also requires more intelligence at the terminal end, since the terminal must recognize the address of its neighbor and pass along the poll. Hub polling is illustrated in Figure 4-13 on page 136. In the diagram, if T2 were not operational, T3 would pass the poll to terminal T1.

Token passing is more common in local area networks and multi-point configurations of intelligent terminals. This technique could technically be considered separate from polling, since there is no primary station—that is, all stations are on equal status. Token passing is similar in some respects to hub polling. A particular bit sequence is designated as the token. Whichever station is in possession of the token is the station allowed to transmit. The token is passed from station to station, together with the privilege of transmitting information. Since the token eventually arrives at each station, each receives the opportunity to send. Token passing is depicted in Figure 4-14 on page 136.

Advantage of Multi-point Connections.   The advantage of multi-point lines is economic in nature. First, only one communications link is required

Figure 4-13
Hub Polling

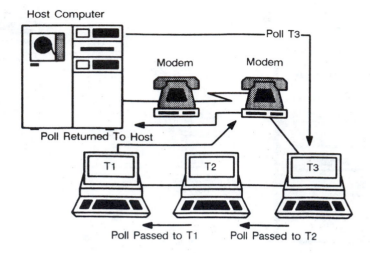

Figure 4-14
Token Passing

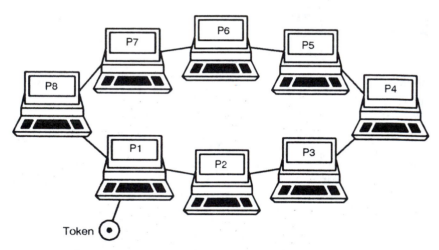

P1 has the token. P1 may transmit data to another station.
If P1 has no more data to transmit, P1 passes the token to P2.

for a host to communicate with a number of terminals; second, if modems are required on the link, fewer modems are necessary. In a true point-to-point link a pair of modems is often required for each terminal, one at the host end and one at the terminal end. For multi-point links, at most one modem per terminal and one at the host are required. In some instances a terminal cluster controller, discussed in Chapter 5, may be used at the terminal end, and if the terminals are sufficiently close to the controller, individual terminal modems will not be necessary—that is, only a host and cluster controller modem will be required. For example, if ten terminals are to be located remotely, ten point-to-point lines would require 20 modems. For a multi-point line, at most 11 modems would be required, possibly only two. Figure 4-15 presents several multi-point configurations, together with their required modems.

Disadvantages of Multi-point Connections.   There are also disadvantages to the multi-point configuration. First, terminals used in this environment must have some amount of intelligence, making them more expensive than terminals in the point-to-point connection. This cost is usually negligible, however, when compared with the savings of medium and modems.

Because the medium is shared among a number of terminals, a terminal may have to wait to transmit its information. If messages are short, the wait time should not be long; however, if messages are lengthy, such as when a microcomputer transfers a file, then the other terminals may be required to wait an inordinate amount of time. Delays also have an impact on response times, and this delay should be factored into the response time calculations for a multi-point line. If *half duplex* lines are used for communication, the modem turnaround time can become significant. For roll call polling, two modem turnarounds are required for each poll message. As in the example in Chapter 3, where modem turnaround time was greater than the message time, such potential also exists in a half-duplex polled environment.

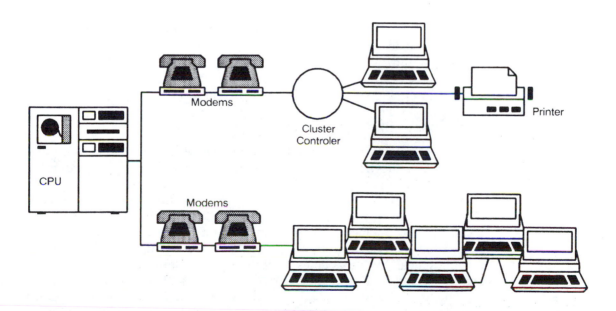

Figure 4-15   Multi-Point Configurations

Asynchronous vs. Synchronous Transmission

Polled terminals usually transmit information a block at a time rather than a character at a time, a transmission mode referred to as synchronous transmission. Although polled environments exist for transmission of one character at a time, referred to as asynchronous or start-stop transmission, the synchronous environment is more suitable because of its ability to transmit blocks of data. Terminals used in a multi-point configuration can also be used in a point-to-point configuration, providing configuration flexibility while simplifying the portion of application design that deals with the terminal interface.

Polling Costs.   The actual polling of devices can be implemented in hardware or software. Software solutions can be expensive because of the number of CPU cycles consumed. When software solutions are employed, the function is usually placed in a front end processor or communications controller, which prevents the main CPU from becoming bogged down in controlling lines. An additional cost of polling results from a portion of the available line capacity being used for exchange of poll messages. This reduces the data capacity of the medium.

SPECIFIC TERMINAL DEVICES

There are four types of terminals that have had or are likely to have significant impact on the data communications industry: teletypewriter-compatible terminals, RJE terminals, IBM 3270 family terminals, and microcomputers.

Teletypewriter-compatible Terminals

The teletypewriter (TTY) family of terminals operates in much the same manner as the teletypewriter equipment originally used in telegraphy. AT&T's ASR model 33 is one example of a TTY machine. (ASR is an abbreviation for automatic sending and receiving unit.) The TTY class of terminals has been the workhorse of the data communications industry since its inception. Originally these terminals were dumb terminals and transmitted in asynchronous mode. Because they are used in so many applications, the capabilities of this family of terminals have been expanded, and TTY-compatibility now exists for both smart and intelligent terminals. This has enabled systems to take advantage of the progress made in terminal development without losing any investment in software designed for TTY devices.

RJE Terminals

IBM 2780 and 3780 Terminals.   The most common example of RJE terminals are *IBM's 2780* and *3780* family of terminals. The 2780 was introduced in 1967; the 3780 is an enhanced version of the 2780, providing larger buffers, larger numbers of records per buffer, space compression, and enhanced control attributes. RJE terminals have card readers, card punches, printers, and communications controllers. They operate in the batch mode and are used to transfer files between a remote site and a host computer(s).

IBM 3270 Terminals.   The *IBM 3270* family of terminals is perhaps the single most successful non-TTY terminal. Together with over 100 competitive, compatible models, it accounts for approximately 30% of the terminal market, with over one million units sold [Brear, 1983; King, 1983]. This line of terminals is called a family because it actually consists of a variety of terminals, printers, and cluster controllers.

IBM 3270 terminals may be attached either locally or remotely and in point-to-point or multi-point configurations, using local or leased lines. The terminal display stations include model numbers 3277, 3278, and 3279; the printers include model numbers 3284, 3286, 3287, 3288, and 3289; and the controllers include model numbers 3271, 3272, and 3274. Figure 4-16 illustrates a number of ways in which these devices may be configured.

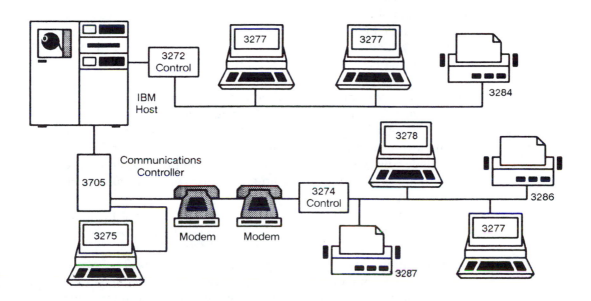

Figure 4-16   A Sample IBM 3270 Configuration

Each of the terminal models has submodels. For example, the 3278 display terminal has models 1, 2, 3, and 4, distinguished by the number of lines that can be displayed and hence the total number of displayable characters, which ranges from 960 per screen for the model 1 to 3440 per screen for the model 4. Printers also come in various submodels, with the distinctions being in print speed, buffer size, controller interface, and allowable distance from the controller. The display terminals are classified as smart terminals.

IBM 3270 cluster controllers, which control up to 32 terminals or printers, differ with respect to how they interface with the system. For example, the 3272 is used for local channel attachment, the 3271 for remote half duplex, and the 3274 for local or remote half duplex. They also vary with respect to the protocol supported, either binary synchronous (BISYNC) or synchronous data link control (SDLC), both of which are explained in Chapter 6. Cluster controllers are responsible for polling terminals, checking terminal status, transferring data between host and terminal, and forwarding screen *formatting* commands to the display terminals. Each control unit contains memory used to buffer data passing between the host and terminals or printers.

Microcomputers

Microcomputers are becoming an important force in data communications networks. Because of their intelligence they can be made to imitate any type of terminal, a relatively important feature for protecting any investment in terminal equipment. Thus, with a microcomputer as a terminal, computer systems can be replaced by different models and the terminals will still be able to communicate with the new system. This compatibility arises either because the new computer system supports the terminals or because the microcomputer has been reprogrammed to imitate a new type of terminal. Furthermore, the microcomputer is capable of performing a number of functions previously required of a host system or other piece of equipment, such as a front end processor (see Chapter 5), functions that include editing of data, code translation, compression/decompression, and local processing such as totaling of invoices and computing extended prices and discounts.

For a microcomputer to be used as a terminal, it must be augmented by two items, a communications interface and software.

Communications Interfaces. A communications interface is standard equipment in a number of systems; in other systems this must be added, usually as a printed circuit board occupying one of the microcomputer's expansion slots. Sometimes these communications interfaces are added to printed circuit boards that provide other functions, such as additional memory. The communications interface enables the microcomputer to be attached to a communications line or modem and to physically receive and transmit data.

Software.   Software is required to provide the interface between the communications line and such microcomputer components as disk and memory. There are many pieces of software available for a variety of microcomputers, and they allow microcomputers to imitate a TTY device, an RJE device, or an IBM-3270–type terminal, as well as a number of terminals compatible with other computer makes.

Other Selection Criteria.   Other factors that should be considered when selecting an intelligent terminal include the CPU, available software, auxiliary storage, and peripherals.

Many of the original microcomputers used an 8-bit *CPU*. Many current systems use either a 16-bit or 32-bit CPU, the difference being the speed with which they are able to transfer data between the memory and the registers and the amount of memory that can be efficiently accessed. In general, the 32-bit systems are faster and can support more memory and devices than the 16-bit and 8-bit processors.

An extensive array of *software* is available for intelligent terminals, including database management, data communications, graphics, programming languages, spreadsheets, word processing, and a host of other applications. Use of these programs can increase the amount of processing done at the terminal and eliminate some of the need for accessing a host system. In selecting software, how it will interact with the host system should be considered.

The amount of *auxiliary storage*—primarily disk and tape, the speed of these storage devices, and the *peripherals* available are important considerations, because these also affect the amount and type of work that can be accomplished at the terminal. For example, a disk's capacity will partially determine the size and number of documents that can be stored at a word processing terminal: If the capacity is large, the terminal will have less need for the (usually) larger storage facilities of the host.

CASE STUDY

The Syncrasy Corporation is considering expanding operations into several major marketing areas. A preliminary analysis has been initiated to determine the costs of expansion; a portion of it has already been completed. System design objectives have been formulated, stating the goals the system will be expected to meet. A feasibility study is underway to determine if the design objectives can be met within the expense restrictions. One part of this study is to determine the number of terminals required in each location. To accomplish this necessitates first estimating transaction time.

Transaction Time

The preliminary analysis has indicated that expansion needs will be adequately met by a single host processor with multiple terminals at remote locations. For one location it has been determined that there are five types of transaction constituting the major transaction load. These transaction types are described in Figure 4-17.

Figure 4-17
Projected
Transactions for
Syncrasy Corp.

| | Transaction Type | | | | |
	Order Entry	Credit Check	Customer Maintenance	Send Mail	Receive Mail
Think/wait time (secs)	10	5	120	60	180
No. of input characters	600	50	150	2000	50
No. of output characters	20	500	500	50	2000
Disk/CPU/ queuing time (secs)	1	0.5	0.5	1.5	1.5
Hourly peak	40	10	4	5	5

Think/Wait Time.   *Think/wait time* for each transaction represents the amount of time the operator will wait or think before or during the entering of the transaction. For example, the long think time for a customer maintenance transaction (120 seconds) reflects the time the operator is obtaining the information from the telephone. Other possible sources of think/wait time are drinking coffee or tea, reading documents, rearranging papers, and so on.

Data Entry (Input-Output) Time.   *Number of input characters* represents the number of key strokes the operator will enter to complete a transaction. Depending on the type of data being entered, operators are capable of entering 5 characters per second or more. In the following analysis, a more conservative key stroke rate of 1.5 characters per second is assumed. *Number of output characters* is the number of characters received in response to the transaction. Both input and output create transaction time delay that is a function of transmission speed. Here, it is assumed that each character transmitted requires 10 bits.

Disk/CPU/Queuing Time.   *Disk/CPU/queuing time* is the amount of time the transaction is held by the processor and the time spend waiting in queues at different places in the system. For this analysis the cumulative times for these activities have been given. In reality, these times are rather difficult to determine.

Disk Access Time.   Each transaction type requires records to be read from or written into the database. For *order entry* transactions, the inventory levels of each ordered item would be adjusted by reading and writing the inventory record for each item, which might require that one or more index tables be accessed and searched. Database access times depend on the type of disk drive used and the organization of the database. Usually there are three major components of disk access time: seek time, rotational delay (latency), and transfer time. Some disks eliminate seek time by providing a read/write head for each track.

CPU Time.   *CPU time* is the amount of time required for the CPU to execute the necessary processing instructions, including those executed by the database management system, the operating system, the data communications software, and the application programs. It is a function of the speed of the processor and memory, as well as the number and type of instructions to be executed, and is generally small relative to disk access time and data transmission time. CPU time is rather difficult to estimate for a non-operational system, and initial estimates could be off significantly. However, since most business transactions tend to be input/output (I/O) intensive, and since I/O time is usually much greater than CPU time, such deviations often have little impact on the final calculations.

Queuing Time.   The third component of disk/CPU/queuing time is the amount of time the transaction must wait in queues for service. Like CPU time, this component is somewhat difficult to determine accurately; unlike CPU time, however, it can represent a significant portion of overall transaction time. A transaction can wait in queues in various places within a system—at the terminal waiting to be polled, at an application or data communications activity waiting to be processed, and at the disk drive awaiting the completion of other disk requests.

Transaction queues can be compared to lines during grocery shopping, when a customer might wait in one line for a parking space, another line for check approval, and a third line for checkout. In the store situation, wait time is a function of line length or customer arrival rate, mean service time for customers in line, number of servers available, and the service convention, such as first-in first-out (FIFO) or last-in first-out (LIFO). The same is true of computer systems. The specifics of how to calculate the disk, CPU, and queuing times are quite complex, and a more detailed analysis can be found in Pritchard, 1976. These times have been provided without derivation for this exercise.

Number of Terminals

The amount of time required to completely process a single transaction is the total of operator think/wait time, data entry (I/O) time, transmission time, and disk/CPU/queuing time. The *minimum* number of terminals required can be found by determining the total time required to process all transactions per given time period, say, 1 hour. Thus, if 1200 transactions per hour were to be processed, each requiring 30 seconds (0.5 minutes) to complete, then the number of terminals required would be

$$\frac{1200 \text{ transactions}}{\text{hour}} \times \frac{0.5 \text{ terminal minutes}}{\text{transaction}} \times \frac{1 \text{ hour}}{60 \text{ minutes}}$$

$$= \frac{600}{60} = 10 \text{ terminals}$$

This is the minimum number of terminals required based on utilization.

For a number of reasons, a user might decide to install additional terminals: There may be more potential operators than there are required terminals, such as in an office in which every employee is given a terminal even though each employee uses it only part of the time. Or, in order to place ATMs more conveniently for customers, a bank might install more ATMs than actually required to meet transaction demand. Additional terminals might also be installed to accommodate expansion, to provide spares, and to provide a margin for calculation error.

It is assumed that all *wait time* components are included in the transaction times. Were this not the case, then the calculated number of terminals would be less than the minimum number required: For instance, if only the transmission time on a multi-drop line were considered, and not the average wait time for polling, the results would not realistically reflect the *total* time of a given transaction, because the calculation ignored wait time for access to the transmission medium.

To determine the number of terminals required for Syncrasy Corp., the approach will be to calculate the single transaction time for each type of transaction, multiply each transaction time by the number of transactions of that type per hour, and then total. Shorter approaches could be taken, but they would be less illustrative. Only the *order entry* transaction is computed in detail; the calculations for the remainder will be left as an exercise.

Transaction time for the *order entry* transaction, then, is given by

transaction time = think/wait time + data entry time
   + transmission time + disk/CPU/queuing time

To determine transmission time means that a transmission speed must be selected; for this exercise a speed of 4800 bps is assumed. Order entry transaction time, then, is

$$10 + \frac{600}{1.5} + \frac{620 \times 10}{4800} + 1 = 10 + 400 + 1.3 + 1 = 412.3 \text{ seconds}$$

The transaction times required for credit check, customer maintenance, sending of electronic mail, and receiving of electronic mail are, respectively, 39.9, 221.9, 1,399.1, and 219.1 seconds. (Perform the necessary calculations yourself to test your skill.) And the total amount of time for all transactions in an hour is

$$(421.3 \times 40) + (39.9 \times 10) + (221.9 \times 4) + (1399.1 \times 5) +$$
$$(219.1 \times 5) = 16,852 + 399 + 887.6 + 6,995.5 + 1,095.5$$
$$= 26,229.6 \text{ seconds}$$

Thus, in one hour's time, 26,229.6 seconds of terminal, communications link, and CPU/disk/wait time will be required. And the number of terminals needed is

$$\frac{26,229.6}{3,600} = 7.29 \text{ terminals}$$

Thus, to provide for the total number of transactions from one location, eight terminals will be needed.

SUMMARY

There is a wide variety of terminals, terminal capabilities, and terminal prices. The industry has been moving toward terminals with more intelligence, providing functions that are simple to use and may also reduce overall communications cost and host processor work. Microprocessors and intelligent terminals have begun to emerge as strong forces in the terminal marketplace. Their flexibility and local processing ability make them very effective in the modern communications network. Ergonomic features are becoming important to terminal selection.

Key Terms

Addressable	Mouse
Asynchronous transmission	Multi-point connection
Block mode	Optical character recognition (OCR)
Cathode ray tube (CRT)	Poll/Select
Compression/decompression	Point-to-point connection
Contention	Primary station
Conversational mode	Remote batch processing
Data editing	Roll call polling
Data formatting	Screen templates
Down-loading	Secondary station
Dumb terminal	Smart terminal
Host computer	Synchronous transmission
Hub polling	Teletypewriter
IBM 2780 terminal	Terminal
IBM 3270 terminal	Token passing
IBM 3780 terminal	Trackball
Intelligent terminal	Universal product code (UPC)
Joystick	Up-loading
Line discipline	Video display terminal (VDT)
Microprocessor	Video display unit (VDU)
Modified data tags	Windowing

Key Terms, continued

Terminal Attributes

Cost	Function keys	Half intensity
Conversational	Editing	Reverse video
Block (page) mode	Cursor control	ASCII
TTY compatible	Host control	EBCDIC
Dumb	Color	Protocol support
Smart	Programmable	Attached devices
Intelligent	Auxiliary storage	Duplex
Printer	Protected fields	Screen size
Speed	Graphics	Character size
Asynchronous	Formatting	Modified data tags
Synchronous	Character sets	CPU
Batch	Keyboard	Interface
Point-to-point	Blink	Portability
Multi-point		

Questions and Exercises

1. Computer-aided design and computer-aided manufacture (CAD/CAM) use terminals in the design process. Graphics capability is essential to this application. What other terminal attributes would be beneficial in such an application?

2. Identify five special types of terminals besides the ten special types already identified at the beginning of the chapter. (Hint: Retail establishments can be a source of at least two.)

3. Why is ergonomic design an important terminal selection criterion? Research the literature and find at least two cases in which employers are being sued as a result of terminal-related incidents.

4. Besides the ergonomic requirements of terminals, what other environmental guidelines should be followed with respect to a terminal work environment—that is, what lighting, noise, and furniture should be available to protect the user? How frequently should breaks be taken?

5. Derive the transaction times for each of the transaction types described in the case study—credit check, customer maintenance, sending of electronic mail, and receiving of electronic mail.

6. A bank has decided to install ATMs in a number of locations. They have determined that there will be two major transactions at the ATMs, withdrawals and checking of account balances. The characteristics for each transaction are given in Figure 4-18. Determine the minimum number of ATMs required if the communications link speed is 2400 bps and assuming that each character transmitted requires 10 bits. Assume also that ATM users are able to enter 0.75 characters per second.

Transaction Type		
	Withdrawal	Account Balance
Think/wait time (secs)	15	15
No. of input characters	10	10
No. of output characters	100	100
Disk/CPU/queuing time (secs)	2	1
Hourly peak	1000	100

Figure 4-18
Projected Transactions

7. What are some reasons that a bank might install more ATMs than the minimum required?

References

Brear, Scott. "Assault on the 3270: Now There Are Choices." *Computerworld on Communications* 17 (September 28, 1983).

"Computerworld Buyer's Guide, Terminals and Peripherals." *Computerworld on Communications* 17 (October 5, 1983).

Foley, J. D., and Van Dam, A. *Fundamentals of Interactive Computer Graphics.* Reading, MA. Addison-Wesley, 1982.

IBM. *An Introduction to the IBM 3270 Information Display System.* Manual no. GA27-2739-7. September 1977.

Jones, James L. "A New Radiation Hazard." *Technological Review,* October 1983.

_____ "Video Radiation: Fears Out of Focus." *Technological Review,* October 1983.

King, John. "Which Is the Fairest Terminal of All?" *Computerworld on Communications* 17 (May 18, 1983).

Martin, Lionel, "Ergonomics: A Growing Concern in CRT Design." *Mini-Micro Systems,* November 1980.

Miller, Frederick W. "CRT Terminals Get Smarter, Cheaper." *Infosystems,* September 1981.

_____ "The World of CRT Terminals." *Infosystems,* June 1982.

_____ "More Than Skin Deep." *Infosystems,* September 1982.

Morris, D. J. *Introduction to Communication Command and Control Systems.* Elmsford, NY: Pergamon Press, 1977.

Popper, Andrew "No Truce Ahead in War Over VDT Safety." *Business Week,* July 25, 1983.

Pritchard, J. A. T. *Quantitative Methods in On-Line Systems*. Rochelle Park, NJ: Hayden Book Co., 1976.

Puzman, Josef, and Porizek, Radoslav. *Communication Control in Computer Networks*. New York: Wiley, 1980.

Raloff, J., "VDTs: User Stress and Eyestrain Largely Due to Job Design." *Science News*, July 16, 1983.

Tanenbaum, Andrew S., *Computer Networks*. Englewood Cliffs, NJ: Prentice-Hall, 1981.

5

Data Communications Hardware

Multiplexers

Concentrators

Front End Processors

Protocol Converters

Diagnostic and Miscellaneous Equipment

Summary of the Physical Layer

Case Study

INTRODUCTION

This chapter concludes the presentation of the physical layer of the OSI recommendation. It discusses the hardware components employed either directly or indirectly in data communications networks, continuing in the direction begun in Chapter 4—from the terminal equipment toward the host processors. The discussion of the various pieces of equipment that are configured in communications networks will also present the advantages and disadvantages afforded by each. In addition, the chapter provides a brief overview of how some network problems are resolved.

MULTIPLEXERS

Multiplexing technology allows multiple signals to be transmitted over a single link. For many years, multiplexing has been used by telephone companies to combine multiple voice-grade circuits into a single high-speed circuit for long-distance communication. In data communications networks, *multiplexers* (muxes) allow multiple terminals or communications links to share a common circuit.

How Multiplexers Function

Remote locations often have multiple devices that must communicate with a host. An obvious but expensive way to do this involves one circuit per device. Another alternative, which was discussed in Chapter 4, utilizes one single line and several smart devices that can be polled. Multiplexing provides yet another way for multiple devices to share a communications link.

Figure 5-1 presents a general mux configuration. A number of communication lines enter the mux from the host side. The mux combines the data from all incoming lines and transmits them via one circuit to a mux at the receiving end. This receiving mux then separates the data and distributes them among its outgoing terminal lines. The number of lines going into the mux on the host side is the same as the number going to terminals (or other muxes) on the remote side.

For the user, the multiplexer appears to function as though there were a number of physical links as opposed to just one. The configuration of one high-speed link and a pair of multiplexers, however, costs less than

Figure 5-1
General Multiplexer
Configuration

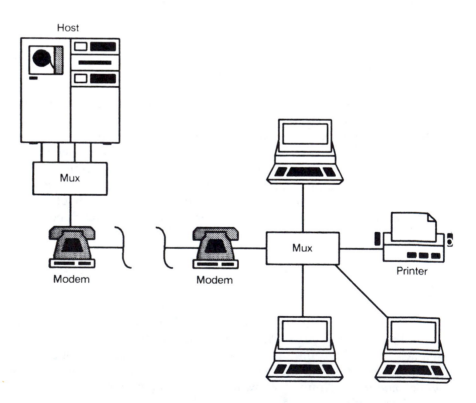

Four host lines combined with one long distance line

does a number of lower-speed links with a pair of modems for each. Furthermore, applications written for a point-to-point terminal connection can be used without modification. The multiplexer makes the line-sharing transparent to the user. In essence, the application sees a point-to-point link.

Types of Multiplexers

There are two fundamental ways in which a communications link is divided among a number of users. The first technique, known as frequency division multiplexing, separates the link by frequencies. The second technique, which has several variations, is known as time division multiplexing; it separates the link into time slots.

Frequency Division Multiplexing (FDM).   *Frequency division multiplexing (FDM)* can be likened to fluid-carrying pipes. Imagine a brewery that uses the novel approach of piping beer directly to the points of consumption, thereby avoiding the cost of bottling. The introduction of a low-calorie brew raises the problem of how to distribute the new product. For instance, one customer, who has been receiving 100 gallons of beer per day, now wants 50 gallons of each product. Constructing a new pipe would be wasteful, since the old one has sufficient carrying capacity. The (logically) easiest solution is to place a divider into the pipe to form two distinct fluid-carrying chambers. Now both brews can be transported without any mixing. By inserting a separator, unfortunately, some carrying capacity has been lost—instead of a capacity of 100 gallons, capacity is now only 90 gallons. This situation is essentially the same as frequency division multiplexing.

In FDM the available bandwidth of the circuit is broken down into subchannels each of which has smaller bandwidths. For instance, in a telephone circuit with a bandwidth of 3100 Hz, a frequency range of 300 to 3400 Hz, and a line carrying capacity of 1200 bps, suppose that instead of one terminal running at 1200 bps it was desired to have three terminals, each at 300 bps. Although arithmetically it appears possible to have four 300-bps terminals on the line, this is impossible, because just as with the separator in the beer conduit, frequency separation of the subchannels must be maintained in order to avoid crosstalk. The recommended separation for a 300-bps circuit is 480 Hz [Held, 1979]. The subchannel separators are referred to as *guardbands*. This situation requires two guardbands of 480 Hz each. Each of the three 300-bps subchannels will therefore have a bandwidth of 713 Hz, derived as follows: 3100 Hz (total bandwidth of circuit) − 960 Hz (two guardbands at 480 Hz each) = 2140 Hz ÷ 3 channels = 713 Hz per channel. Similarly, a 9600-bps channel can be divided into four 1200-bps channels. Frequency separation must be maintained, and the higher the speed of individual channels, the larger the guardbands must become. Figure 5-2 on page 152 illustrates an FDM channel.

Figure 5-2
A Frequency Division
Multiplexer Channel

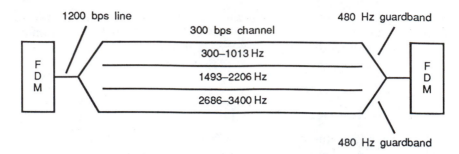

Figure 5-3
A Frequency Division
Multiplexer
Configuration

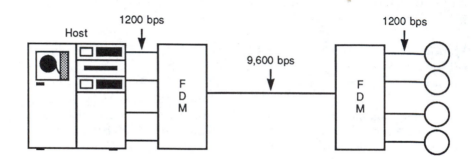

An FDM configuration is given in Figure 5-3. There is no need for modems in this configuration because the FDM functions as a modem by accepting the signal from the Data Terminal Equipment (DTE) and transforming it into a signal within a given frequency range.

Each line in FDM will be mapped onto one of the subchannels. For example, the first line will have its signal passed along the first subchannel, the second line along the second subchannel, and so on, meaning that if terminals on that line are not busy, then that portion of the carrying capacity goes unused.

Time Division Multiplexing (TDM). *Time division multiplexing (TDM)* is roughly equivalent to time sharing systems. As with FDM, TDM has a group of lines entering the mux, one circuit shared by all, and the same number of lines leaving the mux at the other end. Instead of splitting the frequency, however, TDM shares time—that is, each line is given a time slot for transmitting, accomplished by either interleaving bits or characters. Bit interleaving is more common for synchronous (block at a time) transmissions and character interleaving is more common with asynchronous (character at a time) transmissions.

To understand how TDM operates, look at the 4-port TDM in Figure 5-4. This mux combines signals from the four lines onto a single communications circuit. Data entering the TDM from the devices on the input line are placed in a buffer or register. With *character interleaving,* first a

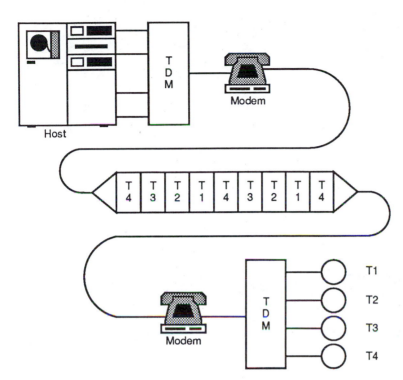

Figure 5-4
A Time Division
Multiplexer

character from line 1 is transmitted, then a character from line 2, then one from line 3, one from line 4, and back again to line 1, to repeat the process. *Bit interleaving* works in essentially the same manner except that a bit instead of a character is taken from each line in turn to form a transmission block. The mux at the other end breaks the data back out and places them on the appropriate line.

As with FDM, each line gets a portion of the available transfer time. However, TDM requires no guardbands, so there is no loss of carrying capacity. And also like FDM, lines are given a portion of the circuit's carrying capacity even though there are no data to be transmitted. Still, the improvement is significant: Instead of only three 300-bps sublines on a 1200-bps line, there can be four lines, each capable of 300-bps transmission. Likewise, a 9600-bps line can be multiplexed into eight 1200-bps lines or four 2400-bps lines.

Statistical Time Division Multiplexing (STDM).   *Statistical time division multiplexing (STDM)* improves on the efficiency of TDM by transmitting data for only those lines with data to send; idle lines take up none of the carrying capacity of the communications circuit. Figure 5-5 on page 154 illustrates this situation. Because neither time slot nor frequency is allocated to a specific terminal, stat muxes must also transmit a terminal iden-

Figure 5-5
Time Division
Multiplexing

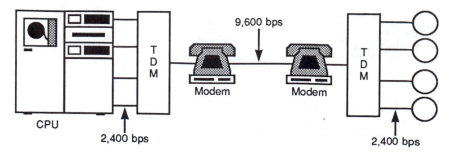

One 9,600 bps line supporting four 2,400 bps devices

Figure 5-6
Statistical Time
Division Multiplexing

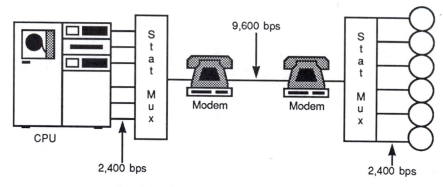

One 9,600 bps line supporting six 2,400 bps devices

tification along with the data block. When all lines have data to transmit, an STDM looks just like a TDM; when only one line has data to send, the entire line capacity is devoted to it.

Under good conditions, an STDM on a 9600-bps line can support five or six 2400-bps lines, as illustrated in Figure 5-6, or three to four 4800-bps lines. The reason for this apparent increase in carrying capacity stems from the unlikelihood that all incoming lines will be 100% busy. If each line is only 50% utilized, then four 4800-bps lines could be placed on one 9600-bps link. STDMs also have internal buffers for holding data from a line in case all lines attempt to transmit at the same time.

Newer stat muxes provide additional capabilities such as data compression, line priorities, mixed-speed lines, integrated modems, network control ports for monitoring the multiplexed line, host port sharing where two or more lines at the terminal end are mapped onto one line at the host end, port switching wherein a terminal can be switched from one port to another, accumulation and reporting of performance statistics, automatic speed detection, memory expansion, and internal diagnostics. All of these features are unlikely to be found in one mux. Different makes offer one or more of these capabilities as standard or optional functions. A few of these features can also be found in TDMs. Because of the higher performance of stat muxes, most of the development and enhancements in the last several years have been devoted to stat muxes.

Multiplexer Configurations

In addition to attaching terminals to muxes, other muxes can be added in daisy chain fashion, a configuration illustrated in Figure 5-7. *Daisy chaining*, also referred to as *cascading*, allows some circuits to be extended to another remote point, useful in a situation with two areas for data entry. With eight terminals in each area, for instance, a 16-port stat mux could provide linkage between the host and area A, and eight lines from area A could travel via an 8-port mux to area B.

The number of ports on a mux can vary, though commonly there are 4, 8, 16, 32, 48, or 64 ports. Multiplexer prices vary according to the number of ports and features provided. For a relatively plain 4-port or 8-port stat mux, prices in 1985 started at about $1500.

Inverse Multiplexer.   There is one additional less common type of mux known as an *inverse multiplexer*; its objective is to provide a high-speed data path between two devices, usually computers. An inverse mux accepts one line from a host and separates it into multiple lower-speed communications circuits. The multiple low-speed circuits are recombined at the other end into a high-speed link, as illustrated in Figure 5-8 on page 156. A 56-Kbps link from a computer to an inverse mux, for example, can

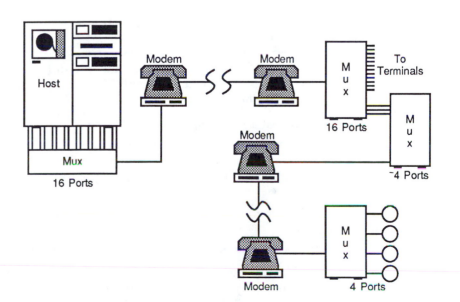

Figure 5-7
Cascading
Multiplexers

Figure 5-8
An Inverse
Multiplexer

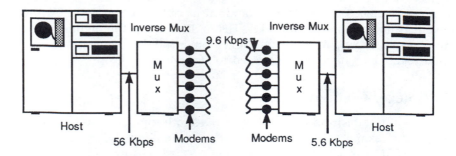

be split into six 9600-bps lines and then back to a 56-Kbps line at the remote end.

Multiport Modem.   A *multiport modem* is another multiplexing device. Essentially it combines modem and T-DM functions into one piece of equipment. Multiple terminal lines of varying transmission speeds enter the multiport modem, and it then multiplexes the data onto one line with a speed at least as fast as the aggregate data rate of all incoming terminal lines.

CONCENTRATORS

A *concentrator* also is a line sharing device. Its primary function is the same as that of a mux, to allow multiple devices to share communications circuits. Because a concentrator is a computer, however, it can participate more actively than a mux in any application. In the early 1970s there was a marked distinction between a concentrator and a multiplexer. As multiplexers took on the additional functions just described, the difference between the two types of devices narrowed. Currently the principal differences between a mux and a concentrator are:

> *Concentrators* are used one at a time; *multiplexers* are used in pairs.

> A *concentrator* may have multiple incoming and outgoing lines, with a different number of incoming lines than outgoing lines; a *multiplexer* takes a certain number of lines onto one line and converts back to the same number of lines.

> A *concentrator* is a computer and may have auxiliary storage for use in support of an application.

> A *concentrator* may perform some data processing functions such as polling devices and data validation.

One possible concentrator configuration is provided in Figure 5-9.

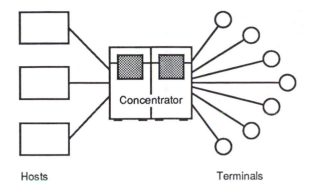

Figure 5-9
A Concentrator
Configuration

Hosts   Terminals

Concentrators with Auxiliary Storage

If the concentrator has disk drives attached, it can assist the host(s) by storing terminal screen templates and by sequencing their display; it can also enable terminals to continue some of their functions if the link between host and concentrator is malfunctioning. With disk storage, the concentrator can also provide store and forward functions: If the communications paths become too busy, data can be stored on the concentrator's disks for later transmission. Message logging functions are also made possible with auxiliary storage devices.

Concentrators can further assist an application by providing data editing, polling, error handling, code conversion, compression, and encryption. Concentrators can also switch messages between terminals and hosts. For example, in a banking ATM environment where three regional processing centers are responsible for authorizing transactions, each city with multiple ATMs could use a concentrator to handle ATM traffic. The concentrator would have three lines, one to a host in each of the three regional processing centers. There would also be one line for each ATM or cluster of ATMs. Based on customer ATM card number, the concentrator would switch each transaction to the processing center closest to the customer's home branch.

FRONT END PROCESSORS

Front end processors (FEP) are employed at the host end of the communications circuit, much like a concentrator is used at the remote end. In many respects, front end processors and concentrators serve the same function. The FEP is intended to take over much of the line management work from the host. An FEP configuration is shown in Figure 5-10 on page 158. *Communications controller* and *message switch* are two other terms that refer to an FEP, the distinction being the piece of equipment emphasized.

Figure 5-10
A Front End
Processor
Configuration

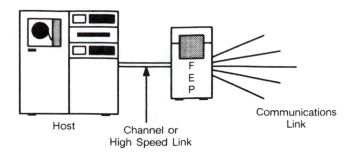

Host

Channel or
High Speed Link

Communications
Link

Special-Purpose and General-Purpose FEPs

An FEP interface with a host system uses one or more high-speed links. The FEP is responsible for controlling the more numerous low-speed circuits. All functions of a concentrator can also be served by an FEP. FEPs may be either special-purpose or general-purpose equipment. Special-purpose FEPs, such as the IBM 3705 communications controller, Amdahl's 4705 communications processor, and Tandem Computer's 6100 communications processor, are designed specifically for data communications. Their operating system and software are totally communications-oriented. General-purpose FEPs, such as minicomputers by Digital Equipment Corporation, Data General, and General Automation, represent the use of general-purpose computers primarily to perform data communications functions.

Communications Controllers

The IBM 370x *communications controllers* or equivalent are extensively used in IBM installations for controlling the communications lines. The 370X family consists of the *IBM 3704, 3705,* and *3725* communications controllers. The 3705 is the model used in this text to describe the functions of controllers. The 3705 can be used locally or remotely. In the remote configuration it actually functions as a concentrator. A local 3705 attaches to a channel on the host system. Remote 3705s attach to a line on a local 3705. These configurations are depicted in Figure 5-11.

The IBM 3704 can control up to 32 half duplex lines; the IBM 3705 controls a maximum of 352 half duplex lines. Full duplex lines can also be attached, but this reduces the total number of available lines. One full duplex line is equivalent to two half duplex lines on the controller. Memory in the controller varies from 32K bytes to 1M bytes. Multiple hardware models are available, varying in the amount of memory, number of lines supported, and networking software available.

Network Control Programs (NCP).   A *network control program (NCP)* is the controller's software. There are several versions available, each with its

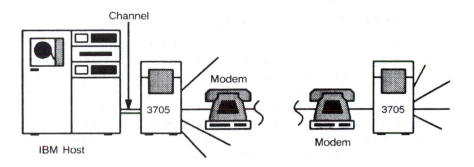

Figure 5-11
Local and Remote
3705 Configurations

own capabilities. The most advanced NCP has advanced communication function (ACF), which supports IBM's Systems Network Architecture (SNA) (see Chapter 8). The NCP acts as interface between the host line-access methods and the lines to attached devices. An *access method* (see Chapter 9) provides input and output services as interface between an application and its associated devices. Access methods make it easier for application programmers to take advantage of the capabilities of different types of devices, capabilities such as polling, dialing, message buffering, code conversion, speed selection, error handling, and collection and reporting of statistics.

Message Switching Processors. A message switching processor functions to route messages to their proper destination, as described earlier in the banking application of concentrators. Message switching equipment can also front end one or more hosts in performing this function.

PROTOCOL CONVERTERS

To communicate with the many different types of data communications terminal devices requires conventions, or protocols. Protocols determine the sequences in which data exchanges may take place and the bit or character sequences required to provide device and line control (see Chapter 6). Not only are there many different devices, but there are a large number of protocols, as well. Each maker of terminals typically has its proprietary protocols, meaning, for instance, that a Burroughs terminal will probably not be able to communicate with an IBM system such as a 3270 terminal. IBM alone has over 25 different kinds of access methods. To bridge these differences, companies have developed *protocol converters*. Basically, a protocol converter allows a terminal to look like something it is not—that is, like a different type of terminal. A protocol converter also enables different computer systems to transmit to and receive from a given terminal model. Protocol conversion is accomplished by hardware, software, or both. This section considers only the hardware approach.

Functions of Protocol Converters

Protocol converters perform a number of functions, the primary one being to convert from one protocol to another. The significance of this function becomes more apparent after studying Chapter 6 on data link protocols. To make such a protocol change involves changing the characters that delimit the data, detecting errors, and providing control of the communications link. And to do this may require reformatting the message data, changing a terminal's address to be compatible with the receiving device, segmenting a message into particular-size blocks or restoring such blocks to a complete message, translating one communications code—such as ASCII—into another—such as EBCDIC, or accommodating device characteristics.

A protocol converter is ordinarily treated as a "black box" on the communications line—that is, as a piece of attached hardware that performs its function in a manner that is immaterial. Protocol conversion may be configured as illustrated in Figure 5-12. One purpose of protocol converters is to protect the user's investment in hardware. Suppose, for example, that a user decides to change computer makes. The old processor from Company X may be kept or it may be exchanged for one from Company Y. If a large number of Company X terminals are involved, and if the user is fortunate, Company Y processors will be able to interface directly with the Company X terminals. If Company Y has no support for the Company X terminals, there are three alternatives; sell the Company X terminals, probably at a great loss, write software that provides the capability, or attempt to find a protocol converter that can convert a Company Y protocol into that required by the Company X terminals.

There are many different types of protocol converters. Some, though not all, of the more common types are:

Asynchronous to synchronous

IBM 3720 to Burroughs poll/select

Burroughs poll/select to asynchronous ASCII

Figure 5-12
Protocol Conversion

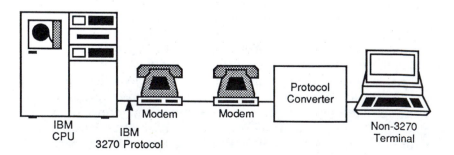

IBM 3270 to NCR poll select

IBM 3270 to IBM 2260 poll select

Teletypewriter to IBM 3270

Asynchronous to IBM SDLC

IBM 2780/3780 to IBM 3270

ASCII printers to IBM 3270

IBM 3270 to IBM SDLC

IBM 2780/3780 to IBM SDLC

PARS (airline reservations system protocol) to binary synchronous

Microcomputers to almost any of the above

An example of protocol converters connecting several different devices is depicted in Figure 5-13. Protocol converters also can function to accommodate differences in the keyboards of different style terminals. Suppose, for instance, that a simple TTY terminal without function keys is to be used in an application that requires function keys. The protocol converter will take a combination of key strokes and map them onto a particular function key, thus allowing a less expensive terminal to be used in an application that usually requires a more sophisticated terminal. Converters also exist to change from one code to another, for example, ASCII to EBCDIC, and to change from one interface to another. A ICOT 352 Asynchronous/3270 protocol converter is pictured in Figure 5-14 on page 162.

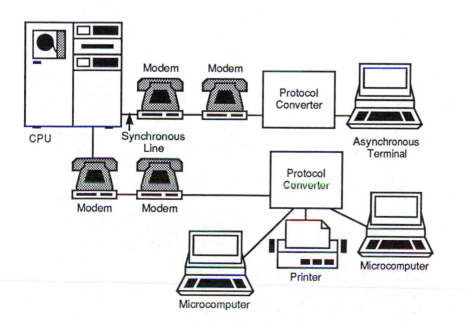

Figure 5-13
Protocol Converters Connecting Different Devices

Figure 5-14
An ICOT 352
Asynchronous/3270
Protocol Converter

Courtesy of ICOT Corporation

DIAGNOSTIC AND MISCELLANEOUS EQUIPMENT

The hardware discussed thus far has been involved in the transportation or receipt of data. Another set of hardware frequently is necessary to perform the following functions:

Provide security of transmission and facilities

Monitor the data

Control the sequences being transmitted

Provide connection for switched communications lines

Provide other functions necessary to control and manage the communications network

A number of these devices are described below.

Security

Security of data transmission and storage is becoming increasingly important. Several pieces of hardware are available to assist in the protection of data.

Call-back Units.   One simple but effective device is a *call-back unit*, which participates in making switched connections. A person attempting to access a system using a switched connection is required to identify himself or herself with an ID and password. The opening connection is severed after the ID and password are entered, and the call-back unit looks in its tables for that user's number, calls the number, and the connection is made.

At least two problems exist with a call-back system. First, the host computer becomes responsible for the costs of the connection. Second, the call-back system prohibits portable terminal connections, making it of little use to the traveling salesperson with a portable terminal. There are, however, some call-back units that allow users with certain passwords to bypass the call back, which can be set for calls at a specific time of day. Of course, this feature has the disadvantage of lowering security.

Encryption Equipment.   Encryption equipment allows transmitted data to be scrambled at the sending location and reconstructed at the receiving end. The U.S. National Bureau of Standards (NBS) has approved a standard called the *data encryption standard (DES)*, which uses a 64-bit pattern as the encryption key. Eight of the 64 bits are for error detection, leaving 56 bits for the actual key, thus providing over 72 quadrillion possible keys (2 to the 56th power). The DES algorithm is available on a microchip, and encryption boxes are now commercially available. Figure 5-15 shows an encryption device installed on a communications link. Encryption is discussed in more detail in Chapter 10.

Line Monitors

Line monitors, also known as protocol analyzers, are used to diagnose problems on a communications link. Like all the equipment studied thus far, line monitors come in a wide variety of models and capabilities. Their basic function, however, is to attach to a communications circuit so the bit patterns being transmitted over the link can be displayed for analysis by a data communications expert, to determine what the problems are. Figure 5-16 on page 164 shows a line monitor. Features commonly available on line monitors are:

Video display

Memory

Recording tape or disk

Programmability

Trap setting for selected bit patterns

Protocol support

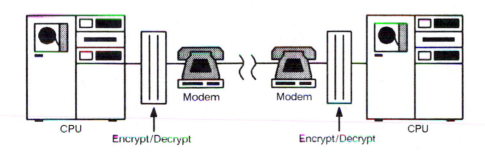

Figure 5-15
Data Encryption Box

Figure 5-16
A Digital Line
Monitor

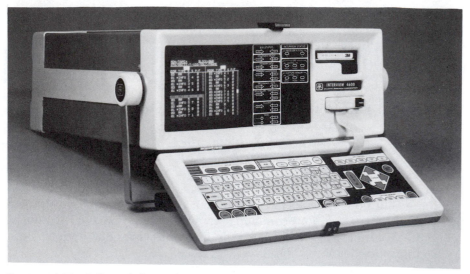

Courtesy of Atlantic Research Corporation

Variable character length support

Multiple interfaces

Multiple speeds

Function keys

Graphics display

If a corporation requires multiple line monitors to cover multiple locations, it is best to use models from one manufacturer. Each manufacturer usually has a number of models, with varying capabilities; this allows the user to buy the minimum required capability. There are two reasons for having a standard for manufacturers. First, education of personnel is easier with only one manufacturer. Even though there may be different models, the operations typically are quite similar, especially for simple functions. Second, and more important, recordings made at one site may be shipped to another and analyzed, and since there is no industry standard recording mode, tape or disk recorded on manufacturer A's machine is probably not readable on manufacturer B's equipment.

Breakout Boxes

A *breakout box* is a passive multipurpose device that is patched into a circuit at an interface. Figure 5-17 shows a programmable breakout box. Once installed it is possible to:

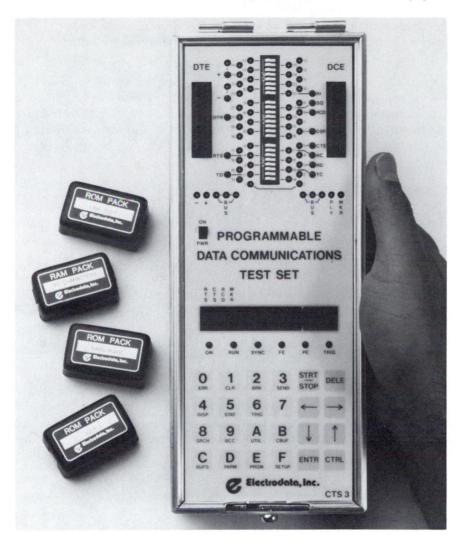

Figure 5-17   A Programmable Breakout Box
Courtesy of Electrodata, Inc.

Monitor activity on the exchange circuits. Each exchange circuit will have a light emitting diode (LED) on the breakout box; if there is a signal on the circuit then the LED will light up.

Exchange circuit leads. One of the causes for failure to communicate properly is crossed leads in the cable. A breakout box allows circuits to be changed without rebuilding the connecter on the cable.

Isolate a given circuit. If a given interchange circuit is used by one device and not the other, then that circuit can be isolated; that is, the signal can be prevented from being passed on to the device that does not accept that lead.

Measure voltage levels on an interchange circuit. This allows the user to detect if the voltages used to carry the signal are within acceptable tolerance limits.

Optionally, breakout boxes can have bit pattern generators and receivers, which allow for both transmission and receiving of a small number of selected bit patterns. This is a beneficial feature because the individual doing the testing is able to determine the effect of a known data pattern on the circuit.

Auto-Call Units (ACU)

An *auto-call unit (ACU)* is used to place a telephone call automatically, without manual intervention. The ACU has the ability of taking the line off hook (the equivalent of lifting the handset from its cradle), detecting the dial tone, dialing the number either through pulse dialing or Touch-tone™ dialing, detecting the ring indicator or busy signal, and detecting call complete or incomplete. *Incomplete* calls can be the result of a busy signal, failure to answer, circuit busy, number out of order, or other similar event. In the United States, ACUs originally could be sold only by the telephone companies. With the Carterphone decision, this policy was changed. The ACU and auto-answer functions are now common in modem equipment. The interface to ACU equipment in the United States is via either the RS-232-C interface or the RS-366 interface. The latter specifically addresses the electrical and functional interface for automatic calling equipment.

Port Concentrator

Multiplexers allow multiple terminals to share one communications link; however, for each terminal attached to a multiplexer there must be one communications port at the host end to receive the signal, which is what makes the multiplexer connection appear to be a point-to-point connection for both terminal and host. All systems have an upper limit to the number of communication ports that may be configured, and, of course, there is a cost to providing ports. A *port concentrator* allows multiple input streams from a multiplexer to be passed to the host through a single communications port. This is beneficial not only in reducing the hardware cost of the host, but also in allowing for expansion beyond the port limitations of a particular processor.

Port concentration requires that a software module be available in the host to receive the multiple terminal messages and route them to the appropriate applications. The functions performed by this software are similar to what must be provided for a concentrator. A port concentrator is illustrated in Figure 5-18.

Port Selectors

The function of a *port selector* is similar to that of a port concentrator. It helps determine which users are granted access in applications where the number of potential terminal users far exceeds the number of available lines, such as reservations systems and library systems. For instance, if a particular system allows a total of 1000 terminals—on either dedicated or switched links—to communicate with a host at one time, and there are 8000 potential users, then obviously not all of these users can have access to the system at once. A port selector, then, can assist in determining which users are granted access. For switched lines the port selector can act as a rotary, allowing users to dial one number and connecting the incoming calls to any available switched port. It can also enable switched users to connect to an unused dedicated port. Port selectors can also sometimes switch to ports on several hosts.

Some port selectors give the user considerable control over how many ports will be used for switched calls, how many can be shared between

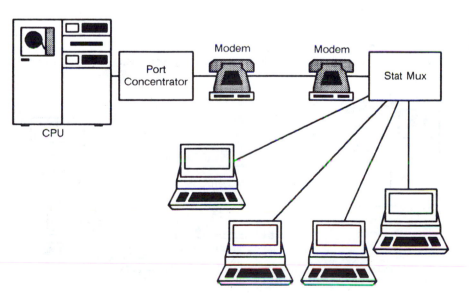

Figure 5-18
A Port Concentrator

dedicated and switched users, and how many can be routed to another host. Thus, the selectable ports and the class of users that may select them can be configured to meet specific needs. A schematic showing how a port selector is used is provided in Figure 5-19.

Cluster Controllers

A *cluster controller*, depicted in Figure 5-20, is designed to support several terminals, and functions to manage the terminals, to buffer data being transmitted to or from the terminals, to perform error detection and correction, and to poll.

The controller may be attached to the host either locally or remotely. While every terminal attached to a cluster controller almost always uses the same communications protocol, the devices themselves may differ. The remote cluster controller in Figure 5-20 has VDUs and printers attached.

SUMMARY OF THE PHYSICAL LAYER

This completes the survey of the physical layer of communications. What follows is a brief review of the different physical components and their

Figure 5-19
A Port Selector
Schematic

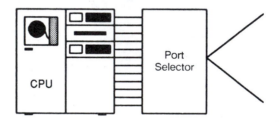

Many terminals: Port selector matches terminal requesting connection with available port (if any).

Figure 5-20
A Cluster Controller

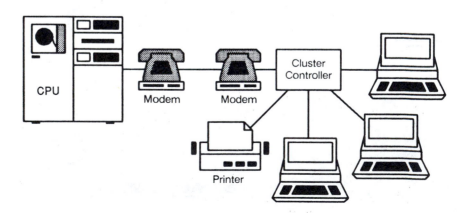

advantages and disadvantages, after which the chapter concludes with a look at a case study that attempts to tie these diverse elements together.

There are a variety of transmission media from which to select. For local area communications the best alternatives are private wires, coaxial cable, fiber optics, infrared radio, and microwave radio. Long distances almost always require that the medium be procured from a common carrier.

The choices for long-distance routes include leased or switched wires, microwave, satellite, and packet distribution networks. The last option is not discussed until Chapter 7. Wire connections obtained from a common carrier may include microwave, satellite, or fiber optics technology. This type of link is treated as a wire because logically it is still a wire link and has the same transmission characteristics—speed and cost—as wire. The most common medium for long-distance transmission is a wirelike medium obtained from a common carrier. Microwave and satellite are usually selected when the volume of data to be transmitted per unit of time is large. Satellite has the added benefit of being able to reach a large number of locations with a small cost for expansion. Propagation delay time is a potential disadvantage of satellite transmission.

There are other physical components to be selected in addition to the transmission media. These include the host computers, terminals, and support equipment such as modems, multiplexers, concentrators, front end processors, security devices, and protocol converters. Speed, cost, functionality, and in some cases security are the determining forces in selecting these options.

When a connection is point-to-point, the configuration is relatively simple. What is needed is a medium with sufficient speed to support the application, plus modems, and line drivers, where necessary. This type of configuration is typical in host-to-host communications, local terminal connections and in remote locations with only one terminal device.

A common case is where a host must interface with multiple terminal devices; in this situation there is a greater number of alternatives. A wide variety of terminal equipment is available with each of the following alternatives.

Multi-point (poll/select)

Multiple point-to-point links

Multiplexers

Concentrators

Concentrators with multiplexers

Front end processors

Front end processors with concentrators and/or multiplexers

Protocol converters

Dedicated links

Switched links

Packet switching networks

The number of potential combinations is enormous. In fact, configuring transmission links to multiple locations quickly becomes a matter of evaluating the many combinations. The difference between the low-cost link and the high-cost link can be significant. Fortunately, there are modeling systems that can sort through the possibilities and perform the time-consuming rate and distance calculations. These models may either be purchased or leased, and some are available on microcomputers. Anyone involved in planning an extensive system or planning multiple systems will surely find any investment in such a model beneficial, even if the model does no more than confirm initial speculations.

CASE STUDY

Seymour Opportunity, vice president of marketing for the Syncrasy Corporation, has convinced the other corporate executives that the future lies not only in mail-order operations, but also in discount computer stores. Wanting to expand into several areas at once, Syncrasy is opening discount computer stores in Chicago, New York City, Atlanta, Houston, Los Angeles, San Francisco, and Kansas City. The home office and computer center are also being moved from Puma Flats to Kansas City. Penny Pincher, the comptroller, has exerted her influence by getting concessions to hold the cost of expansion to a minimum.

The computer stores in Chicago, New York, and Los Angeles will each have five terminals; the other stores will each have three. Mail-order operations will continue, although on a diminished scale. The catalog stores in Kansas City, New York City, and Los Angeles will be located 15, 20, and 40 miles from the discount stores, respectively.

Computer Store Transaction Types

There will be two basic transactions at each of the computer stores: inventory and receipt transactions, and parts and customer inquiries.

Inventory and Receipts.   The first type of transaction deals with inventory control and receipts. Every time a sale is made, the part number, quantity sold, unit price, discount rate, and total amount of the sale are transmitted to the central computer. The line item for each part sold consists of 22 characters, and the total amount of the sale is a 10-character field. The usual response to the transaction is 10 characters. Orders that total more than $1000, however, are an exception. These exceptional transactions, which involve a credit check and which comprise an estimated

30% of all inventory transactions, have 10 additional characters in the response portion of the message. Average processing time for normal orders is 0.5 seconds; for orders over $1000 it is 0.8 seconds. There is an average of 6 items per order, and an average of 20 orders per terminal per hour, with peaks of 40. Peak transaction periods are from noon to 1 P.M. and from 5 to 6 P.M. It is required that 95% of all transactions of this type have a response time of 3 seconds.

Parts and Customer Inquiries.   The second type of store transaction is a parts or customer inquiry. Average input is 10 characters and average response is 500 characters. Average and peak rates for this transaction are both 10 per hour per terminal. A response time of 4 seconds is required. Processing time for these transactions is 1.5 seconds per order.

Catalog Store Activity

Activity in the catalog store operations will decline as a result of having discount stores in the area. Catalog stores will each have eight terminals. Their transactions are the same as those described in Chapter 4. There will be 500 characters of input data and 100 characters for response. Each terminal will average 20 orders per hour, with a peak of 30 orders per hour. Five-second response time is required for these transactions. Processing time is 2.5 seconds per order.

Prices, Equipment, and Mileage

The equipment and mileage prices used in this case study are close to those in effect in early 1985. Only leased transmission lines from a common carrier are considered. Satellite transmission was considered by Syncrasy at the outset, but it was dismissed because of the relatively light amount of traffic from the stores and the effect of propagation delay on response times. The following rates are used in this case study (and in the exercises at the conclusion of this chapter).

Modems.

Speed (bps)	Purchase Price	Monthly Lease Price
1200	$ 500	$ 35
2400	1000	80
4800	2000	150
7200	2750	190
9600	3500	225

Interstate Communication Lines.   The line can handle speeds up to 9600 bps. Line speed is governed by the modem.

First 100 miles $2.25 per mile (including monthly fee)
Next 900 miles (101–1000) $0.94 per mile
Each mile over 1000 $0.58 per mile

Local Communication Lines.   The line can handle speeds up to 9600 bps. Line speed is governed by the modem.

Each mile $4.70

Statistical Multiplexer.

Number of Channels	Purchase Price	Monthly Lease Price
4	$1700	$150
8	2600	225
16	4300	358
32	6500	540

Concentrators.   The price of concentrators can vary enormously. This case uses two configurations. The first configuration will handle up to 32 output lines, which could be point-to-point terminals, multi-point communication lines, or lines to another concentrator or multiplexer. It sells for $30,000, with a monthly lease price of $1,500. The second configuration must be large enough for whatever is required. It sells for $40,000 and leases for $2000 per month. Each of these concentrators will be able to accommodate up to eight incoming lines from the host processor.

Front End Processors.   The price for an FEP is the same as that for a concentrator.

Terminals.   Dumb terminals sell for $750, with a monthly lease price of $50.
    Smart terminals sell for $2,000, with a monthly lease price of $150.
    Intelligent terminals sell for $5,000, with a monthly lease price of $350.

Mileage.   Airline miles are used for determining communication rates between cities. Figure 5-21 lists the mileage between cities.

Figure 5-21
Mileage Chart

	Chicago	Houston	Kansas City	L.A.	N.Y.C.	S.F.
Atlanta	708	791	822	2191	854	2483
Chicago		1091	542	2048	809	2173
Houston			743	1555	1610	1911
Kansas City				1547	1233	1861
Los Angeles					2794	387
New York City						2930

Preliminary Considerations.   A relatively simple case study has been constructed, with relatively few locations and a centrally located computer center. Even so, the variation between media costs of the best and worst cases alone can be significant.

Because of the capabilities they provide, smart terminals have been selected for use. The line time delay for dumb terminals in conversational mode would be excessive, and the current transactions do not warrant the excessive expense for intelligent terminals.

Mileage Costs

In actual practice, several common carriers would be consulted and their bids solicited for the best configuration. If there were many more locations, one of the network modeling systems would also be utilized to analyze all possible routes and provide a listing of the best alternatives. This exercise uses the brute force method.

Long-Distance Line Costs.   Although it is unusual to do so, point-to-point costs will be calculated first. This will enable the best and worst case line costs to be compared. The cost of the Kansas City–Los Angeles link will be computed in detail; mileage and line costs for the remaining cities will simply be listed.

Since mileage rates are different for miles 0–100, 101–1000, and 1001 and over, the 1547 miles between Kansas City and Los Angeles must be broken down into these increments, yielding $100 + 900 + 547$ miles. The cost for the Kansas City–Los Angeles link, then, is

$$(100 \times 2.52) + (900 \times 0.94) + (547 \times 0.58) = 252 + 846 + 317.26$$
$$= 1415.26$$

Monthly point-to-point link charges between the home city and all remote locations are:

Kansas City to:	
Atlanta	$ 930.68
Chicago	667.48
Houston	856.42
Los Angeles	1,415.26
New York City	1,233.14
San Francisco	1,597.38
Total	$6,700.36

Minimum Distance Configuration Costs.   To find the lowest rate based on a minimum-distance configuration, there are many combinations available. The easiest way is to start with the shortest link—Kansas City to

Chicago—and then work outward until all locations are accounted for. A simple program could also be written to evaluate all combinations and pick the shortest route. A network configuration of the shortest routes is given in Figure 5-22. The costs of this network are:

From	To	Distance	Cost
Kansas City	Houston	743 miles	$ 856.42
Kansas City	Chicago	542	667.48
Kansas City	Los Angeles	1547	1415.26
Chicago	New York City	809	918.46
Chicago	Atlanta	708	823.52
Los Angeles	San Francisco	387	521.78
		Total	$5202.92

Local Line Costs.   The costs of local links between the mail-order and discount stores in Kansas City, New York City, and Los Angeles must be calculated in addition to the costs of long-distance lines. These charges are relatively easy to compute since there is a flat rate per mile. The costs are:

Location	Distance	Cost
Kansas City	15 miles	$ 70.50
New York City	20	94.00
Los Angeles	40	188.00
Total		$352.50

The difference between the low-cost and high-cost configurations is $1497.44 per month ($6,700.36 − $5202.92). However, this does not mean that the configuration is finalized. Yet to be determined is whether the capacity of the lines can support the application. For instance, the link

Figure 5-22
A Network
Configuration

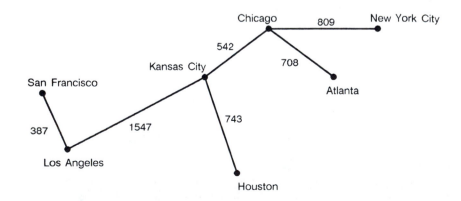

from Kansas City to Chicago must be capable of supporting all message traffic from Chicago, New York City, and Atlanta. If one 9600-bps line is not capable of this, then another alternative will be required, such as linking Houston and Atlanta.

Line Utilization Costs

There are five items to be considered in calculating the costs of line utilization: overhead, response time, aggregate data rate, line contention, and configuration.

Overhead.   Overhead includes costs for several components: control messages, polling, and terminal access. Overhead involves how efficiently the lines are utilized. As the next chapter discusses, some of the purposes of data link protocols are to delimit data, provide error detection and line control, and allow for addressing. Each of these functions requires that additional data be appended to the data message. In this case—and previous examples also—*control message overhead* is approximated by using ten bits per character rather than the actual 7 or 8 bits. While not entirely accurate, this is good enough, and it certainly simplifies calculation.

A second overhead factor is *polling costs*, if a multi-point configuration is being used. Determining polling overhead involves figuring the amount of time a terminal must wait to get polled. This averages out to be:

$$\text{wait time} = \frac{\text{polling interval} \times (\text{number of terminals} - 1)}{2}$$

On the average a terminal will wait for half of the other terminals. Sometimes a terminal will wait for all of the other terminals; at other times there will be no wait at all. Thus, on the average the wait is for half of the other terminals. *Total wait time* is the number of terminals that are waited for, times the polling interval—that is, the amount of time required to send the poll message and wait for reply. The amount of time required for a terminal to send data is *not* factored in because that is included in the contention calculations. Polling is ignored in this example.

The final component of overhead is the additional characters required for *terminal access*. Smart terminals using screen templates, protected fields, and video attributes require a number of characters in order to provide these capabilities. These include not only the characters needed for prompts, but also the control characters that position the cursor, allow for video attributes and protected fields, and so on. The number of additional characters needed to support these capabilities varies from terminal to terminal. Although these additional characters are ignored in this case, the number of characters required for terminal access can be significant. Polling wait time can also be significant, especially with a large number of terminals and half duplex lines with slow modem-turnaround times. These factors must not be ignored in real life.

Calculations

The first line speed calculation will be for response time. Following that, the aggregate data rate for a given link will be considered, making sure there is sufficient capacity to meet all terminals' demands. Contention issues will then be addressed, finishing off with an analysis of configuration.

Response Time: Inventory and Receipts. First, the inventory and receipts transaction are considered. The average number of line items per transaction is six. Each line item consists of the part number, quantity, discount rate, and line item price, with a total of 22 characters per line item. For six line items, $6 \times 22 = 132$ characters are required, plus a 10-character *total* field, giving a total input record length of 142 characters. The response consists of ten characters. The expected response time is 3 seconds. With 0.5 seconds required for processing, this leaves 2.5 seconds to transmit 152 characters, or 152/2.5 = 61 characters per second. At ten bits per character for overhead of the data link protocol (see Chapter 6), a 610-bps line will be required. Thus, a 1200-bps line will be sufficient for this transaction's response time hereafter referred to as *transaction type 1*.

Transactions of this type that are over $1000 in total sales require the same response time, with an additional ten characters in the response and 0.3 seconds of processing time. The system must be able to transmit 162 characters in 2.2 seconds, which is 74 characters per second, or a 740-bps capacity. A 1200-bps line will also satisfy the response time for this transaction, hereafter called *transaction type 2*.

Response Time: Parts and Customer Inquiries. The customer or inventory inquiry transaction requires 10 characters of input and generates a 500-character response, with 4-second response time and 1.5-second processing time needed. The line time allowed is 2.5 seconds. The system, then, must transmit 510 characters in 2.5 seconds, or 204 characters per second. This equates to 2040 bps, necessitating a 2400-bps line. This is hereafter referred to as *transaction type 3*.

Response Time: Warehouse Transactions. The warehouse transaction calculation was done in Chapter 2, where it was determined that 600 characters had to be transmitted in 2.5 seconds, for 240 characters per second or 2,400 bps. This is hereafter called *transaction type 4*.

Overall, then, considering individual terminal response time only, a 2400-bps line will be adequate.

Aggregate Data Transmission Rate. Determining the aggregate data rate for Syncrasy's lines can be started with the line from Kansas City to Chicago, which must support 5 terminals in Chicago, 8 warehouse terminals in New York City, 5 store terminals in New York City, and 3 store terminals in Atlanta. Computation of the aggregate data rate must also consider the peak transaction load. Figure 5-23 contains all of the pertinent information for this analysis.

Transaction Type (Location)	Number of Transactions per Hour	Number of Characters per Transaction	Number of Terminals	Total Number of Characters per Hour
1 (East coast)	28	152	8	34,048
1 (Chicago)	21	152	5	15,960
2 (East coast)	12	162	8	15,552
2 (Chicago)	9	162	5	7,290
3 (both)	10	510	13	66,300
4 (mail order)	30	600	8	144,000
			Total	283,150

Figure 5-23 Transaction Analysis

In Figure 5-23, the Chicago type 1 transactions have been separated from the East coast type 1 transactions. Since peak transaction rates occur during specific hours, and the East coast cities—New York City and Atlanta—are in a different time zone from Chicago, the worst condition of peak traffic on the East coast has been assumed, that is, 40 transactions per hour; average load has been assumed for Chicago. Also, of the 40 transactions, 30% are of transaction type 2. Thus, there are 28 type 1 transactions and 12 type 2 transactions per hour on the East Coast, and 21 type 1 transactions and 9 type 2 transactions in Chicago. The total 283,150 characters transmitted per hour is the product of the number of terminals, number of transactions per terminal, and number of characters per transaction; as indicated in the last column of Figure 5-23.

An aggregate data rate of 283,150 characters per hour equates to approximately 78 characters per second, which is derived by dividing the number of characters per hour by 3600 seconds per hour. The calculations indicate that a 1200-bps line is sufficient to support the aggregate data rate. Thus far, response time is the dominant factor with respect to line speed.

Line Contention. As discussed in Chapter 2, a 2400-bps line is adequate in a point-to-point environment, although not if two terminals attempt to start a transaction at the same time. If a random transaction arrival rate is assumed, the following formula (from queuing theory) may be used to determine the probability of several transactions arriving within the same time interval.

$$P_k(T) = \frac{(LT)^k}{k!} \times e^{-LT} \qquad \text{for } k = 0, 1, 2, 3, \ldots$$

where $P_k(T)$ is the probability that k transactions will arrive in time interval T

L	is the average number of transactions per unit of time
T	is the time interval being considered
e	is the natural base for logarithms
k	is the number of arrivals
$!$	is the factorial function

In this transaction environment there is a total of 840 transactions per hour, derived by summing the products of the number of transactions per hour and the number of terminals performing that transaction as shown in Figure 5-23 on page 177. This results in an average of 0.23 transactions per second (840 divided by 3600). Thus, L in the formula is 0.23. Assuming a time interval T of 5 seconds, which is the time for the longest transaction and which is actually more conservative than necessary, the probability of two transactions arriving within a given 5-second interval is

$$
\begin{aligned}
P_2(5) &= \frac{(0.23 \times 5)^2}{2!} \times e^{-(0.23 \times 5)} \\
&= \frac{(1.15)^2}{2} \times e^{-1.15} \\
&= 0.21
\end{aligned}
$$

The complete probability table is given in Figure 5-24, from which it can be determined that the probability of two or more transactions arriving in one 5-second interval is

$$0.21 + 0.08 + 0.02 + 0.005 = 0.325$$

Figure 5-24
Transaction Arrival
Probabilities

Number of Arrivals	Probability
2	0.21
3	0.08
4	0.02
5	0.005

Thus, two or more transactions will be active in a 5-second time span 33% of the time. Doubling the line speed will allow two transactions within 5 seconds to meet the expected response time. The probability then becomes only 0.10, or 10%, that transactions will contend with each other (the probability that three or more transactions will arrive within 5 seconds). As stated above, a 5-second time interval is actually quite conservative, since it is not entirely devoted to line time, the element of interest. During the 5-second interval, for a given transaction, the line will be idle approximately 50% of the time at a speed of 2400 bps. Increasing the line speed to 4800 bps should adequately eliminate slow response time due to contention.

Configuring the System: East Coast.   It would be most economical to use a short route-line configuration with cascading statistical multiplexers. If the configuration follows a path from Kansas City to Chicago, then Chicago to New York City and Atlanta, and finally New York City catalog store to New York City discount store, as shown in Figure 5-25, by the time the extremities have been reached, a stat mux is likely to have run out of capacity. Each time a line is dropped off, the speed generally steps down. In addition, cascading multiplexers down by five levels will likely result in performance problems. Another problem is the number of terminals in New York City which must be accounted for. Since smart terminals that require some degree of screen handling are being used, a concentrator in Chicago will provide a significant capability to the network, as follows:

Allows terminals to be polled from Chicago rather than Kansas City

Provides for later expansion

Allows for more local terminal and error handling

Can provide some local support in the event the path to Kansas City is malfunctioning

Makes for a more workable configuration than extensive cascading of muxes

Can support higher-speed circuits to the East coast

Configuring the System: West Coast.   A different configuration can be used for the West coast link to Los Angeles and San Francisco: a direct link to Los Angeles and two separate drops—five terminals to the discount stores in Los Angeles and three to San Francisco. This contrasts with the link from Chicago to New York City, with 18 terminals. Cascading muxes are feasible for the West Coast. For the Houston link, a simple 4-port statistical multiplexer on a 4800-bps line can be used. The final configuration is given in Figure 5-26 on page 180.

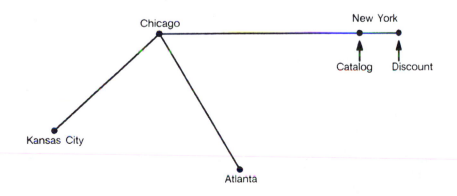

Figure 5-25
Syncrasy East Coast
Network

Figure 5-26
Syncrasy
Configuration

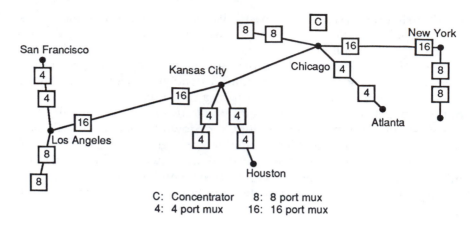

C: Concentrator   8: 8 port mux
4: 4 port mux   16: 16 port mux

Final Costs

The final monthly costs are summarized below, broken down into branches of the network.

Monthly Equipment Cost for Kansas City, Chicago, New York City, and Atlanta Branches of the Network

Multiplexers

2 16-port muxes at $358 each	$ 716
2 8-port muxes at $225 each	450
2 4-port muxes at $150 each	300

Modems

4 9600-bps modems at $225 each	900
4 4800-bps modems at $150 each	600

Terminals

11 smart terminals at $150 each	1650

(Note: two were available from the mail-order store)

Concentrator

1 at $1500	1500
Subtotal	$6116

Monthly Equipment Cost for the Kansas City to Kansas City Branch of the Network

Multiplexers

2 4-port muxes at $150 each	$ 300

Modems

2 4800-bps modems at $150 each	300

Terminals

1 smart terminal at $150   150
(Note: two terminals available from mail-order store)   _____
                                                    Subtotal $ 750

Monthly Equipment Cost for the Kansas City to Houston Branch of the Network

Multiplexers

2 4-port muxes at $150 each $ 300

Modems

2 4800-bps modems at $150 each   300

Terminals

3 smart terminals at $150 each   450
                                                    Subtotal $1050

Monthly Equipment Cost for the Kansas City to Los Angeles to San Francisco Branch of the Network

Multiplexers

2 16-port muxes at $358 each $ 716
2 8-port muxes at $225 each   450
2 4-port muxes at $150 each   300

Modems

2 9600-bps modems at $225 each   450
4 4800-bps modems at $150 each   600

Terminals

6 smart terminals at $150 each   900
(Note: two were available from the mail-order store)   _____
                                                    Subtotal $3416

Total Monthly Costs for the Network

Total equipment	**$11,332**
Total long-distance line costs	**5,203**
Total local line costs	**352**
Total network costs	**$16,887**

Syncrasy will have to sell a lot of equipment to support this $16,887-per-month configuration. Another alternative exists, however: attaching to a packet distribution network (PDN). PDNs are discussed in Chapter 7. Because the amount of data being transmitted is relatively small and because PDNs charge by the number of packets and not by connect time, the overall cost could be lower.

SUMMARY

There are many alternatives available in configuring a data communications system. The hardware components—multiplexers, concentrators, and front end processors—overlap in the functions they can provide. These components can reduce circuit costs significantly; they can also make more efficient use of the circuits and reduce some of the processing load of the hosts. Configuration modeling tools—which have been designed for telephone company or similar common carrier lines—are available to help system designers select the lowest cost or most efficient communications lines.

A wide variety of protocol conversion equipment is available to enable different manufacturers' terminals to interface with host equipment. Such equipment can protect a user's investment in terminals.

Because errors can be encountered in connecting data terminal equipment to data communications networks, diagnostic tools are necessary. With proper use, these tools can reduce the time and effort in tracking down such problems.

Key Terms

Auto-call unit (ACU)	Guardbands
Bit interleaving	IBM 3704, 3705, 3725
Breakout box	Inverse multiplexer
Byte interleaving	Line monitor
Call-back unit	Multiplexer (mux)
Cascading	Multiport modem
Character interleaving	Network control program (NCP)
Cluster controller	Port concentrator
Communications controller	Port selector
Concentrator	Protocol converter
Daisy chain	Statistical time division multiplexer (STDM)
Data encryption standard (DES)	
Frequency division multiplexer (FDM)	Time division multiplexer (TDM)
Front end processor (FEP)	

Questions and Exercises

1. How does a concentrator differ from a multiplexer? How are they similar?

2. Compare and contrast a front end processor and a concentrator.

3. Describe a situation in which a front end processor would be more desirable than a concentrator. Describe a situation in which a concentrator would be preferable to a front end processor.

4. Give a situation in which an inverse multiplexer would be used.

5. Give some examples in which multi-point configurations would be preferable to statistical multiplexing. Give an example where the opposite is true.

6. What is the lowest-cost communications configuration that will link each of the cities in the mileage chart below? Use the same line costs as presented on page 172.

	Cleveland	Houston	Las Vegas	Phoenix	Portland	San Diego	Washington, D.C.
Boston	657	1830	2752	2670	3144	2984	448
Cleveland		1306	2093	2032	2432	2385	360
Houston			1467	1164	2243	1490	1365
Las Vegas				285	996	336	2420
Phoenix					1268	353	2300
Portland						1086	2784
San Diego							2602

7. Using Houston as a central location, what is the cost of a network that would connect Houston to each of the cities in Question 6 via point-to-point links?

8. What line speed would be required to provide a 5-second response time for a transaction that transmits 600 characters of information and receives a response of 350 characters? Assume a processing time of 2 seconds and 10 bits per character.

9. Are there any situations in which an FDM is preferable to a stat mux? If so, what are they?

References

Digital Equipment Corp. *Introduction to Local Area Networks.* Digital Equipment Corp., 1982.

Edwards, Morris. "Modem and Multiplexer Update: Compact and Cheaper." *Infosystems,* November 1981.

Forney, G. David, and Stearns, Robert W. "Statistical Multiplexing Improves Link Utilization." In *Executive Guide to Data Communications,* 2nd ed. New York: McGraw-Hill.

Guy, Kenneth R. "Stat Muxes Help Managers Reduce Data Comm Costs." *Government Computer News,* June 1983.

Harper, William L., and Pollard, Robert C. *Data Communications Desk Book: A Systems Analysis Approach.* Englewood Cliffs, N.J.: Prentice-Hall, 1982.

Held, Gilbert. *Data Communication Components, Characteristics, Operation, Applications.* Rochelle Park, N.J.: Hayden Book Co., 1979.

_____ "Inverse Multiplexing with Multiport Modems." In *Executive Guide to Data Communications,* 2nd ed. New York: McGraw-Hill.

Kelley, Neil D. "Modems, Multiplexers and Concentrators Diagnostics and Control Are Key." *Infosystems,* June 1980.

Miller, Frederick W. "Business Rides Networks on Mux/Modem Links." *Infosystems*, May 1982.

Riviere, Charles J., and Cooper, Richard A. "How Concentrators Can Be Message Switchers as Well." In *Executive Guide to Data Communications*, 2nd ed. New York: McGraw-Hill.

Sudan, Lee. "Mux Ado About Multiplexers." *Computerworld on Communications* 18, (May 2, 1984).

Vacca, John. "Front End Processors." *Computerworld on Communications* 18 (May 2, 1984).

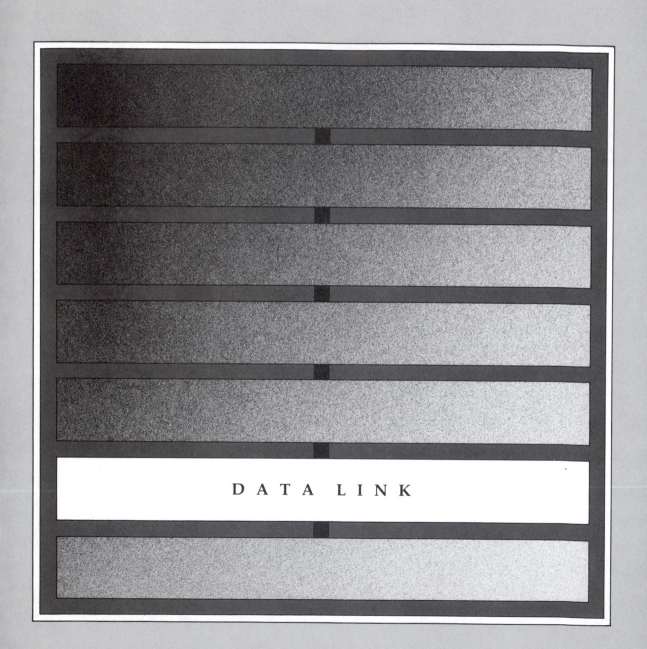

DATA LINK

III

DATA LINK PROTOCOLS: THE DATA LINK LAYER

Chapter 6: Data Link Control

6

Data
Link Control

INTRODUCTION

In this chapter the discussion moves up one layer in the OSI reference model to examine data link protocols. Asynchronous and synchronous transmission are the topics emphasized.

Supplements on asynchronous, character synchronous, and bit synchronous protocols appear at the end of the chapter for those who desire more detail on these topics.

THE DATA LINK LAYER

Chapter 1 presented the function of the *data link* layer: passing data and control information to the next node. In the current context this means

189

sending data across a single link to the next receiving station—terminal, host, concentrator, or the like. There is a difference between a link and a path: A *path* represents end-to-end message routing, whereas a *link* connects one node to an adjacent node or one node to a terminal. In Figure 6-1, the rectangles represent host processors, the circles represent terminals, and the lines represent communications links. Figure 6-1 shows two paths available for communication between node A and node C (A→B, B→C and A→D, D→C), with two links on each path.

Objectives of Transmission Protocols

In order to move data from one point to another, sender and receiver must agree on a transmission protocol, or convention. Protocols have the following objectives: delineation of data, error detection, contention control, transparency, addressing capability, permitting code independence, allowing multiple configurations, permitting system growth, and efficiency. As the various protocols are discussed, it will be seen just how well a given protocol meets these objectives.

Delineation of Data.   Transmission of data includes not only message data, but also control information and (almost always) error detection information. Receiving stations must be able to discern which is which, meaning that the protocol must enable receivers to determine where the data portion of the message begins and ends, where the control portions of the message are and what they mean, and where the error control bits

Figure 6-1
A Communications
Network

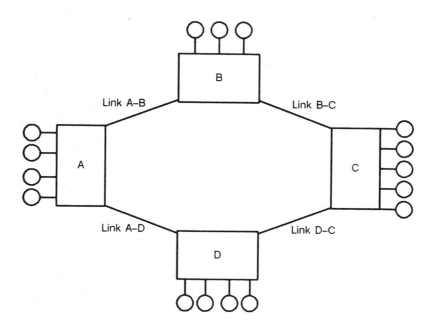

or characters are. In some cases, position within the message indicates the meaning of the field; in others, delineation is the result of framing by specific bit patterns. Examples of both positional and framing delineations are presented later. *Framing* and *enveloping* are terms that describe the process of placing additional data fields at the beginning or ending of another field, or both the beginning and ending. This is one way in which OSI layering is implemented: Each lower layer adds its functional data about the message that has been passed to it from the preceding layer. Delineation of data is illustrated in Figure 6-2(a).

Error Detection.   It is the function of data link protocols to generate, append, and forward error detection codes. (Error detection algorithms are discussed in Chapter 3). Protocols differ with respect to the specifics of their error detection algorithms and with respect to where in the message the error codes are placed. The error detection function is depicted in Figure 6-2(b).

Contention Control.   Data link protocols must establish the circumstances under which a station can transmit and receive data. If two or more stations can transmit at once and thus possibly interfere with one another, then the protocol must control recovery from such a situation.

Transparency.   *Transparency* refers to the ability to transmit any bit pattern as data and have it accepted correctly. This may sound trivial, but it is not. It is true that transparency is hardly ever an issue in transmitting data to terminals and printers, since all transmitted characters are displayable characters in the code set—that is, characters that represent letters, numbers, or special characters such as punctuation. A review of the ASCII and EBCDIC codes in Figures 3-12 and 3-13 (pages 85–87) will reveal that certain bit sequences, such as EOT and STX, are assigned control functions

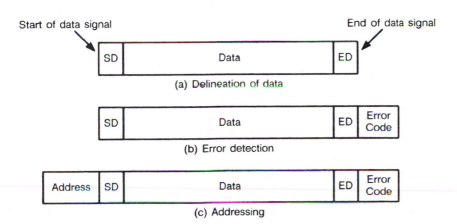

Figure 6-2
Some Data Link Functions

and are not displayable characters. If such special control characters are to be sent as data, the data link protocol must not interpret them as control characters. The transparency issue usually arises when data are transmitted between processors using a protocol designed for terminals or for displayable data. Interprocessor communications include transfer of binary files such as object code and transfer of data files containing binary number fields; transparency allows these binary fields, including characters ordinarily reserved for control purposes, to be accepted as data.

Addressing Capability.   Most data link protocols allow some type of multistation configuration, for example, the poll/select configuration discussed in Chapter 4 on page 133, and the CSMA/CD configuration discussed later in this chapter. For multiple stations to share a circuit, the data link protocol must enable a device address to be appended to the message. Each addressable device in turn must know where in the message the address appears—usually at or near the beginning. Addressing is shown in Figure 6-2(c) on page 191.

Permit Code Independence.   *Code independence* means the ability to successfully transmit data with any coding scheme—ASCII, EBCDIC, BAUDOT, or the like. Code independence enables two different devices—for instance, one that uses ASCII and one that uses EBCDIC—to share a line. As with addressing, code independence is not a requirement, but a desirable characteristic. Some of the protocols to be examined provide no code independence, although higher-level data link protocols usually do.

Allow Multiple Configurations.   Multiple configuration capability enables the system designer to plan a network topology or layout that is consistent with the application and that takes full advantage of the capabilities of the devices being used. In some protocols, only point-to-point or multi-point configurations are allowed. Alternatives such as loop or hierarchical topologies may also be supported, as can be seen from Figure 6-3.

Permit System Growth.   As new hardware components are designed and as features are added to old hardware, the data link protocol should be capable of supporting them. In addition, as the configuration itself expands with additional terminals or hosts, the protocol must not limit this growth. For instance, if the address field contains only eight bits of information, then growth would be limited to 256 distinct devices.

Efficiency.   A protocol with very little overhead is desirable. *Overhead* refers to the number of additional characters or bits that must be appended to the message in order to meet the previously defined objectives, thus allowing more channel capacity to be devoted to carrying data. Although

Host

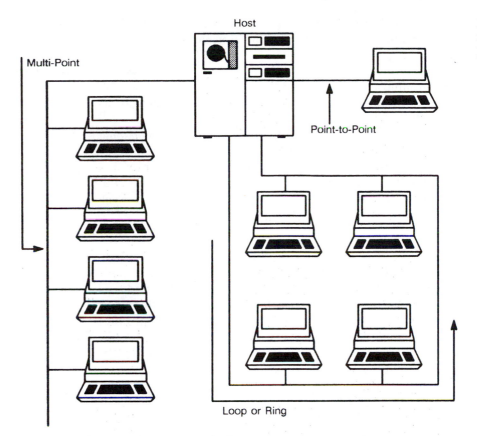

Figure 6-3
Multiple
Configurations

Multi-Point

Point-to-Point

Loop or Ring

data link control is frequently considered as overhead, it really is a necessary function, not just overhead.

ASYNCHRONOUS TRANSMISSION

Asynchronous (async) data link control is the oldest and one of the most common types of data link protocols, and like many of the techniques used in data communications, it is derived from the telegraph and telephone industries. *Asynchronous* is defined by *Webster's New World Dictionary* as "lack of synchronism; failure to occur at the same time."

With asynchronous transmission, data are transmitted one character at a time, and sender and receiver are not synchronized with each other. The sender is thus able to transmit a character at any time, although the receiver must be prepared to recognize that information is arriving, accept the data, possibly check for errors, and store the data in memory. In addition, individual characters can be separated over different time intervals, meaning that there is no synchronization between individual transmitted characters.

Most dumb terminals are async devices, and many smart and intelligent terminals can also communicate asynchronously. Thus, many personal computers use async transmission to communicate with each other and with host systems.

Async transmission is also referred to as a *start-stop protocol*. This term and the terms *mark*—which is the equivalent of a 1 bit—and *space*—which is equivalent to a 0 bit—are holdovers from telegraphy. Start-stop terminology derives from the fact that each character is framed by a start bit and a stop bit, in the following manner.

Compatibility of Sending and Receiving Stations

A communications link is either idling or transmitting data. In the idle state, the line is held in the mark condition—that is, continuous 1 bits. When establishing the communications link, the sending and receiving stations must first agree on the number of bits per character. And if parity is to be transmitted, both must agree on either even or odd parity, and on whether the parity bit is to be checked. (The parity bit could be transmitted but not checked by the data link software or hardware.) Third, they must also agree on a transmission speed, because this determines the time interval at which the line is sampled (see Supplement 1). Some modems are capable of detecting and adjusting to the transmission speed automatically. Such modems first assume maximum supportable line speed and then determine if a lower speed is being used. Finally, there must be agreement as to what signals will terminate the message, since characters can be sent at random intervals, for instance, from a person typing. Usually, a message terminator is either a defined set of characters called *interrupt characters*, a count of a specific number of characters, or a time-out interval, depending on the particular application.

The following discussion assumes that sending and receiving stations have been set up the same with respect to the number of bits sent per character, parity, message termination, and maximum speed of the link (detected by the receiving modem). The line is in the idle state, meaning that a continuous stream of 1 bits is being transmitted. There are seven data bits and one parity bit, and odd parity will be checked.

Initial Transmission

The arrival of a character is signaled by a start bit, which is a change in the state of the line from a mark to a space, or 0 bit. Following the start bit are seven data bits, one parity bit, and a stop bit, which is a return to a 1 bit, or mark condition. If parity does not check or if the tenth bit is not a 1, then an error will be deemed to have occurred. How this is physically accomplished is described in Supplment 1 at the end of this chapter. The

ASCII representation for the character *F* is 1000110; the async representation for transmitting this character is given in Figure 6-4.

Termination

After receiving a character, the line goes back to the idle state until the next start bit is encountered.

Interrupt Characters.   If interrupt characters are being used to terminate transmission, each character received must be examined to determine if it matches one of these characters. If it does, the message is considered complete, and is delivered to the application for which it was intended. This is the usual manner in which async communications are completed. On terminals, the character that is transmitted when the operator presses the return key—usually a carriage return character—is frequently one of these termination characters. Other interrupt characters can also usually be specified.

Character Count.   If a character count is being used to terminate the transmission, then as soon as the specified number of characters have arrived, the message is considered complete, and the data are sent on to the application. If termination was specified to be after 100 characters of data, as soon as the 100th character is received, the message is considered complete for the data link. In actuality, the application may be building a buffer of information in 100-byte blocks. This type of termination is useful when long streams of data are being sent.

Double Buffering.   Terminating data input with manageable-size blocks avoids problems of buffer overflow and buffer contention. Buffer overflow, or overrun, can arise when the data block being transmitted is larger than the receiving buffer area, or when data from a subsequent block are received before the previous block's data have been emptied from the buffer. Either condition leads to lost data. Frequently in such instances the data link protocol uses a technique known as double buffering to avoid missing

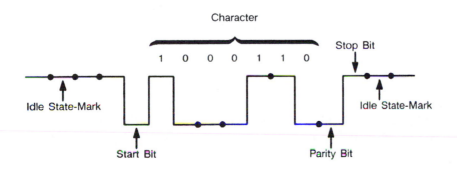

Figure 6-4
Asynchronous Transmission of the Character F

characters. *Double buffering* means there are two (or more) input buffers capable of receiving data. The buffers are alternated: When one buffer is filled, a small amount of time is required to move the data from the input buffer to another part of memory, during which interval another character could arrive. One way to prevent this character from being lost is to start receiving the next message in the alternate buffer. Switching buffers might be used, for example, in an attachment to wire service news bulletins or in transferring data from a microcomputer's disk to the host. Such data may arrive at any time and in variable-length blocks. If termination characters are not inserted at appropriate intervals, then a character count termination can be used to avoid buffer overflow. With manned terminals, character count termination is usually used only for entering fixed-length data fields. Interactive questions with one-character answers often use this technique.

Time-out Interval.   Another termination mechanism is the time-out interval. This method is effective in conjunction with a character count or when data are received from sensor-based or laboratory equipment. In the laboratory situation, a long time interval between data arrival means the entire data stream has arrived or the equipment is out of order. The time-out interval is not a good terminator for data being input by an operator: If the operator takes a break in the midst of input, a time-out interval would prematurely terminate the message. In conjunction with character count, the time-out interval is beneficial when the size of a message can vary. Thus, if the termination character count is 100, say, and the message is 350 characters in length, then by only character count termination, the first 300 characters would be received routinely but the last 50 characters would be held in the buffer until it was filled, which would only occur when the next message is sent. A time-out termination would prevent unnecessary delays in completing such a message.

Effectiveness of Asynchronous Transmission

The following rating of asynchronous transmission with respect to the data link objectives described earlier uses a three-level grading system—poor, adequate, and good. The data delineation and contention control objectives are not rated, since they are both essential functions; exactly how they are implemented, however, can influence the effectiveness rating.

Error Detection.   Parity is not one of the premier error detection algorithms. The requirement of a stop bit at a specific place enhances the parity capability somewhat. It is also possible to append a longitudinal redundancy check (LRC) or cyclic redundancy check (CRC) block check character (BCC), but this is seldom done. On many systems the BCC would have to be checked at a level above that of the data link protocol. Peformance is poor.

Transparency. The use of interrupt characters precludes transparency. Transparency can be achieved, however, with either character count termination or time-out termination. Performance is adequate, but use of transparency requires giving up part of the protocol. Transparency is normally not an issue in async transmission because transmission is usually either to or from a display device.

Addressing. Asynchronous transmission has no limitations with respect to addressing. Performance is good. Addressing is not specifically mentioned in the protocol.

Code Independence. There is no code independence with asynchronous transmission. There must be agreement on the number of bits per character prior to communication. The only possible code independence would involve a switch from one 8-bit code to another, which is not even possible with interrupt characters if the interrupt characters in the two codes are different. Performance is poor.

Configurations. Asynchronous transmission configurations in practice are essentially limited to point-to-point and multi-point. There are no inherent restrictions to this in the protocol. Performance is adequate.

Growth. If unlimited growth originally had been a part of async protocols, then other protocols probably would not have emerged. The protocol is primitive compared to others. Performance is poor.

Efficiency. In the earlier example, ten bits were transmitted for seven bits of data, making the overhead 30% for async transmission, which is relatively high. In addition, transmission speed is limited. Performance is poor.

Why Asynchronous Transmission Is So Popular

Despite the relatively poor rating just given asynchronous transmission, it remains one of the most common data link protocols, and for a number of reasons. Historically, async was the first protocol on the scene, and for a number of years it was the only way to transmit. Consequently, many terminals and controller boards were designed for async operation; the trend has continued as the hardware components continued to be refined. Thus, async technology is well developed, and there is a wide variety of hardware options available at a relatively low price.

Async is also very well suited to many types of applications. People performing data entry in a conversational mode or even in block mode operate at speeds compatible with async protocol. The speed, although limited with respect to other protocols, is still adequate for use with terminal equipment with human operators. Synchronous speeds for these devices are seldom higher than those for async. The primary penalty paid associated with async is its inefficient use of the circuit. Figure 6-5 illustrates the difference between asynchronous and synchronous transmission.

SYNCHRONOUS TRANSMISSION

Synchronous data link protocols can be divided into three groups—character oriented, byte-count oriented, and bit oriented, which is the newest technology and the basis for many of the emerging data communications systems. With synchronous transmission, sender and receiver are synchronized with each other. Synchronous modems contain clocks that are put in time with each other by a bit pattern transmitted at the beginning of a message. For long messages these sync patterns are periodically inserted within the text to ensure that the modems remain synchronized. Synchronized modem clocks are one feature that separates asynchronous modems from synchronous ones, for although there is a clocking function in async transmission, the clocks are not synchronized. Another difference between asynchronous and synchronous transmission is that instead of transmitting character by character, synchronous transmission involves a block at a time. Block transmission means the sending and receiving modems must be in sync with each other; failure to remain synchronized will lose data.

CHARACTER SYNCHRONOUS PROTOCOLS

Framing vs. Positional Protocols

Some protocols are positional, whereas others use a framing technique, as previously mentioned. *Framing* protocols rely on the use of reserved characters or bit patterns to define fields within a message. For instance, for a message that contains both header and text fields, a framing protocol

Figure 6-5
Asynchronous vs.
Synchronous
Transmission

a) Asynchronous

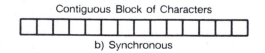

b) Synchronous

would use a special character to designate the start of the header, another to designate the start of the data, and a third to indicate the end of the data. This is illustrated in Figure 6-6. A *positional protocol*, on the other hand, relies on either fixed-length fields or character counts or both to delineate data. With a positional protocol, for example, each message format would indicate the number of data characters being transmitted in the first 16 bits, and the device address in the next 16 bits, followed by the data for the indicated number of characters, and finally the block check character. It is possible to use both framing and positional modes in a procolol, as in the use of beginning and ending bit patterns with fixed-length control fields within the message (except for the data portion).

Character synchronous protocols differ from byte count synchronous and bit synchronous protocols in that character synchronous message control is oriented toward specific transmission codes and specific characters within those codes. For example, in the ASCII code (see Chapter 3), a specific character (STX) is used as a control character indicating the start of text or message. Other types of data may be transmitted prior to the text, such as a message header. In bit-oriented protocols, specific characters have not been defined to perform these control functions.

Character Synchronous Standards

There are both corporate and national standards for specifying how character synchronous protocols are to be implemented. National standards include American National Standards Institute (ANSI) standards X3.1, X3.24, X3.28, and X3.36, all of which pertain to various aspects of character synchronous transmisssion. The IBM binary synchronous communications (*BSC* or *BISYNC*) protocol also has become accepted as a de facto industry standard communications protocol, and is supported by many manufacturers. It has become one of the common protocols interfacing between systems from different vendors. Because it is so common, BISYNC is used as a model of the *binary synchronous protocol* in the following discussion. More details on binary synchronous transmission can be found in Supplement 2 at the chapter's end.

Binary Synchronous Protocols: BISYNC

BISYNC was introduced by IBM in 1967 as the data link protocol for remote job entry, using the 2780 work station. Since that time it has come to be

Start of Header Character	Header	Start of Text Character	Message	End of Text Character

Figure 6-6
Framing for a Character Synchronous Message

used in many other applications and with many other devices. Only three data codes are supported by BISYNC: 6-bit transcode (SBT), ASCII, and EBCDIC. Technically there is no reason why other codes could not be used. SBT is an old code whose current use is minimal.

In order to synchronize sending and receiving modems, one or more synchronization characters are transmitted at the beginning of each transmission block. The receiving modem uses this bit pattern to establish timing and get in step with the sender. To maintain timing for long transmission blocks, additional sync characters are inserted at regular intervals. The number of sync characters required for synchronization is dependent on the equipment being used, although two or three is the usual number. Figure 6-7 depicts a message with BISYNC control characters for synchronization (SYN), the start of text (STX), and the end of text (ETX).

Point-to-Point Mode.   BISYNC supports both point-to-point and multipoint configurations. In the point-to-point mode, contention is used to determine which station is granted the right to transmit. In the contention mode, both devices on the communications link are considered equal. During transmission, one station must gain control of the link, usually by issuing a bid for the line. If the other station is ready to receive messages, it grants control of the link to the requesting station. If both stations should simultaneously issue a bid, some mechanism of resolution is required. For example, each station could generate a random delay interval before retrying the bid, making it unlikely for both to issue a bid at exactly the same time. Another alternative is for both to agree ahead of time on which station has priority in case of simultaneous bidding. Short one-character sequences are used to bid for the line. Point-to-point configurations can be via either switched lines or leased lines. Line bidding and data exchange sequences are illlustrated in Figure 6-8.

Multi-point Mode.   In the multi-point environment, one station is designated as supervisor and the others as tributary or secondary stations.

Figure 6-7
BISYNC Control
Characters

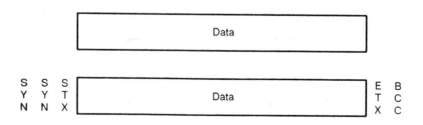

SYN	Synchronization character
STX	Start of text character
ETX	End of text character
BCC	Block check character—LRC or CRC

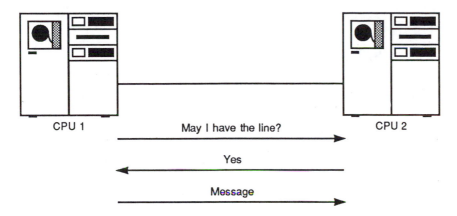

Figure 6-8
Line Bidding
(Contention Mode)

The supervisor maintains absolute control over the link; secondary stations remain passive and monitor the link. Secondaries may transmit only when permitted to do so by the supervisor. Thus, all data transfers are initiated by the supervisor. Up to seven characters are allowed for addressing, providing an extremely wide range of addresses (in excess of 100 billion different addresses if only 40 different characters are used). All transfers of data are between the supervisor and the secondary stations. The protocol does not allow for direct transfer of data between secondary stations. Polling sequences are relatively short, consisting of the sync characters, an optional EOT (end of transmission) character, the station address, and a one-character control sequence. The EOT character ensures the state of the line at the beginning of the poll. For some devices, additional pad characters are transmitted; they assist with synchronization and, in some older equipment, ensure that the transmitting buffer is emptied of the last control character being transmitted. Polling is illustrated in Figure 6-9 on page 202.

Message Control.   Each transmitted block can have an optional header field for message control, designating such things as routing information, priority, and message type [IBM, 1970]. The beginning and ending of text is identified by framing the data with control characters. For instance, an STX character signals that the data portion of the text is starting. One of a number of characters—such as ETX, ETB, or EOT—can be used to identify the end of a block of data, depending on whether an intermediate or final block is being transmitted. If the message is lengthy, it is ordinarily broken into segments or blocks. The ETB control character designates the end of the transmission block; ETX signals the end of the text; and EOT means end of transmission. If a message were broken into four different transmission blocks, for example, the first three blocks would terminate with the ETB control character, and the last would terminate with the EOT character.

Figure 6-9
Polling Example

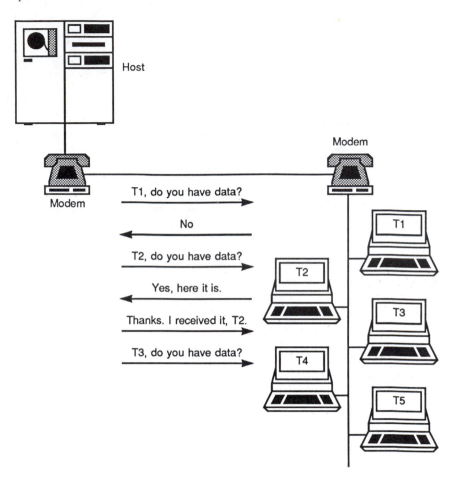

Host

Modem

Modem

T1, do you have data?

No

T2, do you have data?

Yes, here it is.

Thanks. I received it, T2.

T3, do you have data?

T1

T2

T3

T4

T5

Transparency.   Transparent transmission with BISYNC is rather cumbersome. Supplement 2 at the end of the chapter discusses the implementation in some detail. The original version of BISYNC was used for RJE, so transparent data transmission was unnecessary. Only the later uses of BISYNC created the need for transparency; the implementation is workable but inelegant.

Error Control.   Error control is either CRC, or LRC with VRC. CRC is used with EBCDIC or 6-bit transcode, and with ASCII when configured for transparency. LRC and VRC are used with nontransparent ASCII.

BISYNC's Half Duplex Nature.   One limitation of BISYNC is that it is essentially a half duplex protocol, so each message transmitted must be acknowledged by the receiver before the next can be sent. This is not a major concern for many applications, especially those involving terminal data entry, for which the amount of time required to acknowledge is small compared with the speed of data submission. For host-to-host communications, on the other hand, this can be quite restrictive. Consider a file transmitted between two processors: It would be quite efficient for the sender to transmit several blocks before requiring an acknowledgment, and for the acknowledgment to be transmitted in parallel with the data— that is, in full duplex mode. Unfortunately, the only benefit to using BISYNC on a full duplex line is that it eliminates modem turnaround time.

The half duplex nature of the BISYNC protocol is also inefficient in conversational applications. A session to prompt a user for an employee's last name on a point-to-point connection would work essentially as indicated in Figure 6-10.

Host		Terminal
May I have the line?	$\longrightarrow$	
	$\longleftarrow$	Yes.
Transmit: What is the Last Name?	$\longrightarrow$	
	$\longleftarrow$	I got your message
	$\longleftarrow$	May I have the line?
Yes.	$\longrightarrow$	
	$\longleftarrow$	Johnson
I got your message.	$\longrightarrow$	

Figure 6-10
Line Bidding and Conversational Exchange

To overcome this problem, there is now a limited conversational mode that allows the receiver to acknowledge receipt of a message and send data at the same time. Another extension allows multiple blocks to be transmitted without individual acknowledgment, acknowledgment being made one time for the entire group of blocks.

Effectiveness of the BISYNC Protocol

Error Detection. When CRC is used, BISYNC error detection is quite good. But CRC is not supported in every instance. The alternative of LRC and CRC is adequate. Performance is adequate to good.

Transparency. Transparency is possible but not cleanly implemented with BISYNC. It is an obvious add-on to the protocol. Performance is good, but implementation is poor.

Addressing. A wide range of BISYNC addresses is possible—from one to seven characters in length. Performance is good.

Code Independence. There is no code independence with BISYNC. Only three codes are supported, and it is not possible to convert from one to another. Transparency can be used to provide limited code independence as long as the number of bits in the new code is the same as that for the old. Performance is poor.

Configurations.   BISYNC configurations are essentially limited to multipoint and point-to-point modes on switched or leased lines. Performance is adequate.

Growth.   As with async protocols, if BISYNC had a sufficient number of desirable characteristics, there would be no bit-oriented protocols. The manner in which transparency was added indicates somewhat its limitations at meeting expansion requirements. Performance is adequate.

Efficiency.   BISYNC is quite efficient with respect to the number of control characters required to transmit a message. If the messages are very short, then the amount of overhead is more significant than when the messages are lengthy. This is because there is a fixed number of control characters that must be transmitted regardless of the text length. Thus, when the text is short, the ratio of control characters to text characters is larger than when the text is long. Contrast this with the asynchronous case, where the number of control bits is directly proportional to the number of characters transmitted. Performance is good except in those applications where full duplex operations could be used or where the half duplex nature of the protocol impedes progress.

BYTE COUNT SYNCHRONOUS PROTOCOLS

Byte count synchronous protocols are character oriented. The difference between them and BISYNC is in how they signal the beginning and ending of messages. *Byte count* refers to the fact that the number of characters in the message is given in a required message header, as illustrated in Figure 6-11. The header is of a fixed length, and the data field is of variable length.

The advantage of byte count protocols is principally in the area of transparency. With the byte count provided, it is obvious where the message begins and ends: The beginning is x characters from the beginning of the message, where x represents the length of the header. The data then span the byte-count number of characters. Following that may be a block check character or CRC characters. Since there is no need to scan the input

Figure 6-11
A Byte Count
Message Format

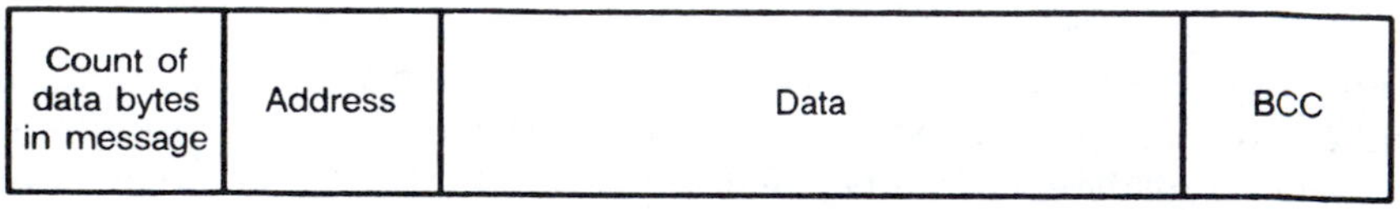

Count of data bytes in message	Address	Data	BCC

stream for termination characters, any bit pattern can be represented within the data stream.

Message Sequence Numbers

Some implementations of byte count protocols also include *message sequence numbers*. Each transmitted message is given a number, in order, thus allowing multiple messages to be transmitted without any acknowledgment. If, for example, three bits are used for sequencing messages, eight different sequence numbers—0 through 7—can be generated; when the count reaches 7, the next number assigned is again 0. This allows up to seven messages to be transmitted before being acknowledged. To be able to send multiple messages without an acknowledgment can save a significant amount of time, especially on slower links or links with a high modem turnaround time.

Effectiveness of Byte Count Synchronous Protocols

The ratings of byte count synchronous protocols are much the same as for BISYNC, the differences being in transparency and efficiency. *Transparency* is much more straight forward than BISYNC's implementation. And byte count protocols have greater efficiency if message sequencing or true full duplex operations are allowed. An example of a byte count synchronous protocol is Digital Equipment Corporation's DDCMP protocol. Its message sequencing allows 256 message numbers.

BIT SYNCHRONOUS PROTOCOLS

The first bit-oriented synchronous data link protocol was introduced by IBM in 1972. It was appropriately named *synchronous data link control (SDLC)*. Since then, numerous other bit-oriented data link controls have surfaced. The major *bit synchronous protocols* are:

SDLC Synchronous data link control, from IBM.

BDLC Burroughs data link control, from Burroughs Corporation.

UDLC Universal data link control, from Sperry Corporation.

CDCDLC Control Data Corporation data link control, from Control Data Corporation.

ADCCP Advanced data communications control procedure, an ANSI standard data link protocol. (ADCCP is frequently pronounced *add-cap*).

HDLC High-level data link control, a standard of the International Standards Organization.

LAPB Link access procedure—version B, designated as the data link protocol for the X.25 packet distribution networks. LAPB is an adaptation of HDLC.

All of these bit synchronous protocols operate similarly. HDLC and ADCCP are closely related on message formats. HDLC is said to encompass all the functionality of IBM's SDLC. Despite the fact that there are both national and international standards, SDLC is used in the following discussion as the model for bit-oriented data link protocols because it is used in many IBM installations and thus is part of the majority of bit synchronous applications. Furthermore, many vendors also support SDLC in order to provide connection to IBM networks and devices. More detailed information regarding SDLC may be found in Supplement 3 at the end of this chapter.

Synchronous Data Link Control (SDLC)

Synchronous data link control (SDLC) operates in full duplex or half duplex modes on nonswitched lines in both point-to-point and multi-point configurations. In half duplex mode it allows switched, point-to-point configurations. In addition, it is possible to configure stations in a loop, as depicted in Figure 6-12. Data are transmitted in one direction around the loop in a manner similar to hub polling. In all configurations, including point-to-point, one station is designated as the primary station and the others as secondary stations. The primary is responsible for controlling the link and determining which station is allowed to transmit.

The Frame. The basic unit of transmission in SDLC is the *frame*; its general format is presented in Figure 6-13. The *flag* field is used to indicate the beginning and the ending of the frame. The bit pattern for the flag—01111110—is the only bit pattern in the protocol that is specifically re-

Figure 6-12
An SDLC Loop
Configuration

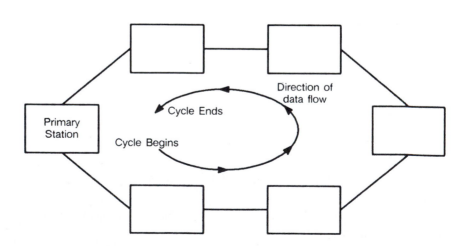

8 bits	8 bits	8 bits	Variable	16 bits	8 bits
Flag 01111110	Address	Control	Data (Optional Octets)	Frame Check Sequence	Flag 01111110

Figure 6-13
A SDLC Frame Format

served; all other bit patterns are acceptable. This is discussed further in the upcoming section on "Transparency." The second field within the frame—the *address* field—is eight bits wide, making a maximum of 256 unique addresses representable. Other data link protocols, such as *ADCCP* and *HDLC*, allow the address field to be expanded in multiples of eight bits, which significantly increases the number of addressable stations per link. The *control* field—also eight bits in length—identifies the frame type as either unnumbered, informational, or supervisory. Of these three types, only the first two are used to transmit data, with the primary data transport frame being the information frame.

Following the control field is the data field, which is the only optional field. This field is always omitted for supervisory frames, is optional on unnumbered frames, and is almost always present on information frames. The only restriction on the data field is that the number of bits must be a multiple of eight, each 8-bit group being called an *octet*. This restriction does not mean that an 8-bit code must be used; in fact, any code is acceptable. But if necessary, the data being transmitted must be padded out with additional bits to maintain an integral number of octets. If the data being transmitted consist of five BAUDOT characters, for instance, then at five bits each, only 25 bits of data would be required and an additional seven bits would have to be appended to complete the last octet.

Following the optional *data* field is a frame check sequence, for error detection, which is 16 bits in length. The final field of the frame is the flag that signals the end of the message. The bit pattern for the ending flag is the same as that for the beginning flag, thus allowing the ending flag for one frame to serve as beginning flag for the next.

SDLC is a positional protocol. That is, each field except the data field has a specific length and location relative to adjacent fields. Thus, there are no special control characters (except for the flag characters) to delimit the data or headings in the message. For control frames, which are either unnumbered or supervisory, the control function is encoded in the *control* field. Unnumbered frames have five bits available to identify the control function, so 32 different function types are available. The supervisory frame has only two bits available, and thus a maximum of four functions can be defined.

Number Sent (Ns) and Number Received (Nr) Subfields.   For information frames, the *control* field contains two 3-bit fields known as the *number sent (Ns)* and *number received (Nr) subfields*. The Ns and Nr counts are used to sequence messages. Three bits allow for eight numbers, 0 through 7. When transmitting an information frame the sender increments the Ns field value. Numeric roll-over occurs at 7, that is, the number following 7 is 0. This allows seven messages to be sent before acknowledgment is required. The Nr field is used for acknowledging receipt of messages. Every time a message is received, the receiver increments the Nr count, which represents the number of the frame expected next. Thus, an Nr count of 5 means message number 5 should arrive next. The Ns and Nr counts are compared every time a frame is received to make sure that no messages have been lost.

Although the ability to receive up to seven frames without acknowledgment improves performance, it also places a burden on the sender, which must be ready to retransmit any unacknowledged frames. Since this requires that messages be saved in the sender's buffers until acknowledged, this can create problems for systems with small buffers or memory. Examples of how the Ns and Nr fields are used are found in Supplement 3.

Both ADCCP and HDLC allow the control field to be expanded to provide for larger Ns and Nr counts, as illustrated in Figure 6-14. When expanded to 16 bits, the Ns and Nr fields can both be seven bits in length; this allows 128 sequence numbers, and up to 127 messages can be transmitted before being acknowledged. This is especially beneficial with satellite links, where because of the 0.5-second propagation delay for response, a small number of unacknowledged frames could create undesirable delays. For example, if 10,000-bit blocks are being transmitted on a 1-Mbps satellite link, then theoretically 50 blocks could be transmitted every half-second. With 3-bit Ns and Nr fields, the transmission time for 43 blocks would be lost and only about 1/7 of available capacity could be used.

Transparency.   Transparency is implemented in SDLC by bit insertion, also known as bit stuffing. Since the beginning and ending flags use the only reserved bit sequence, their bit pattern—01111110—must never appear in the data portion of the record. This is accomplished by inserting a

Figure 6-14
Control Fields for
Information Frames

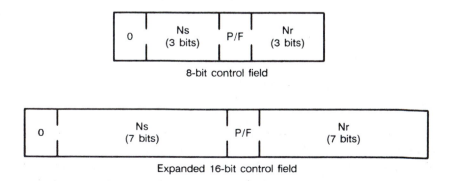

8-bit control field

Expanded 16-bit control field

0 bit after encountering five consecutive 1 bits in the data. After the control field, the receiver looks for two specific bit patterns, the ending flag and five consecutive 1 bits. If the ending flag is encountered the receiver knows that the preceding 16 bits are frame check characters and that all bits between the end of the *control* field and the start of the frame check are data. If, on the other hand, five consecutive 1 bits arrive followed by a 0 bit, then the receiver also knows that the 0 bit has been inserted for transparency. The inserted 0 bit is then stripped out and the receiver continues evaluating the input stream. An example of transparency is included in Supplement 3.

Effectiveness of the SDLC Protocol

Error Detection. SDLC uses CRC-16 to detect errors. Performance is good.

Transparency. Transparency was designed into the SDLC protocol. It is effected by inserting a 0 bit after five consecutive 1 bits. Performance is good and the overhead is minimal.

Addressing. SDLC is limited in addressing capability because it can use only eight bits, which can represent at most 256 devices. Other bit synchronous protocols that allow the address field to expand rate higher in this category. Performance for SDLC is poor, for others good.

Code Independence. All of the bit synchronous protocols provide code independence. The only restriction—a minor one—is that the data field must be an integral number of octets. Performance is good.

Configurations. Almost any combination of half duplex, full duplex, point-to-point, multi-point, dedicated, or switched links are supported in SDLC. In addition, loop configurations are allowed. Performance is good.

Growth. Ability to accommodate growth and new developments was one of the original design objectives of SDLC. Thus far it has been flexible enough to satisfy all new developments. Despite being a relatively new protocol, it has gone through a period of significant expansion and new development in communications equipment and applications. Performance is good.

Efficiency. Like BISYNC, SDLC has a fixed overhead. Each information frame has 48 bits appended for flags, control, addressing, and error detection. If the data to be sent consists of only a few bits, then the amount of overhead is high. In the typical situation, performance is good.

ISOCHRONOUS PROTOCOLS

The *isochronous* data link *protocol*, which is seldom used in business data communications, is a blend of asynchronous and synchronous protocols. Like async, each character is framed by its own start and stop bits. Like synchronous, the modems supply timing and are synchronized with each other. Data are transmitted a character at a time, but the time between characters is always an integral multiple of character intervals. When the cost of electronics hardware was higher, isochronous transmission provided speeds higher than those supported by async and at a lower cost than synchronous. In synchronous transmission the entire message must be built before it can be sent. Async and isochronous, in contrast, can transmit as the message is being generated. When memory was quite expensive, the cost of synchronous transmission was greater than for the other two protocols. The isochronous protocol is now virtually extinct.

CARRIER SENSE MULTIPLE ACCESS WITH COLLISION DETECTION PROTOCOL

Carrier sense multiple access with collision detection (CSMA/CD) is used as the data link protocol in a number of *local area networks (LAN)*, specifically, in the Ethernet LAN designed by Xerox, Digital Equipment Corporation, and Intel. Where specifics are required in the discussion that follows, Ethernet serves as the example.

CSMA/CD is a broadcast protocol. The typical CSMA/CD configuration consists of a length of cable with stations attached (a *bus network*), as illustrated in Figure 6-15; a *ring network*, shown in Figure 6-16, can also be

Figure 6-15
The CSMA/CD Bus
Configuration

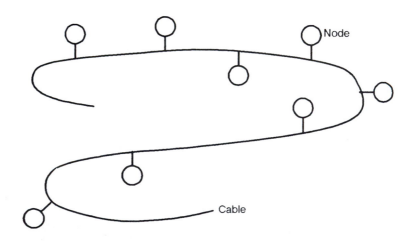

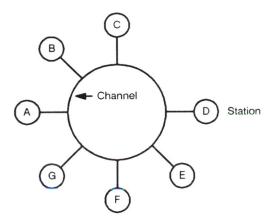

Figure 6-16
Ring Architecture

used. Each station attached to the LAN has a unique address. Messages are broadcast or sent across the medium, and all stations receive the message. Each recipient examines the address field to determine if it is the addressee. Only the station(s) to whom the message is addressed act upon the message.

There is no supervisor station in Ethernet; all stations are equal. When a station has a message to send, it "senses" the carrier on the channel (CS, or carrier sense) to determine whether a message is being transmitted. If a message is in progress, the station waits until the circuit is clear. Any station detecting a clear channel is free to transmit (MA, or multiple access). On occasions when two or more stations attempt to transmit at the same time, the messages collide, since the medium only allows one message at a time, and the collisions are detected by all monitoring stations. Any station detecting the collision reinforces it by also briefly broadcasting data, further jamming the circuit. After a collision, the stations responsible for it wait for a randomly selected time before attempting to transmit again, to decrease the probability that the same two stations will cause another collision.

Efficiency.   The efficiency of CSMA/CD is quite high when the amount of data traffic is light. As the number of stations and message traffic increases, so do the number of collisions, which decreases the efficiency of the communications link.

CSMA/CD transmits messages in frames similar to those used by SDLC. The CSMA/CD frame consists of a 64-bit preamble, a 48-bit destination address, a 48-bit source address, a 16-bit field indicating the message type and how to interpret the data, a variable-length data field, and a 32-bit CRC field. The size of the data field ranges from 46 to 1500 octets. The CRC field is 32 bits wide rather than 16 as in HDLC and BISYNC; this improves error detection. The 64-bit preamble, which consists of alternating 1 and 0 bits, allows the receiver to become synchronized with the sender. The CSMA/CD frame format is given in Figure 6-17.

Effectiveness of the CSMA/CD Protocol

Error Detection.   As implemented in Ethernet, a 32-bit CRC is used. This improves over the error detection provided with 16-bit CRC. Capability is very good.

Transparency.   Transparency is inherent in the CSMA/CD protocol. The data field is in a fixed position. There are no message termination flags or control characters to be concerned with. Capability is good.

Addressing.   CSMA/CD address fields are 48 bits wide, which allows for an extensive address range. The Ethernet specification limits the number of stations to 1024. Capability is good.

Code Independence.   CSMA/CD's only restriction on code independence is that an integral number of octets must be transmitted. Capability is good.

Configurations.   Ethernet has basically two configurations, bus and ring, as illustrated in Figures 6-15 and 6-16 on pages 210 and 211. The access protocol is not limited to these configurations, however; star and other configurations can also be used. Capability is good.

Growth.   Growth with the CSMA/CD protocol is inhibited by performance when large numbers of stations desire to transmit. The addressing scheme is not an inhibiting factor. Capability is adequate.

Efficiency.   Efficiency of the CSMA/CD protocol is good when there are few collisions. As the number of collisions increases, efficiency decreases. Capability is adequate to good.

TOKEN PASSING PROTOCOLS

The *token passing protocol* is most frequently implemented in a ring-architecture local area network, as depicted in Figure 6-18. Bus implementation

Figure 6-17
The CSMA/CD
Message Format

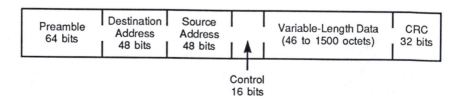

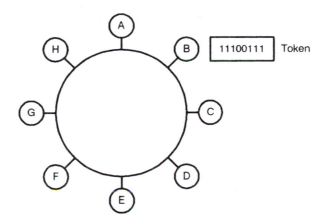

Figure 6-18
A Token Passing Ring

is also possible. Data are passed around the ring from station to station in one direction only. Since all nodes on a token passing loop are considered equal, a mechanism is needed to determine which station has the right to transmit data on the medium. A predefined bit pattern called a token is used to identify who has transmission rights.

In Figure 6-18, node B has possession of the token, giving B the right to transmit data to another station on the ring. Maintaining possession of the token, node B transmits its data to the next node on the ring, which examines the message's address to determine whether it is the recipient. If not, the node forwards the message to the next node. The node that is the intended recipient of the data keeps the data and forwards an acknowledgment, which could be the message itself. On receiving the acknowledgment node B passes the token to node C, giving it the right to transmit data. Of course, if node C has no data to send, it immediately passes the token to its neighbor.

There are a number of token passing variations. In some systems, a packet of messages is sent around the ring. When the packet arrives at a node it removes the data addressed to it and appends its own messages to the others in the transmission block. Usually the block's maximum size is predefined, so a vacant spot must be obtained in order to transmit the message. Ring networks are usually designed so that a failed node will not disrupt the passing of data between the other nodes.

The advantage of a token-passing ring is its predictability. For a given configuration the average wait time and transmit time can be determined and will not vary significantly. With the CSMA/CD protocol, in contrast, when the number of stations and messages increases, wait time for use of the medium can be unpredictable. One of the criticisms of token passing is the potentially long delay time between transmissions from one station when the number of nodes is large, as it takes the token longer to reach a node wishing to transmit.

Effectiveness of the Token Passing Protocol

Error Detection.   Error detection in token passing is determined by the specific implementation. If CRC is used then the capability is good.

Transparency.   Particular implementations of token passing can provide good capability.

Addressing.   Addressing capability is implementation-dependent with the token passing protocol.

Code Independence.   Token passing code independence depends on implementation.

Configurations.   The configuration of token passing is usually a ring or bus. Capability is fair.

Growth.   The growth of token passing protocols is inhibited by performance when large numbers of stations are configured: The more stations there are, the longer it takes for the token to reach a given node. Performance could degrade with a large number of stations. Capability is adequate.

Efficiency.   The efficiency of token passing is very predictable, given a specific number of stations. Peformance is good.

SUMMARY

Although there are a number of other data link protocols in existence, those described in this chapter are the ones most commonly used. The question is, which of them should be selected for a given application? First, the network designer must choose a protocol supported by the hardware vendor. Almost all vendors will support some version of asynchronous, character synchronous, and bit synchronous protocols. CSMA/CD and token passing are found primarily in local area networks. Second, the type of hardware used in an application partly dictates the data link protocol. Most terminals will support one or possibly two protocols. The exception is the intelligent group of terminals, which can support a wide variety of protocols. Third, the network support provided by the vendor affects the choice of data link protocol. Many of the newer network systems have been designed around a bit-oriented synchronous protocol; however, since not all users have compatible terminals, accommodations are frequently made to support other protocols, such as BISYNC. In actuality, one does not select a protocol and then gather the equipment to support it; rather one selects a network design, a hardware vendor, and associated hardware, all of which dictate a particular protocol.

Most current technology and development is based on bit-oriented synchronous protocols, of which there are a number of implementations and for which several standards exist, both international and U.S. The industry trend is toward higher-speed transmission and efficient use of the data link, a trend that definitely favors synchronous transmission protocols.

Key Terms

ADCCP	Interrupt characters
Asynchronous	Isochronous protocol
Binary synchronous protocol	LAPB
BISYNC	Local Area Network (LAN)
Bit synchronous protocol	Mark
BSC	Message sequence numbers
Bus network	Number received (Nr) subfield
Byte count synchronous protocol	Number sent (Ns)
Character synchronous protocol	Octet
Code independence	Positional protocol
Carrier sense multiple access with	Ring network
collision detection (CSMA/CD)	Synchronous data link control (SDLC)
Data link	Space
Double buffering	Start-stop protocol
Enveloping	Synchronous
Frame	Token passing
Framing protocol	Transparency
High-level data link control (HDLC)	

Questions and Exercises

In answering some of the questions below, it will be helpful to refer to the supplementary material at the end of the chapter.

1. Make a chart that compares the overhead of asynchronous, BISYNC, and SDLC protocols. Make the chart for message sizes of 50, 100, 500, and 1000 characters. The chart should look essentially as follows:

Number of	Number of Bits Transferred		
Text Characters	ASYNC	BISYNC	SDLC
25			
50			
100			
500			
1000			

In filling out the chart, assume a start, stop, and parity bit for async. For BISYNC, assume six control characters, (SYN SYN STX ETX plus two for BCC). For BISYNC you should also include a point-to-point line bid (SYN

SYN ENQ), and two acknowledgments (SYN SYN ACK0 and SYN SYN ACK1) of four characters each. One acknowledgment is for the line bid and one for the data. For SDLC, assume a frame overhead of 48 bits. Count the adknowledgment as 16 bits, since ordinarily several frames will be acknowledged at once. Which is the most efficient protocol and under what conditions? Assume 7-bit characters for each case.

2. Name five implementations of bit-oriented synchronous data link controls. List those features indicated in the text that distinguish some of them from SDLC.

3. What is *transparency*? Why is it necessary?

4. What are the advantages and disadvantages of using BISYNC on a full duplex line?

5. How do asynchronous and synchronous protocols differ? In what respects are they the same? How do their modems differ?

6. What advantages does SDLC have over BISYNC?

7. Is there an analogy to CSMA/CD in other communications disciplines such as radio or television? If so, in what respects are they similar?

8. Describe data link objectives in which CSMA/CD is inefficient.

9. In what respects does contention in BISYNC differ from that of CSMA/CD?

10. Diagram a sequence of message exchanges between two stations using SDLC that shows the changing of the *Ns* and *Nr* fields.

11. Is transparency a requirement of code independence? Justify your answer.

12. Can there be a start/stop flag in the address or control field of an SDLC message? If not, why not? If so, why does it not terminate the message?

References

Alusic, Donald. "Isochronous Communications—A Data Transmission Bridge." *Infosystems*, September 1975.

Hewlett-Packard Corp. *Guidebook to: Data Communications*. Santa Clara, CA: Hewlett-Packard Corp., 1977.

IBM. *General Information—Binary Synchronous Communications*. Manual No. GA27-3004-2. Research Triangle Park, NC: IBM, October 1970.

_____ *IBM Synchronous Data Link Control General Information*. Manual no. GA27-3093-2. Research Triangle Park, NC: IBM, 1979.

McNamara, John E. *Technical Aspects of Data Communication*. Bedford, MA: Digital Press, 1977.

Sherman, Elton. "Implementing Distributed Networks with SDLC." *Digital Design*, March 1977.

Shoch, John F., et al. "The Evolution of Ethernet." *Computer* 15 (August 1982).

Tanenbaum, Andrew S. *Computer Networks*. Englewood Cliffs, NJ: Prentice-Hall, 1981.

Tropper, Carl. *Local Computer Network Technologies*. New York: Academic Press, 1981.

Supplement 1
Asynchronous Transmission

Asynchronous transmission is transmission a character at a time. Sending and receiving stations are not synchronized with each other, which means that a sending station can send a character at any time, with no prescribed interval to the next character. Of course, the receiving station must also be ready to accept a character at any time. This supplement provides additional details on how this is accomplished. An asynchronous point-to-point line with a transmission speed of 1200 bps is assumed.

UART Processing Chip

At the heart of asynchronous transmission is a processing chip called the universal asynchronous receiver/transmitter (UART). The UART accepts characters via parallel transmission from the terminal or host and places them on the circuit serially. It also accepts bit serial transmissions from the communications line and passes the characters to the data terminal equipment in bit parallel fashion.

Detecting Incoming Characters

To detect an incoming character, the UART samples the state of the communications circuit at a rate 16 times the expected bit rate. On a 1200-bps line, one bit passes every $1/1200 = 0.000833 = 0.833$ milliseconds, so a sampling of the line is taken every 52 microseconds. Figure 6-19 illustrates this situation. The line is sampled so frequently in order to identify immediately when the state of the line has changed from the mark condition to the space condition. When a line transition is detected, the sampling interval is changed to ensure that the line is always being sampled in the middle of a bit interval. This is far safer than attempting to interrogate the line at the beginning or ending of a bit, when a slight timing error could cause the bit to be missed. Thus, when it appears that a start bit has arrived, there is a delay of $7/16$ of a bit interval (0.364 milliseconds in the

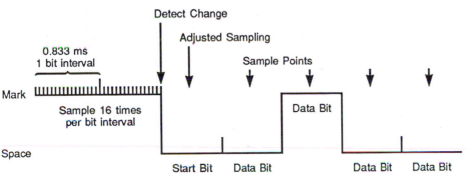

Figure 6-19
Asynchronous Line
Sampling

current example) before the line is sampled again, so that the sample is taken approximately in the middle of the bit interval. If the line is in the space condition, it is assumed this represents a start bit. Line sampling timing is adjusted to sample the line during every bit interval (every 0.83 milliseconds), and the line can be sampled once for each bit, and nearly in the center of the bit interval.

As discussed earlier in the chapter, four items must be agreed on by sender and receiver before asynchronous communications can begin—line speed, number of bits per character, presence of a parity bit, and message termination characters. Line sampling makes use of the agreed-on line speed.

Receiving Incoming Characters and Parity Check

Knowledge of the number of bits expected per character is used to receive the bits making up each character. This discussion assumes seven bits per character, one parity bit, and odd parity.

Having detected the start bit, the UART then assembles the next seven bits that should make up the character. The ninth bit, the parity bit, is received and checked against the seven bits already received. If parity does not check, then a parity error message is sent to the transmitter so the character can be retransmitted. If parity does check, then the next bit is examined to see if it is a stop bit or a mark condition. If a stop bit or mark condition is not detected, then a transmission error is assumed to have occurred. If everything is correct, the UART returns to sampling the line. It is necessary to know how many bits compose a character, as well as whether parity is being transmitted and checked, in order to know when to expect the stop bit.

Message Termination

If termination characters have been specified, the communications process driving the line must examine the character to determine if it matches any of the defined termination characters. If there is no match, then the character is placed in memory awaiting the rest of the message. If an interrupt character is detected, then appropriate action is taken, depending on the interrupt character.

For example, when two interrupt characters have been designated—backspace and carriage return, then backspace would cause the end-of-buffer pointer to be decremented by one, and the next character transmitted (if not another backspace) would be placed in the buffer over the last received character. Since every key stroke in asynchronous transmission is transmitted immediately to the host (with dumb terminals, anyway), then hitting an incorrect character followed by backspace transmits two characters to the host, the incorrect character and the backspace character. On the other hand, if the *carriage return* character is received, then the end of the message has been indicated. The buffer of data is made available to the application program by the operating system, indicating that input is complete. In some older systems, each character received interrupts the CPU so the character could be stored in memory. The more efficient approach has been taken here—the operating system is interrupted and the application awakened only on message completion.

Data Overruns

A UART usually has two registers available for receiving data from the line and two for receiving data from the data terminal equipment (DTE). This allows a received character to be checked for parity and placed into memory while another character is being received. Even so, data overruns are still possible, especially when an intelligent or smart terminal is transmitting data from its buffer. At such a time the data may be transmitted at intervals much faster than operator typing speeds. Even when the line speed is not exceeded, the receiving hardware or software may be incapable of receiving a continuous stream of characters at that speed. One solution to this problem is to increase the interval between transmitting characters.

Supplement 2
Binary Synchronous Transmission

Binary synchronous (BISYNC) protocols transmit data a block at a time. This requires that the sender and receiver be in sync with each other. To achieve this timing, synchronous modems contain clocks synchronized with each other during transmission. This timing can be compared to joggers and their watches: The jogging watch can be set to a pace related to the length of the runner's stride and the distance to be run. The watch determines the necessary number of strides per minute and emits a beep every time the jogger's foot should strike the ground. There must be synchronization between the watch's beeping tone and the runner's feet. Likewise, the clocks in the synchronous modems must be in time with each other so the receiving modem will look for an arriving character at the correct time.

Establishing Synchronization

To establish this timing ordinarily requires two or more synchronization (abbreviation, SYN) characters. The sending station prefixes all transmissions with a number or SYN characters. If the modems are not in sync

when the first SYN character arrives, the entire character will not be received correctly, although the receiving modem will be aware that a character stream is arriving. The second SYN character assures synchronization. Additional SYN characters are transmitted with equipment that
requires more than two characters for synchronization. SYN characters are
hexadecimal 32 in EBCDIC, hexadecimal 16 in ASCII, and hexadecimal 3A
in SBT; these are the three codes supported by BISYNC.

Like the asynchronous protocol, BISYNC is aware of the number of
bits per character. Also as in asynchronous transmission, a single chip
interfaces with the line. The line is continuously monitored, awaiting the
SYN character that signals the beginning of a message. A copy of the SYN
character is maintained in a register and compared with the data received.
When the first SYN character appears to have arrived, the next character
is checked to determine whether it also is a SYN character. The first SYN
character sets *bit* synchronization, the second sets *character* synchronization. Once synchronization is established, individual characters can be
received and processed.

Transmission Control Characters

BISYNC uses a number of special transmission control characters to indicate the beginning of the data or header information, the end of the data
or transmission block, the end of transmission, acknowledgments of data
received, and so on. A listing of these follows.

SYN.   The SYN character establishes *synchronization*. It precedes all message blocks and may be inserted in long messages to maintain
synchronization.

STX.   *STX* indicates the *start of text*; what follows it are data.

SOH.   *SOH* means *start of header*. The optional header field follows. Headers may contain application-dependent data such as transaction codes and
terminal ID.

ETX.   *ETX* indicates *end of text*. It tells when a complete text message has
been received. If lengthy text is broken into blocks for transmission, only
the final block will contain the ETX character.

ETB.   *ETB* Signals the *end of the transmission block*. It requires an acknowledgment. See *ETX*, above.

ITB.   *ITB* marks the *end of an intermediate transmission block*. In some cases
a number of blocks may be transmitted without being acknowledged. An
ITB character is used to signal the end of these blocks. The actual character
used to represent the ITB is *IUS* in EBCDIC and *US* (unit separator) in
ASCII and SBT.

EOT.   *EOT* means *end of transmission* and is used to terminate a transmission. It differs from *ETX* in that *ETX* signals the end of a logical message. Multiple messages may comprise one transmission; *EOT* signals this condition. Following the transmission of *EOT*, the transmitting station relinquishes control of the link. All stations are reset following *EOT*. *EOT* can also be used as a response to a poll and to signal an error condition that precludes message completion.

ACK0.   *Positive acknowledgment* is signaled by *ACK0*, which is actually a two-character sequence consisting of a DLE character (see below) plus a character that is code-dependent. In ASCII, *0* is the second character. BISYNC uses *ACK0* and *ACK1* in an alternating acknowledgment scheme.

ACK1.   *Positive acknowledgment*. See *ACK0* above. *ACK1* is a two-character sequence consisting of *DLE* (see below) and a second code-dependent character, a *1* in ASCII.

NAK.   *NAK*, meaning *negative acknowledgment*, is used to indicate that the previous block was received in error and should be retransmitted. It is also used as a negative response to a poll message.

ENQ.   *ENQ*, meaning *inquiry*, is used to bid for the line in contention mode, to initiate a poll or select message, or to ask that a response to a previous transmission be resent.

DLE.   *DLE—data link escape;*—is used to implement transparency. It is also used to form other control characters such as *ACK0*.

WACK, TTD, RVI.   These are used for special control situations, defined later. Each represents a special kind of positive acknowledgment.

Control for Long Messages.   Messages, particularly long ones, can be broken into blocks for transmission to minimize the amount of data that might have to be retransmitted in case of errors and to accommodate buffer sizes in the receiving equipment. In the case when all intermediate blocks can be transmitted before acknowledgment is required, the ITB control character is used to terminate the block. If *ETB* is used instead, each block must be acknowledged. Alternating acknowledgments—ACK0 and ACK1—are used to provide a small amount of error control. *ACK0* is always a positive response to a line bid or to selection.

Transmission Sequences

In the examples that follow, the character sequences should be read from left to right, with the first character transmitted appearing on the left. *BCC* represents the block check character, either LRC or CRC.

Point-to-Point Contention Mode. In point-to-point contention, a station must first bid for and be granted access to the line. This sequence is given in Figure 6-20.

Figure 6-20
A BISYC Contention
Mode Line Bid

Line Bidder		Responder	Comment
SYN SYN ENQ	$\longrightarrow$		Line bid
	$\longleftarrow$	SYN SYN ACK0	Positive response
SYN SYN STX text ETB BCC	$\longrightarrow$		Message block 1
	$\longleftarrow$	SYN SYN ACK1	Positive response
SYN SYN STX text EOT BCC	$\longrightarrow$		Last block
	$\longleftarrow$	SYN SYN ACK0	Positive response

At this point the line is available for either station to issue a bid. A negative response to the line bid would be *NAK*. If a station were unable to receive data for some reason, it would *NAK* the line bid.

Multi-point Mode. A polling sequence with positive and negative responses is shown in Figure 6-21. A selection sequence is portrayed in Figure 6-22.

Figure 6-21
BISYNC Polling

Supervisor	Secondary	Comment
SYN SYN address1 ENQ $\longrightarrow$		Poll to station 1
	$\longleftarrow$ SYN SYN EOT	No data to send
SYN SYN address2 ENQ $\longrightarrow$		Poll to station 2
	$\longleftarrow$ SYN SYN STX data EOT BCC	Data sent
SYN SYN ACK0 $\longrightarrow$		Positive response
SYN SYN address3 ENQ $\longrightarrow$		Poll to station 3

Figure 6-22
A BISYNC Selection

Supervisor	Secondary	Comment
SYN SYN EOT SYN SYN address ENQ $\longrightarrow$		Selection
	$\longleftarrow$ SYN SYN NAK	Negative response; unable to receive
SYN SYN EOT SYN SYN address ENQ $\longrightarrow$		Retry
	$\longleftarrow$ SYN SYN ACK0	Positive response
SYN SYN STX text ETX BCC $\longrightarrow$		Data sent
	$\longleftarrow$ SYN SYN ACK1	Positive response
SYN SYN EOT $\longrightarrow$		End of data

In the selection sequence in Figure 6-22, the station being selected at first gave a negative acknowledgment to the selection, a *NAK*. A printer would respond in this manner if its buffer was not empty and it was unable to accept more data. A positive acknowledgment was given to the subsequent selection, and the data was transmitted. *EOT* in the selection stream ensures the status of the link.

WACK. On occasion a station may wish to positively acknowledge receipt of a block and also advise the sender that it is not ready to receive the next block, such as when a printer with limited buffer size is out of paper or otherwise unable to empty its buffer. The WACK character is used both to positively acknowledge receipt of a block and also to tell the sending station to wait before transmitting further. *WACK* is a two-character sequence—*DLE* followed by a code-dependent character (a semi-colon in ASCII and a comma in EBCDIC). The message sequence for *WACK* is presented in Figure 6-23.

Sender		Receiver	Comment	
SYN SYN ENQ	$\longrightarrow$		Line bid	**Figure 6-23**
	$\longleftarrow$	SYN SYN ACK0	Positive response	BISYNC WACK
SYN SYN STX text ETB BCC	$\longrightarrow$		Data	
	$\longleftarrow$	SYN SYN WACK	WACK	
SYN SYN ENQ	$\longrightarrow$		Line bid	
	$\longleftarrow$	SYN SYN ACK0	Positive response	
SYN SYN STX text ETX BCC	$\longrightarrow$		Data	
	$\longleftarrow$	SYN SYN ACK0	Positive response	

The WACK response in Figure 6-23 delays the sender from transmitting the remainder of the text block. The sender would continue prompting the station with *ENQs* until the receiver is able to receive. A positive response to *ENQ* will allow the sender to continue with the message.

TTD.   Sometimes a sending station becomes temporarily busy and so is unable to continue sending its message. If the sender wants to maintain control of the communications circuit during such an interval, it can do so with the temporary text delay (TTD) control sequence. *TTD* consists of *STX* followed by *ENQ*. The transmitting sequence for this is given in Figure 6-24. The TTD sequence must be repeated within 2 seconds to avoid time-out. The usual time-out value of 3 seconds avoids a long wait for a station that is not on line.

Sender		Receiver	Comment	
SYN SYN ENQ	$\longrightarrow$		Line bid	**Figure 6-24**
	$\longleftarrow$	SYN SYN ACK0	Positive response	BISYNC TTD
SYN SYN STX ENQ	$\longrightarrow$		TTD	
	$\longleftarrow$	SYN SYN NAK	Response to TTD	
(within 2 seconds)			Avoid time-out	
SYN SYN STX ENQ	$\longrightarrow$		TTD	
	$\longleftarrow$	SYN SYN NAK	Response to TTD	
SYN SYN STX text ETB BCC	$\longrightarrow$		Data	
	$\longleftarrow$	SYN SYN ACK1	Acknowledgment	

RVI. When a receiving station has a high-priority message to transmit to a sending station, the receiver can indicate this by acknowledging a message with a reverse interrupt (RVI) character sequence. *RVI* is a two-character sequence—*DLE* plus a code-dependent second character (< in ASCII and @ in EBCDIC). *RVI* acknowledges the message received and alerts the sender to relinquish the line as soon as possible, so the station that has been receiving can assume control of the link. An RVI sequence is illustrated in Figure 6-25. *RVI* does not cause the sender to immediately discontinue transmission; the sender will continue transmitting until its buffers are empty and it is capable of receiving data.

Figure 6-25
BISYNC RVI

Sender		Receiver	Comment
SYN SYN ENQ	⟶		Line bid
		⟵ SYN SYN ACK0	Positive response
SYN SYN STX text ETB BCC	⟶		Data
		⟵ SYN SYN RVI	Reverse interrupt
SYN SYN STX text ETX BCC	⟶		Empty buffer
		⟵ SYN SYN ACK1	Acknowledgment
SYN SYN EOT	⟶		Transmit end
		⟵ SYN SYN ENQ	Line bid
SYN SYN ACK0	⟶		Positive response
		⟵ SYN SYN STX text ETB BCC	Priority message

Transparency

In its original use with RJE, the only BISYNC characters that needed to be transmitted were the control characters and displayable characters. As BI-SYNC's functions were expanded to include the transfer of binary data, transparency was added. Unfortunately this add-on solution was inelegant. Transparency means that any bit sequences can be included in the text, even those that are also used as control characters. Without transparency a data byte that looks like an ETX character would prematurely terminate the message, since the link protocol would interpret the two characters following the phony ETX as CRC, the CRC check would probably fail, and the block would be negatively acknowledged, thus causing the block to be retransmitted over and over until a retry limit was reached.

The data link escape (DLE) character is employed to provide transparency, essentially inserted before any control characters. That is, *DLE STX* initiates transparent mode, and *DLE ETX, DLE ETB, DLE ITB,* or a like sequence terminates the block. The DLE character can be used in this manner with the STX, ETB, ITB, ETX, ENQ, DLE, and SYN control characters.

This all seems rather straight forward, as if all that was needed was to frame the message with DLE STX and DLE ETX. Unfortunately, it is still possible to have within the text two adjacent characters that form a DLE

ETX sequence, which would prematurely terminate the message. The solution to this problem is to insert *DLE* before each *DLE* in the text. Thus, what has happened is that one character has been picked to represent transparency. Since this character may also appear in the text, it has to be accommodated within the text. The text is scanned for any DLE characters; for each one found, an additional *DLE* is inserted. The data stream is scanned on the receiving side as well, whenever two DLE characters are encountered next to each other, one is discarded, thus ensuring that the *only* DLE ETX sequence is at the end of the block. The insertion of *DLE* will, of course, change a DLE ETX data sequence into a DLE DLE ETX sequence. *DLE ETX* in this case is *not* construed as a termination. The DLE DLE grouping indicates that *DLE* is for data and not control. A before-and-after image of a sample text message is given in Figure 6-26.

Supplement 3
Synchronous Data Link Control

This SDLC discussion is focused on the control field functions and the Ns and Nr message sequencing concept. Transparency and loop configurations were briefly discussed earlier in the chapter; additional information regarding these subjects can be found in the IBM reference manuals on SDLC [IBM, 1979].

The control field provides the ability to designate the type of the frame—unnumbered, supervisory, or informational—and to acknowledge receipt of frames.

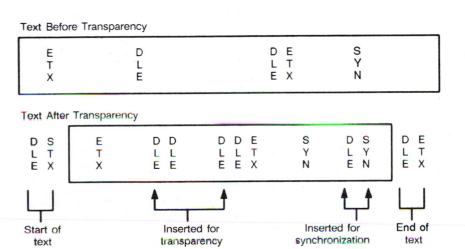

Figure 6-26
A Sample Text
Message

Unnumbered Frames

Unnumbered frames are used for control functions such as resetting a station's Ns and Nr counts to zero; causing stations on switched lines to disconnect; rejecting a frame received in error; and transmitting data such as broadcast or status messages that do not need a sequence check. The general format of the unnumbered control field is given in Figure 6-27. The first two bits—11—identify the frame as unnumbered. The code bits are used to identify the frame function, initialize station, reject frame, disconnect, and so on. The five bits allow for 32 different functions. The existing control functions for unnumbered frames are given in Figure 6-28.

Figure 6-27
Control Field Format:
Unnumbered Frame

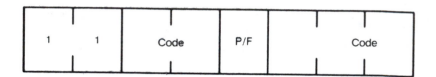

| 1 | 1 | Code | P/F | Code |

Figure 6-28
Unnumbered Control
Functions

Code for Unnumbered Control	Function
UI	Identifies an information frame as unnumbered.
SNRM	Sets normal response mode. Resets Ns and Nr count fields.
DISC	Places secondary station in disconnect mode.
RD	Indicates a secondary station request to disconnect.
UA	Signals a positive acknowledgment to an SNRM, DISC, or SIM command.
RIM	Indicates a secondary station request for initialization.
SIM	Primary initializes secondary. Ns and Nr counts are set to 0.
DM	Indicates that a secondary station is in disconnect mode.
FRMR	Signals that an invalid frame has been received.
TEST	Means that a test frame has been sent to a secondary station, which will respond with a test frame.
XID	Requests an ID exchange.

P/F Bit. The P/F (poll/final) bit, which is common to all of the control fields, is set when a station is being polled and when the final frame for a message is sent. Just as in BISYNC, messages can be broken into blocks for transmission; all but the last such block will have the P/F bit set to zero. The P/F bit also is used in loop configurations to specify optional and mandatory responses to polling.

Supervisory Frames

The control field format for the supervisory frame is given in Figure 6-29. The first two bits—10—designate the frame as supervisory. The P/F bit is as described above. The *receive count* field (explained below) is used to acknowledge receipt of frames. The *code* field is two bits wide and therefore can represent only four different control functions, three of which have been specified thus far. Two control functions are used to indicate whether the station is ready to receive (RR) or not ready to receive (RNR) data. The third control function (REJ) is used to reject a frame.

Information Frames

The information frame is the primary conveyer of data; its control field format is given in Figure 6-30. Unlike the other two types of frame, only the first bit—0—is used to designate the frame as informational. The P/F bit is as described above. The *send count* (Ns) and *receive count* (Nr) fields are each made up of three bits. As discussed earlier in the chapter (page 208), the Ns field is used by a station to count the number of messages sent to another station. The Nr field is a count kept by a receiving station of the number of messages received from another station. Each station maintains separate Ns and Nr count fields for each station with which it communicates. When a station is initialized by the supervisor, the Ns and Nr counts are set to zero, so the Nr count becomes the message number

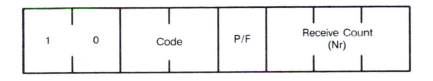

Figure 6-29
Control Field Format:
Supervisory Frame

Figure 6-30
Control Field Format:
Information Frame

the receiving station expects next. The first message sent is message number 0. After either count reaches 7, the next increment rolls the count over to zero, meaning that, at most, seven messages can be sent before an acknowledgment is necessary.

Example: How Ns and Nr Counts Are Used

This example illustrates the values of the address field, the frame type, the Ns and Nr counts, and the P/F bit, in that order.

Supervisor						Secondary Station				
Address	Frame Type	Ns Count	Nr Count	P/F Bit		Address	Frame Type	Ns Count	Nr Count	P/F Bit
A	RR	0	0	1	⟶					
					⟵	A	RR	0	0	1
B	RR	0	0	1	⟶					
					⟵	B	I	0	0	0 data
			1		⟵	B	I	1	0	0 data
			2		⟵	B	I	2	0	0 data
			3		⟵	B	I	3	0	1 data
B	RR	0	4	0	⟶					
C	RR	0	0	1	⟶					

The supervisor station polls the secondary stations. The supervisor uses a supervisory frame to indicate that it is ready to receive. The P/F bit is set to 1 to indicate that station A is being polled. The Nr count is set to zero, indicating that the next frame expected from station A is frame number 0. Station A has no data to send and thus responds with a supervisory frame indicating that it is ready to receive and that the next frame expected from the supervisor is frame number 0. The final bit is set to 1 in this instance to indicate that there are no data to send.

Station B is then polled. Station B does have data to transmit, and uses the information frame to do so. Four frames are required to transmit the entire message. For the first three frames the P/F bit is set to 0 to indicate that more frames will follow. The last frame in the message has the P/F bit set to 1. The Ns count for station B is incremented with each *message*. The Nr count is incremented following the receipt of each *frame*, although the supervisor sends no acknowledgement in this case until the final frame is received. On receiving the final frame, the supervisor acknowledges receipt of all messages at once with a supervisory frame. The P/F bit is not set on this frame, since station B is not being polled.

Much of the efficiency of bit-oriented data link protocols stems from their ability to transmit multiple frames without acknowledgment and to transmit in full duplex mode. This avoids the wait times required by other protocols like BISYNC, which require that each message be acknowledged before another may be sent.

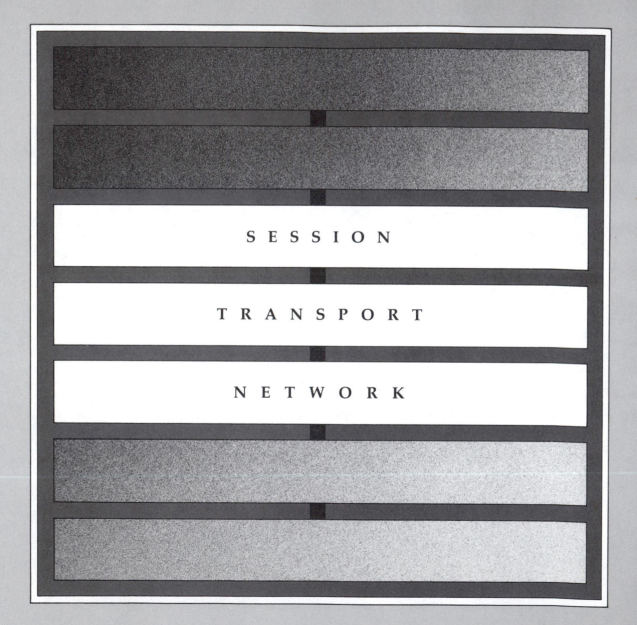

IV

NETWORKS AND SYSTEM SOFTWARE: THE NETWORK, TRANSPORT, AND SESSION LAYERS

7

Introduction to Networks and Packet Switching

INTRODUCTION

This chapter and the next move up one more step in the OSI layers, to discuss the network layer. At the conclusion of this chapter, you will be familiar with computer networks and the terminology specific to them, computer network routing algorithms, and network configurations. In addition, you will have knowledge of packet distribution networks and their advantages and disadvantages, as well as several specific packet switching systems.

TERMINOLOGY

Network/Node/Computer System.   The term *network* as used in Chapters 7 and 8 means a network of computer systems and their attached communications devices, such as terminals and multiplexers. The focus, however, is on computer-to-computer communications links. Each computer system is called a *node*; *computer system* is the term used rather than processor or computer because of the existence of multiple processor systems. Thus, a node is one or more processors that collectively serve as a termination point for a communications link with another node. The size of the node is immaterial to this discussion; it can be a large, mainframe system or a microcomputer system or any size in between.

Link-Path-Circuit.   A *link* is a circuit established between two adjacent nodes—that is, with no intervening nodes. A *path* is a group of links that allow a message to move from its point of origin to its destination. In this chapter, *circuit* refers to either a link or a path, depending on the context.

Session/User.   *Session* refers to a communications dialogue between two users of a network. A *user* can be a terminal operator, an application, or any other originator of messages. In some systems, sessions are quite formal, with well-defined conventions for establishing, continuing, and terminating the dialogue.

Packet Switching/Packet Distribution Network (PDN)/Circuit Switching.   *Packet switching* refers to the technology of transmitting a message in one or more fixed-length data packets. A packet switching network is also sometimes referred to as a *packet distribution network (PDN)*, *public data network* (also *PDN*), or *value-added network (VAN)*. Henceforth, the abbreviation *PDN* will be used. A PDN generally connects a user and the nearest node in the PDN. The PDN routes the data packets to their final destination either by finding the best route for each packet (packet switching) or by establishing a fixed path for the entire session, known as *circuit switching*. Telephone companies use circuit switching to establish switched communications. The path may not be the same each time, but only one path is used per session (except in the event of path failure).

Store and Forward.   In a *store-and-forward* system, messages are logged at nodes along the path and then forwarded to the next node. In some instances, the message is logged at each intermediate node in order to provide message accountability, a desirable feature for financial transactions involving large sums of money. Instead of having each node store the message, the message can be stored only at those nodes incapable of immediately forwarding the message, which is more typical of time-based message delivery systems such as electronic mail or systems where messages are given delivery priorities. In the latter case, a low-priority message can be stored temporarily while higher-priority messages are forwarded; the lower-priority messages can be forwarded when the congestion is cleared up.

Local Area Network (LAN)/Long-Distance Network.   There are two broad categories of networks, *local area networks (LAN)* and *long-distance networks*. An LAN is almost always privately controlled with respect to both data terminal equipment (processors, terminals, and so on) and data communications equipment (media, repeaters, and so on). An LAN serves a limited geographical area, typically within one building or building complex. The maximum allowable distance between nodes varies with the system, but it is generally a few miles. A long-distance network, on the other hand, usually consists of data terminal equipment owned or controlled by the user, together with data communications equipment provided by a common carrier. In a few instances long-distance networks have been implemented as totally private networks, as in the instance of a power distribution company that had already installed a network of private communications links. An LAN is depicted in Figure 7-1, and a long-distance network in Figure 7-2 on page 236.

Network Architecture/Topology.   The general configurations used to describe networks are sometimes referred to as *network architecture* or network *topology*. Several of the common topologies are described below, in the "Network Topology" section.

THE NETWORK LAYER

Functions of the Network Layer

The OSI network layer performs three major functions: network control, routing, and congestion control. Whereas the data link layer is concerned

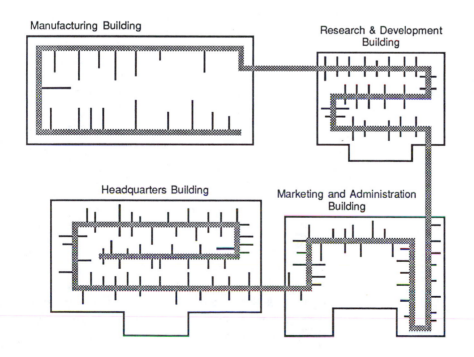

Figure 7-1
A Local Area Network Connecting Devices in a Building Complex

Figure 7-2
A Long Distance
Network

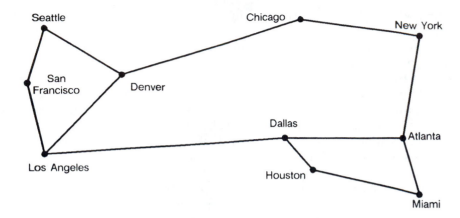

with getting data between two adjacent nodes, the network layer is concerned with end-to-end routing, or getting the data from originating node
to ultimate destination. Thus, the network layer must be aware of the
alternatives in paths, path selection, and addressing of messages.

Network control involves sending node status to other nodes and reacting to the status received from other nodes, which status information is
used to determine the best routing for messages. Where priorities of messages are allowed, it is the responsibility of the network layer to enforce
the priority scheme.

Congestion control means reducing transmission delays that might result
from overuse of some circuits or because a particular node in the network
is busy and unable to process messages in a timely fashion. The network
layer should adapt to these transient conditions and attempt to route messages around such points of congestion. Not all systems can adapt to the
changing characteristics of the communications links, however. In some
instances, specifically, broadcast-type systems, there is very little that can
be done to overcome this problem.

NETWORK TOPOLOGY

Network topologies come in several varieties, defined by the manner in
which the nodes are connected: star, hierarchical, interconnected, ring,
bus, or combinations of these.

Star Network

A star, or centralized, network is illustrated in Figure 7-3. In a *star network*,
one node serves as a message switch, accepting a message from one node
and forwarding it to the destination node.

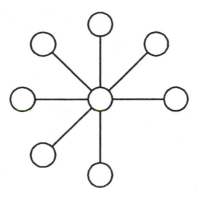

Figure 7-3
A Star Configuration

Advantages and Disadvantages.   A star configuration has several advantage. First, it makes for a short path between any two nodes, there being a maximum of two links, or hops, to traverse. And if the message is to go from the central node to a peripheral node, or vice versa, then only one hop is required. Thus, the time needed for a message to get from source to destination can be quite short. On the other hand, having the central node involved in the transmission of every message can lead to congestion at the central site, with consequent message delays, and exacerbated even further when the central node is functioning for more than just message switching. If, as is frequently the case, the central node is also the central processing system, higher-priority processing requirements could make the processor temporarily unable to attend to communications functions, which is more likely to occur in a uniprocessor system than in a multiple processor system.

A star configuration also provides the user with a high degree of network control. Since the central node is in direct contact with every other node, and all messages flow through it, a centralized location exists for message logging, gathering of network statistics, and error diagnostics and recovery. In some situations, however, this centralized control and dependence on a centralized system is considered a disadvantage rather than an advantage. In a network of computers from several different colleges, for instance, all of the peripheral nodes become somewhat subservient to the central node, which subservience may not be palatable to the computer centers at the other locations. Furthermore, the peripheral nodes may object to having communications between two peripheral nodes routed through the central node.

Expanding a star network is quite easy, for only the new node and the central node need be involved. All that is required is to obtain the communications link, connect the two, and update the network tables in the other nodes. Some instances also require that a new system generation be performed for the other nodes. If adding a new node exceeds the limits of memory allocated to the network routing tables, then a new system generation is usually required. For relatively dynamic networks it is common to allocate space for potential nodes in order to reduce the number of system generations that must be performed.

Star systems have a relatively low reliability. The loss of the central node is equivalent to loss of the network, and failure of a peripheral node has little impact on the network as a whole: Only messages bound for that node are undeliverable. The best candidate for central node is a fault-tolerant system, which is almost immune to failure.

Star systems have an additional disadvantage in a long-distance network: possibly higher circuit costs. This is exemplified in the case study in Chapter 5, in which the point-to-point configuration has a monthly circuit cost almost $1500 higher than that of the shortest path configuration.

Hierarchical Network

Hierarchical topology, shown in Figure 7-4, is also referred to as a tree structure. There is one root node (node A in Figure 7-4). Directly connected to node A are several nodes at the second level. Each of these can have a number of cascaded nodes attached. This type of network closely resembles corporate organization charts, and corporate computer centers are one instance in which this topology can be found: With the corporate computer center as root node, division systems are attached directly to the root, regional systems to divisional systems, districts to regions, and so on. Corporate reports from a lower level are easily consolidated at the next higher level, and the network generally mirrors the information flow pattern in the corporation. Thus, information flowing from a district in one division to a district in a different division would need to go through the root or corporate node. As with a star system, this allows for a great deal of network control.

Figure 7-4
A Hierarchical
Configuration

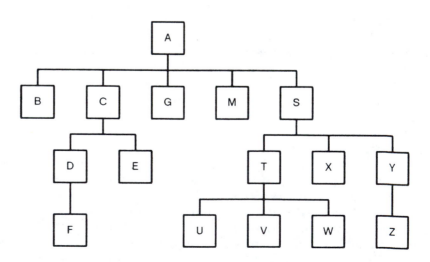

Advantages and Disadvantages.   Media costs for the hierarchical system are likely to be less than for star topology, assuming that the lower-level nodes are in closer proximity to the next higher level than they are to the root. It is possible, of course, to devise configurations in which media costs are higher than for a centralized system. The number of hops for a hierarchical system can be quite large. If node F in Figure 7-4 needed to send a message to node Z, the message would have to pass through six nodes (F→D→C→A→S→Y→Z). In hierarchical topology, the number of instances of this type of data transfer is presumably small compared to the number of messages that remain within one branch of the tree.

Expansion and reconfiguration of a hierarchical network can pose problems. For instance, in the configuration of Figure 7-4, to split node C into nodes C and K, with D and F under C, and E under K, would require more work than in the star configuration. Node K would have to be linked to node A, node E unlinked from C and relinked to K. Although this may not sound difficult, it costs time and money to change circuits from one location to another, especially with circuits provided by a common carrier. As with most configuration changes, network routing tables must be updated, and a system or network regeneration may be needed.

Failure of the root node in a hierarchical configuration is less costly than in a star configuration, but it does present a serious problem of reliability. In fact, the failure of any node other than those at the extremities will make it impossible to reach it or any of its subordinate nodes. Congestion at the root and higher-level nodes is also a potential problem.

Interconnected (Plex) Network

Two forms of interconnected (*plex*) architecture are portrayed in Figure 7-5 on page 240. In the fully interconnected network (Figure 7-5(a)), every node is connected to every other node with which it must communicate. In the past, fully interconnected topology was required because the available network software was not sophisticated enough to perform the routing and forwarding functions. The more typical topology does not require all nodes to be connected. Message traffic patterns are used to determine where links should be installed. As might be expected, the cost of the links in a fully interconnected network is high. The number of links required for an interconnected network of n nodes is $\dfrac{n(n-1)}{2}$.

Advantages and Disadvantages.   The performance of an interconnected system is generally quite good, since direct links can be established between nodes with high amounts of data to exchange. Costs can also be controlled because interconnected topology is capable of the shortest or least expensive configuration. In fact, any of the other topology types can be mimicked by an interconnected topology, although routing and control mechanisms would probably be different.

Figure 7-5
Interconnected
Configurations

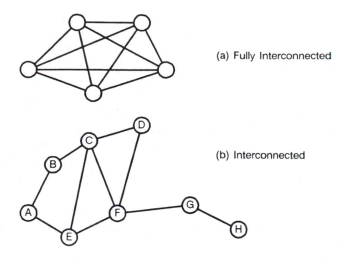

(a) Fully Interconnected

(b) Interconnected

The expandability of interconnected configurations ranges from terrible to good, depending on where the new node is inserted. In a fully interconnected network, expansion is costly and time-consuming because a link must be established to every node with which the new node must communicate. Yet, adding a node at the extremity of the network is quite simple, such as node H in Figure 7-5(b).

The impact of node failure depends on the specific configuration. In some instances, alternate paths around a failed node are available, such as node C in Figure 7-5(b). The loss of node F in the figure will isolate nodes G and H from the rest of the network. Since all nodes in interconnected topology are equal, control is distributed rather than centralized.

Ring Network

Ring architecture is depicted in Figure 7-6. The typical ring configuration has data flowing in one direction around the ring, especially true in local area networks. In some implementations, the use of two channels allows data to flow in both directions. The usual ring implementation uses either carrier sense with multiple access (CSMA) or token passing to determine which station is allowed to transmit information. Token passing and CSMA were discussed in Chapter 6. In a ring network, one node might be designated as the primary station and the others as secondary stations, as required in the SDLC ring configuration. This implementation is generally referred to as a *loop* rather than a *ring*. However, all nodes are typically at the same level of priority, and consequently there is less control than in the star and hierarchical topologies. This can be advantageous or disadvantageous, depending on the user's perspective. Some users prefer a considerable amount of central control over their network. All enhancements and monitoring are done centrally. Other users view the nodes as

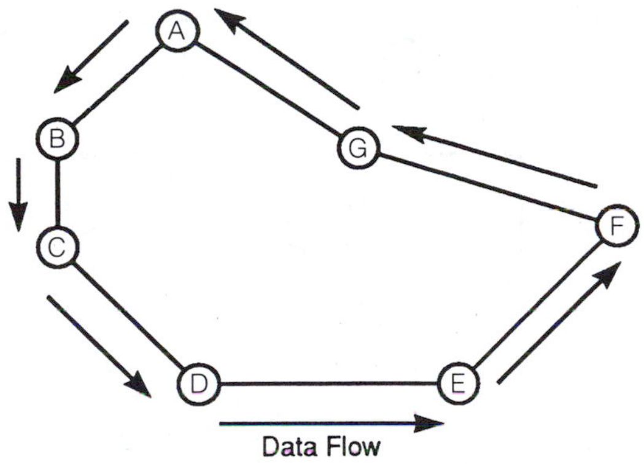

Figure 7-6
A Ring Configuration

Data Flow

autonomous entities and central control is undesirable. One node is thus allowed to make any local changes which do not affect the network.

The number of hops a message must take is a function of the number of nodes in the network, n. On the average, a message must pass through $n/2$ links. When token passing is used, it serves as a flow control mechanism, and congestion is not as apparent as with star, hierarchical, or interconnected architectures.

Reliability of the ring is high, assuming that messages are routed to the next node when one node fails—that is, the ring remains unbroken, which is the usual case. Thus, when a node fails, only that particular node is lost, and all other nodes can communicate as usual.

Expandability is easily achieved with ring architecture. Only the two adjacent nodes are physically affected; one link must be abandoned and two new ones added.

Ring architecture usually costs less than the star or hierarchical network. The links are usually chosen to minimize media costs.

Bus Network

Bus architecture is like a ring, but without the ends being connected. A bus, shown in Figure 7-7 on page 242, is defined as a conductive medium to which multiple devices (in this case nodes) can be connected. Bus topology and ring topologies are common in local area networks. In the usual implementation, all nodes on the bus are equal, so control is distributed. The number of hops is irrelevant to the bus configuration in an LAN, since all nodes are connected to the same medium. Token passing and CSMA access can both be used. The most common bus implementation currently is CSMA.

Advantages and Disadvantages. Reliability on bus networks is good, unless the bus itself fails. The loss of one node has no effect on any of the

Figure 7-7
A Bus Configuration

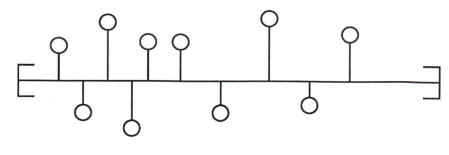

Figure 7-8
A Bus Configuration
with Spurs

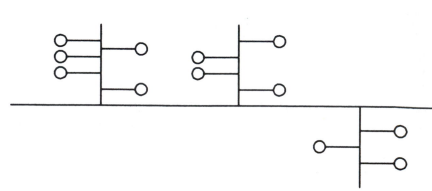

other nodes. Cost comparisons with other topologies do not make much sense, since bus architecture is limited to an LAN.

Expandability is excellent with bus architecture. All that is required to add a new node is to tap into the medium. The ability to add new nodes is one of the strengths of bus architecture.

Bus Configuration with Spurs.   Another LAN topology can be derived from bus interconnections; this is illustrated by Figure 7-8. The different branches, or spurs, might represent cables on different floors in a building or in different buildings. These individual buses are connected to a common bus. If the distances involved are great, repeaters must be used to enhance the signals.

Combination Networks

Combinations of the above topologies are sometimes integrated into one network. One such combination is a backbone network—for instance, a ring—with spurs attached. The backbone nodes can be dedicated to message transfer and data communications while the other nodes are used for both data processing and data communications. In widely distributed systems with a large number of nodes, this helps reduce the number of hops, the length of the links, and congestion problems. If the backbone is implemented as a ring or with multiple paths available, reliability is also high.

Summary of Network Topologies

Figure 7-9 summarizes the different types of topology with respect to cost, control, number of hops (speed), reliability, and expandability.

Topology Type	Cost	Control	Number of Hops	Reliability	Expandability
Star	Can be high	Very good	Maximum of two	Poor	Good
Hierarchical	Can be high	Good	Can be many	Fair	Fair to good
Interconnected					
Full	Highest	Distributed	One only	Good	Very poor
Other	Can be lowest	Distributed	Can be many	Good	Good
Ring	Good	Distributed	Can be many	Good	Good
Bus	Good	Distributed	N/A	Good	Good

Figure 7-9 Network Topology Characteristics

MESSAGE ROUTING

Routing, one of the functions of the network layer, is achievable through a number of algorithms used to direct messages from the point of origination to final destination. Determination of message routing can be either centralized or distributed. Routing itself can be either static, adaptive, or broadcast, and is governed by a network routing table resident at each node. The network routing table is a matrix of other nodes together with the link or path to that node. Thus, if a message destined for node X arrives at node K, the network routing table is consulted for the next node on the path from K to X. Network routing tables can also contain more information than just the next link, e.g. congestion statistics. The following discussion does not cover all varieties of routing techniques. For more detail, the reader is referred to Tanenbaum (1981) and Kuo (1981).

Centralized Routing Determination:
The Network Routing Manager

In centralized determination of routing tables, one node is designated as the network routing manager to whom all nodes periodically forward such status information as queue lengths on outgoing and incoming lines and the number of messages processed within the most recent time interval. The routing manager is thereby provided with an overview of network functioning, where bottlenecks are occurring, and where facilities are under utilized. The routing manager periodically recalculates the optimal paths between nodes and constructs and distributes new routing tables to all nodes.

Disadvantages of Centralized Routing Determination. The disadvantages of this form of network routing are manifold. That the routing manager can receive many messages from the other nodes increases the probability of congestion, a problem that can be exacerbated if the routing manager is itself a node used to accept and forward messages. And networks are sometimes subject to transient conditions such as when the internode transfer of a file saturates a link for a short period of time. By the time this information is relayed to the routing manager and a new routing is calculated, the activity may have already ceased, making the newly calculated path less than optimal. And some nodes will receive the newly calculated routing tables before others, leading to inconsistencies in how messages are to be routed. For example, suppose that under the old routing mechanism the route was A→B→D→X, whereas the new path is A→C→D→X, as indicated in Figure 7-10. Also, the new path from node B to node X is B→A→C→D→X. Now, if node B receives its new routing chart while node A is still using the old chart, then for a message destined from A to X, A will route it to B and B will route it back to A, continuing until A receives the new routing table. In addition, transmission of the routing tables themselves may bias the statistics being gathered to compute the next routing algorithm.

An additional problem with centralized route calculations is the amount of processing power needed—a considerable amount of CPU time could be consumed. Reliability of the routing manager is also an important factor. If this node fails, then either the routing remains unchanged until the system is recovered, or an alternate routing manager must be selected. The best situation is to have alternate routing managers available in case the primary routing node fails. This is implemented most easily by having the routing manager send the alternates "I'm alive" messages at predefined intervals; if the backup manager fails to receive this message within the prescribed interval, it assumes the manager has failed and takes over, its first responsibility being to broadcast the fact that network status messages should now be routed to it.

Figure 7-10
A Network
Configuration

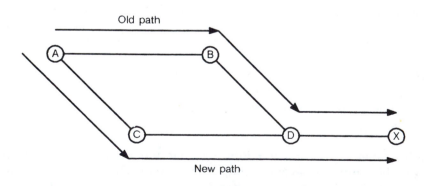

Distributed Routing Determination

Distributed routing determination relies on each node to calculate its own best routing table, which requires each node to periodically transmit its status to its neighbors. As this information ripples through the network, each node updates its tables accordingly. This technique avoids the potential bottleneck at a centralized route manager, although the time required for changes to flow through all of the nodes may be quite long.

Static Routing

The purest form of static routing involves always using one particular path between two nodes; if a link in that path is down, then communication between those nodes is impossible. Fully interconnected networks sometimes used to utilize this approach. That is, there was only one path between any two nodes—the link between them; if the link was down, the available network software was incapable of using any of the potentially alternate paths. Fortunately, that type of system has largely disappeared. In general, static routing now refers to the situation in which a selected path is used until some drastic condition makes it unavailable, at which time an alternate path is selected and used, until manually switched or a failure occurs on the alternate path or the original path is restored.

Weighted Routing. When multiple paths exist, some implementations weight each path according to perceived utilization. The path is then randomly selected from the weighted alternatives. For example, Figure 7-11 shows three paths from node A to node X, via nodes B, C, and D. Suppose the network designers had determined that the path through node B would be best 50% of the time, through node C would be best 30% of the time, and through node D would be best 20% of the time. When a message is to be sent from node A to node X, a random number between 0 and 1 is generated: If the random number is 0.50 or less, the path through node B is traversed; if the random number is greater than 0.50 and less than or

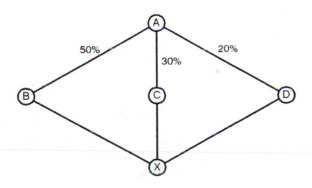

Figure 7-11
Weighted Routing

equal to 0.80 then the path through node C is selected; otherwise the path through node D is selected. The path may alternate, but each path is used with the same frequency as in the routing tables. This type of routing can only be changed by altering the route weighting in the routing tables.

Adaptive Routing

Adaptive routing is occasionally referred to as dynamic routing. (Although in some instances a distinction is made between these two terms, this text makes no such distinction. Adaptive routing differs from static routing by attempting to select the best current route for the message or session, being defined by several different parameters.

Quickest Link.   The simplest adaptive routing algorithm is to have a node pass along the message as quickly as possible, with the only restriction being to not pass it back to the sending node. Thus, the receiving node looks at all potential outbound links, selects the one with the least amount of activity, and sends the message out on that line. There is no attempt to determine if that path will bring the message closer to its destination. This type of algorithm is not very efficient and will cause messages to be shuffled to more nodes than necessary, thereby adding to network congestion. The message could conceivably be shifted around the network for hours before arriving at its destination.

Best Route.   The more intelligent adaptive routing techniques attempt to select the best route, as determined by one or more of the following parameters: the number of required hops, the speed of the links, the type of link, and congestion. Routing of this type requires current information on the status of the network. If a node is added to the network or if one is taken off the network, that information must be relayed to the nodes doing route calculation. Knowing the speed of the links as well as the number of hops is important. Traversing two links at 4800 bps is more costly than traversing one link at 2400 bps. The line time for both will be the same, but some time is lost in receiving and forwarding the message. Avoiding congested areas will prevent messages from being stuck on inbound and outbound queues. In the configuration of Figure 7-12, if node B is transmitting a file to adjacent node C, the route from node A to node C through B is the shortest but probably not the quickest at that time. The route through nodes E and D would be more efficient, since the link from B to C is congested.

Examples of Route Selection Algorithms

Tandem EXPAND Network.   The Tandem EXPAND network uses a routing mechanism that is dynamic in nature—that is, lying somewhere between static routing, where routes seldom change, and adaptive routing,

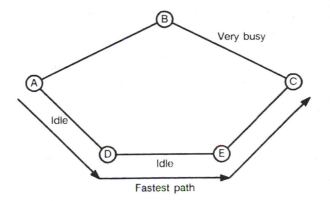

Figure 7-12
Routing Based on
Congestion

where routes can change frequently. Each link in the network is given a weighting based on its speed. Each node maintains a network routing table containing information about the paths to all other nodes. The best route —determined from the speed of the link and the number of hops that must be traversed—remains in effect until the topology of the network changes. Thus, when a node is added to or removed from the system, the information regarding its links is broadcast to all other nodes in the network, thereby updating the network routing tables and potentially changing paths. Link failures are also reported to other nodes so routing tables can be changed. Congestion is not considered in determining the best route, only the current information on the addition or deletion of nodes and changes in the active status of links. When the best link is down, an alternate next-best link is automatically selected. When the preferred link is returned to service, the network automatically switches back to it. It is also possible to define multiple links between two nodes.

In EXPAND, a path is not altered unless the topology changes. The only accommodation made for congestion is the ability to add multiple links between two nodes. The multiple links will be shared, allowing a higher rate of data exchange between the nodes.

TYMNET. In *TYMNET,* a packet switching network, every request for a connection causes a route for that session to be determined, centrally. Once established, the route remains static for that session, unless there is a path failure, in which case a new route is established. Each link in the TYMNET system is rated with respect to capacity, link type, and congestion. These factors are coupled with the application type to determine the best path. Thus, a satellite will be highly rated for the transfer of large volumes of data in which response time is not critical, such as file transfers and large outputs to a printer. Terrestrial links carry more weight for conversational types of sessions. These factors are periodically forwarded to the route manager node from the other nodes. Congestion or loading is also used to evaluate routes. If a node has reported that it is extremely busy, then the routing calculations will give a higher weight to less busy nodes.

ARPANET. *ARPANET,* the first packet switching network, originally used an adaptive routing with distributed determination. Each node, called an interface message processor (IMP), computed its own routing table. The routing table contained the expected time to reach each destination plus the amount of time to reach each of its neighbors. Periodically, each IMP would transmit its routing table to each of its neighbors. An IMP would evaluate the routing table received from its neighbor; if it determined that the time to get to that neighbor plus the time the neighbor had to get to a specific destination was less than the current IMP's time to get to that destination, then the routing table was updated. For instance, suppose that node A's path to node X requires 500 milliseconds to traverse, that the next node on the path is node B, and that node A has determined that the access time to neighbor node C is 50 milliseconds, then when A receives node C's routing table, it will search every entry to calculate path times, and if C's path time to node X is less than 450 milliseconds, A will update its routing table to reflect this lower time, the time to C plus C's time to X.

ARPANET's routing technique had one major flaw, messages sometimes would get stuck in loops between nodes because of inconsistencies in routing tables. As a result the above implementation was abandoned in favor of a newer one. The current strategy is still a distributed version, with nodes transmitting their path calculations to adjacent nodes. Added to the prior version is a database maintained by each node of the network topology and an increased routing table exchange interval, which has eliminated the looping problems.

Broadcast Routing

A third type of routing is broadcast routing, exemplified by the CSMA/CD type of link protocol discussed in the preceding chapter. Routing is quite easy, the message is broadcast to all stations, and only the station to whom the message is addressed accepts it. Token passing, described in the previous chapter, is most commonly used in ring architectures: the data flow in one directional only, being passed from node to node along the medium until the destination is encountered, at which point the receiving node removes the message. Alternatively the message is passed back to the originator as an acknowledgment, and the originator then removes the message and passes the token to its neighbor. The network layer of the OSI recommendation has little function in broadcast routing and token passing networks.

INTERCONNECTION AND GATEWAYS

Since 1970, the computer industry has been very active in implementing both long-distance and local area networks. Despite attempts at standardization, no standard has yet gained acceptance. In some respects this is fortunate, since early in the development of a concept is rarely the time to standardize. Unfortunately, however, there now exist a multitude of different implementations and frequently a need to interface them. In fact, it was recognition of this need that gave rise to the OSI reference model.

The types of networks that need to be connected are: one local network to another, a local network to a long-distance network, and a long-distance network to another long-distance network. When networks are connected, the networks can be heterogeneous, or they can be homogeneous, such as when two local area networks of the same type are connected because each has been extended to the maximum allowable length or because they are owned by separate entities.

Bridges

An interconnection between like networks is referred to as a *bridge*, which is relatively simple compared to a connection between heterogeneous networks. The function of a bridge that connects two homogeneous networks—say, A and B—is first to monitor all messages from network A with messages addressed to nodes in B, and second, to accept those network A messages with network B destinations and transmit them to network B. Of course, the bridge does the same for network B messages destined for network A. This situation is depicted in Figure 7-13.

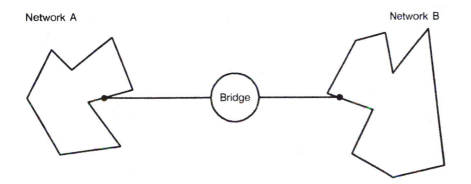

Figure 7-13
A Bridge Network Interconnection

Network A & B are of the same type, e.g. packet switching networks.

Interconnecting Heterogeneous Networks

In the heterogeneous case, the interconnnection may be complicated by differences between the lower two levels of the OSI recommendations: At the physical level the electrical signals and connectors may differ, and at the data link level there may be gross differences in message format (such as HDLC on one side and BISYNC on the other), error detection, addressing, message headers, and so on. Differences might exist at higher OSI levels as well.

There are even more extreme differences when connecting a long-distance network to a local area network. The speed of an LAN is quite high, typically over 1 Mbps, whereas the speed of long-distance links is frequently 9.6 Kbps or slower. This difference alone places a large burden on the interconnection system, which must serve as a large buffer to exchange data from high-speed to low-speed devices. In addition, there are likely to be differences in message size, addressing, data link protocol, error detection, and flow control. More subtle differences might be found in the message acknowledgment conventions and error rates and recovery. The LAN may require all messages to be acknowledged, and within a short period of time, whereas acknowledgment in the long-distance network may be for multiple messages, with a relatively long acknowledgment interval.

Gateways

The interface between two different networks is called a *gateway*. A gateway functions to reconcile the differences between the two networks, as pictured in Figure 7-14. The functional components of the gateway are the network interfaces and the translator process that forms the heart of the gateway.

Example of a Network Gateway Interconnection.   A corporation with the same type of local area networks in its Milwaukee and St. Louis offices

Figure 7-14
A Gateway Interface

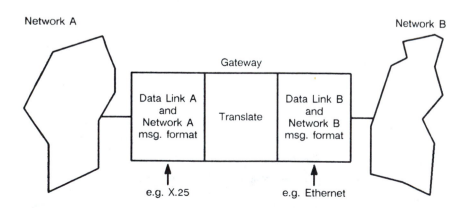

desires to connect the two LANs with a long-distance network link so that electronic mail, document images, and data can be exchanged, as presented in Figure 7-15. There are two gateways, one in Milwaukee and the other in St. Louis. To further simplify matters, the connection between the two is a single communications link with a speed of 9600 bps using an HDLC data link protocol. To transmit a 10,000-character document image from Milwaukee to St. Louis, the LAN formats the message as though the recipient were local. This requires that both the sending and receiving addresses be present and use a 32-bit CRC for error detection, a data field of 1500 characters, and a transmission speed of 10 Mbps. (This is essentially a description of an Ethernet LAN; see Chapter 8.)

The gateway machine that is monitoring all messages in the Milwaukee LAN detects the message with a St. Louis address, accepts it, and translates it into HDLC format. (The sending station's address is probably included at the beginning of the data.) The message can be broken into smaller blocks and transmitted to the St. Louis gateway machine, where the opposite procedure is performed to make the message acceptable to the St. Louis LAN. Meanwhile, back in Milwaukee, the additional message frames are arriving at a pace greater than the long-distance channel can accommodate, which means that the gateway in Milwaukee must either buffer these messages or hold the sender off until the first frame is com-

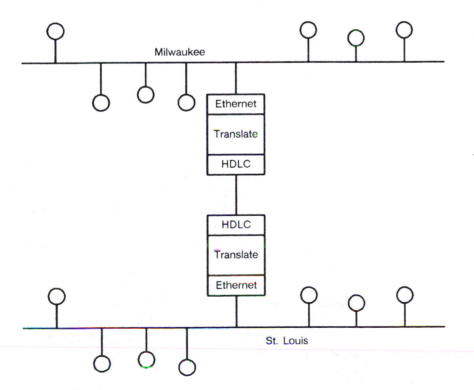

Figure 7-15
A Gateway

pletely transmitted. A combination of both procedures could also be used; that is, the gateway could accept data until the buffer was full and then hold off further frames. Alternatively, the gateway could operate in a store-and-forward manner.

More detailed information regarding network interconnections can be found in the September 1983 issue of *Computer* (vol. 16, no. 9), which features network interconnection problems and solutions. Network interconnection promises to be one of the great challenges facing the data communications industry in the near future.

PACKET DISTRIBUTION NETWORKS

The concept of a packet distribution network was first introduced in 1964 by Paul Baran of the Rand Corporation. Baran defined a process of segmenting a message into maximum-size packets, routing the packets to their destination, and reassembling them to recreate the message. In 1966, Donald Davies of the National Physics Laboratory in Great Britain published details of a store-and-forward packet switching network. In 1967, plans were formulated for what is believed to be the first packet switching network, ARPANET, which became operational in 1969, with four nodes (since expanded to more than 125 nodes).

All packets in a packet distribution network are of a fixed size, often 128 or 256 characters. Eliminating variations in packet size makes management of buffers less of a problem and evens out the message traffic patterns.

Terminology

A packet distribution network (PDN) is variously referred to as an *X.25 network, a packet switching network, a value-added network (VAN)*, or a *public data network*. Packet distribution and packet switching both refer to the manner in which data is transmitted—that is, as one or more packets with a fixed maximum length. The X.25 designation stems from CCITT's recommendation X.25, which defines the "interface between *data terminal equipment (DTE)* and *data circuit-terminating equipment (DCE)* for terminals operating in the packet mode on public data networks" [Tanenbaum, 1981]. The term *public data network*, which derives from the X.25 recommendation, is somewhat of a misnomer, since packet switching networks have also been implemented in the private sector. The term *value-added network* is applied because the network proprietor adds not only a communications link, but message routing, packet control, store-and-forward capability, network management, compatibility between devices, and error recovery.

PDNs and the OSI Layers

Only three OSI layers—physical, data link, and network—have been described for PDNs, because a PDN is responsible for message delivery. Although all seven OSI layers exist for the user, the application, presentation, session, and transport layer functions are the responsibility of the user portion of the network. The functions of the physical and data link layers have already been described (Parts 2 and 3). The network layer is responsible for message sequencing, flow control, call setup and clearing, and internetwork connection. Message sequence numbers provide message accountability and allow reordering of packets. Call setup and clearing functions establish and delete message paths.

Current PDN Implementations

The use of PDNs has increased significantly since the first PDN was established, and most countries that use computers currenty have access to at least one. In the United States, in addition to the privately implemented ARPANET, there are General Telephone and Electronics Corporation (GTE) *TELENET* and Tymshare Corporation's *TYMNET*. Implementations outside of the United States include *DATAPAC* in Canada, *TRANSPAC* in France, *EURONET* in Europe (essentially an extension of *TRANSPAC*), Britain's Packet Switching Service (*PSS*), West Germany's *DATEX-P*, and Japan's Nippon Telephone and Telegraph (NTT) *DDX-2* system. Interconnections exist between these networks, providing international networking capabilities at a reasonable cost.

The general configuration of a PDN is given in Figure 7-16 on page 254. A number of the CCITT recommendations, covering different aspects of PDN access and use are listed in the figure at the points where they apply; the function of each is described below.

The terminal in a PDN can be a computer, a terminal, or any entity requiring data transmisssion services, even another network, although the point of interface would then be a processor of some type.

Connection Options

A PDN provides up to three types of connection options: the permanent virtual circuit, the switched virtual circuit, and datagram service.

Permanent Virtual Circuit. A *permanent virtual circuit (PVC)*—is usually selected when two nodes require almost continuous connection. A PVC is akin to a leased communications link, as described in Chapter 2.

Switched Virtual Circuit. The second connection option, which is the most common, is a *switched virtual circuit (SVC)*. When a session is established between two users, an end-to-end circuit is determined and allo-

Figure 7-16
A PDN General
Configuration

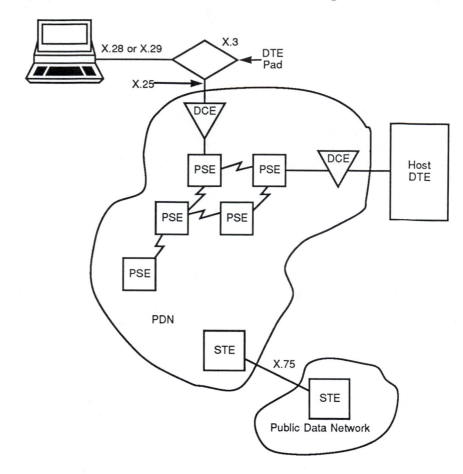

cated for the duration of the session; this is analogous to a switched communications link.

Datagram Service. The third type of connection option is a *datagram*, which is a message that fits into the data field of one packet. Since a temporary path is established for each datagram, two datagrams from the same source can have two different circuits established. Datagram service, which avoids the overhead of establishing a virtual circuit, has the potential for fast service for short, isolated messages.

Certain features of datagrams make them undesirable for many applications. First, the arrival order of datagrams is not guaranteed, since each datagram sent by a particular node may take a different route. Second, and more important, arrival itself is not guaranteed, since the PDN establishes datagram arrival queue depths, and a datagram is discarded if the queue is full when the datagram arrives. This problem is compounded by the fact that recovery of lost datagrams is the responsibility of the user, not the PDN, making datagrams best suited to messages of relatively low importance and messages where speed is more critical than the possibility of loss, such as in process control environments and certain military situations. In process control, for example, an imminent nuclear reactor meltdown is time-critical, and the time to set up a virtual circuit in an attempt to avert the problem may be too long. Datagram service, though included in the X.25 standard, has seldom been implemented in existing systems.

Example of a Packet Distribution Network

This example follows a message as it proceeds from the starting terminal to its destination address, using the typical case of switched virtual circuit connection.

Establishing the Virtual Circuit.   The user connects to the PDN by dialing the nearest PDN access port (a local telephone call in most large cities). After a log-in procedure, the address of the other node is supplied. The PDN then goes through the process of establishing the virtual circuit. The call establishment sequence is as follows:

A **call request** packet is sent from the sending node to the receiver. The call request is delivered to the receiver as an **incoming call** packet. The receiver may accept or reject the call.

If the receiver wishes to accept the connection, it transmits a **call accepted** packet that is presented to the sender as a **call connected** message. This establishes the connection, and data exchange may begin.

To terminate the connection, either node can transmit a **clear request** to the other. The recipient of the clear request acknowledges the disconnect with a **clear confirmation** control packet.

Data Exchange.   Once the virtual circuit has been established, data exchange can begin. The recommended data link protocol is *link access procedure, version B (LAPB)*, an HDLC-type protocol (see Chapter 6). There are also other data link protocols that have been specified for use on an interim basis, since there are so many pieces of data terminal equipment that do not support LAPB. The data portion of the frame is restricted to a specific maximum length, recommended at 128 octets, with 16, 32, 64, 256, 512, and 1024 specified as options. The Ns and Nr fields are defaulted to three bits each, as in SDLC, but they may optionally be expanded to seven bits. In the defaulted situation, up to seven frames can go unacknowledged, although the X.25 specification recommends that no more than three be sent before acknowledgment. This acknowledgment limit can be altered at the discretion of the implementer, and would almost always be increased when the Ns and Nr fields are expanded to seven bits.

The PDN uses a portion of the data field for control information—circuit addressing, packet sequence numbers, and packet confirmation. Three or four octets are used in information packets for this purpose, four when the sequence numbers are 7-bit entities.

Packet Assembly/Disassembly (PAD).   The first step in sending the data is to assemble the packets, a function performed by a *packet assembly/disassembly (PAD)* module. The PAD function is not considered a part of the PDN; rather, it is the responsibility of the data terminal equipment. However, since many of the terminals used in PDNs lack the intelligence to perform this function, most PDNs still provide this capability. PAD functions are specified in the CCITT X.3 standard. The PAD acts on one end to transform a message into one or more packets of the required length, and then reassembles the message at the other end. The PAD is also responsible for generating and monitoring control signals such as call setup and clearing.

Once the message has been transformed into packets, the packets are passed to the PDN in accordance with the X.25 interface. The PDN then moves the data through the network for delivery to the destination. The standards do not discuss the internal workings within the PDN, such as routing and congestion control. The receiving PAD takes the information form the data portion of the packet and reassembles the message.

PDN Equipment

Two types of machines have been defined for use within a PDN: packet switching equipment (PSE), which accepts and forwards messages, and signaling terminal equipment (STE), which is used to interface two different PDNs according to CCITT standard X.75.

Advantages and Disadvantages of the PDN

PDNs have several advantages. For one, the user is charged for the amount of data transmitted rather than for connect time. Applications that send low volumes of data over a relatively long period of time will find the charges for a PDN lower than for either leased lines or switched lines. The PDN also gives access to many different locations without the cost of switched connections, which usually involve a charge for the initial connection plus a per-minute use fee. Access to the PDN is usually via a local telephone call, which also reduces costs (that is, until telephone companies begin using measured billing). Maintenance of the network and error recovery are the responsibilities of the PDN.

There are also disadvantages to using a PDN. Because the PDN is usually shared, users must compete with each other for circuits. Thus, it is possible for message traffic from other users to impede the delivery of a message. In the extreme case, a virtual circuit to the intended destination may even be unobtainable. This is also true for a switched connection from a common carrier. If the number of data packets to be transferred is great, then the cost of using a PDN can exceed that of leased facilities. Because the PDN is controlled by its proprietor, the individual user is unable to make changes that might benefit an individual application, such as longer messages or larger packets, longer message acknowledgment intervals, and higher transmission speeds, all set by the PDN administrators.

SUMMARY

This general overview of networks started by defining a number of terms common to all networks. It then looked at several ways in which network systems could be configured, and discussed a number of routing algorithms. Following that it looked at several specific networks and the routing algorithms they use, and then briefly reviewed the problems associated with network interconnection.

Packet distribution networks have evolved into an efficient, effective networking alternative to private networks. PDNs offer circuit acquisition, message routing, error detection, correction, and maintenance. Interconnection of PDNs provides users with an instant international network. The cost of a PDN is reasonable so long as the number of data packets being transferred is low. However, this advantage comes at the price of contending with other users for the facility and a lack of control over network operations. The success of packet switching networks has made them a potential standard for future network implementations as well as for gateways between different network systems.

Key Terms

ARPANET	Packet distribution network (PDN)
Bridge	Packet switching network
Circuit	Path
Circuit switching	Permanent virtual circuit (PVC)
Computer system	Plex
Data circuit-terminating equipment (DCE)	Public data network
	Session
Data terminal equipment (DTE)	Star network
Datagram	Store and forward
DATAPAC	TELENET
Gateway	Topology
Local area network (LAN)	TRANSPAC
LAPB	TYMNET
Link	User
Long-distance network	Value-added network (VAN)
Network	Virtual circuit
Network architecture	X.3
Node	X.25 network
Packet Assembly/Disassembly (PAD)	X.75

Questions and Exercises

1. Why are there only three layers defined for PDNs? Do the other OSI layers exist? Explain.

2. What are the advantages and disadvantages of centralized routing calculations?

3. What are the advantages and disadvantages of local route determination?

4. List two network configurations for which calculation of routes is not required. Why is it unnecessary to determine a message route in each of these configurations?

5. How does a bridge differ from a gateway?

6. What functions are performed by a gateway?

7. What functions are performed by a bridge?

8. Why is datagram service generally unsuited to business applications?

9. Are there any business applications for which datagram service is useful? If so, list them.

10. Would a PDN be a suitable network for the Syncrasy Corporation's network of catalog and discount stores (see Chapter 5)? What would be the advantages and disadvantages of using a PDN for that application?

References

"Banking on Packet Switching." *Computerworld on Communications* 17 (September 28, 1983).

Benhamou, Eric, and Estrin, Judy. "Multilevel Internetworking Gateways: Architecture and Applications." *Computer* 16 (September 1983).

Edwards, Jeri. *Network Protocols*. Cupertino, CA: Tandem Computers, Inc., September 1982.

Freeman, Harvey A. "Network Interconnection." *Computer* 16 (September 1983).

Hanson, David. "Building Up Value-Added Nets." *Computerworld on Communications* 18 (June 6, 1984).

Hinden, Robert, Haverty, Jack, and Sheltzer, Alan. "The DARPA Internet: Interconnecting Heterogeneous Computer Networks with Gateways." *Computer* 16 (September 1983).

Institute of Electrical and Electronic Engineers (IEEE). *Computer Networks: A Tutorial*. Document no. EH0162-8. Geneva, Switzerland: IEEE Computer Society, 1980.

International Telegraph and Telephone Consultative Committee (CCITT). *CCITT Recommendation X.3, Packet Assembly/Disassembly Facility (PAD) in a Public Data Network*. Geneva, Switzerland: CCITT, 1980.

_____ *CCITT Recommendation X.25*. Geneva, Switzerland: CCITT, June 1980.

_____ *CCITT Recommendation X.28, DTE/DCE Interface for a Start-Stop Mode Data Terminal Equipment Accessing the Packet Assembly/Disassembly Facility (PAD) in a Public Data Network Situated in the Same Country*. Geneva, Switzerland: CCITT, 1980.

_____ *CCITT Recommendation X.29, Procedures for the Exchange of Control Information and User Data Between a Packet Assembly/Disassembly Facility (PAD) and a Packet Mode DTE or Another PAD*. Geneva, Switzerland: CCITT, 1980.

Kuo, Franklin F. *Protocols and Techniques for Data Communications Networks*. Englewood Cliffs, NJ: Prentice-Hall, 1981.

Redell, David D., and White, James E. "Interconnecting Electronic Mail Systems." *Computer* 16 (September 1983).

Schneidewind, Norman. "Interconnecting Local Networks to Long-Distance Networks." *Computer* 16 (September 1983).

Tanenbaum, Andrew S. *Computer Networks*. Englewood Cliffs, NJ: Prentice-Hall, 1981.

_____ "Network Protocols." *Association for Computing Machinery (ACM) Computing Surveys* 13 (December 1981).

Thornton, James E., and Christensen, Gary S. "Hyperchannel Network Links." *Computer* 16 (September 1983).

Wen-Ning and Gitman, Israel. "Routing Strategies in Computer Networks." *Computer* 17 (June 1984).

Supplement
Packet Distribution Networks

This supplement covers CCITT standards X.3, X.28, and X.25, and omits discussing standards X.75 and X.29. CCITT standards X.28, X.29, X.3, and X.25. cover the interface between data terminal equipment (DTE) and data circuit-terminating equipment (DCE) in a single packet distribution network. Standard X.75 covers the interface between two different PDNs. Standards X.28 and X.29 are quite similar: X.28 discusses the interface between the packet assembly/disassembly (PAD) and a start-stop (asynchronous) terminal; X.29 covers the same situation for a packet mode terminal (a terminal capable of performing PAD functions). In general, X.29 refers to the network–host interface; it covers the PAD–PAD interface, as well. Because of the similarity between X.28 and X.29, only X.28 is discussed.

The X.3 Standard

The packet assembly/disassembly (PAD) interfaces to start-stop terminals, packet mode terminals, or other PADs.

Basic Functions of the PAD.   When a PAD interfaces with a start-stop terminal, the message characters arrive at the PAD one character at a time and must be grouped together into a packet for transmission over the network. While building the buffer for the data terminal equipment (DTE), the PAD can also perform a limited amount of editing on the data, restricted to deleting characters from the buffer or deleting the buffer's entire contents. Editing is enabled by the user and is done on receiving the proper editing control signals. The PAD knows to transmit a packet whenever the packet reaches the designated packet size, a message termination character is received, or after no characters have been received for a specified amount of time. The receiving PAD must take the data from the user data field and send them one character at a time to the receiver, including framing the character with start and stop bits as necessary, and adding a parity bit if required by the DTE. In addition to the handling of packet assembly/disassembly functions, the PAD is also involved in control and error functions: It is responsible for a portion of the setup and clearing of virtual calls, pacing of data to the DTE, and reacting to reset and interrupt conditions.

PAD Operations Parameters.   PAD operations are controlled by a set of PAD parameters, which in most cases the user can tailor to the operations of the particular terminal and application. The parameters of significance to business applications follow. They show the flexibility available with a PAD.

Echo. The PAD can optionally echo a transmitted character back to the DTE. Some terminals require this feature in order to display the character on the terminal's output device.

Termination Characters. The user can specify virtually any character as a termination character. Termination characters signal the PAD to end a message and to forward the packet to the network.

Timer Delay Interval. Another way that a message can be terminated is via timer delay, which can be specified at values from 0 to 255, in twentieths of a second. When no characters have arrived within the delay interval, the PAD assumes the message is complete and transmits the packet. A timer delay value of 0 means there can be no delay interval in completing the message. The maximum specifiable delay is 12.75 seconds.

XON/XOFF Capability. Some DTE equipment can announce its readiness to accept data via XON and XOFF signals. *XON* means the device is able to receive a certain number of characters, related to the device's buffer size. When the buffer is filled to a certain threshold, then the device transmits the *XOFF* signal to the sender, which holds the sender off until the buffer is emptied below the threshold. The PAD allows this capability of the device to be enabled or disabled.

Break Signal. The DTE can transmit a break signal to the PAD, that is, a sequence of 0 bits over a designated time interval. The user can specify the action the PAD is to take on receiving such a signal: do nothing, transmit an interrupt packet to the host, reset itself, transmit a break message to the host, remove itself from the data transfer state, or discard the output to the DTE.

Padding. On receipt of a carriage return character, some devices—especially the mechanical ones, such as printers—require a certain amount of time to move the printing mechanism to the beginning of the line. In order to provide sufficient time for carriage return, pad characters are sometimes inserted after the carriage return. The PAD allows from 0–7 pad characters to be transmitted to the DTE after a carriage return. Padding can also be specified to follow a line-feed character.

Line Speed. Nineteen different speeds are available, ranging from 50 bps to 64 Kbps. Once set, the line speed may not be changed. This read-only parameter allows a host to ascertain the speed of the device with which it is communicating.

Line-feed after Carriage Return. The PAD can be instructed to always insert a line-feed character following a carriage return. This option provides output line spacing for the receiving device.

Folding. This parameter allows the length of the output to be adjusted to the device. The folding parameter can be any value from 0 to 255. A zero value means no folding is to take place; any other value represents the number of characters to transmit to the receiving device before auto-matically inserting the formatting characters, such as carriage return or line feed.

Editing.   The PAD can perform the limited editing functions of character deletion and line deletion. One parameter enables this capability, and there is one parameter to store each of the line and character delete codes. If the PAD is editing-enabled and receives a character that matches the character delete parameter, the last character in the edit buffer is deleted. This works just like the backspace on most terminals. Similarly, if a line delete character is received, the entire contents of the edit buffer is deleted. The edit buffer can also be displayed.

The X.28 Standard

The X.28 specifications define the manner in which a start–stop terminal interfaces with a PAD, whose functions and options have just been defined. The data terminal equipment can access a PAD via a switched or a leased connection. The speed of the connection is determined by the capability of the DTE and by the PDN administrators.

The PAD expects 8-bit characters from the DTE and transmits 8-bit characters to the DTE. When looking at the characters for control purposes, the PAD looks at only the first seven bits. The eighth bit may either be parity or data; if data, then the first seven bits should not match any of the control functions, like editing.

The major portion of the X.28 standard defines the signals exchanged between DTE and PAD, including how to interrogate and alter the PAD parameters, the definition of the break signal, call establishment sequences, network user identification procedures, call clearing, and fault conditions.

The X.25 Standard

The X.25 specification defines the interface between data terminal equipment and the network for terminals operating in the packet mode, including the interface between the PAD and the network. The specification first briefly discusses the X.21 and X.21bis interfaces, that is, the general interfaces between synchronous and asynchronous devices, respectively. That is followed by a brief discussion of the LAPB data link protocol, which is very similar to HDLC and SDLC. Frames are formatted as described for SDLC. For information regarding this portion of the X.25 recommendation, the reader is referred to the SDLC description in Chapter 6.

At the network level, the objective is end-to-end routing. To provide the information necessary for end-to-end routing, a portion of the data or information field is used by the PDN. The shortest message that can be transferred is three characters in length, because at least three characters of the information field are required by the PDN for routing and control. These three characters contain fields for general format identification, logical channel identification, and packet-type identification. Additional fields are defined in some packets, particularly those used for control. A representative sample of these fields is given in Figure 7-17.

General Format Identification (GFI). The general format identification (GFI) is the first field of the data field of the frame. The GFI indicates the format of the remainder of the data field. The four bits of the GFI designate the sequence number modulus for the packet and also indicate whether the packet is a datagram, information packet, call setup packet, or control packet. The sequence number modulus operates like the Ns and Nr fields in HDLC.

Logical Channel Identification. The logical channel identification field consists of two parts, the logical channel group number and the logical channel number. The group number occupies the four bits following the GFI. With four bits, 16 different channel groups can be specified. The eight bits following the channel group identification is the logical channel address. There may thus be 256 different logical addresses per channel, providing a total of 4096 different circuits or logical addresses in the network.

Packet Type. The third octet designates the packet type, in six broad categories—call setup and clearing, data and interrupt, datagram, flow control and reset, restart, and diagnostic. Each category except *diagnostic*

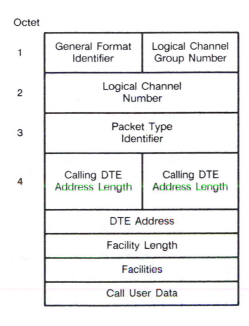

Octet

| 1 | General Format Identifier | Logical Channel Group Number |

Figure 7-17
Call Request and Incoming Call Packet Format

is further broken down into subtypes, for example, the call setup and clearing subtypes of incoming call, call connected, clear indication, DCE clear confirmation, call request, call accepted, clear request, and DTE clear confirmation.

Information Field. The defaulted recommended length of the information field is 128 octets, but X.25 provides for optional lengths of 16, 32, 64, 128, 256, 512, and 1024 octets. Message sequence numbers are used to account for packets. By default, the modulus for sequence numbers is 8, with 128 a suggested alternative. The sequence numbers work like those in the Ns and Nr fields of SDLC. A window size n is set that restricts a sender to transmitting at most n messages without acknowledgment. The default window size is 2 for a modulus of 8. The window size can be changed if the user has been given the option of *flow control parameter negotiation* which enables the user to change the packet size, sequence number modulus, window size, and circuit speed.

Optional Parameters. There are a number of other parameters that network administrators may optionally put under user control, for instance, the barring of all incoming calls. In this case, DTE will be allowed only to initiate calls. By the same token DTE can be barred from initiating calls and allowed only to receive calls. Further, a user can elect to reverse charges so the recipient of the call becomes responsible for the packets transmitted.

The user might be allowed to alter the datagram queue length, which determines the number of incoming datagrams that can queue up before datagrams begin to be discarded. Thus, if queue depth is set at 16, then 16 datagrams will be allowed in the inbound queue. If 16 datagrams are waiting when another arrives, the late arrival will be discarded.

Finally, the user is able to specify whether a closed or bilateral closed user group should be established. Closed user group members are allowed to communicate only with each other. In a bilateral closed user group, two DTEs that agree to communicate can do so, but communication with all other DTEs is prohibited. Options added to these closed groups allow for incoming and outgoing communications with the rest of the user community.

Datagrams. The X.25 specification also covers the use of datagrams. The datagram message is restricted to 128 octets. The user can elect to receive acknowledgment of datagrams in three instances—if the datagram is rejected, discarded, or accepted, result conditions that are returned to the user only when requested by the user. The user may optionally receive the capability to specify whether notification be given on nondelivery or delivery of a datagram. Datagrams are given sequence numbers, and there is an acknowledgment window that operates the same as with virtual circuits.

Local Area
and
Vendor Networks

INTRODUCTION

Chapter 7 introduced the subject of networks and discussed packet switching networks. This chapter continues discussing networks, specifically, local area networks and computer vendor networks.

THE PRIVATE BRANCH EXCHANGE

Private branch exchange (PBX) systems have changed dramatically in the last ten years. They are currently one of the ways a *local area network (LAN)* is

265

implemented. This section, which does not describe PBX systems in detail, is meant to indicate the potential of PBX as a medium provider and switch for LAN systems.

History of PBX

The PBX system has been a standard fixture in offices for many years. As business offices grew, so did the required number of telephone installations. This increased demand eventually became a drain on the telephone companies' ability to supply individual telephone lines. PBX equipment was meant to alleviate the problem. In essence, a business could become a telephone branch switching office.

One of the basic assumptions of telephony is that telephone calls are relatively infrequent and of short duration. Telephone switching systems therefore have been set up with capacities of approximately 10%–20%. Thus, no more than 20% of the subscribers in a given exchange are able to place a call at a given time [McNamara, 1977]. The same assumption was brought to PBX installations, excluding intra-office connections. Thus, for a business with approximately 50 telephones, sufficient line capacity would be installed for only approximately 10–20 outside calls [Digital Equipment Corp., 1982]. Add to this the intracompany calls made within the same business location (which do not utilize outside line capacity) and the total number of connections possible is greater than 20%.

Early models of the PBX system used operator-controlled switchboards, as frequently seen in movies and television. Until 1967, the only vendors of PBX systems were the telephone companies. With the Carterphone decision, the market opened up for other vendors to design and sell PBX equipment. This spurred developments such as electronic switching, computer-based PBX systems, and finally digital PBX systems, all technology developing concurrently with the evolution of the local area network.

A business office that has already installed a modern PBX system, with telephone wires strung everywhere, and every desk and work station having its own telephone or telephone receptacle, could implement an LAN to automate the office. But rather than pay heavy additional costs to install new cables, the office could use the existing PBX medium. This is just what numerous businesses have done, especially those that do not require the extremely high data transmission rates of coaxial cable.

Digital Branch Exchange

The maximum data transmission rates currently supported by a PBX-based LAN are approximately 56 Kbps for synchronous transmission and 19.2 Kbps for asynchronous. Higher rates are likely to be available soon. The new wave in PBX systems is digital PBX, sometimes referred to as *digital branch exchange (DBX)*. This system uses digital transmission not only for data, but also for voice. Digital telephone sets, some integrated into terminals and work stations, transmit digital rather than analog signals. The more common analog telephone sets can also be used when accompanied by an analog-to-digital conversion board. Digital PBX systems eliminate the need for modems for every connection within the system. Interfacing the data network with the outside telephone network may require changing the digital signals to analog for transmission along telephone companies' wires. This, too, is likely to change in the future as telephone companies gradually convert to digital networks.

The integration of voice and data on the PBX network has altered its characteristic usage. Previously, PBX served exclusively for relatively infrequent calls of short duration. With the integration of data into the network, it is now common to have terminals and host processor connected for the entire workday, with relatively continuous data exchange. This has dictated changes in the operations of the PBX system. To provide enough circuits for both periodic voice transmission and continuous data transmission, multiplexing of connections has been implemented. This makes the system appear to be 100% available to all user categories.

A rather interesting, state-of-the-art LAN PBX system has been installed at the University of Chicago. This installation uses three digital PBX systems linked with a local microwave circuit for direct inward-dialing service. The reader is referred to Harris and Sweeney (1983) for a good description of the components and connections in this type of system.

BASEBAND VS. BROADBAND REVISITED

The discussion of transmission media in Chapter 2 briefly covers the differences between *baseband* and *broadband transmission* for coaxial cable. In fact, baseband and broadband transmissions are not limited to coaxial cable; both could also be implemented via twisted wire pairs or fiber optics. In practice, such transmission on twisted pairs makes little sense because the bandwidth is too small. The following discussion assumes coaxial cable as the medium, since that is the medium in common use.

In baseband transmission, the entire bandwidth of the cable is used to carry data, which are represented on the cable as voltage fluctuations. In baseband, the data become the signal. In broadband transmission, a frequency division multiplexing technique allows multiple, high-speed and low-speed channels on one cable, and permits the cable to be used for nondata purposes such as video. A discussion of one potential use of a broadband system follows.

Coaxial cable has a bandwidth of approximately 400 megahertz (MHz), which can be broken into a number of channels, each of which will support a particular function. For instance, the total bandwidth can be separated into a voice channel, video channel, high-speed data channel, low-speed data channel, and switched channels.

Harris and Sweeney (1983) suggest the following channel allocations, which are illustrated in Figure 8-1.

One band can span the frequency range of ten to 25 MHz to be used for low-speed data transmissions. A band that spans the range from 55 to 75 MHz could be used for switched voice or data transmissions. Another band, from 175 to 210 MHz, could be dedicated exclusively to high-speed data exchanges. A third, from 210 to 240 MHz, could be assigned for video transmission.

A 10-Mbps channel using CSMA/CD access could be implemented on the high-speed data band, yielding a band equivalent to that of the base-band *Ethernet* system. The low-speed data band could be separated into a number of 56-Kbps circuits as well as lower-speed 9600-bps circuits. Because video requires a channel capacity of approximately 6 MHz, there could be five video channels allocated on the bandwidth. The interface with the broadband system is via modems or similar devices. On the low-speed channels, almost any type of terminal could thus be easily attached. The high-speed channel could be used to attach devices capable of transmitting at higher speeds, such as work stations and processors.

Advantages and Disadvantages of Broadband Transmission

From this description, broadband transmission may seem the obvious way to go—it provides flexibility as well as a channel that is equivalent to many of the baseband systems. However, there are some disadvantages to broadband. A broadband system is inherently more complex than a baseband system, for the channels must be carefully designed and allocated among users. By comparison, a baseband system does not need the same amount of planning and design. A broadband system is somewhat more expensive

Figure 8-1
Suggested Broadband
Frequency Allocation

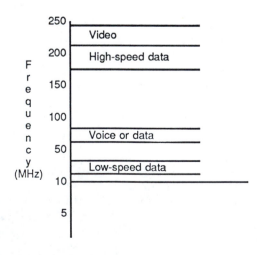

to implement, on the order of $100 more per station [Frank, 1983]. Baseband is more suitable for the extremely high transmission rates sometimes required for communication between large-scale processors. It is an all-digital medium with a high transmission rate capacity. Current implementations on coaxial cable operate at 50 Mbps; and fiber optic systems have been announced with data rates of 275 Mbps.

For an LAN user interested in the transfer of data only, a baseband system is the easiest to implement. With careful prior planning, a baseband system could be implemented initially, and later converted to a broadband system, if necessary. Future uses of LANs will probably require the flexibility and diversity provided by a broadband system, which allows almost any device to interface with the system, with both high-speed and low-speed interfaces available. More important, broadband also easily accommodates voice and video.

LOCAL AREA NETWORKS

Local area networks are networks of devices confined to a limited geographical area. The actual distances involved are dependent on the implementation, with a maximum usually at a few miles or less. This makes the LAN highly suitable for single or multiple building complexes. Although LAN technology has been largely developed for data communications, it has other uses. Voice transmission, for both telephone and voice generation and recognition, is available in a number of systems. The PBX-based systems in particular require this option. Another desirable characteristic in some systems is video transmission, for teleconferencing and educational purposes. The data transmission rate required for video is quite high and currently precludes the use of PBX or wire pair facilities. Video transmission requires a bandwidth of approximately 6 MHz. The only LAN media that can accommodate all three—data, voice, and video—are broadband coaxial cable and fiber optics.

Typical Applications of the LAN

Typical applications of the local area network are office automation, factory automation, process control, and the connection of multiple processors for high-speed data exchange. These applications have several things in common: a variety of devices in a limited geographical area working on a number of different applications and requiring high speed and reliability. A variety of types of devices need to be connected to the LAN. In the office automation environment, for instance, there are several varieties of terminals (dumb, smart, and intelligent), various types of printers, and small, medium, and large computer systems. In addition there may be special-purpose devices such as plotters, graphics terminals, optical scanning equipment, and voice synthesizers/recognition, to name a few.

A number of distinct functions can be performed in each application area. Again using office automation as an example, some stations might be involved in word processing applications and electronic mail, another in generating graphics images, some performing data entry, others performing batch file transfers, and still others processing on-line transactions. Each function has its own unique processing and data transfer requirements.

Requirements of LANs

Speed and Reliability.   A common requirement of LANs is that they be fast and reliable. This means the medium should be capable of supporting high transmission rates and that all stations have access to it. No one station should be capable of consuming the medium's entire bandwidth for any appreciable length of time. Reliability means that the system should be able to continue functioning regardless of the failure of individual components. If a supervisor processor is required, then alternates should be designated in case of supervisor failure.

Specialist Functions: The Server.   Sometimes there is a requirement for specialist functions, processes, or nodes, referred to as servers. A *server* is a routine, process, or node that provides a common service for one or more stations in the network. The database server is perhaps the best example. In the OA environment there may be one or more nodes that hold most of the business's database. Other nodes in the network frequently need portions of the data stored at this node. The database node provides a service for the other nodes—database storage, access, and update. If document preparation is one of the office activities, one node can be designated as the archive for all completed documents. A document needing to be updated or reproduced can be requested from this node and transferred to the requesting station. The server node must also reconcile multiple requests for the same records or documents when necessary. In some instances multiple users working on the same record or document can produce undesirable contention and deadlock.

Contention and Deadlock.   Contention for data resources arises when multiple users concurrently access the same records. For example, when two different text processing operators are charged with modifying a contract, neither one aware of the other, each will obtain a copy of the current contract, make changes to it, and return the amended document. Of course, the operator who last replaces the document destroys the other's work.

These problems can be avoided with special controls on records, files, or documents. The usual such control is a lock that disallows concurrent access or concurrent update, although lock controls can create deadlock, as when user A reads and locks record 1 and user B reads and locks record 2, and then A attempts to read record 2 while B attempts to access record 1: Without arbitration, A and B might both wait forever, since A cannot proceed while needing a resource controlled by B, and B cannot proceed while needing a resource controlled by A. This deadlock condition is illustrated in Figure 8-2.

	USER A	USER B
T		
I	Reads and locks record 1.	Reads and locks record 2.
M	Attempts to read record 2.	Attempts to read record 1.
E	Waits.	Waits.

Figure 8-2
Deadlock Situation

Interfaces.   A communications interface unit is required to connect a device to the transmission medium. For baseband coaxial cable networks such a unit is commonly called a transceiver. For broadband coaxial cable or twisted pairs using analog transmission the interface unit is a modem or similar device.

This, then, is the basis for a local area network: multiple devices of different types and capabilities working on diverse applications in a limited geographical area, all requiring reliability and rapid response together with a number of common services that all or most of the devices must have available.

LANS may be oriented toward general or specific interfaces. The general interface LAN attempts to allow as many different devices from a variety of vendors to attach to the network, giving the user a wide variety of options in selecting equipment. The specific interface LAN is oriented toward a specific manufacturer's equipment, frequently computer vendor products such as Tandem's *fiber optic extension (FOX)* LAN, for which the only attachable devices are Tandem processors.

THE ALOHANET

The prototype of many of today's LANs comes from a network that does not generally qualify as a LAN, the *ALOHANet*, developed by the University of Hawaii (UH) and placed in operation in 1971. UH had a unique problem to resolve in establishing a data communications network in the islands—how to link the main computer center in Honolulu with outlying campus and research facilities, some of them in areas where telephone service was poor. The distances involved and the ocean made it impractical to establish private communication lines. Satellite communications might have been a good solution, except that the technology was still in its early stages.

The solution adopted by UH was ultra-high-frequency radio broadcast utilizing two broadcast frequencies—one emanating from the Honolulu computer center to all outlying stations, and one from outlying stations to the central station. Outlying stations were not allowed to transmit directly to one another. The transmission rate was 9600 bps.

Stations on the inbound channel operated in contention mode for the right to broadcast, much like the CSMA/CD broadcast protocol described in Chapter 6. Outbound message traffic was not subject to contention at all, since only the central station was allowed to broadcast on that channel. All remote stations monitored the central station's frequency and accepted those messages addressed to them.

System performance was quite good when the number of stations was small. As more stations were brought on-line, however, contention on the inbound channel increased, as did the number of collisions. Modifications have since been made that reduce the number of collisions and also in-crease performance. One of these improvements is the slotted ALOHA protocol.

Slotted ALOHA Protocol

In the *slotted ALOHA protocol*, transmit time is essentially broken into time intervals of a length that transmits the maximum-size block or packet. Variations of the slotted technique exist, but the general idea is that one station may not occupy successive transmission slots, thus helping to avoid contention. For example, consider two stations, each with a long message to send, with one message requiring multiple transmission packets. Using nonslotted CSMA/CD, station A would transmit its first packet, wait for the medium to clear, and then attempt to transmit packet 2. Station B, also waiting for a quiescent channel, transmits at the same time as Station A; a collision occurs and both stations back off for a random interval. In the slotted protocol, on the other hand, station A would not have the option of transmitting in two successive slots. Taken to the extreme, the slotted protocol is identical with time division multiplexing. In the ideal form it approaches statistical time division multiplexing. The slotted protocol, or variations thereof, is used in both bus and ring architectures, the two most common LAN configurations.

IEEE STANDARDS

In 1979, the Institute of Electrical and Electronics Engineers (IEEE) arrived at the same conclusion for LANs that the International Standards Organization had earlier arrived at for networks in general—that is, the number of unique networks was expanding, and consideration had to be given to interconnecting these different models. In 1980, therefore, the IEEE began to evaluate the LAN environment in order to recommend an LAN standard. By mid-1984, two standards had been adopted: *IEEE 802.3*, which describes an Ethernet-type standard (see below), and *IEEE 802.4*, which describes a token passing LAN.

Adopting The OSI Reference Model

One of the first actions of IEEE was to endorse the International Standards Organization OSI reference model, correctly observing that the top three layers were application-oriented and that the next two were interface layers between application and transmission functions. As a result, only the bottom two layers—divided into three separate layers—were chosen for the LAN standard. The lowest layer encompasses the physical medium, either twisted wire pairs, coaxial cable, or fiber optics. The second layer designates the physical attachment to the medium and includes the techniques for encoding data onto the medium and decoding data from the medium. The third layer, the data link layer, includes CSMA/CD, token ring, or token bus protocols. A data link control function sits above each of the protocols to reconcile the differences among them and provide a clean interface with the applications.

IEEE Standards Project 802

The standards committee—known as IEEE Standards Project 802—faced a monumental task. In 1979 there were 44 identified LAN implementations, groupable into seven different categories [Myers, 1982]. Committee members represented a variety of vendors, users, and academic institutions, all with disparate experiences, applications, and ideas as to how LANs should be implemented. For example, the needs of process control differ somewhat from those of office automation. A guaranteed response time is relatively unimportant in the automated office. In process control a guaranteed response time is critical. The manufacture of silicon chips, for instance, is a combination of a number of time-sensitive photographic, chemical, doping, and heat processes. If an LAN is used in the process control cycle, then it is essential that a node controlling a time-sensitive operation be assured of a guaranteed access window into the network. As described in Chapter 6, such guarantees are impossible to make in the CSMA access structure, whereas they are quite predictable in the token passing protocols.

General Problems of Standards Adoption.   Standards adoption committees seem to find themselves in one of four situations. The first is to specify a standard for something that does not yet exist, which was the situation with the COBOL and Ada programming languages. The second is when numerous technologies have been attempted but only one found acceptable. This is true of the bit-oriented data link control protocols, where a number of slightly different standards exist but most meet some subset of the standard. The third category involves standardization prior to a technology's development, as with the CODASYL DBTG efforts in 1969–1971. This situation implemented a standard database access language (extended to include a database implementation as well) during the early period of database development, prior to the evaluation of the relational model database management system. The fourth is when several viable alternatives have been proven.

LAN standardization fits into this fourth category. Several already viable alternatives had to be allowed to appeal to all vested interests. The alternative would have been to select one option, which would have resulted in the fragmentation of the remaining groups. In such a no-win situation, IEEE Standards Project 802 opted for the former approach.

Committee Recommendations

Topology and Data Link Protocol.   Rather than proposing a standard representing a single approach, the committee opted to propose a standard representing two topologies—*ring* and *bus*—and three data link protocols—*carrier sense with multiple access and collision detection (CSMA/CD)* for bus topology and *token passing* for either ring or bus topologies. Users and implementers are thus free, within standard guidelines, to adopt a strategy that meets the requirements of their particular application. The initial proposals also included minimum requirements for speed, number of accessible devices, and distance. Some of these restrictions eliminated a number of alternatives where the minimum speed characteristic cannot currently be met, such as low-speed PBX implementations.

Transmission Medium.   The question of transmission medium has been left open. The committee recommended twisted pairs and coaxial cable—both baseband and broadband. A decision on fiber optics has not yet been made because of the variety of currently available technologies and because research is still ongoing. Microwave, radio broadcast, and infrared transmission have been recognized as possible alternatives for internetwork and interbuilding connections.

Addressing.   Various addressing alternatives were proposed. On one hand, users of large networks are interested in internetwork connections involving addresses that are internationally unique. On the other hand, some users desire local access only and are concerned about the extra address space required for international addressing. The compromise proposal allows both alternatives. The scheme for local access only uses a 16-bit address, and the internationally unique address uses 48 bits. The latter was a concession to the Ethernet lobby, which had already adopted a 48-bit address; the alternative was a byte-expandable address space that allows up to seven bytes, or 56 bits with eight bits reserved for control. The 48-bit address plus eight bits for control was replaced in later recommendations by a straight 48-bit address plan.

Voice and Video.   Not specifically addressed by the IEEE standards are voice and video transmission. Voice is extremely difficult to implement on baseband coaxial cable transmissions. In PBX systems, the bandwidth is usually insufficient to support video images. A token passing implementation using broadband coaxial cable could be used for each of these; other implementations might preclude either voice or video.

The proposed IEEE standards will at best limit the implementation options for LANs, and at worst serve as a tutorial on prominent implementations of LAN systems.

IBM'S PLANS

IBM, the largest computer vendor, has yet to release an LAN system. It is generally accepted that IBM will at some time in the future support a token passing ring or star network using twisted wire pairs as the medium. In May 1984, IBM released some additional clues as to its intentions, by providing customers with wiring plans. The plans specify a star-based topology using twisted wire pairs [Dix, 1984], cabling that is characteristic of PBX systems. Regardless of the approach taken, it is very likely that any IBM LAN will have a significant impact on LAN technology.

ETHERNET

Ethernet has probably been the most publicized of the LAN implementations. Loosely based on the ALOHANet, Ethernet was originally proposed in 1972 by Xerox Corporation, which was later joined by Digital Equipment Corporation and Intel Corporation in the efforts to implement and standardize an LAN. What follows is the "standard" or most current guidelines for Ethernet implementation.

Ethernet Specifications and Effectiveness

In formulating the specifications for Ethernet, the designers focused on 11 requirements of an LAN: high data transmission rates, distance, ability to support several hundred devices, simplicity, low error rates and good error detection, efficient use of shared resources, stability under high load, fair access to the medium, ease of installation, ease of reconfiguration, and low cost [Shoch and Hupp, 1982]. The resulting specifications are described below.

Transmission Rates and Distance.   Ethernet uses coaxial cable with base-band transmission at 10 Mbs, and a maximum allowable distance between stations of 2.5 kilometers (1.55 miles). Both transmission speed and distance have been considerably less in experimental and certain production implementations. Experimental speeds have been more on the order of 1–3 Mbps; and some commercial implementations have yet to achieve the specified speed of 10 Mbps. The 2.5-kilometer distance is sufficient for most applications. For greater distances, two or more interconnected LANs can be used.

Ease of Installation and Reconfiguration and Error Characteristics. Because coaxial cable is the medium, adding and removing stations without disrupting the network is relatively easy. The technology for tapping into the network, developed by community antenna TV (CATV), allows stations to be added while the network is live. Thus, it is quite easy to configure and reconfigure the network. As mentioned in Chapter 2, coaxial cable provides very low error rates, which—coupled with 32-bit CRC—provide excellent error characteristics for the net.

Number of Supportable Devices and Medium Accessibility.   The specifications state that a maximum of 1024 devices may be attached to the network, although the range of allowable addresses is much larger. (The 48-bit address field yields over 281 trillion unique addresses.) This width field was chosen, not to support so many devices, but to allow for unique international addressing. A very large office complex where it is likely that more than 1024 devices will be required, can resolve this by interconnecting two or more nets. There is also a tradeoff regarding the number of supported devices and ability to access the net: As the number of stations increases, so does the probability of contention for the medium. A limit of 1024 stations is realistic.

Performance Under Heavy Load, and Efficiency.   The ability to configure 1024 devices on the network does not necessarily mean that all the devices will be supported satisfactorily. One of the potential problems of the CSMA/CD protocol is performance under heavy load. Prototype office networks with over 200 stations have not proven much of a stress to the Ethernet system. Other stress tests have been run: Ten stations were placed on the net, each with a 10% medium load of 1 Mbps, making for an aggregate load of 10 Mbps, sufficient to completely fill the bus. Station utilization varied from 93% to 96%, with an average of 94% [Myers, 1982; Shoch and Hupp, 1980], which is quite good. This test was close to a best case for the network, since there were relatively few stations. Other tests [Liu, Hilal, and Groomes, 1982; Stuck, 1983] indicate that network efficiency can deteriorate under heavy loads. More testing with real applications will be necessary to properly evaluate performance and potential bottlenecks.

Installation and Data Packets.   Stations are attached to the network via a transceiver (interface to the medium) and a controller, which performs the CSMA/CD and packet assembly/disassembly functions, buffers messages, and recognizes the station address. Data are transmitted on the Ethernet in packets, with a minimum data field width of 46 characters (octets) and a maximum of 1500 characters. The minimum allows the network's most distant station to detect a message before transmission ends; without this delay, some stations would have difficulty knowing whether a collision had occurred. Likewise, each station waits a propagation delay interval after sensing the end of a message to ensure that the message has cleared the channel. Both the sender's address and the receiver's address are transmitted. The frame check sequence is a 32-bit CRC. A 16-bit data field designates the message type. The general format of a data packet is given in Figure 8-3.

Cost.   Because of the popularity of the Ethernet, processing chips are being produced that allow a station to interface with the network. The cost of these chips can be expected to decline, thereby reducing the cost of adding a station. The current costs to interface with the LAN vary with the type of device. Representative costs in 1984 were approximately $800 for a personal computer interface (logic board and software) and $1700 for controller board and software for a mini- or super-minicomputer.

Unfortunately, the Ethernet does not solve all users' problems. The deficiencies of CSMA/CD have already been mentioned, as has the difference between baseband and broadband technologies. There are certain other attributes not provided by Ethernet: The broadcast technology prohibits full duplex operations, which would be possible in broadband systems, but not in baseband, limiting somewhat interstation message exchange. In addition, no provisions have been made for priority of stations or messages, which would be advantageous with respect to access to the channel in process control applications. The ability to assign priorities to stations has been part of other implementations, however. Naturally, priority schemes run counter to the design objective of fair access to the medium.

OTHER LOCAL AREA NETWORKS

Although every LAN implementation is not mentioned here (since there are over 45 companies providing some type of network), several deserve

64-bit Synchronization Pattern	48-bit Destination Address	48-bit Source Address	16-bit Field Type	Data 46–1500 Octets	32-bit CRC

Figure 8-3   An Ethernet Packet Format

mention either because of the architecture or the number of implementations.

Attached Resource Computer (ARC)

Datapoint's *attached resource computer (ARC)* net, one of the early commercial offerings, has gone through several generations since its introduction. The ARC network is a token passing bus-and-star architecture using baseband coaxial cable as the medium. Network nodes are either for database processing or for application processing. Though each node can have its own disk, a database node is meant to serve as a central repository of data to be shared by the application nodes. The maximum distance spanned by the ARC network is four miles. In the near future, Datapoint intends to implement a digital switching system that supports both voice and data.

Wangnet

Wangnet, Wang Laboratories' local area network, is a broadband network with four bands provided—the Wang band, utility band, interconnect band, and peripheral band. The *Wang band*, which supports a speed of 12 Mbps and uses a CSMA/CD access protocol, serves for Wang's stronghold, office automation. The primary applications run on this band are document editing, electronic mail, and document archiving and retrieval. The *utility band*, with seven video bands available, can provide video channels for education or teleconferencing. The *interconnect band*, which is broken into 16 64-Kbps high-speed lines and 64 9600-bps low-speed lines, enables non-Wang (RS-232-C or RS-449) terminals to interface with the network. The *peripheral band* allows direct connection of six Wang work stations, one to each of six channels. The maximum distance spanned by the Wangnet is four miles.

Fiber Optic Extension (FOX)

Tandem Computers offers a proprietary *fiber optic extension (FOX)* LAN to which only Tandem systems can be connected. A Tandem node consists of from 2 to 16 processors attached to two high-speed buses, an X bus and a Y bus. Each bus has a data transmission rate of 13.6 million *bytes* per second. The FOX LAN allows up to 14 nodes to be connected by a dual fiber optic cable. The cable itself consists of five fiber optic conductors that mirror the two high-speed buses connecting the processors within one node. Two fibers are used to represent one bus and to allow full duplex operations; that is, there is an X receive fiber and an X send fiber as well as a Y send and Y receive. The fifth fiber optic cable is a spare. The rated speed per fiber is 1 million *bytes* per second, with an aggregate data rate of 4 million *bytes* per second (32 Mbps). Data can be transmitted in either direction, and the shortest distance is selected for transmission. The architecture for the FOX LAN is a ring with a maximum length of 1 kilometer.

As with other components of Tandem systems the FOX LAN is fault-tolerant—any portion of the network can fail and the LAN will continue to function.

HIGH-SPEED LOCAL AREA NETWORKS

Ethernet and similar LANs are well suited to office automation and process control environments, where the messages to be exchanged are generally quite small, and users do not require extremely high-speed transmission. This is in contrast with an LAN consisting of only large computing systems, in which application the LAN could be used to transfer large files, provide database service to multiple hosts, and provide high-volume printing and tape archiving. To be successful in this segment of the industry, the LAN must be capable of operating at channel speeds or greater. This application of an LAN is sometimes called back-end processing, a term derived from comparison with front-end processing. Whereas the front-end processor is responsible for handling the communications lines to terminals and other hosts, the back-end processor is responsible for database, printing, archiving, and certain processing functions.

Hyperchannel (HC)

The most widely used high-speed LAN is Network Systems Corporation's *Hyperchannel (HC)*. A representative Hyperchannel configuration is given in Figure 8-4. The HC uses a bus architecture on a baseband coaxial cable with a CSMA bus access protocol and a transmission speed of 50 Mbps. The length of the network is dependent on the type of coaxial cable used; nominal distance is 1000 feet, but distances up to 3000 feet have been attained with higher-quality cable [Thornton and Christiansen, 1983]. Future plans include a fiber optic link, the Datapipe, which will have a capacity of 275 Mbps and a range of 30 miles.

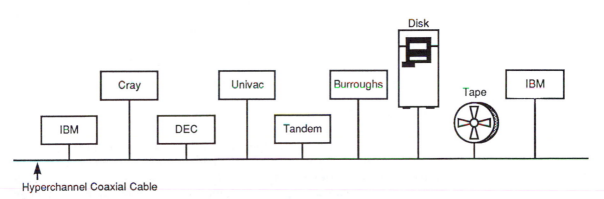

Figure 8-4   A Representative Hyperchannel Configuration

Each node in Hyperchannel can be connected to up to four cables. The additional cables provide backup and increase the aggregate data transmission rate. They also reduce the probability of collisions on the medium: If many collisions are detected, say in the situation where only one cable is used, then the CSMA access protocol is augmented with a priority scheme, thus reducing contention and enabling higher-priority messages to be transmitted first.

HC Interfaces. HC interfaces to many different CPUs have been implemented, including systems from Control Data Corporation, IBM, Cray, Univac, Digital Equipment Corporation, Tandem, and Burroughs, to name a few. In addition, it is also possible to attach HC to controllers for IBM-compatible tape and disk drives, common memory, and high-speed data communications channels such as AT&T's T1, T2, and T3 services and satellite. The ability to attach to tape, disk, and memory allows these units to function as servers for the rest of the system. Thus, any CPU can have access to a common database, use the tape drives for archiving, logging, or data access, and share a common memory. Access to these facilities also can reduce data redundancy and minimize the amount of independent storage connected to each CPU.

HC Adaptors. Each device is connected to the cable by an adaptor, which serves as interface between the medium and the CPU's channel or controller and enables different devices to share the channel without any concern about each other's characteristics. The adaptors are buffered, which allows them to receive data from the bus and hold data to transmit while waiting for access to the bus. The size of the adaptor's buffer determines the size of the data transfer. Buffer sizes are 4000 and 8000 characters and block sizes are 2000 and 4000 characters. Only half the buffer is used for transmission, to allow room for data to be received into the buffer. Adaptors also exist that allow one HC net to interface with another. The connecting link between two HCs must be quite fast, for example, satellite.

The HC has proven very successful for high-speed LAN applications. Network Systems Corporation has continued its research and development efforts in expanding both the capabilities of the system and the number of devices to which it can interface.

HIGH-SPEED STANDARD

In 1979, the X3T9 Committee of the American National Standards X3 Committee was formed to deliberate local distributed data interfaces (LDDI), with the objective of developing an interface standard for a 50-Mbps channel supporting distances up to 1 kilometer. No standard has yet been adopted, but the committee has formulated a proposal for a high-speed standard, one that endorses the OSI reference model and focuses on the physical and data link layers. The proposal outlines a priority-oriented access strategy on a bus medium. Each station would be given a message slot on the medium via a priority designation that essentially determines its position in a time division multiplexing scheme. Furthermore, the proposal has a provision for priority messages.

Example of Proposed Access Strategy.   One of the nodes on a small local area network with nodes A, B, and C, in that order of priority, has just finished transmitting a message. The first available time slot belongs to station A, but before A can transmit, it must wait long enough for any station with a high-priority message to transmit; if no such message appears, then A can transmit. Station B must wait a sufficient time for A's message to appear; if none is forthcoming, then B can transmit. Station C must wait for B's message to arrive before it can transmit. This algorithm helps avoid the collisions that can occur under a pure CSMA/CD approach.

The proposal also suggests a message frame consisting of the sending and receiving addresses (16 bits each), a 16-bit text-length field, a variable-length text field, and a 32-bit frame check sequence.

VENDOR LONG-DISTANCE NETWORKS

Vendor offerings play a major role in network implementation and configuration, and almost every major vendor offers a network. Vendor networks compete with each other, with X.25 networks, or with common carrier networks, although the last might be excluded because common carriers typically provide circuits but not the higher-level network requirements, such as routing, error detection, and packet assembly/disassembly.

The following section is devoted to one particular network, *IBM's system network architecture (SNA)*, which has become a de facto industry standard. Currently, interfacing with an IBM network is likely to be via an SNA interface. In the future, interfacing will be via either SNA or IBM's anticipated LAN. A brief look at some other industry offerings follows the SNA discussion.

SYSTEMS NETWORK ARCHITECTURE

SNA, announced by IBM in 1974 as the basis for future data communications implementations, is not a product per se; rather, it is a concept of how to implement data communications on IBM systems. The SNA network actually consists of a number of hardware and software components in a well-defined configuration. Initial implementations were criticized as being incomplete and requiring an excess of computer resources. Over time, the original weaknesses have been eliminated, with major releases of significant new features in 1976, 1979, and 1983.

Why SNA?

For years, IBM has been the leader in computer sales and installations. The move to SNA was prompted not by competition from the outside, but by competition from within the organization. Prior to 1974, the implementation of communications systems had been somewhat random: If a new terminal was developed, a new or modified access method and data link protocol were likely to accompany it. By 1974 IBM was offering more than 200 different models of communications hardware, 35 different device access methods, and over a dozen data link protocols. Continuing this product proliferation would have given IBM an enormous burden for support and maintenance. SNA was the result of the corporate objective of integrating all these functions into one cohesive network architecture.

The objective of any network is to enable different users to communicate with one another. *Users* are either real people working at a terminal or operator's console or they are applications that request data or provide data or both. A user is also an entity with some degree of intelligence. Thus, a terminal is not a user, though the terms *terminal operator* and *terminal* are frequently used synonymously.

SNA Layers

SNA, like the OSI reference model, is a multilayered architecture. Depending on the presenter's perspective, there are either 7, 6, or 4 layers; usually, only 6 or 4 layers are cited. The discrepancy between a 6-layer and 4-layer definition is explained by the fact that layers 3 through 5 are sometimes referred to as a single layer known as the *half-session* layer. Although the lowest layer, the physical layer, is not usually specified in SNA, such a layer obviously must exist; it is included in the following discussion as the seventh layer. The layers defined are given in Figure 8-5. The six layers are named in parentheses, where applicable.

Figure 8-5
SNA Layers

Layer 1	Data link control
Layer 2	Path control
Layer 3	Half-session layer, consisting of:
	Transmission control (Layer 3)
	Flow control (Layer 4)
	Presentation services (Layer 5)
Layer 4	Services manager (Layer 6)

Hardware Components. The first layer encountered is the (nonexistent) physical layer, which defines the connectors and electrical signals needed to provide communication. It is also used here to define the hardware components of the system. SNA defines four distinct hardware components, called *physical units (PU)*. Physical units come in four types, numbers 1, 2, 4, and 5, with no PU currently assigned to number 3. These device types are listed in Figure 8-6.

Physical Unit	Hardware Component
Type 1	A terminal device, e.g., 3278
Type 2	A cluster controller, e.g., 3274
Type 4	A communications controller, e.g., 3705
Type 5	Host, e.g., 4341 and 3084

Figure 8-6
SNA Physical Unit Types

The hardware configuration, then, consists of IBM or IBM-compatible CPUs, communications controllers, terminal cluster controllers, and terminals, printers, or work stations, connected by any of the media discussed in Chapter 2. The preferred data link protocol is SDLC, but accommodations have been made for BISYNC as well.

Logical Units and Sessions

Users of SNA are represented in the system by entities known as *logical units (LU)*. An LU is usually implemented as a software function in a device with some intelligence, such as a CPU or controller. The dialogue between two system users is known as a *session*. Since a logical unit is the agent of a user, LUs are involved in requesting a session with another LU.

For example, suppose a terminal (operator) desires to retrieve a logical record from a database. Each of these users—the terminal and the database application—will be represented by a logical unit. The terminal LU will request a session with the database application LU, and the application LU can either accept or reject the establishment of a session. Rejection is typically for security reasons, or because the requesting LU lacks authority to establish a session with the LU, or because of congestion, meaning the application LU has already entered into the maximum number of sessions it can support. If the session is granted, then the two users establish a communications path and continue to communicate until one of them terminates the session. Figure 8-7 on page 284 shows several sessions between users communicating through their respective logical units.

Session Types.   There are many different types of sessions that can be requested—for instance, program to terminal, program to program, or terminal to terminal. Each of these categories can be further stratified as to terminal type (interactive, batch, or printer) and application type (batch, interactive, word processing, or the like). To further complicate matters, one logical unit can represent several different users, and two users can have multiple sessions in concurrent progress.

Figure 8-7
Several SNA Sessions

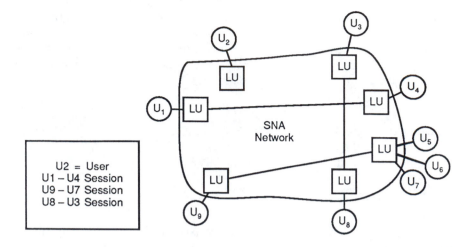

U2 = User
U1 – U4 Session
U9 – U7 Session
U8 – U3 Session

System Services Control Point (SSCP)

A supervisor or intermediary is involved in establishing a session. In SNA this extremely important entity is known as the *systems services control point (SSCP)*; it resides in the host processor, that is, the CPU. The SSCP is the software controlling its host's portion of the network. The devices controlled by the host and its SSCP represent a *domain*.

Early versions of SNA had only one SSCP and thus only one host computer, so all of the network was controlled by this one host. In 1979 the system was enhanced to allow multiple host systems, and hence multiple domains, because large networks were being implemented between different, but equal, organizations (one organization wishing not to be subservient to another), and because of the added capability of establishing multiple control points in large networks.

Within a given domain the SSCP is the controlling entity. It is responsible for the physical and logical units within its domain. In fulfilling this obligation, it manages its units, including unit initialization, maintaining the status of individual units, taking units on and off line as necessary, and serving as mediator in the establishment of sessions.

Intradomain Communication

If user A in one domain is attempting to converse with user B in the same domain, communication is established as follows. The logical unit representing user A sends a message to the SSCP requesting a session with user B. On behalf of user A, the SSCP contacts the user B LU to request a session and to also provide information about user A, including user A's access profile and type. User B either accepts or rejects the session request. If the session is rejected, then user A is so notified. If user B accepts the invitation to enter into a session with A, then a communications path must be established.

Path Allocation: End-to-end vs. Virtual Routing.   Path establishment was easy in the early implementations because there was only one path between LUs. Nowadays, two routing methods are supported, end-to-end routing and virtual routing. In *end-to-end routing*, for which at least one of the nodes must be a type 5 physical unit or terminal, the path is determined and maintained through the entire session (unless the path is broken). In *virtual routing*, there is no permanently established path; instead, each node consults its routing table to determine to which node the message should be forwarded. The path control half-session layer is responsible for path allocation. Each available path is given a weighting that assists in route determination. A route might be selected based on best use, according to such factors as security, speed, and propagation delay (as for satellite links). Up to five different paths between any two LUs can be described.

Addressing

For one device to talk to another, an address is required. In SNA, addresses are 48 bits in length. Even though this is the same length as for other addressing schemes (such as Ethernet and IEEE 802), with potential for international addressing the addresses are not compatible, for the address field is broken into subfields.

Figure 8-8 on page 286 illustrates a two-domain SNA configuration. Addressable components in SNA are called *network addressable units (NAU)*, which can be an SSCP, an LU, or a PU. Within one domain there are also subareas. A *subarea* consists of a communications controller (e.g. 3705) and all its NAUs, or a host/SSCP together with all of the locally attached NAUs. Figure 8-8 shows one subarea. NAUs within one subarea are known as *local addresses*. An example is a 3278 terminal attached to a cluster controller. The SNA 48-bit address is segmented into a 32-bit subarea address and a 16-bit address for an NAU within that subarea. Communication between users in different domains works much like that for a single domain, except that the SSCPs in both domains are involved—that is, the request goes from an LU to its SSCP to the SSCP in the other domain and then to its LU.

Additional SNA Terminology

Network Control Program (NCP).   The *network control program (NCP)*, which resides in a communication controller such as the 3705, controls communications lines and the terminals attached to the communication lines. It works in conjunction with the virtual terminal access method

Figure 8-8
The IBM SNA
Network

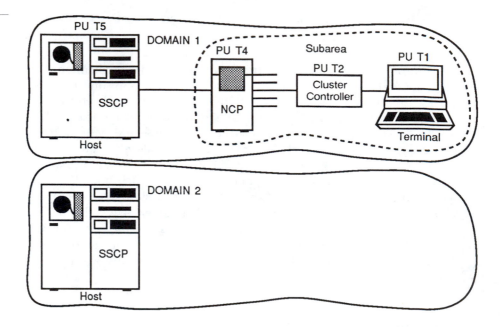

(VTAM) that resides in the host. VTAM serves as the interface between application programs and the network.

Advanced Communications Facility (ACF).   The *advanced communications facility (ACF)* was introduced in 1979. It provides such features as interdomain communication, improved error and testing capability, and dynamic device configuration.

Network Performance Analyzer (NPA). The *network performance analyzer (NPA)* provides performance information for the system, including information on lines, buffers, errors, queue lengths, and data transmission rates.

Network Problem Determination Aid (NPDA).   The *network problem determination aid (NPDA)* collects, maintains, and reports information on error conditions within the network. It also allows for testing of the system concurrent with production operations.

SNA continues to evolve as a network offering. It has recently been extended into office automation, including support for document distribution, storage, and retrieval. Another recent addition is enhanced support for program-to-program communication. An interface with IBM's upcoming LAN is surely in the works.

TANDEM'S EXPAND NETWORK

Tandem's EXPAND network, a proprietary network that links Tandem nodes, has the objective of extending the architecture of a single Tandem system—consisting of from two to 16 processors—to a network of systems. Fault tolerance is included in the network, since there can be multiple links between adjacent nodes and multiple paths between nodes. Figure 8-9 illustrates a potential configuration. Up to 255 nodes can attach to the network, giving a maximum of 4080 processors in a fully expanded network (255 nodes, with 16 processors per node).

Primary Backup Processors

To provide a fault-tolerant network, the network software resides in two different processors, one primary and one backup. Both primary and backup processors are active, meaning the backup is not a hot standby processor. The backup processors in a number of other fault-tolerant systems are passive. That is, they do not perform a processing function of their own, but simply wait on a standby basis to take over if the main processor should fail. In Tandem systems, each processor is assigned some portion of the entire workload and thus actively participates in the processing function. The software residing in the backup processor is relatively dormant, receiving periodic network status information. In addition to having the software and hardware backed up in case of failure, the network can also be configured so there are at least two paths to each node. Thus, if a processor fails, the backup takes over; if a line fails, the alternate path is used; or if any single component (in some cases, multiple unrelated components) should fail, the backup components are automatically utilized and the system continues to operate.

Topology of EXPAND

There are no restrictions with respect to the topology of the network. The nodes can be configured as a ring, bus, star, or virtually any other config-

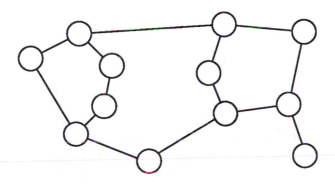

Figure 8-9
A Potential EXPAND Network

uration. Routing tables are locally determined, based on the transmission speed of the links and the number of hops. Neither congestion nor line type is taken into consideration in determining the path. The information regarding the line speed is provided during system generation. If a link in the path should fail, the next best path is determined and automatically used. When the malfunctioning link is returned to service, the original path is reactivated. When multiple links exist between two nodes, as illustrated in Figure 8-10, all links are active, thus providing a wider data path between the two nodes. When two paths exist, only one will be active at any one time, the alternate path being used only if the primary path fails.

EXPAND Data Link Protocols

The data link protocols used by EXPAND are either binary synchronous or HDLC. The links do not all have to be of the same type; some can be binary synchronous and others can be bit synchronous. Nodes can also be attached to the network via packet switching networks and Tandem's satellite transmission protocol.

Terminals

Terminals gain access to the network through the node to which they are attached, and the terminals can be attached to the network via any communications protocol. One of the design objectives of EXPAND was to make the network as transparent as possible. Thus, a user in Dallas, Texas, can access data or applications on a node in London almost as easily as on a home node, the only difference being that the file name includes the name of the node on which the file resides. The file and network system are then responsible for determining the path to the data and retrieving them. In addition to running jobs remotely or accessing data remotely, users can establish themselves as users on another node. Logically, the user appears to be a local user on that node. By default (that is, without specifying a remote system as part of the file or application name), all jobs will be initiated on that node and all data accessed on that node. If care is

Figure 8-10
A Multi-Link
EXPAND Network

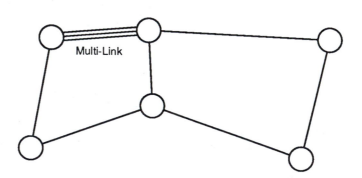

Multi-Link

taken in application design, applications designed to run and access files on one node can also be used to access remote files or run remotely as well, meaning no reprogramming would be required to run such a program locally or remotely. Programs can also access data in multiple remote locations as well as locally.

Security on EXPAND Network

Network security on Tandem systems is implemented differently from security on a single node.

Single-Node Security.   With a single node, the premise is that all users can cooperate, so barriers are built that secure data and applications by establishing user groups and individual accounts within a group. Files can then be secured based on four attributes—read, write, execute, and purge, attributes that dictate who may look at data in a file, change data in the file, execute the file if it is a program, and remove the file from the system. Each attribute can be restricted to an individual user, a group of users (all individuals within a given group), any individual user at that node, or to the omnipotent user of the system, SUPER.SUPER, which has access to all files on that node.

Network Security: Remote Passwords.   In the network environment the basic premise is that no remote user should have access to the node. To grant access, therefore, barriers must be taken down, meaning that remote passwords must be established so a user at one node can have access to another node. These remote passwords must specify the user group and user ID within the group as well as the node names. In addition, the remote passwords must be established on both nodes, and the names, group number and individual user number, and passwords must agree. An example may clarify this situation.

Suppose every node on an EXPAND network has an accounting group established, each one assigned a group number. If there is a user named ACCTING.MANAGER on both nodes A and B, then that name must be associated with the same user group and user number. Group and individual numbers vary from 0 to 255, so the user might be assigned to group 20 and user 255. (The individual with user number 255 is considered the manager of the group and has the ability to add and delete users from the group.) For network access between nodes A and B, this user ID must be established on both nodes. This is insufficient for network access, however, for which remote passwords must also be established. To do this, a user must be logged on to the system on which the password is to be established. The following shows the log-on sequence for ACCTING.MANAGER on node A and the establishment there of the remote passwords to node B:

LOGON ACCTING.MANAGER, (PASSWORD 1)

REMOTEPASSWORD \B, (PASSWORD 2)

REMOTEPASSWORD \A, (PASSWORD 3)

The same procedure would need to be performed on node B. Password 2 must agree with the remote password established for that user on node B, and password 3 must also agree. It is also possible to permit access in one direction only, so a user on node A could be granted access to node B, but on node B the same user would not have access to node A.

The security attributes of files include user, group, and any user for the network environment. For example, the file security attribute O represents a user on the local node, and U represents the user in the network environment. Thus, the read, write, execute and purge attributes can be set to local access only or to network access, and for individual, group, or any user.

EXPAND Network Expandability

New nodes can be introduced to the EXPAND network without interruption to any except the adjacent nodes, if the expansion has been planned for. One of the system generation parameters is the number of expected nodes, which determines the size of the network routing tables. Thus, one could specify 100 nodes for the network, even though fewer actually existed, and additional nodes could be added later, since sufficient space would already be available for them in the routing table. If the number of nodes in such a network exceeded 100, then a new system generation would be required. The information that a new node has been added to the system is propagated through the network by each node passing the information to its neighbors. Similarly, the information that a node has been removed from the network is transmitted from node to node until all have received it. Information regarding a new node, the deletion of a node, or a change in the status of a link stimulates the nodes to recalculate their network routing tables to reflect the change.

The largest EXPAND network user is Tandem itself, having over 200 nodes in offices in Europe, North America, and the Pacific Basin. This network includes terrestrial links from common carriers, X.25 links, and satellites. Applications include electronic mail, inventory, accounting, order entry, and other business functions.

In summary, EXPAND offers flexibility in how the network is configured and provides almost transparent access to applications and files that are distributed about the network.

DIGITAL EQUIPMENT CORPORATION'S DECNET

DECnet is the network system of Digital Equipment Corporation (DEC). In 1975, DEC announced its equivalent to IBM's SNA, the digital network architecture (DNA). Like SNA, DNA is a concept; its implementation is found in DECnet, which represents the software and hardware components for the network. Henceforth, only the term DECnet is used.

The objective of DECnet is to allow DEC systems as well as systems from other vendors to communicate on a common network. Flexibility was key in the implementation—flexibility to allow a variety of processors and terminals. It was to encompass point-to-point, multipoint, full duplex, half duplex, asynchronous, synchronous, process-to-process, down-line loading, remote file access, multiple configurations and low price.

History of DECnet

DECnet's implementation was in phases. Phase I, released in 1976, did not meet the system's objectives. The number of processors on the network was limited, and it gained the reputation of using an excessive amount of processing time and lacking transmission speed between nodes. Furthermore, for two nodes to communicate with each other, they had to be directly connected. It was not possible to send a message from one node to another through an intermediate node. Phase II, released in 1978, corrected some of the problems encountered in the first phase. Additional capabilities such as interfaces to non-DEC processors were added. Phase III, released in 1980, included the ability to transmit data through an intermediate node and expanded the number of nodes that could realistically be supported. Interfaces with IBM's SNA and with X.25 networks were also added.

DECnet Layering

DECnet is implemented as a layered architecture similar to the OSI reference model and IBM's SNA. Of the five layers defined—physical, data link, transport, network services, and application—the first four are similar to those in the OSI model. The names of the third and fourth layers are reversed—that is, the network layer of the OSI is called the transport layer in DEC's implementation, and vice versa. There is no session layer as such. The presentation and application layers of the OSI model are included in a single layer in the DEC system.

The data link layer uses the DEC DDCMP character synchronous protocol, a byte count protocol discussed in Chapter 6. Messages are routed via network routing tables maintained at each node, and transmitted as datagrams or via virtual circuits. The initial phases provided only datagram-type service. In this mode, packets could not be delivered, duplicate packets were possible, and packets could loop around the system and eventually be discarded. The ordering of packets was not guaranteed, meaning that packets could arrive out of order. With this service, packets had a field for counting the number of hops through which the packet had passed. Every time the packet was received by a node, the hop count was incremented. Packet looping could be detected by interrogating the hop count; if the count exceeded some predefined threshold, the packet would be discarded.

In addition to interfaces with foreign networks, DECnet has also been enchanced to interface with Ethernet LANs.

MICROCOMPUTERS IN NETWORKS

Advantages of Microcomputers

Microcomputers are becoming increasingly important elements of computer networks. This trend, which started in the early 1980s, is continuing because of their numerous advantages:

Relatively low cost

Ability to operate as a variety of terminals

Compact size

Ability to operate in office environments

Relatively wide-ranging processing capabilities

Large base of applications software

Large base of network-related software

Low Cost.   The cost of microcomputers has steadily declined since their introduction. Currently they are price competitive with many smart terminals that have significantly narrower processing capabilities. Furthermore, because microcomputers can emulate a wide variety of terminals, they make a sound investment. That is, if the user changes hardware vendors or data communications products, the micro will probably be able to function in the new environment. Generally, what is required to enable a micro to emulate a terminal is a synchronous or asynchronous logic board and certain software. With these components, a micro can function as either an asynchronous or synchronous terminal, and within each of these data link protocols, it can represent a variety of terminal types, such as IBM 3270, IBM 2780, and DEC VT100.

Fewer Special Requirements.   Because most microcomputers are designed to operate in an office environment, they have none of the special requirements for air conditioning or power that typify many larger systems. Their compact size means they fit in about the same desk space as a conventional terminal or typewriter. These attributes help keep their overall cost down.

Ease of Use and Versatility.   Next to cost, perhaps the most significant reason that micros have become important components of data communications networks is their ease of use and wide-ranging processing capabilities, including the ability to function as multiple terminal types, cited above, and the applications and network software available, plus an increase in processing power and storage capacity that has expanded the range of applications. Programs once available only on mainframe systems are now available on micros: scientific and statistical packages, simulation models, database management systems, and others. With large-capacity disk drives, significant amounts of data can be stored or down-loaded from a host system for processing, information that can then be printed locally and distributed to other systems within the network. This not only provides more local control of such functions, but can also reduce the workload of the host system.

Micros basically participate in two different kinds of network configurations—networks of microcomputers or personal computers, and as work stations in networks with larger systems as hosts. Within each of these configurations, the network can be either a local area network or a long-distance network.

Personal Computer Networks

Personal computer (PC) networks have grown significantly in number, as has the number of companies supplying PC networking software and hardware. Especially significant has been the growth of PC LANs. Both large and small businesses have found PCs to be a cost-effective tool, and many smaller businesses have acquired several PCs. When more than one PC exists in an office, a frequent requirement is to have them share resources such as data, software, printers, and disks.

Resource Sharing. PC LAN software provides the mechanism for resource sharing. For example, a medical clinic might maintain a patient-information database that must be accessible to different office personnel for billing, making appointments, and processing insurance claims. A PC LAN will allow multiple PCs to share this information. In addition, one printer can be shared among multiple users, letters and correspondence can be exchanged between different work stations, and software can be exchanged between systems, where not prohibited by licensing agreements. (Most PC software is licensed for use on one system only or for a specified number of systems. PC LANs do not necessarily remove such restrictions.)

Sharing PC resources is also exemplified by the following education application: To make computer instruction programs economically feasible for a school, hardware components are frequently shared by users. Rather than having disk drives and printers attached to every processor, one or more processors can act as hosts to others. In Figure 8-11 on page 294, one micro computer is attached to all the disk drives and printers. A student at one of the micros will enter a request to run a program resident

Figure 8-11
A Micro as Host to
Other Micros

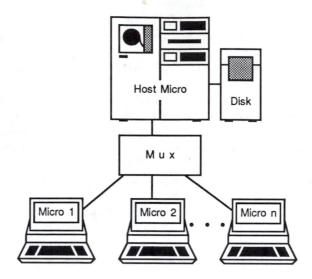

on the host's disk, and this software will be loaded into the memory of the student's processor. If the student needs to print the output of their program, the output data are transferred to the host and printed when the printer is available. In this configuration, the cost per education station is minimal, since it is unnecessary to purchase disk drives and printers for each computer.

Multi-tasking.   One outgrowth of PC networks is a pressure to enhance some of the existing microcomputer software. In the operating system environment, for instance, multi-tasking operating systems have become quite beneficial, and numerous operating systems are now available that allow the micro to handle several concurrent job streams. Thus, data communications transfers can be taking place while one or more applications are being processed. For example, one document can be transferred to another work station while a new document is being edited and an electronic mail program is awaiting receipt of a mail message.

Database technology must also change to provide database integrity during concurrent processing. Most PC database management systems have been designed for operation by a single user, so there is generally no concept of record-level or file-level locking or contention resolution. Two users could conceivably update the same record at the same time, in which case one database application could destroy the update posted by another, as occurs when two applications read one record and both alter the record before writing it back into the database. This is illustrated in Figure 8-12. With systems of this nature, operations need to be scheduled so only one operator is updating at a given time or so concurrent updating is arranged to avoid the multiple update problem.

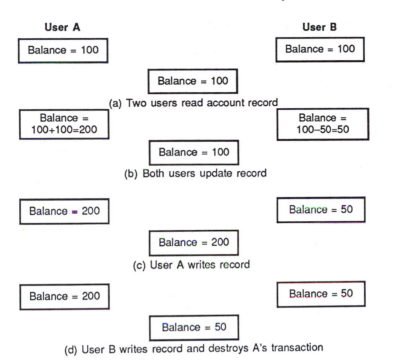

Figure 8-12
A Database
Contention

Cost. The cost of a PC–LAN connection differs from supplier to supplier. The typical configuration includes a printed circuit board, software, and connectors to attach to the medium, and the cost of such attachments generally start at around $500.

Long-distance PC Networks. Long-distance networks consisting only of micros are generally informal networks used mostly by computer hobbyists, primarily for bulletin board and information exchange applications. The most common long-distance network use of PCs is to connect the PC as a work station to a larger host computer. In this configuration the PC can serve as a terminal device, as a stand-alone or network processor, or as a terminal device performing some local processing in support of an application.

Versatility. One advantage of a PC is its ability to emulate almost any type of terminal. In fact, the PC can assume several identities, depending on the type of work being performed. In one application it might perform local data entry before passing a batch of data along, emulating an RJE terminal; at another time it might operate in page mode, like an IBM 3278; and at other times it might appear as a conversational TTY-like device. When not performing terminal functions, it can be used as a local processor. It is this flexibility that makes the PC an attractive network component.

Other Applications of PC Networks

The applications of PCs in a network environment are manifold, the most obvious being to use them simply as a terminal when connected to the host and as a local processor when not attached to the host, since this requires no additional processing at the host or microcomputer level. This type of use, however, does not fully exploit their potential.

Using Host Database.   One of the more integrated uses of PCs is to extract data from a host database, down-load them into a PC, use local applications such as spreadsheet software and graphics to manipulate the data locally and print the results on a printer or plotter attached to the PC. This is illustrated in Figure 8-13. When used in this manner, data must be extracted from the database, formatted, and transmitted to the micro, where they may need additional formatting to make them compatible with the PC's application software.

For example, in a personnel situation in which a union contract is due for renegotiation, with the union requesting a salary raise, additional holidays, a shorter workweek, and additional benefits, the personnel manager can use a PC spreadsheet to evaluate the options, as follows: On the host system a high-level database query language can extract the necessary data from the company database, including salary, seniority, and benefits for union employees. The query language can output the extracted data to a disk file on the host system. Next, the data can be formatted for transmission to the PC, which consists of compressing the data, to economize on line usage, and segmenting the data into record sizes compatible with the PC software. The data can then be transmitted to the PC and stored on disk. To again format the data on the PC, the data can be decompressed

Figure 8-13
Data Extraction from
Host to Micro

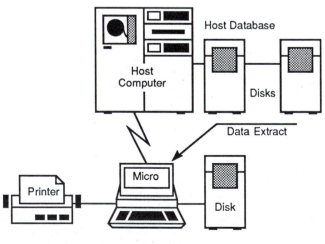

Spreadsheet Processing

and formatted into a differential file format acceptable to the spreadsheet software. The data can then be loaded into the spreadsheet program and analyzed. Various scenarios of wage and benefit packages can be evaluated and graphs produced indicating the impact of the different proposals.

Participating in Host Application.   Another use of a PC is as an active participant in an application system running on the host. When data have been entered on the PC, a local process will edit the data to ensure they meet editing characteristics. The data can then be compressed (to minimize utilization of the communications link), encrypted for security, and transmitted to the host. The PC could also be responsible for the display and sequencing of screen templates, which not only eliminates that portion of the data being transmitted over the communications link, but also assumes some of the processing load usually required of the host node.

Efficient Use of Terminal Operators.   Another possible advantage of microcomputers as opposed to smart or dumb terminals is the ability to keep an operator productive even when the host is unavailable. For instance, using a less intelligent terminal in an application where the data are ordinarily entered directly into a database residing on the host, a failure of either the host or the communications link would result in the operator's being unable to continue with data entry. With a microcomputer, however, it is possible for the operator to continue with data entry and to have the data stored locally. When communications to the host computer are reestablished, the transactions already entered can be forwarded to the host. If the microcomputer's operating system supports multi-tasking, then the stored transactions can be forwarded while the operator enters additional transactions.

Home Computers.   Network applications involving personal computers in the home have started to emerge. Home banking is being implemented in some areas, enabling customers to transfer money between accounts and to pay bills. Videotex applications enable consumers to shop at home and to obtain information from a variety of sources such as news wires, stock exchanges, and travel agencies. When the home computer has become as common a household appliance as the telephone, its use in computer networks is likely to expand even further.

PCs and Host Processing

Whether the use of microcomputers in communications networks brings about a significant savings in host processing remains to be seen. In one installation, it has been found, the amount of host CPU savings was slight—approximately 5% [Campbell, 1984]. On the other hand, microcomputers might actually increase the load on host processors, since they will open up new kinds of applications. The ease of access to host data, coupled with local processing and output, will likely aid the development of previously impractical applications. These new applications will surely increase demand for host computer services.

CASE STUDY

The Syncrasy Corporation, once again expanding, intends to open retail outlets in a number of other cities. A tentative list of these new cities is given in Figure 8-14. To accommodate the additional retail outlets, the number of terminals and work stations in the Kansas City world headquarters will be expanded to approximately 250. These terminals and work stations will be involved in order processing, inventory management, document generation, network management, electronic mail, personnel management, and software development. There is to be a great deal of sharing among users in the facility, such as between the software developers and the documentation group, as well as the exchange among work stations of both large and small documents. In addition, world headquarters will be required to generate, store, and transmit graphics and video training films. Since graphic images use a high number of data bits, the system must be capable of transmitting a lot of data, and at the approximately 6-Mbps transmission speed required for video.

Figure 8-14
Expansion Cities

Seattle	Detroit	Rome
Phoenix	Denver	Oslo
Boston	Montreal	Hong Kong
Miami	Toronto	Sydney
Dallas	London	Tokyo
Washington, D.C.	Paris	Mexico City
Philadelphia	Frankfurt	

Network Requirements

Each of the cities on the network will have at least one processor on the network, and the existing network, discussed in Chapter 5, might be abandoned if a better configuration exists.

Reliability.   The requirements of the new network include high reliability between the major centers in New York, Chicago, Kansas City, and Los Angeles and between the European cities. For the Pacific area, however, it has been decided that distance and the related communications costs prohibit the redundant links required for reliability. Reliability for Syncrasy means that all nodes can continue to communicate should a link fail, and that all remaining nodes can still communicate should a node fail.

Low Cost.   The second design criterion is cost. Syncrasy wants the lowest-cost network that can provide the necessary functions.

World Headquarters Requirements

The world headquarters' entire complex is located in three buildings that are close enough to allow use of a local area network.

Transmission Medium.   The first question was whether to use a baseband or broadband system. Since video images as well as data transmission are required, either two separate baseband systems or one broadband system will be necessary. A broadband local area network was selected.

Because of the high volume of data to be exchanged, it was considered necessary to have a very-fast-data channel as well as multiple lower-speed channels for interfacing with a variety of devices. Syncrasy's relatively modern PABX system, which uses wire pairs for transmission, was considered for the network medium. Its advantages include the integration of voice with data, and avoiding the cost of installing a separate data delivery medium. However, since the data-carrying capacity of the PABX telephone system is significantly less than that required, an LAN vendor was selected. The medium chosen was coaxial cable using broadband. The channel configuration of the chosen local area network is similar to that depicted in Figure 8-1 on page 268.

U.S. Network Configuration

The long-distance network in the U.S. must, of course, interface with the local area network, with the gateway function being performed by a processor attached to both networks.

Backbone Network.   The need for reliability in the four major U.S. cities demands a loop configuration, as depicted in Figure 8-15. As a minimum, the network routing algorithm must be able to alter paths in the event of the failure of a node or link. This type of configuration is sometimes called

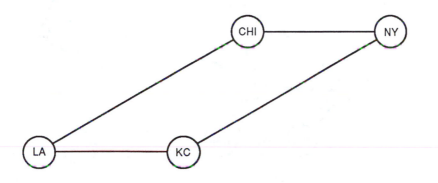

Figure 8-15
A Backbone Network

a *backbone network*, and the nodes are referred to as *backbone nodes*. From the mileage chart given on page 172, in Figure 5-21, it can be determined that the backbone network in Figure 8-15 is the minimum-distance configuration.

One possible United States configuration is depicted in Figure 8-16. The backbone network serves as the delivery system for many of the nodes, such as from Seattle to Boston. However, a message sent from Seattle to San Francisco will not make use of the backbone system.

Syncrasy has decided that the backbone nodes should be dedicated to the network task; so they will *not* be used for application processing. This decision was made because the amount of anticipated message traffic is sufficient to allow dedicated backbone nodes. To increase the reliability of the backbone network, fault-tolerant computers were chosen.

Remaining U.S. Network.   Three primary options were considered in configuring the remainder of the network: leased media, switched media, and public data network (PDN). Which of these is most cost effective is a function of distance and message traffic. Distance becomes a factor when determining the rates charged for leased and switched connections, it is usually not a factor with respect to PDN rates. Message traffic affects the connect time for switched connections and the packet charges for a PDN.

For all U.S. nodes not in the backbone network an analysis was performed to determine which of the three options would be most cost-effective. The analysis for the Seattle node follows.

Seattle–San Francisco Line Costs.   The following rate information on the three options for connecting the Seattle node to the San Francisco node

Figure 8-16
A Possible United
States Network

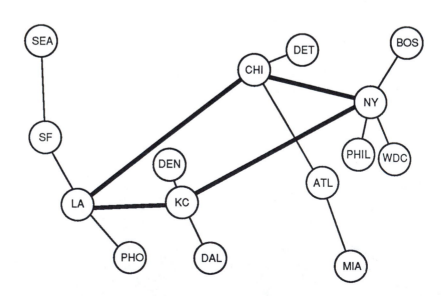

(the closest) are only approximate and are intended for use only in this case study. Actual rates may vary. Leased line rates are given in Figure 8-17, switched telephone rates in Figure 8-18, and PDN rates in Figure 8-19.

First 100 miles	$2.52 per mile (includes monthly service charge fee)
Next 900 miles (101–1000)	$0.94 per mile
Each mile over 1000	$0.58 per mile

Figure 8-17
Leased Line Rates, Seattle to San Francisco

First minute of connect time	$0.60
Each additional minute	$0.40

Figure 8-18
Switched Line Rates, Seattle to San Francisco

Connection charge per node	$400 per month
Packet charge	$1.50 per 1000 packets
Packet size	128 characters

Figure 8-19
PDN Charges, Seattle to San Francisco

Additional comparison information must be derived. To evaluate the switched connections, the number of connections per day and the total amount of connect time must be approximated. Seattle, being a relatively low-volume node at a network extremity, will not be involved in store-and-forward operations. In contrast, the San Francisco node will originate and receive its own messages and will forward messages to and from Seattle and other nodes. It is estimated that there will be three connections per day, requiring 250 minutes total connect time. A message traffic of 30,000 characters per day is also anticipated. A 23-day workmonth is assumed. The total distance between Seattle and San Francisco is 810 miles.

Leased line charges are

(first 100 miles × $2.52 per mile) + (710 miles × $0.94 per mile)
$$= 252 + 667.40 = \$919.40$$

Daily switched line costs are

(3 connections × $0.60 per first minute) + (247 remaining minutes × $0.40 per minute) = 1.80 + 98.80 = $100.60

Monthly switched line costs are therefore

23 days × $100.60 per day = $2313.80

No additional telephone service charges are included in the analysis because telephones are already installed on the premises. If one or more telephones were dedicated to data communications, then their cost would have to be included.

PDN charges are derived as follows: Two stations must be connected at a fee of $400 each. There are 30,000 characters transmitted per day, which at 128 characters per packet is 235 packets. This assumes that all packets are full, which will not be the case. A message of 140 characters requires two packets to be sent. The 30,000 characters transmitted per day was approximated to include this variance. There is a charge of $1.50 per 1000 packets, and there are 23 work days per month. Thus, the monthly PDN charges are

$$(2 \times 400) + \left(\frac{30,000}{128} \times \frac{1.50}{1000} \times 23\right) = 800 + (235 \times 0.0015 \times 23)$$
$$= 800 + 8.11 = \$808.11$$

This analysis shows that PDN will be the most economical link between Seattle and San Francisco. This configuration has the added benefit of allowing the Seattle node to transmit directly to any node with a PDN port, meaning that such messages would not always need to be routed through San Francisco.

Break-even Point.   One more computation will complete the analysis of the link between Seattle and San Francisco A break-even figure will show the amount of message traffic necessary to make the cost of a leased line the same as that for a PDN. (From the above analysis, it seems unlikely that a switched connection will ever be practical.) The break-even number of characters per day, x, is given by

$$(2 \times 400) + \left(\frac{x}{128} \times 0.0015 \times 23\right) = \$919.40$$

$x = 442{,}991$ characters per day

This is not a significant amount of message traffic; a 120-page typed document, at 80 characters per line and 55 lines per page, with no compression, exceeds this amount.

The above calculations assumed that neither node had a PDN port, and that there was one connection charge per node. However, if one of the nodes already had a PDN connection, then the cost for that port should not be included, or should be distributed throughout the network. Thus, if San Francisco already had been configured with a PDN port, then the PDN cost would decrease by $400, or the cost of that port should be apportioned among the nodes that must be connected to San Francisco.

San Francisco–Los Angeles Line.   A similar analysis was performed for the San Francisco–Los Angeles connection. A switched line was not considered in this instance because message traffic from Seattle to other nodes without a PDN port can be routed through San Francisco. A leased line was the most economical in this instance. The analysis follows.

The leased line rates between San Francisco and Los Angeles are different from those given in Figure 8-18 because the link is intrastate. A leased line is available for $425. Since approximately 200,000 characters per day are transferred between the two cities, PDN charges are

$$400 + \left(\frac{200,000}{128} \times 0.0015 \times 23\right) = 400 + 53.90 = \$453.90$$

International Lines.   All the European cities will be connected by a backbone network. The connections between Europe, the United States, Canada, Mexico, Japan, Australia, and Hong Kong will be made via X.25 networks. The amount of message traffic between these entities does not warrant the use of leased facilities.

Configuring the other parts of the network is left as an exercise.

SUMMARY

This chapter has looked at local area networks and vendor implementations. LAN technology has experienced rapid growth since the mid-1970s. There are currently over 45 providers of LAN systems, using twisted pairs, coaxial cable, fiber optics, and PBX systems to move data. Attempts have been made to establish standards for LAN implementations, most notably by the IEEE (Institute of Electrical and Electronics Engineers). Because of the diversity of applications for which LANs are used and because of the variety of existing implementations, multiple standards have been adopted that allow for bus or ring topologies using CSMA/CD or token passing access methods. Additional standards are likely to appear in the future. The Hyperchannel is an example of a very-high-speed LAN. IBM, which currently has no LAN implementation, has announced a recommended office wiring plan, and has been offering information regarding LAN implementations, leading to the speculation that IBM will introduce a ring or star token passing LAN in the near future.

The most significant vendor network offering is IBM's system network architecture, which was designed to consolidate their data communications offerings, at one time a wide variety of devices, access methods, and protocols. SNA provides an architecture for the design of data communications systems through a body of software and hardware components, not just a single product. SNA is continually being enhanced to accommodate new hardware and implement new capabilities. Most computer vendors provide a network architecture to accompany their systems. Although these architectures can differ significantly from IBM's SNA, they all share the same objectives.

Microcomputers are very likely to play an increasing role in data communications networks and in network processing. Their general ease of use and wide range of available software may form the basis of new applications and capabilities.

Key Terms

Advanced communications facility
  (ACF)
ALOHANet
Attached resource computer (ARC)
Backbone network
Baseband transmission
Broadband transmission
Bus
Carrier sense with multiple access
  and collision detection (CSMA/CD)
Digital branch exchange (DBX)
Domain
End-to-end routing
Ethernet
Fiber optic extension (FOX)
Half-session
Hyperchannel (HC)
IEEE 802.3
IEEE 802.4

Local area network (LAN)
Logical unit (LU)
Network addressable unit (NAU)
Network control program (NCP)
Network performance analyzer
  (NPA)
Network problem determination
  aid (NPDA)
Physical unit (PU)
Private branch exchange (PBX)
Ring
Server
Session
Slotted ALOHA protocol
Subarea
System network architecture (SNA)
System services control point (SSCP)
Token passing
Virtual routing
Wangnet

Questions and Exercises

1. What features of a PBX make it unsuitable for a local area network? What features make it attractive?

2. Compare and contrast Ethernet with the Hyperchannel.

3. Is a broadband LAN superior to a baseband LAN? Justify your answer.

4. List the four types of physical units in SNA.

5. What is a half-session layer in SNA? What is its purpose?

6. Explain how a session is established in SNA.

7. Why are there multiple LAN standards?

8. Is having multiple LAN standards beneficial? Justify your answer.

9. How do Ethernet, the IEEE 802 standard, and SNA addressing differ? How are they the same?

10. Describe what a gateway between Ethernet and SNA must accomplish.

11. Suppose that the message traffic between New York City and Boston is 600,000 characters per day. If the cost of a leased line is $650, which will be

more economical, a leased line or PDN? Assume that New York City already has a PDN port. How many characters must be exchanged for a leased line to cost the same as a PDN?

References

Baer, David M., and Sturch, Jim. "An SNA Primer for Programmers, Part 1." *Computerworld on Communications* 17 (November 14, 1983).

_____ "An SNA Primer for Programmers, Part 2." *Computerworld on Communications* 17 (November 21, 1983).

Bellamy, John. *Digital Telephony.* New York: Wiley, 1982.

Benhamou, Eric, and Estrin, Judy. "Multilevel Internetworking Gateways: Architecture and Application." *Computer* 16 (Sept. 1983).

Burr, William E. "An Overview of the Proposed American National Standard for Local Distributed Data Interfaces." *Communications of the ACM* 26 (August 1983).

Campbell, B. W. "The Planning Side of Success with Micros." *Data Communications* 13 (Oct. 1984).

"Controversy Hits Market for Local Area Networks." *Mini-Micro Systems* 14 (March 1981).

Cypser, R. J. *Communications Architecture for Distributed Systems.* Reading, MA: Addison-Wesley, 1978.

Dalal, Yogen K. "Use of Multiple Networks in the Xerox Network System." *Computer* 15 (October 1982).

"DECnet's Phase III Expands Communications." *Mini-Micro Systems* 12 (March 1980).

Digital Equipment Corp. *Introduction to Local Area Networks.* Digital Equipment Corp. 1982.

Dix, John. "IBM Announces Wiring Scheme Eliminating Coaxial Cable." *Computerworld on Communications* 18 (May 14, 1984).

Frank, Howard. "Broadband Versus Baseband Local Area Networks." *Telecommunications*, March 1983.

Franta, William R., and Heath, John R. "Hyperchannel Local Network Interconnection Through Satellite Links." *Computer* 17 (May 1984).

Harris, Fred H., Sweeney, Frederick L., Jr., and Vonderohe, Robert H. "New Niches for Switches." *Datamation* 29 (March 1983).

IBM. *Systems Network Architecture, Concepts and Products.* Manual no. GC30-3072-1. Research Triangle Park, NC: IBM, 1981.

_____ *Systems Network Architecture—Sessions Between Logical Units.* Manual no. GC20-1868-2. Research Triangle Park, NC: IBM, 1981.

IEEE Society. *Tutorial Local Network Technology.* IEEE Catalog no. EH0208-9, 1983.

Kuo, Franklin F. *Protocols and Techniques for Data Communications Networks.* Englewood Cliffs, NJ: Prentice-Hall, 1981.

Levy, Walter A., and Rothberg, Michael. "Coaxial Cable Finds a Home." *Mini-Micro Systems* XIV (March 1981).

Liu, Ming T., Hilal, Wael, and Groomes, Bernard H. "Performance Evaluation of Channel Access Protocols for Local Computer Networks." *Proceedings of the COMPCON Fall 82 Conference* (1982).

Loveland, Richard A. "Putting DECnet Into Perspective." *Datamation* 25 (March 1979).

McNamara, John E. *Technical Aspects of Data Communications.* Bedford, MA: Digital Equipment Corporation, 1977.

Metcalfe, Robert M., and Boggs, David R. "Ethernet: Distributed Packet Switching for Local Computer Networks." *Communications of the ACM* 19 (July 1976).

Myers, Ware. "Toward a Local Network Standard." *IEEE Micro* (August 1982).

Schneidewind, Norman. "Interconnecting Local Networks to Long-Distance Networks." *Computer* 16 (Sept. 1983).

Shoch, John F., and Hupp, Jon A. "Performance of an Ethernet Local Network— a Preliminary Report." *Digest of Papers—COMPCON Spring 80.* Los Alamitos, CA: IEEE Computer Society, 1980.

————— "Evolution of the Ethernet Local Computer Network." *Computer* 15 (August 1982).

Stuck, Bart W. "Calculating the Maximum Mean Data Rate in Local Area Networks." *Computer* 16 (May 1983).

Tanenbaum, Andrew S. *Computer Networks.* Englewood Cliffs, NJ: Prentice-Hall, 1981.

Thornton, James E., and Christiansen, Gary S. "Hyperchannel Network Links." *Computer* 16 (Sept. 1983).

Tropper, Carl. *Local Computer Network Technologies.* New York: Academic Press, 1981.

Yasaki, Edward K. "Is There a PBX in Your Future?" *Datamation* 29 (March 1983).

Network System Software

INTRODUCTION

This chapter discusses some of the major software components of a data communications network. In the OSI recommendation, software exists at every level from the data link level up. Thus, this chapter covers functions of the six highest levels of the reference model. Consistent with prior approaches, the discussion moves from the level closest to the terminals toward the host processor.

The next chapter covers security, editing, formatting, message routing, and various other software functions, with special emphasis on how all these components can be integrated into a comprehensive applications support system. The discussion there is confined to software residing in the front-end processor or communications controller, and host processor. Not discussed is the software that resides in terminals, cluster controllers, or concentrators.

At the conclusion of this chapter you should know how the database, operating system, application, and data communications software are related to each other, how transactions flow through a system, and the functions provided by access methods and transaction control processes.

SOFTWARE OVERVIEW

Applications Software

A generic software configuration is depicted in Figure 9-1. At the heart of the system is the applications software. The objective of applications software is to solve a business or scientific problem. A few years ago this used to also mean the solving of system problems such as interfacing to terminals and files. Currently, most systems software is intended to remove the application from systems and communications functions so the user can concentrate on the application. To support this objective, software such as database management and data communications access methods and teleprocessing monitors have been developed. These provide functions common to most application programs and insulate the applications from the details of file and device access.

Operating System

The *operating system (OS)* assists the applications by scheduling jobs, initiating jobs, allocating resources, managing memory, providing input/output (I/O) interfaces, enforcing process priorities, preventing one process from interfering with another, assisting with process-to-process communication, and providing a man–machine interface. The operating system is the overall manager of the processor. The operating system also handles multi-processing and multi-tasking, both of which are quite important in the efficient operation of an on-line system.

Figure 9-1
An Applications
Environment

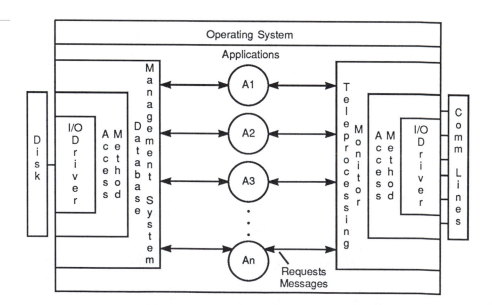

Multi-Processing and Multi-Tasking.   Multi-processing allows more than one process to share the memory and system processor, implemented in a variety of ways. *Multi-tasking* is the ability of one process to work concurrently on tasks for multiple users. One way this is implemented is to make programs reentrant. *Reentrant code* allows multiple users to share a program, thus reducing the amount of memory required. Essentially this is done by separating the users' data from the executable code. Each user has a unique set of data, but all share the executable code. Different users will probably be at different logic points in the code. For the code to be shared by users, one task must be prohibited from modifying the code file. Reentrancy is equivalent to running multiple copies of the same program, one for each user, without incurring the additional memory overhead of one separate code file for each user.

Database and File Management Systems

The database and file management systems organize data into files and provide access to the data based on one or a number of different keys or data items. A file manager performs a rather small subset of the database management functions.

The basic features of a *database management system (DBMS)* are a data definition language (DDL), a data manipulation language (DML), data independence, recovery, query and report writer language, data dictionaries, interfile relationships, data integrity, security, contention resolution, and deadlock detection and correction. There are a number of additional attributes, but these are the essential ones. A more complete set of database management system functions is given in Figure 9-2.

Data manipulation language (DML)	Data definition language (DDL)
Integrity	Security
Data independence	Recovery
Statistics	Concurrent use
Reorganization	Utilities
Query report writer	Host language interfaces
Data editor	User views
Data dictionary	Database design aids
Deadlock detection/resolution	Distributed databases
Transaction definition/recovery	

Figure 9-2
Database Management System Features

Data Definition Language (DDL).   Once a database has been designed, the data elements, records, files, and file relationships must be defined.

This is done with a *data definition language (DDL)*. The data are described as to data names, type and size of the data elements, how the data elements are grouped together to form records, and which records are combined to form files. Relationships between files can be defined explicitly by establishing pointer fields or implicitly by storing the same data on different records. In the latter case, the data are associated by virtue of the fact that the records contain a common field.

Both physical and logical views of the data must be defined. The physical view of data—also referred to as the schema—describes how the data are physically stored on disk, together with supporting structures such as indices for access methods. The logical description—also referred to as the subschema—shows how a user views the data.

Data Manipulation Language (DML).   A *data manipulation language (DML)* provides the means to access, update, and delete data in the database. In some systems it is implemented as a host language interface.

Query and Report Writer Language.   Query and report writers allow the user to extract data from the database and format them for reports, thus eliminating some of the need to write report programs. Most of the current systems support a high-level natural language as interface, enabling nontechnical personnel to create their own reports.

Host Language Interface.   A *host language interface* allows one or more programming languages to be used to retrieve and update the database. The most popular host language in business is currently COBOL, but FORTRAN, PL/1, Ada, Pascal, C, and most of the common programming languages have interfaces with one or more database sytems. The interface might be an integral part of the language or it could be separate from the language. For example, the CODASYL committee's recommendation for a language interface includes verbs for manipulating records, such as GET, FIND, MODIFY, INSERT, and DELETE. Since these verbs are outside the usual syntax of their languages, when using a separate command language for database access, a precompiler must translate the database calls into acceptable language or procedure calls.

Recovery.   *Recovery* restores the database to a consistent state following a failure. For example, in a banking application in which money is being transferred from a savings account to a checking account, if the system fails after the money is removed from the savings account but before it is deposited in the checking account, the database would be inconsistent. Recovery will either back out the transaction or take it forward to its completion.

Data Dictionary.   A *data dictionary* is a database about the data. It is an important tool for the database administrator to provide standards and control within the database itself. The dictionary contains such information as data item names, lengths, type, and edit rules.

Integrity and Security.   *Integrity* and *security* can be provided in various ways: Security might include access rules and profiles. Integrity is concerned with the consistency of data. In a personnel database, for instance, an employee's record would not be deleted without first ensuring that all the employee's dependents were also removed, so the DBMS might include integrity rules prohibiting such actions.

Design Aids.   Design aids assist the database administrator in tuning and designing the database, including the providing of statistics, models, and programs for indicating how data can be most effectively grouped into records.

Data Independence.   *Data independence* means the ability to make changes in the physical storage of data without requiring massive changes in the applications that use the data. For example, if the size of a zip code field is expanded from five to nine digits, ideally the only programs that should require modification are those making use of that particular field. If a new field is added to a record or a new file is added to the database, then ideally only those programs needing access to that field or file should require changes. There are many existing systems that do not provide this level of data independence.

User Views.   User views are also commonly referred to as subschemas. Different users are likely to have different views of data. For instance, in a personnel database, an application that mails a corporate newsletter to employees might have a view of each employee's name and address, whereas a payroll application might have a view of name, employee number, social security number, salary, and number of dependents; both applications are accessing the same physical files, but the data required by each would be different.

Concurrent Use, Interference, and Contention Resolution.   Users can sometimes intefere with each other's use of data. To illustrate: Suppose Mr. and Mrs. Smith have a joint checking account with a balance of $1000, and both make a transaction at the same time at different branches: Mr. Smith deposits a $2000 check while Mrs. Smith cashes a $200 check. The important point here is that the two different users are accessing the same record in an attempt to update it. Mr. Smith's transaction is processed first, and the record updated to show a balance of $3000. Then Mrs. Smith's transaction, which cancels Mr. Smith's deposit, deducts $200 from the $1000 balance and the record is updated to show a balance of $800. This situation is illustrated in Figure 9-3 on page 312.

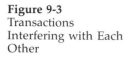
Figure 9-3
Transactions
Interfering with Each
Other

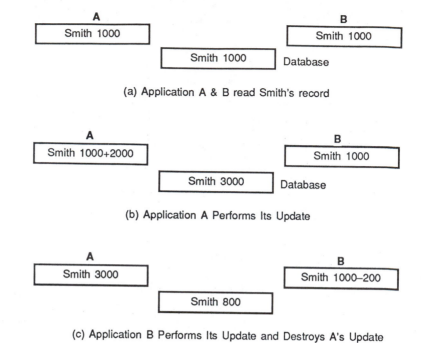

(a) Application A & B read Smith's record

(b) Application A Performs Its Update

(c) Application B Performs Its Update and Destroys A's Update

The most common way to avoid such interference problems is to place locks on records. This means, essentially, that whenever a user intends to update a record (and sometimes when just reading it), the record must be read with a lock that prevents other users from accessing the record during the time it is undergoing change.

Deadlock Resolution.   Locking of records solves the *contention* problem, but creates another problem, known as deadlock or deadly embrace. *Deadlock* occurs when two or more transactions are accessing locked records. Suppose, in the simplest case, that user A has locked record X and user B has locked record Y. User A attempting to access record Y cannot proceed until Y is unlocked, and user B attempting to access record X cannot proceed until X is unlocked. Both users could potentially wait forever. How deadlock detection and correction are viewed varies with the database system. Some systems make it the user's obligation to detect and correct deadlock, whereas others make it the responsibility of the DBMS. Contention and deadlock problems both become more acute when transactions access and lock records on multiple nodes, which means the records are locked for longer periods of time because of the relative slowness of the communications circuit and because different lock managers are usually involved, one at each node.

Access Methods.   Database *access methods* provide the the user with alternative paths for accessing data. With personnel files, for instance, an employee's file might need to be accessed via the employee's name, employee number, and social security number. Although data can be physically organized in only one way, access methods provide alternate routes to the data. If its is desirable to retrieve employee names in alphabetical order, but the personnel records are physically stored in ascending employee number order, then an index sequential access method could be established to provide sequential retrieval by name. The DBMS would use this access method to create and maintain an index of last names and addresses, as shown in Figure 9-4. To find the record for employee Adams, for instance, would mean looking first in the index and then following the pointer to the actual record. The index sequential access method is only one of several methods for retrieving data from a database.

Transaction Control Process

Whereas the DBMS provides an application with access to data, application access to terminals or other nodes is provided by a *transaction control process*

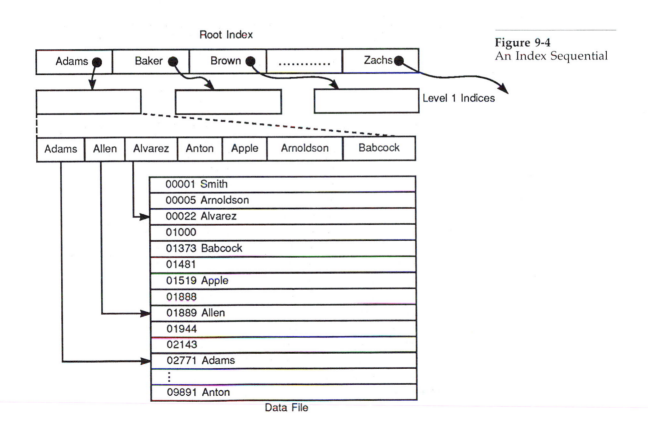

Figure 9-4
An Index Sequential

(TCP), also referred to as *a teleprocessing monitor (TP)* or *message control system (MCS)*. In the absence of a TCP, a *data communications access method* can fulfill this function. As the DBMS allows applications to share data and insulates the applications from the physical details of data storage and provides data independence, the TCP enables different terminals to interface with multiple applications and insulates an application from the physical differences between terminals and between network nodes. As the DBMS uses different access methods to provide multiple paths to data, the TCP uses different terminal access methods to give access to different terminal types. A more detailed description of the transaction control process and its associated access methods is found later in this chapter.

Device Drivers.   At the extremities of the processor are device drivers, also called *I/O drivers*. On the DBMS side these are disk and tape drivers, and on the data communications side these are line drivers. Such software processes provide a low-level interface with the physical devices, lines, disk drives, or tape drives they control. Line drivers are quite system dependent.

Other Software Functions.   Embedded in the various levels of software just described are other software functions, such as security, formatting, and data editing. Their exact place of implementation varies from system to system. Data editing, for instance, can be performed by the terminal, the TCP, or the application. These topics are discussed in Chapter 10.

Example of Transaction Flow

An application must first open, or connect to the TCP. Applications in some systems run under control of the TCP, and the connection is inherent in their being started. In other systems the applications are relatively independent of the TCP, so they communicate with each other via an interprocess communication facility. Regardless of the implementation, however, a data path always exists between the application and the TCP. Once open, the application issues a read request, indicating its readiness to accept a message for processing. The TCP, which controls all of the terminals in turn, initiates a *read* on all terminals under its control. At this point, each application is awaiting a transaction from the TCP, and the TCPs are awaiting data from the terminals. When a terminal transmits a transaction, the TCP examines the transaction and determines which application should process it, and passes the transaction to the application. The application then requests records from the DBMS, which returns the requested data to the application for processing. The processing results are passed back to the TCP, which determines if another application process must become involved in the transaction. Assuming that only one application is all that is required, the TCP then forwards the result back to the terminal that initiated the transaction. The application posts a new *read* request to the TCP, and the TCP does likewise to the terminal.

ACCESS METHODS

Data communications access methods give system users easier access to terminal devices. They relieve users from the device-specific attributes of terminals, and provide connection, disconnection, and data transfer services to the applications. As with TCPs, the scope of access methods differs with the vendor and even within different access methods from one vendor. A generic description is provided below, with a specific implementation included in the supplements.

Application–Terminal Connection

Several approaches have been used to provide access methods. One approach is to have one application process tied to a terminal, as illustrated in Figure 9-5. This is characteristic of IBM's *basic telecommunications access method (BTAM)* structure. The application interfaces with the terminal or line through the access method, or in some cases with the access method embedded in the application itself. The advantage of this approach is simplicity—A TCP is complicated, whereas the application per terminal or line is relatively simple. The disadvantages of the application–terminal connection are: changes in the terminal environment can cause changes in the application; reduced flexibility, because of the restriction of one application per terminal or line; operational problems resulting from moving a terminal from one application to another; larger-size applications programs, because one application process usually must perform more functions to handle all the transactions from one source; and a larger number of processes, because the sharing of applications among lines is more limited.

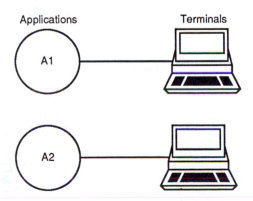

Figure 9-5
Terminals Linked to
Applications

Multiple Transaction Process

A second approach to access methods is for one very large process to handle multiple transaction types attached to one or more lines, as depicted in Figure 9-6. This configuration gives a single terminal access to multiple transactions. The problems with this environment stem from the complexity of the process: A change in any subapplication supported by the overall process requires a change in the entire process, which makes coding and maintaining the process much more difficult. Furthermore, a problem in one portion of the process can disable all other included transactions.

Accessing a Terminal

Because an access method separates the application program from the terminal access logic, access methods can be used with or without a TCP, depending on the environment. Figure 9-7 illustrates two situations, TCP present and TCP absent. The access method performs fewer functions when the TCP is present because some functions are performed by the TCP. In the following discussion, *application* means either a TCP working on behalf of the application or the application program itself; thus, it will be unnecessary to determine whether a TCP is present or not.

The first requirement of accessing a terminal from a program is to connect the two. The access method serves as an intermediary in this case. Either the application initiates a connection by issuing an open or connect request to the access method, or the terminal initiates the action by issuing an application log-on request through the access method. Once the con-

Figure 9-6
Multiple Transaction
Process

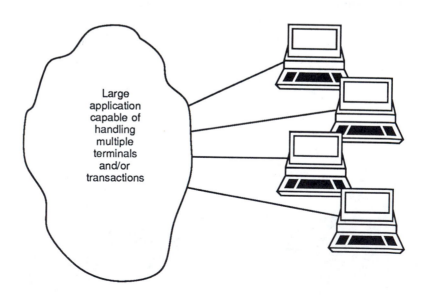

Large application capable of handling multiple terminals and/or transactions

Figure 9-7
Application-Terminal
Connection

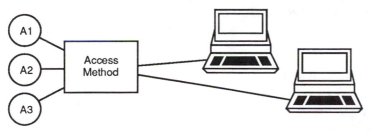

(a) Access method connecting terminals and applications

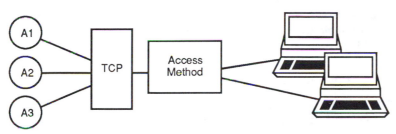

(a) TCP connecting terminals and applications

nection has been honored, a communication path exists, and the two can exchange data. Connection requests can be denied for security reasons or because the application or device is already occupied. Many access methods support numerous terminal protocols, which makes it easier for the application programmer to interface with multiple terminals, since the access method can accommodate the terminal differences.

In the absence of a TCP, the access method makes the connection between an application program and a terminal. In some implementations the connection is very static—that is, the application and terminal are attached to each other and the terminal can run only those transactions provided by that particular application. For another application process, the two must be disconnected and the terminal reconnected to the other application. Other systems provide more flexibility in making the connection between a terminal and an application. IBM's *virtual telecommunications access method (VTAM)*, described in the supplement, provides several algorithms by which terminal–application connections are made.

TRANSACTION CONTROL PROCESS

The transaction control process (TCP) provides the direct interface between the application environment and the data communications environment. A TCP is also sometimes referred to as a teleprocessing monitor or a *mes-*

sage control system (MCS). This section covers the general functions of the TCP. The supplements to this chapter present two specific implementations.

TCP Configuration

The configuration of the transaction control process is depicted in Figure 9-8. Since the TCP serves as a switch between applications and terminals, it must be aware of the terminals attached to it, the transactions that can be submitted, and the applications responsible for processing those transactions. It performs a switching function between applications and data communications lines. In this environment, any terminal can access any application visible to the TCP. Implementation can be as a monolithic process, as in Figure 9-9(a), or as multiple processes, as in Figure 9-9(b).

Single Threading vs. Multi-Threading

With *single threading*, a process accepts an input, processes the input to completion, and produces an output, being then ready to accept another input for processing. If a TCP were to operate in this manner it would accept an input from one terminal, send the transaction to an application process, wait for the response, and send the result back to the terminal, resulting in potentially long delays for the other terminals.

To efficiently perform the very complex function of coordinating multiple terminals and applications, the process must be multi-threaded. With *multi-threading*, different operations are processed concurrently.

Figure 9-8
A Generic TCP
Configuration

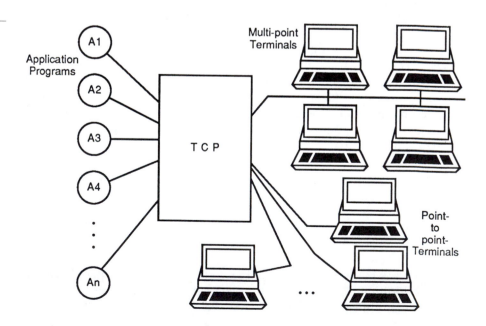

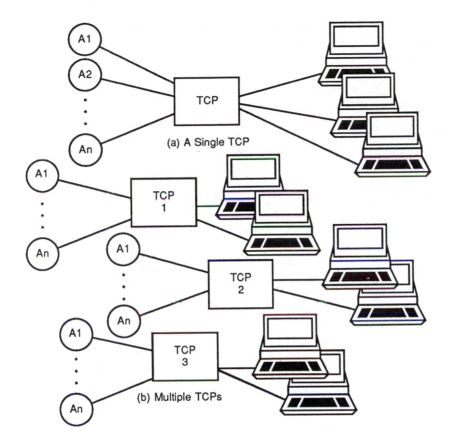

Figure 9-9
Multiple TCPs

(a) A Single TCP

(b) Multiple TCPs

The difference between single-threading and multi-threading can be likened to what happens in a grocery store when people queue up at the checkout counter, with the checkout clerk representing the TCP process and the customers the terminals. The clerk ordinarily operates in a single-threaded manner, processing one customer and one customer only until the total order has been tabulated and the money collected before turning to the next customer. If an object is unpriced, everyone waits while an assistant locates the price. Looking up the price is analogous to accessing a disk, with the assistant as the DBMS. Everyone waits while the price is being determined, the check written and verified, and comments about the weather are exchanged. To improve efficiency the clerks could be multi-threaded: Everyone in the queue would get attention. The clerks would maintain separate totals for each customer while a missing price was being located, the clerk could move on to the next customer and process their order. While the checks were being written, another customer could be served. The multi-threaded clerk must be much more flexible than the single-threaded clerk. Multiple totals will be accumulated, items will be taken from the correct basket and placed in the proper sack, and the bill will be delivered to and collected from the proper customer. Multiple application threads, then, are active within a multi-threaded process at the same time. A comparison of single-threaded and multi-threaded processes is graphically presented in Figure 9-10.

Maintaining Context.   An additional requirement of multi-threaded processes is to maintain context. Whereas each single-threaded transaction is completely self-contained, in a multi-threaded process, a complete activity might be separated into several parts, and somewhere, some process must keep track of the parts that are completed and those yet to be performed, and continue the transaction from the point at which it was discontinued. In some instances the action to be performed is contingent on a previous activity. For instance, in searching a database for an employee named Smith, an application might select and display the first ten Smiths plus additional identifying information, and if none of the ten names was cor-

Figure 9-10
Single-Threading vs.
Multi-Threading

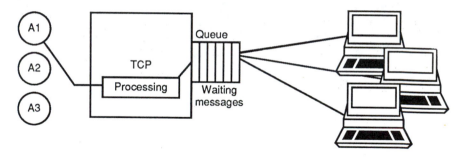

(a) Single Thread: Only One Transaction Active

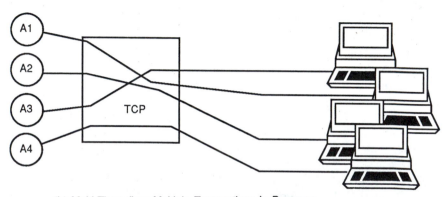

(b) Multi-Threading: Multiple Transactions in Progress

rect, the next ten would be displayed, and so on until the proper Smith was found. The search for the next ten names is contingent on where the previous search stopped.

Like the multi-threaded grocery clerk, the TCP must handle multiple customers at once. For example, suppose the TCP controls four terminals—T1, T2, T3, and T4—and three applications—A1, A2, and A3. At the start of the system, all four applications request to open, or connect to the TCP. The TCP records this information and issues a command to open, display the first screen, and post a *read* on each of the four terminals. At this point, the TCP is awaiting input from the terminals or a process. A chronological record of its activities is outlined in Figure 9-11. This type of interleaved processing continues throughout the workday.

Accept update transaction from terminal T2

Write T2's transaction on audit log

Accept inquiry transaction from T4

Route T4's request to application A1

Receive *write complete* on T2's audit log write

Begin transaction for T2

Route T2's transaction to A2

Receive inquiry transaction from T3

Route T3's transaction to A1

Receive A1's return message for T4

Write response to terminal T4

Receive A2's return message for T2

End T2's transaction

Receive inquiry transaction from T1

Receive request for next ten records from T4

Send T1's request to A3

Receive notice that T2's transaction has ended

Send response to T2

Send T4's request together with stored context to A1

Figure 9-11
Multiple TCP
Transaction Threads

Although in Figure 9-11 the context was maintained in the TCP, it could have been maintained within the application or the terminal. The TCP or a terminal is the most logical place for maintaining context, although to do so at a terminal requires that the terminal be smart or intelligent. The application is not as logical a place because multiple copies of one application can be used to increase efficiency, in which case the TCP would have to send a transaction to the same process that worked on the first part of the transaction requiring some context at the terminal or TCP. Furthermore, saving context in applications programs makes them more complex. Some designers prefer to remove this type of complexity from the application. Since many TCP processes are supplied by software houses or computer vendors rather than being written by the end user, it benefits the user to have the complexity placed in the TCPs and not in the applications.

Memory Management

In order to manage the context information and accept data from both terminals and applications, the TCP must provide *memory management* functions. At any point in time it can receive a message from either terminals or applications; multiple messages will be queued up at one time. The way in which TCPs manage memory varies. Essentially they must have enough memory available to provide storage for terminal and application messages as well as context data. Sometimes this requires virtual memory algorithms similar to those employed by some operating systems—that is, disk is treated as an extension of memory and data are swapped back and forth between real memory and disk areas.

Transaction Routing

The TCP must provide transaction routing, either based on a transaction code embedded within the data or on context data and a transaction identifier or an indicator such as a function key, light pen, or touch screen. Transaction routing requires that the TCP know which application handles a given transaction and the path or connection that leads to that application. Transaction routing could be table driven, in which case the TCP would look up the transaction ID in a table providing directions to the proper application process. Alternatively, a procedural interface with a case statement or similar construct would result in a program call or a message being sent to that process.

In order to fulfill its responsibility of message routing, the TCP must know about processes. Furthermore, if an application fails, the TCP should be able to request that it be automatically restarted. If a transaction arrives for an inactive process, the TCP should also be able to activate the process. If one application receives multiple transactions so that response times become degraded, the TCP should be able to initiate additional copies of that process to enhance performance. By the same token, if a process has been inactive for a long period of time, the TCP can optionally be directed to delete that process.

Transaction Log

The TCP is a logical place to implement transaction logging. A *transaction log* captures the transaction inputs, usually on tape or disk. Once captured, the system can assure the user that the transaction will be processed. This does not mean that the transaction will be successfully completed (errors could prevent that); it does mean that the transaction will not be lost by the system should a failure occur. In addition to its use in recovery, transaction logging is sometimes required by auditors, especially in financial transactions. Electronic Data Processing (EDP) auditors will periodically check transaction sources and trace them through the system to determine if they were correctly processed. If transaction logging is implemented, as soon as a transaction is received from a terminal or other node, it is written on the log file. Usually the TCP appends additional information to the message, such as a date-time stamp, *transaction ID*, or similar identifying information. Sometimes the completion of a transaction is also logged. In recovery situations this eliminates the possibility of a transaction being processed twice.

Synchronizing Database Logging and Transaction Logging. In some systems the transaction log is synchronized with the database logging function to ensure that a message once received by the system will be processed, and that no duplicate transactions will be processed in the event of failures. At least one commercially available system provides such synchronization, and even guarantees that transactions that must be reprocessed in the event of a failure will be processed in the original order. This last is an important feature in banking applications such as when an account with a $100 balance first has a $500 check deposited and then a $200 check cashed. In the compressed recovery situation, the transactions could possibly be submitted in reverse order, meaning the check cashing transaction would be rejected for insufficient funds, leaving the account in an inconsistent state.

Security

Since a TCP can be a focal point for on-line transactions entering the system, it is a logical place to collect statistics and provide for security. There are a number of statistics necessary to effectively manage a network system that can be collected in the TCP, including the number of transactions, types of transactions, number of characters transmitted to and from a terminal, application processing time per transaction, and number of transactions per terminal. Security at the terminal and transaction level could be enforced at the TCP. Since all on-line transactions for terminals managed by a TCP must be routed through it, the TCP is a logical place to implement security, possibly through security server processes.

Message Priorities

If message priorities are desired within the on-line system, the TCP is in an ideal position to assist with implementing them. Every message received could be examined for priority, or priorities could be assigned by the TCP. For instance, priorities could be established according to the source and type of message. Priority messages could then be given service first and routed to special server applications to expedite messages.

It is necessary to establish test environments when designing an online system and after the system has become operational. The TCP can provide features to make testing and debugging easier, including the ability to examine the transactions received by the TCP and the format of messages input to and output from the TCP. The TCP should also allow operational systems to be run concurrently with test systems.

Figure 9-12 summarizes the activities of a TCP. Many of these functions are also performed by an operating system; in fact, a comprehensive TCP is essentially an operating system run by another operating system.

Figure 9-12
TCP Activities

Provides a user interface with the TCP subsystem

Manages memory

Provides an interface between applications and terminals

Manages applications

Logs messages

Participates in recovery

Provides transaction definition

Edits data fields

Formats data for terminals and applications

Routes messages to server processes

Gathers statistics

Provides testing and debugging facilities

Assists in providing security

Assists in implementing a priority system

SUMMARY

Data communications software works closely with the applications, database, and operating software to provide the functions required of today's systems. Two of the major components of networking software are access methods and transaction control processes.

In some cases, access method software provides the linkage between application programs and terminal devices. In all cases, access methods provide an interface with different terminal devices, providing terminal and application independence. Transaction control processes also provide a link between applications software and terminal equipment. A TCP will also use the access method software to interface with terminal devices. The functions provided by TCPs in interfacing applications and devices go beyond those provided by the typical access method. These added capabilities include data edits, message switching, data formatting, and transaction definition and recovery.

Key Terms

Access method	Message control system (MCS)
Basic telecommunications access method (BTAM)	Multi-processing
	Multi-tasking
Contention	Multi-threading
Database management system (DBMS)	Operating system (OS)
	Recovery
Data communications access method	Reentrant code
Data definition language (DDL)	Single threading
Data dictionary	Telecommunications access method (TCAM)
Data independence	
Data manipulation language (DML)	Teleprocessing monitor (TP)
Deadlock	Transaction control process (TCP)
Host language interface	Transaction log
I/O driver	Virtual telecommunications access method (VTAM)
Memory management	

Questions and Exercises

1. Describe the functions of a data communications access method.

2. Describe the functions of a TCP.

3. Compare and contrast the functions of a TCP and a data-communications access method.

4. Compare and contrast the operations of a TCP and an operating system.

5. Why are audit (log) trails important?

6. Other than the banking example given in the chapter, describe two transactions that could create inconsistencies in a database if not recovered in the same order in which they were originally processed.

7. Why is multi-threading of a TCP an attractive feature?

8. Is the saving of context necessary for multi-threading? Why or why not?

9. Is it necessary for all user transactions to be recoverable units? If so, why? If not, give an example of a transaction that would not have to be recovered if the system failed.

References

IBM. *Introduction to VTAM Logic*. Manual no. SY27-7256-3. IBM, 1976a.

_____ *OS/VS TCAM Concepts and Applications*. Manual no. GC30-2049-1. IBM, 1976b.

_____ *Customer Information Control System/Virtual Storage (CICS/VS) System Programmer's Reference Manual.* Manual no. SC33-0069-4. IBM, 1981.

_____ *Advanced Communications Function for VTAM General Information: Concepts.* Manual no. GC27-0463-3. IBM, 1982a.

_____ *Customer Information Control System/Virtual Storage (CICS/VS) General Information.* Manual no. GC33-0155-1. IBM, 1982b.

_____ *Customer Information Control System/Operating System/Virtual Storage (CICS/OS/VS) Installation and Operations Guide.* Manual no. SC33-071-3. IBM, 1982c.

Lim, Pacifico Amarga. *CICS/VS Command Level with ANS COBOL Examples.* New York: Van Nostrand Reinhold, 1982.

Tanenbaum, Andrew S. *Computer Networks.* Englewood Cliffs, NJ: Prentice-Hall, 1981.

Supplement 1
IBM's Virtual Telecommunications
Access Method (VTAM)

The *virtual telecommunications access method (VTAM)* is one of a number of telecommunications access methods supported by IBM. VTAM and the *Telecommunications access method (TCAM)* are currently the most important of the access methods because both support systems network architecture (SNA). The basic functions of VTAM include attachment of applications to terminals and control of messages between applications and terminals, providing terminal-specific access attributes, application and terminal configuration definition and alteration, buffer and device management, and debugging aids.

Network Configuration

A network configuration file describes the VTAM environment of communication controllers, local terminals, and SNA nodes. Two tables are maintained by VTAM to define devices—a major node table and a specific node table. The major node table contains information regarding application groups, NCPs that reside in communications controllers, local 3270 devices, and switched and local SNA devices. Switched SNA devices are physical or logical units that can be attached to the network via switched communications links; local SNA devices are physical or logical units attached directly to the channel. A pointer from the major node table is used to link major nodes to specific nodes. The specific node table contains information about specific terminals and cluster controllers. Addresses for terminal devices are created from a combination of the major node address and the specific node table addresses. These two tables are built from the configuration file when VTAM is initialized. Applications are not defined in these tables.

VTAM may be used in conjunction with a TCP, in which environment its functions are limited primarily to terminal interface. In the description that follows the full functions of VTAM are discussed. In the TCP environment some features may be unutilized or not as highly utilized as in the stand-alone configuration.

Establishing Communication

Once initialized, VTAM is ready to perform its primary function of establishing communications between terminals and applications. In SNA this is referred to as a session—that is, a communication between two logical devices. Sessions can be established by either the application or the terminal.

Application-Initiated Communication. Before an application can communicate with a terminal, it must first establish a connection to VTAM, by invoking an OPEN macro. Via this process, VTAM creates the buffers and control blocks necessary for communication between the application and terminals. Having established a session between the application and VTAM, the application can then request attachment to a specific terminal, accomplished by a request to OPEN a destination. If the terminal is available, VTAM establishes the connection. A terminal will be unavailable if it is off line, reserved for some reason, or already attached to another application. In the latter case the request is queued, to be granted when the terminal becomes available. An application can also gain access to a terminal by having the connection privilege passed to it by an application already connected to the terminal. A terminal can be connected to only one application at a time, but one application can be attached to multiple terminals.

Terminal-Initiated Communication: The Network Solicitor. A terminal can also request connection to an application. In such a case, the terminal would have been initially defined as a monitored terminal, meaning that a special application program known as the network solicitor will be initially attached to the terminal and will monitor it for application connection requests. Users can either write their own network solicitor program or use one provided as part of the VTAM system. The solicitor takes inputs from the monitored terminals and passes control to the requested application if the application is willing to communicate with the terminal. When the session between the application and the terminal is finished, the terminal is passed back to the network solicitor program, which resumes monitoring the terminal. The VTAM solicitor process is illustrated in Figure 9-13 on page 328.

Figure 9-13
The VTAM Solicitor
Process

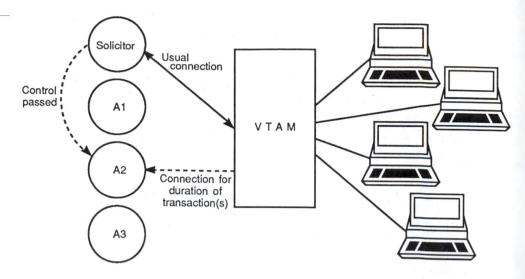

Input-Output Processing

Two types of I/O processing can be specified between an application and a terminal—record mode and basic mode. *Record mode* allows full duplex transmission, and either the application or the terminal is capable of initiating communication. In record mode, VTAM provides device formatting services. *Basic mode* is a half duplex transmission mode, with the application controlling the conversation—that is, the terminal can transmit only on solicitation of information from the application. Basic mode can be used to communicate with asynchronous and BISYNC terminals. When operating in basic mode the application is primarily responsible for device characteristics. It must insert line control characters in the text and recognize them in messages returned from the terminal.

For VTAM to communicate correctly with a terminal it must know in which of the two modes it must operate as well as terminal characteristics. For each of the operating modes, there exists a device control table containing the control routines for all types of supported devices. VTAM picks the control procedures from this list and builds a device access table for that particular terminal. The initial table with all of the routines is referred to as a skeleton table. The skeleton table might contain, for example, a routine common to all terminals and then several procedures tailored to a specific terminal type. VTAM then builds a terminal access table for a specific terminal by selecting the common routine and one of the specific terminal procedures.

Diagnostic and Debugging Tools

VTAM offers the user a complement of diagnostic and debugging tools, including the following.

A **buffer trace** logs the contents of input and output buffers, enabling the user to determine the changes made to the data by VTAM.

NCP line traces enable the user to trace one line at a time, providing information about line parameters.

Storage pool traces yield information about whether the storage pools maintained by VTAM are being used efficiently or inefficiently.

Formatted dumps can reveal all or a part of VTAM's working environment.

In addition, VTAM assists the user in handling both hardware and software errors and in attempting recovery from abnormal terminations and hardware failures.

Supplement 2
IBM's Customer Information Control System (CICS)

The customer information control system (CICS) is a TCP provided by IBM and is one of the more widely used TCP products. Its primary function is as an interface between terminal users on one side and application programs and database or file requests on the other. To do this, CICS manages both terminals and application processes. It runs on 370, 4331, 4341, 303x, and 308x processors under OS/VSE, OS/VS1, MVS/370, or MVS/XA operating systems.

CICS Partition

CICS occupies a large partition within an IBM mainframe computer. Part of the partition houses CICS code, message buffers, and data, and part is used by the application programs that CICS manages, as depicted in Figure 9-14 on page 330. Unlike VTAM, in which a terminal is logged onto only one application at a time, CICS provides the linkage between applications and terminals. This means that a terminal can use multiple application processes without being attached to a specific process or being transferred from one to another. Terminals are controlled by CICS, not by the application programs. In a number of respects CICS functions like an operating system in managing its region: It starts and stops tasks, manages the memory in its partition, provides application interface with devices, and implements a priority system to determine which task will be run first.

Installation Options: Customized or Preconfigured

In installing a CICS system, the user has two basic options, customize the installation to the particular system and applications or install a system

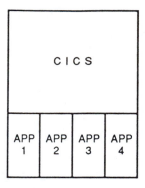

preconfigured by IBM. To customize, the user must decide which functions are required and include those code modules that support the selected functions. The tailored system that results can provide greater economy of memory resources and efficiency of operation. The preconfigured system takes less work to install, and several preconfigured systems are available that incorporate different combinations of commonly used functions. Regardless of the initial approach taken, the CICS system can be tuned later for increased or decreased functionality and for more efficient operations.

Intersystem Communication (ISC) and Multiregion Operation (MRO)

More than one CICS environment can be run within one system, and these different CICS environments can communicate with each other. Likewise, different nodes in a systems network architecture (SNA) network can run CICS, and these CICS systems can communicate using the facilities of SNA, thus allowing a terminal operating under control of one CICS system to communicate with applications or terminals under the control of another CICS system and providing for a distributed network. Communication with other nodes is referred to as *intersystem communication (ISC)* and communication between two CICS systems on one node is called *multiregion operation (MRO)*. Several CICS systems can be used in one node for separation of functions, such as separating an operational system from a development system, or separating a very secure set of transactions or applications from more commonly used transactions or applications. Despite the fact that each CICS system can control different terminals or applications, the databases, terminals, and applications can be shared between the CICS systems via MRO or via direct access to the databases.

CICS Tables

To fulfill its function of interfacing terminals and applications, CICS must have a knowledge of application processes, files, destinations, and terminals, which are described by tables created during the initialization process. These tables, which can be modified later to add, delete, or amend the descriptions, are created by invoking macro instructions. Just as multiple CICS systems can be generated, so too can multiple tables. Thus, tables can be generated for distinct production, development, and testing environments. At any given time, one CICS system will have only one set of tables for each resource—file, application, terminal, or destination. In order to install one CICS system, the user may be required to define up to 15 such tables per set, describing terminals, applications, transactions, control, system recovery, and system initialization.

Terminal Control Table.   *The terminal control table (TCT)* contains descriptions of terminals; a terminal can communicate with CICS only if it is described in this table. In interfacing with terminals, CICS uses the support of one of IBM's access methods, either VTAM, VTAME, BTAM, or TCAM, depending on the type of terminal being supported. For example, the 2780 and 3780 RJE terminals and most asynchronous devices are supported under BTAM, and SNA interfaces are supported under VTAM. Some terminal types—such as 3270 devices and some asynchronous devices—are supported by several access methods. The TCT contains such information as the access method interface, where error messages are displayed on the terminal, terminal type, line size, screen size, and terminal address.

Physical and Data Description Maps.   The interface between terminals and applications is via two map sets, physical maps and data description maps. A set of physical maps describes the screen layout for terminals, with one such map for each screen displayed on a given terminal. A set of data description maps represents the application's view of the data. The two map sets can be created in one of two different ways, by basic mapping support or by a screen definition facility. The basic mapping support (BMS) subsystem enables the programmer to define the screen formats and input and output data formats by use of macro commands. The on-line screen formatting facility known as the screen definition facility (SDF/CICS) enables the user to interactively create the screen formats and resulting maps. SDF/CICS also provides the ability to edit existing maps and test the formats on-line.

Because there are two maps, one terminal-oriented and one application-oriented, independence between the terminal and application is achieved. Thus, the terminal can be changed without a corresponding change in the application. Likewise, application changes can be made without changing the screen layout, so long as no new fields are required. In COBOL the symbolic map takes the form of a data division entry. The physical map resides in the CICS load library.

CICS Load Library Tables.   Applications written in COBOL are able to reference CICS routines by embedding CICS commands in the COBOL source. A CICS precompiler translates these commands into a format acceptable to the COBOL compiler. The same is true when PL/1 is the application language. Compiled and link-edited application programs are placed into a CICS load library.

A number of tables describing the application programs in the load library are used to associate a transaction with the application programs that will process that transaction. A transaction is identified by an identifier that is one to four characters in length. A transaction can be initiated from either a terminal or an application program or based on a particular event or at a specified time. Usually, the terminal user enters the transaction identifier or selects it from a menu of available transactions. The tables are used to identify which program is to process a particular transaction, whether the transaction is to be audited and backed out if necessary, the estimated duration of the transaction, and if the program is to be loaded at CICS initialization time or is to reside in memory permanently.

Quasi-Reentrancy

CICS programs written in COBOL are called quasi-reentrant, which means they can be shared by more than one terminal at a time. Each terminal will have its own copy of data and all terminals will share the same code. At certain points in the program, reentrancy may not be allowed, since an instruction could be changed or an address modified. Thus, sharing is allowed only at specified points, such as when the process must be suspended while awaiting disk access. PL/1 programs are fully reentrant, and at any time one task can be suspended and another allowed to execute the code.

Efficiency can be gained through multi-threading in CICS and through reentrancy or quasi-reentrancy in the application programs. Having multiple terminals simultaneously access one process reduces the amount of memory required for application code.

File and DBMS Access

CICS provides access to files and database management systems. File access to indexed sequential access method files (VSAM ISAM) and direct access method (DAM) files can be made directly through CICS calls, whereas access to IBM's IMS and SQL database management systems can be made through application program calls. Interfaces also exist that allow access to non-IBM database management systems.

Logical Units of Work and Sync Points

Transaction backout and journaling is provided as an option to the user. For long transactions, the user can specify synchronization points that become recovery points. The work performed between synchronization points, termed *logical units of work (LUW),* are units of recovery, so one transaction can have no sync points and be an LUW, whereas another transaction could define several sync points. In the latter instance, once a sync point is reached its unit of work is committed and thus will not need to be backed out in the event of a failure. This is depicted in Figure 9-15.

Diagnostic and Tuning Aids

CICS provides aids for diagnosing problems and tuning the system. A command interpreter allows a user to create a CICS call, execute it, and receive a response without coding an application, thus enabling the user to interactively test a transaction or parts of a transaction. An on-line debugging aid named the *execution diagnostic facility (EDF)* allows an application to be tested, and permits the CICS application calls to be intercepted, examined, and changed if necessary. The responses to the calls can also be trapped and modified.

An EDF allows the code to be tested and also provides for the generating of exception conditions for testing error routines. Other diagnostic aids include the gathering of statistics for system tuning, and dumping of buffers, tables, and the entire region or partition in which CICS resides. Statistics gathered include the number of transactions, amount of CPU time consumed by transaction, amount of paging, peak loads, number of terminal I/Os, the number of times a given application is used, and file statistics regarding reads, adds, and updates. Two utilities are available to assist in formatting and reporting these statistics—*performance analysis reporting system (CICSPARS)* and *service level reporter II (SLR).* The statistics help determine response time and use trends so that system tuning and upgrades can be effected in a timely manner.

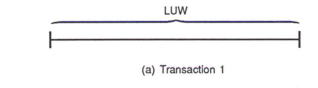

(a) Transaction 1

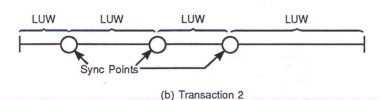

(b) Transaction 2

Figure 9-15
Transactions: Sync Points and Logical Units of Work

Supplement 3
Tandem Computer Inc.'s Pathway™

Pathway™ is a transaction control program (TCP) from Tandem Computers Inc. It is the data communications portion of its database management system, ENCOMPASS.™ Pathway serves as the interface between terminals and applications processes called servers. Its primary function is to accept input from a terminal, edit the data, route messages to one or more servers that perform the processing and database accessing necessary to satisfy the request, accept responses from the servers, and route the response messages back to the terminal. Pathway is also a focal point for the recovery system. It is generally recommended that transactions be started and terminated by the TCP.

Development Environment

The development environment of Pathway™ is depicted in Figure 9-16. The development process consists of defining screen templates for display on the terminals and preparation of procedural code in a COBOL-like language called *screen COBOL*. These programs specify the transaction control and routing logic. Screen templates can be defined within screen COBOL or by use of *Pathaid*, a screen generation utility process. Regardless of the manner of generation, the screen description is included within the screen COBOL program that displays the template on the appropriate terminal, as detailed in the following section.

Figure 9-16
Pathway™
Development
Environment

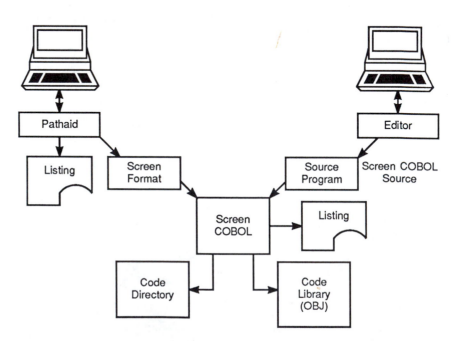

Screen Formats: Pathaid.   Pathaid is a utility that enables Pathway™ users to create and maintain screen formats. Ease of use was one of the design goals of Pathaid, and as a result, end users are usually able to participate in the development process by generating the screen templates they need. When the user starts the Pathaid process, a menu of alternatives is presented, including options for creating a new screen, changing an existing screen, and displaying help information. If the *new screen* option is selected, the user is asked to name the screen. A cleared terminal screen is then presented, which the user can "paint" to fit the application. In the example screen template given in Figure 9-17 on page 336, the text appears as documentation or prompts. In formatting the screen the user can move the cursor around at will. There are also functions to insert and delete lines or characters.

Field Description.   When the screen has been formatted to the user's satisfaction, a function key is pressed to proceed to the second part of screen definition, *field description*. From the screen painting the system is aware of the prompt names and field width. In the field description phase each input field is presented to the user for further definition: The user is asked to specify field name, field type (alphabetic, numeric, etc.), minimum field width, whether the field is required or optional, and display characteristics of the field (protected, highlighted, etc). When this phase is completed, the screen is stored on disk for inclusion into screen COBOL programs that will display it. Essentially, the screen definition becomes a copy library for a screen COBOL program.

Screen Cobol

A screen COBOL program provides the procedural steps that sequence the screen templates to be displayed, edit the terminal inputs, format messages, begin and end transactions, handle error conditions, route messages to the proper server processes, accept responses from the servers, and display the responses on the terminal.

Screen COBOL itself is a COBOL derivative. COBOL was chosen as the base language because of the large body of COBOL programmers in the business community. Several major modifications were made to COBOL syntax in order to support the handling of terminals and application programs. First, all READ and WRITE verbs were removed from the language, making it impossible to directly access disk, tape, or peripherals other than terminals and processes. There are advantages and disadvantages to this decision. One advantage is that screen COBOL cannot be used as an application language. Code produced by the screen COBOL compiler is pseudocode interpreted by the Transaction Control Program (TCP). Since interpreted code is executed more slowly than object code, users are discouraged from performing application processing in the TCP. Input from and output to devices other than a terminal or process was considered unnecessary. The disadvantage is that input message logging

```
*********************************************************************
*                                                                   *
*    E M P L O Y E E    M A I N T E N A N C E    S C R E E N         *
*                                                                   *
*********************************************************************
*                                                                   *
*    EMPLOYEE NUMBER _____                                    *
*                                                                   *
*    LAST NAME  _____                           *
*                                                                   *
*    FIRST NAME _____  MIDDLE INITIAL  _                 *
*                                                                   *
*    STREET ADDRESS _____     *
*                                                                   *
*                   _____     *
*                                                                   *
*    CITY  _____                           *
*                                                                   *
*    STATE _____   ZIP CODE  _____      *
*                                                                   *
*    COUNTRY _____                          *
*                                                                   *
*    TELEPHONE (____) ____-_____                                    *
*                                                                   *
*    SEX (M or F) _                                                 *
*                                                                   *
*    MARITAL STATUS (M, D, S, or O) _                               *
*                                                                   *
*    DEPARTMENT _____                    *
*                                                                   *
*    CURRENT JOB CODE _____                                  *
*                                                                   *
*    HIGHEST EDUCATION LEVEL  __                                    *
*                                                                   *
*    HIRE DATE  __-__-__                                            *
*                                                                   *
*********************************************************************
*                                                                   *
*    F1  = ADD RECORD          F2  = GET RECORD                      *
*                                                                   *
*    F3  = UPDATE RECORD       F4  = DELETE RECORD                   *
*                                                                   *
*    F5  = GET NEXT RECORD     F6  = GET PRIOR RECORD                *
*                                                                   *
*    F15 = HELP SCREEN         F16 = EXIT BACK TO MENU               *
*********************************************************************
```

Figure 9-17   Screen Template for Page Mode Terminal

can be accomplished only through a server process, thereby creating an unnecessary delay.

In the second modification of COBOL, the file section of the data division was eliminated (since no I/O is allowed, it was unnecessary), and a screen section was added. The description of screen templates is kept in this section.

In the third modification, several new verbs were added to the syntax: DISPLAY, ACCEPT, SEND, and RECEIVE were established to display and obtain data on or from a terminal and send and receive data to or from a process. Extensions were also made to the PERFORM verb to allow case statements. The new PERFORM syntax is PERFORM ONE OF – – – – DEPENDING ON (VARIABLE). This last verb is especially powerful for invoking the proper procedure based on function key values the terminal user has pressed. For instance, if F1, F2, F3, and F4 represent add, modify, delete, and retrieve record, respectively, the PERFORM verb could be used as follows:

PERFORM ADD-RECORD, MODIFY-RECORD, DELETE-RECORD,
    GET-RECORD DEPENDING ON FUNCTION-KEY.

Other verbs added to support the recovery system include BEGIN-TRANSACTION, ABORT-TRANSACTION, and END-TRANSACTION.

A typical screen COBOL program would consist of the following logic flow:

Display screen on terminal

Accept data from terminal

Edit input data

Format input message for servers

If transaction is an update transaction, begin transaction

Based on displayed screen and operator input, send data to server

Receive response from server

Format response message for terminal

End transaction if a database update transaction

Display response on terminal

Proceed to next display screen

Screen COBOL Code File.   As previously mentioned, screen COBOL programs are compiled into a pseudocode that is interpreted by the TCP. The compiler places the pseudocode into a code file that might contain the images of multiple programs. An entry is also made in a directory file to allow the program to be efficiently retrieved. Multiple versions of a program can be maintained in the code and directory files, enabling users to automatically maintain a history of screen programs as well as to switch the active program while the system is running. This latter feature has many benefits: If a new program is found to be in error after implementation, a switch to the previous version can be made while the system is running. Likewise, a new version can be implemented to replace a previous version, allowing some changes to the system to be made on the fly.

A utility exists to perform dictionary and code file maintenance. Utility functions include deleting programs, changing the current active program, renumbering the programs, and copying programs from one directory to another. Since each compile creates a new version rather than replacing the previous version, dictionary and code file maintenance is periodically necessary.

Pathway™ Operations Environment

The Pathway™ operations environment—termed a *requester–server environment*—is depicted in Figure 9-18. Servers are application processes and requesters are screen COBOL programs. The requester sends a message to a server process requesting some function to be performed. The server processes the request and returns an appropriate response. One server can receive requests from multiple requesters, and one requester can send messages to several servers. Servers can be written in any language supported by Tandem systems, including COBOL, FORTRAN, MUMPS, BASIC, and TAL, a block-structured language similar to Pascal.

To start the operational system, an environment must be defined. The environment consists of a named Pathway™ monitor process, one or more TCPs under control of the monitor, terminals that will be attached to a TCP, and server processes with which the TCPs will communicate. Most

Figure 9-18
Pathway™
Operations
Environment

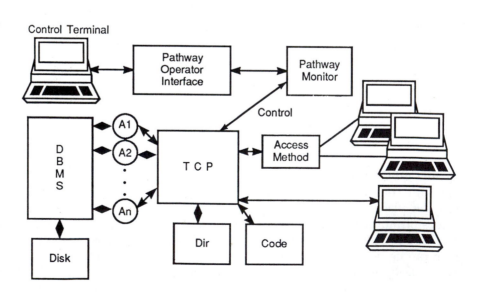

of these characteristics can be changed while the system is operating. The description of the environment is input to an operator interface program, PATHCOM. The interface process allows the Pathway™ subsystem to be started, stopped, and altered.

Monitor Process.   The monitor process provides services to the TCPs, including starting and stopping server processes, assisting in error situations, starting and stopping TCPs, and starting and stopping the subsystem under its control. Since multiple monitors can exist, multiple Pathway™ subsystems are possible.

TCP.   The heart of the Pathway™ system is the TCP, which in many respects resembles an operating system, for it manages memory, fetches programs from disk, provides multiple environments, and assists with I/O. The TCP has within its workspace a buffer for storing and executing screen COBOL programs. The startup parameters it is provided include the names of the terminals it will control, the initial screen program for each terminal, and the servers with which it will communicate. Each terminal is controlled by only one TCP, but servers can receive requests from multiple TCPs. On startup, the TCP fetches the initial program from the code file, loads it into its memory space, and begins to execute it. The TCP provides multi-threading capability by running one program for each terminal it controls. Its operational characteristics can best be explained by way of an example.

Example of Pathway™ TCP.

The initial log-on screen displayed on the terminal is followed by a master menu screen, then application menu, and application transactions. This description proceeds through these actions, and illustrates how the TCP, terminals, and servers interact.

Starting.   The TCP is given parameters that describe the terminals and servers. Using these parameters, it opens the terminal, allocates memory for the first screen COBOL program to be executed for that terminal, retrieves the program from the disk, and begins interpreting the program. The program indicates that a log-on screen is to be displayed on the terminal. When the operator enters the required information and presses the proper function key, the data are read from the terminal's buffer into a buffer maintained by the TCP. The action to be taken at this point is coded in the screen COBOL program. The message from the terminal is edited and passed to a server, which verifies the password and performs any required security logging. On completion, the result is passed back to the screen COBOL program being executed by the TCP. If the log-on is approved, the log-on screen COBOL program calls the master menu program, which the TCP brings from disk into its memory work area so it can begin interpreting it.

Master Menu. The master menu program displays a master menu on the terminal, showing the available application options, such as personnel, payroll, and inventory. The user selects an application—say, personnel, and the master menu program calls for that application program, which the TCP brings from the screen COBOL code file into its memory area so it can begin to interpret it. The program displays the personnel functions available—*add, find, modify,* and *delete an employee*—and the operator selects one of the functions—say, *add an employee.* This invokes a procedure within the screen COBOL program.

Application Transactions. The selected procedure displays the employee data screen on the terminal and awaits the return data. When the data are received, they are edited and formatted. A transaction is started for recovery purposes and the formatted message, together with the transaction ID, is passed to a personnel server, which inserts the record into the database and returns a successful completion result to the screen COBOL program. The transaction is ended, which causes the audit buffers to be written. The program displays the result on the screen, awaiting the next input from the operator. At this point the operator can indicate the wish to exit from the *add employee* function, which returns the personnel menu. Exiting from the personnel menu automatically returns the master menu.

Context

Context, or the remembering of related operations for a given terminal, is ordinarily maintained in the TCP. This allows the servers to be written and maintained context-free, which is much simpler.

While this processing is being done on behalf of one terminal, a similar process can be taking place for the other terminals supported by that particular TCP. Thus, each terminal has a screen COBOL program driving it, and each terminal can be working on different applications and has its own context.

Flexibility

This type of operation provides considerable flexibility. Since one program can call another, many different sequences of programs and screens are available. One terminal can access any application within the system or a restricted subset of applications available via the coding in the screen COBOL program. Application programs can be written as single-threaded programs, typically relatively small, easily maintained processes. Multiple servers can be called on to satisfy a single transaction, as in a banking application in which one server handles checking accounts, another savings accounts, and a transfer transaction would send a message to each of these servers.

Throughput

The Pathway™ system also assists in throughput management. Servers with a high volume of transactions can be declared *static servers*, meaning they are always running and available for transactions. Multiple copies of one server can also be declared so there are multiple servers to handle a high volume of transactions. Servers not highly used or used only during peak transaction periods—termed *dynamic servers*—can be created as needed. If such servers do not receive a transaction within a user-defined interval, the server is stopped. The combination of these capabilities allows new servers to be activated as needed and to be discontinued when no longer needed. Thus, during normal times only perhaps three static servers might be necessary to provide the application support, and during busy times two more dynamic servers will be automatically started, analogous to a grocery store adding clerks when checkout lines grow too long. The user can also specify how long the transaction queue to a server must be before a dynamic server is created. Dynamic server creation is illustrated in Figure 9-19. As the transaction rate increases, the number of servers also increases.

Tuning Aids

The TCP and the monitor can optionally record and display statistics regarding the operation of the Pathway™ subsystem, including the use of the buffers, message sizes, terminal activity, and memory management. These statistics can be used to tune the system for greater efficiency. The gathering of statistics is a function that can be turned off or on by the user.

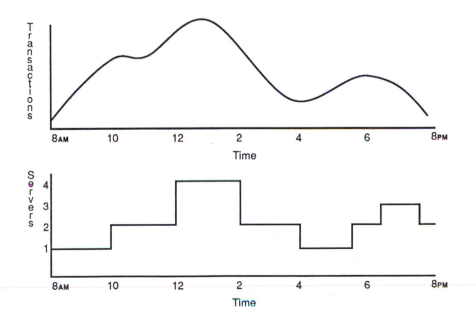

Figure 9-19
Dynamic Servers
Adapt to Meet
Transaction Volume

In summary, the Pathway™ system provides message routing between terminals and applications processes, message formatting, transaction definition, load balancing, and statistical information regarding the operation of the Pathway™ environment. Application modules can be added or deleted from the system during operation, as can screens and screen COBOL programs. The operator interface provides the ability to start, stop, and alter the system configuration. Multiple Pathway™ environments can co-exist in the system, and each can have one or several TCP programs under its control.

APPLICATION

PRESENTATION

V

ANALYSIS AND MANAGEMENT: PRESENTATION AND APPLICATION LAYERS

10

Application and Presentation Layer Software

Security

Data Editing

Formatting

Error Detection and Recovery

Other Software Functions

INTRODUCTION

This chapter continues the discussion of software begun in the preceding chapter. At the chapter's conclusion, you should be familiar with a number of the more common data communications software functions: security, encryption, data editing, message and screen formatting, data compression, and error detection and recovery.

SECURITY

Security is a delaying tactic. It does not prevent unauthorized access to a system, but simply makes it more difficult. Such delay should be long enough either to make unauthorized access too costly or to give time to detect and apprehend the perpetrator, or both. In the first case, the rewards of unauthorized access would be less than the cost of breaking into the system. In the second, the attempted penetration would be detected and further attempts squelched. From the system owner's perspective, the cost of security should be no more than the potential loss from system penetration.

Vendor-Provided Security

The security features provided by the vendors of software systems tend to be superficial, and they are generally found only in vendor-provided user interfaces such as command interpreters and operator- or programmer-level interfaces. When provided, such facilities are generally limited to a particular user group and ID classification, together with an optional password for log-on. Usually there are also additional protections at the data level, including levels of access to files, and within the operating systems, including safeguards prohibiting one process from interfering with the data of another process or viewing the data of an active or recently terminated process. This section is not concerned with this aspect of security; instead, it addresses security concerns that directly affect the data communications network.

One reason that vendor systems provide so little security is that user security needs vary significantly. Some installations require little or no security. In others, such as financial and military applications, security is a primary concern. Thus the user is usually left to implement the security levels relevant to specific applications. Since security incurs a cost in additional processing time for security checks, disk access to validate user IDs, and memory space for user profiles and device profiles, any vendor security offering would almost have to have levels of implementation to appeal to a broad group of users. Software houses and original equipment manufacturers (OEM) frequently implement security features within applications designed for a particular line of business. An OEM will purchase a computer from the manufacturer, add some value to the system, and then resell it to an end user. In some instances the OEM also places their name plate on the equipment.

Physical Security

A good place to start to establish a secure system is with physical security. Since physical security is independent of particular hardware or software, it can be planned long before the installation of the network and hardware. By preventing access to physical components of the system such as terminals, communications circuits, processors, and modems, the likelihood of unauthorized access is significantly decreased. Of course, it will not prevent an authorized user from misusing the system.

Data Communications Environment vs. Batch Systems.   Physical security is more difficult to maintain for data communications systems than for batch systems because almost all batch system equipment resides in just a few locations. Computer rooms are typically secure, with dedicated rooms, lockable doors, and limited personnel access. Usually, system operators or system programming staff are present, and they are able to detect and prevent unauthorized access. The opposite is usually true of data communications sytems. At the host end, security can be equivalent to that of a batch system. However, office terminals are frequently located on open-access desks or in private rooms with unlockable doors. In addition, control of physical access to the building housing this equipment might be lax or even nonexistent. During normal working hours, of course, personnel in the area can help prevent unauthorized personnel from using the equipment, but that is seldom the case in off hours. Furthermore, some remote nodes may be relatively operator-free, without access controls.

Sensitive Applications.   For extremely sensitive applications, all equipment should be located in secure areas with controlled personnel access. Guards or closed-circuit television monitors should be used to monitor areas housing terminals and communications circuits, thus providing the same level of security as in the computer room. Nonsecure transmission media such as radio wave broadcast should be avoided where possible. If radio broadcast must be used, *all* transmitted data should be encrypted, for if only the sensitive data are encrypted, this identification of sensitive data aids the potential penetrator. Switched lines should be avoided, if possible. Where they are in use, they should be disconnected during the hours they are not required, thus preventing unauthorized use via telephone.

Encryption

Encryption should be used with all media carrying sensitive data. The particular encryption algorithm chosen should be capable of deterring unwarranted use by making the cost or time to decipher the message too great.

Data Encryption Standard (DES).   One of the most common yet controversial encryption algorithms is the *data encryption standard (DES)* adopted by the National Bureau of Standards. The controversy surrounds the effectiveness of the standard. In 1976 it was estimated that it would take an average of 91–2000 years to break the DES code [Diffie, 1978, Kinnucan, 1978; Meyer and Tuchman, 1978; Solomon, 1978]. Opponents of the algorithm countered that the code could be broken in 6 minutes to 12 hours at a cost of $20–$5,000 [Solomon, 1978]. The primary criticism centered on the fact that only 56 bits are used for the encryption key. With the increasing speed and lower cost of computer hardware, most critics and proponents agreed that the algorithm had an effective life of approximately 10 years, meaning it is now nearing the end of its effectiveness.

Figure 10-1
Encryption
Configurations

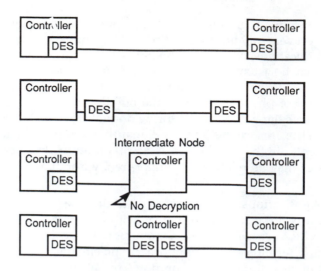

Most DES algorithms make use of integrated circuits designed for that purpose. The chips may be integrated onto processor or controller boards or used in stand-alone external boxes. The encryption devices can be placed between individual nodes or at the origin and destination of the message. Figure 10-1 illustrates several configuration options. If the encryption devices are placed at each node, some degree of security is lost, since the message must be decrypted at each intermediate node, thus increasing the likelihood of interception. In end-to-end encryption, only the text body can be encrypted, and end-to-end addressing must remain clear so that intermediate nodes can perform the routing correctly.

How the DES Algorithm Works. The DES algorithm uses a 56-bit encryption key (plus 8 bits for parity) to encrypt and decrypt the data. Known only to the sender and receiver, the encryption key locks and unlocks the meaning of the message. In general, unencrypted data (called plain text) are translated into encrypted data (known as cipher text) by *rearrangement* of the order of the bits, *substitution* of one bit or character for another, or a combination of the two techniques. There must exist a deterministic algorithm that takes the plain text to its equivalent cipher text so that the same data used with the same key always yield the same cipher text. The process must also be reversible so the data can be reclaimed. The DES algorithm uses 16 iterations of a combination of rearrangement and substitution. Each of the 16 iterations is essentially the same and involves the following actions:

1. A 64-bit data entity is broken into two 32-bit pieces.

2. One piece is rearranged and augmented, yielding a 48-bit group.

3. The 56-bit encryption key is manipulated to produce a 48-bit entity.

4. The 48-bit key and data string are exclusively ORed together and a 32-bit string is extracted.

5. The 32 bits are again rearranged.

6. This 32-bit string and the untouched 32-bit data half are exclusively ORed, forming a new 32-bit entity.

7. The resulting 32-bit string is then used as input to step 2.

With 16 such iterations, a 56-bit key yields over 70 quadrillion possible outputs. Lengthening the key to 128 bits or more would, of course, further extend the number of possible encrypted strings and increase the average expected decryption time. The lack of a longer key string is cited as one of the current weaknesses of the DES.

Example of Encryption

The complexity of the DES algorithm provides its usefulness, but makes the working through of an example quite tedious. However, the basic mechanics can be illustrated with the less complex algorithm outlined in Figure 10-2. The second step in the figure is a rearrangement step; the third through sixth steps form the substitution phase.

1. Divide the plain text into groups of 8 characters. Pad with blanks at the end as necessary.

2. Select an 8-character key.

3. Rearrange the characters by interchanging adjacent characters—that is, making the first character the second and the second the first, and so on.

4. Translate each alphabetic character into an ordinal number—that is, A becomes 1, B becomes 2, and so on, with a blank being a zero.

5. Add the ordinal number of the key to the results of step 3.

6. Divide the total by 27 and retain the remainder (which will be between 0 and 26).

7. Translate the remainder back into a character to yield the cipher text.

Figure 10-2
Example Encryption Steps

The algorithm of Figure 10-2 can be illustrated by applying it to the plain text string, DATA COMMUNICATIONS, and using the key PRO-

TOCOL. The first eight characters are encrypted in Figure 10-3; the remainder is left as an exercise.

Figure 10-3
Example of
Encryption

1. DATA COM   Separate into groups of eight.

2. ADATC MO   Rearrange the characters.

3.   01   04   01   20   03   00   13   15   Translate characters to decimal.

4.   01   04   01   20   03   00   13   15   Add key values.
       16   18   15   20   15   03   15   12
       17   22   16   40   18   03   28   27

5.   17   22   16   13   18   03   01   00   Remainder after division by 27

6.   Q   V   P   M   R   C   A   space

Unlike anagrams, which simply substitute one letter for another, encrypting a letter in the plain text can produce different letters in the cipher text. Thus, the clear text letter A is encrypted as both the letter Q and the letter P. The algorithm of Figure 10-2 will work only for text containing letters. The more general case could use ASCII or EBCDIC decimal equivalents and a divisor of 128 or 256.

For encryption to be useful, the key must be derived as randomly as possible and changed frequently, and the key value should be carefully safeguarded. Additional iterations with a different key will also impede unwarranted decryption. Thus, in step 6 of Figure 10-3, the cipher text QVPMRCA could be used as plain text and another algorithm with a different key applied, which is analogous to the iteration process in the DES algorithm.

Other Encryption Algorithms. Other encryption algorithms have been proposed; although none have gained the acceptance of the DES. One of the more promising, referred to as the trap door or public key method, utilizes large prime numbers and two keys, one key made public and the other kept secret by the message recipient. The public key encrypts the data; the private key decrypts the cipher text. For further information regarding this method, consult Solomon (1978).

User Identification and Authentication

Encryption is only one aspect of security. In most systems the first level of security is user identification and authentication. User identification runs the gamut from simply providing a user name to the exotics of voice print and palm print or fingerprint identification, the latter usually being employed only in high-security systems like those of the intelligence and military communities. In business applications, identification is generally via user name, or by badge, in which case the system must be equipped with a badge reader.

After identification comes authentication, which requires the user to provide additional information ostensibly known only to that particular user—something the person knows (like a password) or has (like an ID card) or something unique about them (such as a fingerprint or voice print).

Passwords.   *Passwords* are the most common form of authentication. They are maintained in a file of information about system users, typically including user ID, password, defaulted security attributes for any files created, and possibly an access profile. Because this file contains the information needed to access any portion of the system, it should be carefully secured and encrypted.

Passwords should be changed frequently, either centrally by the network administrators or in a decentralized manner by the users. Centrally changed passwords are assured of being changed regularly and assigned on a random basis. The major flaw of this approach is in the timing of their distribution to users: Dissemination of new passwords must be timely and well coordinated. The logistics in a large, distributed network are considerable. Furthermore, the distribution process is likely to be the weakest element in the security system: Since passwords are usually distributed in written form via mail or courier, there is ample opportunity for unauthorized users to obtain them.

Decentralized password changes rely on users to change their passwords regularly, either by themselves or through their managers. Individual users can change their passwords without leaving any written record of the password, and they can make changes as often as they like. The password file periodically can be centrally examined, and if users have not changed their password within a specified period of time, they can be so notified or their access privileges can be revoked. The biggest problem with user-assigned passwords is that they are typically non-random, since users like to select a password that is easy to remember, like their initials, birth date, or names of loved ones. Unfortunately, this type of password is also more easily guessed by a potential intruder.

Ultrasensitive Applications.   Identification and authentication are usually insufficient for sensitive applications, since it is also necessary to identify what functions a given user may or may not perform. The two most common ways of controlling user access is by adding layers of identification and authentication, or by employing user or application profiles.

Layered IDs.   Layers of identification and authentication help to screen access to sensitive transactions. Once users have been logged on to the system via the initial identification procedures, they can be asked to provide additional identification and authentication information every time they attempt to access a new application or a sensitive transaction within an application. Thus, in a banking application, an operator might be required to provide another password or authorization code in order to transfer funds from one account to another. The advantage of layered IDs is that each application or transaction can have its own level of security, so that applications that are not sensitive can be made available to everyone, and those that are very sensitive can be protected with one or more levels of security. The disadvantage of layered IDs is that the user must remember several different authentication codes, thus increasing the probability of their being written down and made accessible to others.

User Profiles.   A *user profile* contains all the information needed to define the applications and transactions a user is authorized to execute, such as when a user in a personnel application is authorized to add new employees, delete employee records, and modify all employee data fields except salary. The profiles maintained in a user file can be very detailed, covering each application or transaction, or relatively simple, with only a brief profile. In the case of a brief profile, for example, a user might be assigned an access level to the system for each of four functions—read, write, execute, and purge—specifically, level 8 read access, level 6 write access, level 8 execute access, and level 2 purge access. Each file and transaction would also have an access profile, and the user would be granted access as long as the access number was equal to or greater than that of the file or transaction. Thus, if the payroll file had access attributes of 8, 8, 10, and 10 for read, write, execute, and purge, respectively, the user just described would only be able to read the information in the file because the read-access meets or exceeds the file requirements. A write-access of 6 is insufficient to allow the user to write to the file.

The advantage of the brief profile is its simplicity. Its disadvantage is the difficulty in stratifying all users across all applications and files in this manner. Of course, such a profile could be provided for all files or applications, which then becomes a complex profile that is difficult to maintain and administer.

Menu Selection and User Profiles.   User profiles can be very effective when used in combination with a menu selection system that displays user options on the terminal so the user can select the transactions or applications to perform. If a user profile is available, the menu can be tailored to the individual user, and the only transactions the user will see are those to which the user has access. Thus, in the example above, the user who could only read the payroll file would see only that option displayed on the menu, whereas the payroll manager would likely have all options displayed. The security of the system is enhanced by denying users visibility to transactions and files to which they have no access.

Time and Location Restrictions

Time and location, in conjunction with identification and authentication, can play an important part in bolstering security. Time intervals can be established during which a transaction is legal. In a stock trading application, for instance, buying and selling stock on the exchange is limited to a specific time period, so any attempt to trade stock outside of that period would be rejected. Or in a personnel application, it would be prudent to restrict to normal working hours those transactions that affect employee salary or status. This kind of security can be further enhanced by halting sensitive portions of the application system during nonworking hours.

Transactions can also be restricted by location. For instance, a money transfer transaction would be disallowed from a bank teller terminal if such transactions had to be initiated by a bank officer. In a manufacturing plant, a shop floor terminal would be unable to initiate an accounts receivable or payable transaction, such transactions being limited to a set of terminals in a given location, implemented by either attaching applications to specific terminals or by terminal identification coupled with its location and a transaction profile. A terminal profile could list the location of the terminal and the transactions valid from that terminal. Time and location restrictions in conjunction with user controls provide a hierarchy of security precautions.

Switched Ports with Dial-In Access

Perhaps the most vulnerable security point of any system is a switched port that allows dial-in access. The dangers of this should be evident: It enables any person with a telephone and a terminal to access the system. For that reason, extra security precautions should be taken. The switched line should be operational only during the periods when transactions are allowed. In a university environment, for instance, this might be 24 hours a day. In an order entry application, this would likely be between 8 A.M. and 8 P.M. During the period when transactions are disallowed, the line should be disabled. A call-back unit as described in Chapter 5 can be used to ensure that only calls from authorized locations are received.

User identification and authentication procedures and the restriction of allowed transactions become of greater concern when switched lines are used. The telephone numbers of the switched lines should be safeguarded as carefully as possible. In high-security installations a manual answer arrangement should be used, thus allowing person-to-person authentication as well as the usual application-based authorization.

Another method used to stall unauthorized users of switched lines is to hide the carrier tone until an authentication procedure has been provided, a solution that is most practical when telephones are manually answered. This method is meant to foil pirates (hackers) who try to gain access to systems by randomly dialing business telephone numbers until a computer installation is reached.

Recognizing Unauthorized Access Attempts

As was said at the outset of the discussion of security, all of the techniques discussed are simply delaying tactics, their implementation may not provide adequate security. A tight security system should recognize possibly unauthorized access attempts and provide some type of corrective assistance. In the movie *Wargames*, a computer was used to rapidly generate passwords until a correct one was found. Even relatively unsecure systems would discourage this type of activity. A very simple way to counter such attempts is to mark the terminal down altogether, or to temporarily retire the terminal, meaning that the system would not accept input from that terminal for a specified period of time. Such an algorithm might work as follows: After, say, three unsuccessful access attempts, no input from that terminal would be accepted for 5 minutes. Assuming a 6-character password of only letters and numbers, which gives over 2 billion possible passwords, then if a billion of these were tried, with a 5-minute delay between each try, over 9500 years would be needed to gain access.

There is a second algorithm employed in some systems that acts to simulate a successful log-on. After some number of unsuccessful log-on attempts, the user receives a successful log-on message. Rather than actually being granted access to the system, the user is provided with a fake session. While this session is being conducted, security personnel can determine the terminal from which access is being made and the types of transaction the user is attempting to run. This type of simulated session can also help keep the penetrator busy while security personnel are dispatched to the location for investigation. Again, switched connections make such an activity more difficult, especially with respect to apprehension.

Automatic Log-Off

People are often the weakest link in security. All too frequently, operators write their passwords on or near the terminal, or they leave the area with their terminal still logged on, allowing anyone to perform transactions on their behalf. This not only jeopardizes the security of the system, but can also place the employee's job in jeopardy. The system can assist operators by logging off any user who has not entered a transaction within a certain amount of time, say two minutes. Then, operators who leave their terminals for more than two minutes would have to go through the identification and authentication procedures on returning. Alternatively, the user could be required to go through an authentication procedure for every transaction. Unfortunately, this adversely affects operator performance. The first alternative is relatively simple to implement on most systems, and if the log-off interval is chosen well, operator efficiency will be unimpeded.

Transaction Logs

Transactions logs are an important adjunct to security. Every log-on attempt should be logged, including date and time, user identification, unsuccessful authentication attempts (with passwords used), terminal identification and location, and all transactions initiated from that terminal by that user. If a number of unsuccessful log-on attempts are made, the information could also be written on the console of the operator or security personnel so that other action—such as investigation—can be initiated. Transaction logs are also of benefit to Electronic Data Processing (EDP) auditors and diagnostic personnel.

DATA EDITING

Data editing has been a part of data processing almost since its inception.

Batch Verification and Editing

In the batch environment the data were collected in source form and then entered into machine-readable form, such as punched card, paper tape, magnetic tape, or disk. The next operation was likely to be a *verification* process. With punched cards this meant passing the cards through a verifier. Essentially, another operator would re-enter the data so the verifier could compare the second input with the original; if there was a difference, a notch would be cut in the card and a correction made. This means that the transfer from source document to machine-readable form was performed twice. Once in machine-readable form, the data would be checked by an editing program to ensure that they conformed to predefined constraints. Records that did not pass the edit checks were rejected and printed on an exception list for immediate correction, or they were removed for later correction and placed in subsequent batch runs. The records that initially passed the edit checks were input to batch programs that processed the data.

Problems with Batch Editing.   There are several problems inherent in such a system. They can be illustrated with the following personnel transaction—hiring a new employee. New employees must fill out several forms with such information as name, address, telephone number, social security number, and dependents. The forms are checked by a personnel administrator to ensure they are complete, placed in a collection basket, and forwarded to the data processing department, where they are distributed to data entry personnel for translation into machine-readable form—punched cards for this example.

After being punched, the cards are verified and input to the edit program. A card that fails the edit test is reunited with its source document to determine whether the data are punched incorrectly. If not, then the source documents are sent back to the point of origination for correction, and the process begins again.

Compared to an on-line system, the problems with such a system are excess handling, increased potential for document loss, separation of data capture from data entry and verification, and slow reaction of the system to data entry or edit errors. Because the data are captured in one location and processed in another, they must be packaged and transmitted. Each handling or move increases the probability of loss. The personnel ultimately responsible for entering the data into the system are less able to catch errors than the personnel who are involved in the original capture of the data. Finally, if errors in the data are encountered, it may take several hours or days for the corrections to be made.

An on-line system avoids these problems because the personnel who capture the data are also usually the ones who enter the data into the system. Errors in input are immediately flagged and corrected at the source. In addition, the resulting database is more current and accurate.

Edit Test Types

There are numerous types of edit tests employed in on-line systems and batch editing systems. The most common of them follow.

Existence. A field can be designated as optional or mandatory. Mandatory fields must be provided. The edit checks for a mandatory field checks that some entry has been made in that field.

Class Tests. A class test checks a data field for class or type, most commonly numeric and alphabetic. For example, the first name of an employee would be checked to ensure that it contained only letters, and a social security number field would be checked to ensure that it contained only numbers. More sophisticated systems contain additional classes of data, such as dates and currency types.

Size Tests. A size test can ensure that a minimum and possibly maximum number of characters have been entered. For example, a size test might require a U.S. postal zip code to have either five or nine digits, and a state abbreviation exactly two characters. It is seldom necessary to specify a maximum data size in an edit check since the amount of space allocated on the input record or the database record will establish the maximum length. However, in some instances field lengths greater than the current required use are established. This allows for ease of future expansion. For example, the field for a U.S. postal zip code could have been sized at ten digits during the era of five-digit zip codes. In this situation a user could accidently enter a code greater than five digits, and thus a maximum size edit would be prudent.

Range Tests.   Range tests ensure that data fall into prescribed ranges. An employee's salary may be checked to ensure that it is within salary guidelines; a hospital patient's age may be checked to make sure it falls between 0 and 120 years. Range checks can also be used to flag unusual data entries and mark them for special attention, such as in the following example of a city tax assessment system. When the tax base was computed, a key-punch error gave a 10-year-old automobile an assessed valuation of $7 million rather than $700. This incorrect figure was used in calculating the amount of property tax each resident would have to pay so the city could meet its budget. The owner of the car refused to pay a tax in excess of $200,000 and the city had to borrow money. A range check in the edit program could have alerted the tax assessors to such inconsistencies or to excessively high property valuations.

Value Tests.   Value tests are similar in some respects to range tests. Where a range test checks the limits of a field's value (such as, is the field greater than zero and less than 100?), a value test checks for discrete values, such as M or F for sex, or O, A, B, or AB for blood type.

Hash Totals.   In data entry and other applications where groups of numbers are entered, a hand-computed total may also be included as input. When the data are edited, the total is recomputed and compared with the input total. If the two agree, it is assumed that the data were input correctly; otherwise the batch is rejected and checked for errors. A related technique is the checksum, which is a number computed from the input data by the sending system and transmitted to the receiver so that when the edit tests are performed, the checksum can be computed again and checked.

Data Consistency vs. Data Accuracy

The more that is known about a set of data, the more accurate the edit checks can be. However, edit checks do not ensure the accuracy of the data, only their consistency. Thus, when a blood of type O is mistakenly key punched as type A, the value is consistent with acceptable values, even though the datum is in error.

When to Perform Edit Tests

Data editing can be employed at any point in an on-line system, preferably as close to the terminal as possible. For an intelligent terminal that would be at the terminal itself. When intelligent terminals are not being used, the edit tests could be performed at the TCP or in the application program, with the TCP being the better of the two. Performing the edit tests as close to user input as possible decreases the amount of processing required for records that do not pass the tests.

FORMATTING

Formatting of application messages is a function of the OSI presentation layer. When working in page mode, formatting also includes screen formatting, which is generally done by the access method or the TCP. Data or message formatting can include encryption, as discussed earlier.

Data Compression

A message can also be compressed, and by a number of techniques, all of which attempt to reduce the size of the message and thus allow more efficient use of the communication links.

Repeating Character Compression.   Perhaps the most common *compressions* technique is repeating character compression. This algorithm replaces repeating characters with one character plus a character count. For instance, with a 40-character address field, an address consisting of only 15 characters would contain 25 blanks, which by repeating character compression would be replaced with a byte count field and a character field, as illustrated in Figure 10-4.

Figure 10-4
Data Compression

123 Main Street

_____   Uncompressed

00000000011111111112222222222333333333334
12345678901234567890123456789012345678 90

1
123 Main Street6   Compressed

In Figure 10-4 the "16" represents a binary encoded byte. Thus, up to 255 bytes can be represented. It is also necessary to be able to distinguish a byte count field from an actual data field, which can be done by setting the high-order bit in the field to *on* (and thus limiting the repeat count to 127 characters). Alternatively it can be done by using two bytes for the repeat count, the first byte being a reserved flag byte to indicate that compression is being used, and the second representing the actual character count. The important aspect of compression is that the system be able to distinguish repeat counts from actual data.

Common Word Compression.   Common word compression is a technique whereby commonly used words can be represented by one or two bytes. For example, in a hospital application, common words like *patient, insurance, bill, x ray, doctor*, and *nurse* can each be represented by one character. Again, the encoding or compression scheme must include a flag of some sort to distinguish compressed data from uncompressed data.

Front End Compression.   Front end compression is a technique whereby records with like beginnings are compressed. This algorithm is similar to that of repeating character compression, except the repetition is of the first characters in a record. It is used more frequently in database management systems for index compression than in data communications applications. Figure 10-5 gives an example of front end compression performed on a subset of a personnel file that is arranged by employee last name.

Uncompressed	Compressed
LAMB, CAROLYN	LAMB, CAROLYN
LAMB, MARY	6MARY
LAMB, RICHARD	6RICHARD
LAMBDEN, RON	4DEN, RON
LAMBDIN, PEGGY	5IN, PEGGY
LAMBERT, DONNA	4ERT, DONNA
LAMBIRD, GEORGE	4IRD, GEORGE

Figure 10-5
Front End
Compression

Other Types of Formatting

Other types of formatting may also be required. At each of the OSI levels above the physical level, headers and control characters can be added to a message. Header information would include transaction identification, originating terminal, time stamp, transaction type, destination information, routing information, sequence numbers, and so on. An example of the type of formatting that *could* be done at each of the OSI levels follows.

Application Layer Formatting.   The basic concern at the application level is to provide the data that will be sent to the application layer on the receiving side. Formatting by the application layer is meant to organize the data into fields and to order the fields into records. Some systems, such as the U.S. bankwire system, use variable-length fields, with separators as field delimiters. Most business systems use fixed-length fields organized into records of variable or fixed length, as would be found in a COBOL program. The only requirement is that the sending and receiving applications agree on the message format. The application can also attach a descriptive header to the message, possibly containing a transaction identification, date and time stamp, originating terminal or application, and an indentifier telling the receiving application what to do with the message—for instance, add to database, modify a database record, or database inquiry. One possible message built by the application level is given in Figure 10-6 on page 362.

Presentation Layer Formatting.   The application layer passes the message to the presentation layer. In the example of Figure 10-7 on page 362, the only change made by the presentation layer is compression.

Figure 10-6
Application
Formatted Message

Trans ID	Name	Address

Figure 10-7
Presentation Layer-
Compression

Trans ID	Name (Comp)	Address (Compressed)

Session Layer Formatting. The next layer is the session layer, which is responsible for establishing the connection, *recovery* should the session be disrupted, flow control, and dialogue rules. For the message in Figure 10-8, the session layer has appended only a message sequence number, which can be used for recovery and possibly flow control. This is not the same sequence numbers as the data link control sequencing for HDLC.

Transport Layer Formatting. The transport layer in this example assists in making the connection between the session layers at each node; however, this activity does not affect the message. The transport layer also breaks a long message into smaller transmission blocks if necessary and enables its peer on the receiving side to reconstruct the message. Since the message is relatively short, the transport layer adds nothing to the message.

Network Layer Formatting. One function of the network layer is routing. In performing this function it can append the routing information to the message, as illustrated in Figure 10-9.

Data Link Layer Formatting. At the data link layer, the control information is included in the message. This includes the headers, block check characters, and transparency control characters if needed. The changes to the message at this level are described in Chapter 6.

Device Formatting. The formatting of messages is only one part of the formatting that must be effected. The other factor in data communications

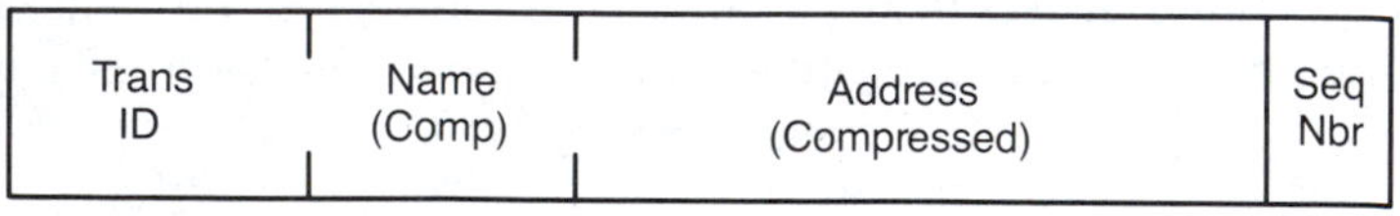

Figure 10-8
Session Layer-
Sequence Number

Trans ID	Name (Comp)	Address (Compressed)	Seq Nbr

Routing Header	Trans ID	Name (Comp)	Address (Compressed)	Seq Nbr

Figure 10-9
Network Layer-
Destination Header

is device formatting—that is, preparing the message for display on a specific type of terminal, printer, log file, or similar output device. Device management is a function of the presentation layer. For page mode terminals, the message and data fields within the message must be defined by control or escape sequences. The formatting capabilities are described in Chapter 4. For printed output, field alignment, page numbering, titles, subtitles, column headings, and carriage control must be inserted at either the presentation layer or the application layer. For log files, record blocking and message formatting must be accomplished. Again, this can be done either at the application level or presentation level or both.

ERROR DETECTION AND RECOVERY

Certain aspects of error detection and recovery have already been discussed in previous chapters, specifically with regard to the various redundancy checks and the send and receive counts in HDLC. These checks provide detection of lost or garbled messages, and the recovery technique is usually to retransmit the message or messages from the point of error. There is another level of recovery in data communications systems, the recovery of the system once a message has arrived and before its response has been returned and the message processed. In the ideal situation this type of recovery is coordinated with database recovery as well. Although individual implementations may differ somewhat in their approach, the basic elements of such a recovery system are outlined in this section.

When a message arrives at a node there is a certain amount of processing that must be accomplished to satisfy the message requirements, such as to immediately forward the message to the next node, store the message and forward it as time allows, or process the message and return the results to a terminal or other output device. During this processing cycle the application(s) processing the message, or the system itself, may fail. This section discusses how recovery might be effected. Not all systems adopt the approach discussed here; of those that do, some have yet to implement all the features in the following discussion.

When a node receives a message and acknowledges receipt to the sender, responsibility for the message is transferred from the sender to the receiver, meaning that the receiving node must be able to recreate the message and ensure its correct processing in the event of almost any possible failure. Designers of simple terminal systems sometimes take the view that it is the responsibility of the terminal operator to resubmit any possibly lost messages in the event of a failure, an approach that can be justified only on the grounds that it is easier than implementing more sophisticated software that would resolve most of the problems automatically. Although it is true that such recovery systems slow the system and increase processor utilization, these resources still usually cost less than does relying on an operator to recover transactions, usually without sufficient knowledge of what occurred.

Message Logging (Safe Storing)

To be sure that a message can be recreated, it should be logged to a file *before* being acknowledged. The object of the recovery process is to close all the time windows of vulnerability and create a system in which no messages are lost and all are processed exactly once. If message receipt is acknowledged and the message logged to an audit file, there is still a small window of time—perhaps on the order of 50 milliseconds—during which a system failure could prevent the message from being recreated, such as after acknowledgment has been returned and the write to the log file initiated, but before the write has been completed, in which case the message will have been lost. Furthermore, it is insufficient to initiate the write to the log file and acknowledge the message before the log write is successfully completed, because queues on the log device could delay the write, or a file error could occur that prevents the write from being completed, in which case acknowledgment will have already been sent and a failure could again cause the message to be lost.

Database—System Consistency. In addition to the message being logged, a transaction must be started for update transactions. A transaction is a logical collection of processing activities that either will be completely accomplished or will leave the database in the same state as before the transaction started.

This somewhat complicated sounding idea is actually very simple. It is like the situation of door-to-door vacuum cleaner salesperson: Calling on a customer starts a transaction, at the end of which the salesperson either leaves with the equipment (and the demonstration pile of dirt that had been spread on the carpet) and the customer still has all of the money, or the customer has the vacuum cleaner and the salesperson leaves with some of the money. In the first instance the transaction is unsuccessful for the salesperson and everything is exactly as it was prior to the beginning of the transaction, personal feelings excepted. In the second case the transaction is completed and a new state of consistency attained. But the following combinations do *not* happen: (1) the customer keeps all the money and the vacuum cleaner, or (2) the salesperson gets some of the customer's money and keeps the vacuum cleaner, leaving the customer with only the dirt on the carpet.

The same is true of an on-line transaction. The database and the system must be left in a consistent state at the conclusion of the transaction. Suppose a message requires two records in the database to be altered, record A, with contents M, and record B, with contents N. The message starts a transaction that changes the contents of A to Y and the contents of B to Z. At the conclusion of the transaction the database can be in only two possible states: Records A and B contain either M and N or Y and Z. The combination of M and Z and the combination of N and Y are inconsistent states, so if a failure should occur when record A has attained the value Y and record B still has the value N, recovery must be invoked. The recovery process must either roll the value of record A back to M or roll the value of B forward to Z. To make the example more specific, you can imagine that record A is a checking account record, record B a savings account record, and the transaction a transfer of funds between accounts. This transaction is used in the following discussion.

Message Processing

Once the message has been written to the log file (also referred to as *safe storing* the record), the acknowledgment returned to the sender, the data are edited, and a transaction started, the message can be processed. The transaction is forwarded to an application process. The unique transaction ID created when the transaction began is passed along with the message.

Database Update.   The application accesses the two records to be updated in the database and issues a *database write* request for both records. Before the updates are posted to the database, the database management system writes the before-and-after images to an audit file. After the audit writes have been completed the writes to the database can be initiated. Just as it was incorrect to acknowledge the message before completing the write to the log file, it is incorrect to write to the database before the before-and-after image writes are completed, for to do so would create a small time window that would make recovery impossible—that is, the database could be updated before the audit writes are made. If a failure occurs prior to capture of the audit images on disk or tape, the transaction might be unrecoverable.

Response Message.   Having completed the database updates, the application prepares a response and returns it to the TCP. The TCP then ends the transaction by writing an end transaction record to the transaction log and ensuring that all audit buffers have been written to the audit file. After both of these events have occurred, the transaction is completed and the response message can be sent back to the originating terminal.

Recovery Is Possible After Safe Storing

Recovery following failure is a joint effort between database and data communications system. At any point subsequent to the safe storing of the original message, recovery to a consistent state is possible. Suppose, for instance, that a failure occurs after the application has received the message and modified the first but not the second database record. The database system begins the recovery process first. When the system is restored to operational status, the transaction will be observed to be incomplete. The database management recovery system will use the before images it captured to restore the database to its state prior to the beginning of the transaction. That is, the before image of the updated record is written back to the database, thus erasing the update.

Next, the database recovery process sends a message to the TCP advising that the transaction has been stopped and the before images have been posted. The TCP retrieves the message associated with that transaction, starts a new transaction, and forwards the message to the application.

Retry Limit.   The same transaction could fail again, always possible because of problems with database files being full, indices being full, or unusual data conditions, such as division by zero. To protect against an infinite recovery loop, the recovery system should have a retry limit that prevents a transaction from being restarted indefinitely.

Audit Trails.   Like security systems, recovery systems are not completely reliable. If system failure includes failure of the device (tape or disk) containing the transaction and database audit logs, then automatic recovery becomes impossible. In such instances a database backup version is reloaded and as many after images as possible are reposted to the database to bring it forward in time. Those images on the medium that failed are not available, of course, so some processing is lost. To limit the exposure due to failure of the audit media, many systems allow the user to have multiple copies of the *audit trails*. For instance, if both a tape drive and a disk drive are available, then although for most recovery processes the disk drive would be used because of the random access capability it provides, the tape could be used when the disk is inaccessible. The next chapter contains further discussion regarding transaction design in an on-line system.

OTHER SOFTWARE FUNCTIONS

Some of the capabilities discussed in previous chapters can also be implemented in software. These functions include the gathering of statistical information, polling, speed conversion, queue handling, flow control, network control, buffering, blocking and deblocking, dialing and answering a telephone line, performance monitoring, and the person–machine interface.

SUMMARY

Security is a delaying factor used to deter unauthorized personnel from gaining access to a system and to provide time to catch those who try. Security of systems and networks is of growing concern to system implementers. Security can be implemented at multiple levels within a system. There is an overhead to implementing security precautions, and the cost of the security system should not exceed the potential loss from unauthorized use of the system.

Reliability and presentation of data are very important to the success of any system. Many software functions in a data communications network handle these requirements. Data are encrypted to prevent unauthorized disclosure, compressed to economize on-line time and disk storage, edited to eliminate as many errors as possible, and formatted to make them understandable and presentable. Data are formatted for output as well as for exchange between processes and media.

The error detection and recovery discussed in this chapter is different from the error checks made by VRC, LRC, and CRC discussed earlier. This chapter discussed error detection and recovery in connection with system and application recovery. The data communications and database systems should work together to provide a comprehensive recovery that leaves the system in a consistent state, with no transactions lost or processed more than once. The recovery system should also recover the users of the system and establish or help establish their restart points.

Key Terms

Audit trail	Password
Authentication	Recovery
Compression	Safe store
Data editing	Security
Data encryption standard (DES)	User profile
National Bureau of Standards	Verification

Questions and Exercises

1. Complete the encryption example for the message DATA COMMUNICATIONS started in Figure 10-3 on page 352.

2. Describe a number of physical security features and how they protect unauthorized access.

3. Investigate the security features of a system to which you have access. Describe the strong and weak points of the security provided.

4. Why is data compression helpful in a communications network?

5. Using the recovery mechanism described in this chapter, discuss how recovery would be implemented if a failure occurred (a) after safe storing the message and prior to sending it to the application, and (b) after all the database writes have been completed (assume two writes) but before the end of the transaction.

6. What will happen in an on-line system if a data edit check fails?

7. Investigate an application to which you have access and describe the data edit checks it uses. If you do not have access to an application, pick one, describe two data records used in the application and the edit checks you would use for those fields.

8. Design an input record for registering a student in a class. Describe the edit checks that could be used to verify the data.

References

Berg, John L. "Security Report." *Infosystems* 22 (July 1975).

Bryce, Heather. "The NBS Data Encryption Standard: Products and Principles." *Mini-Micro Systems* 14 (March 1981).

"Cryptography and Data Communications." *Infosystems* 22 (July 1975).

Diffie, Whitfield. "The Outlook for Computer Security." *Mini-Micro Systems* 2 (October 1978).

"Encryption Algorithm: Key Size is the Thing." *Datamation* 22 (March 1976).

Kinnucan, Paul. "Data Encryption Gurus: Tuchman and Meyer." *Mini-Micro Systems* 2 (October 1978).

Meyer, Carl H., and Tuchman, Walter. "Putting Data Encryption to Work." *Mini-Micro Systems* 2 (October 1978).

Solomon, Richard J. "The Encryption Controversy." *Mini-Micro Systems* 11 (February 1978).

Tanenbaum, Andrew S. *Computer Networks*. Englewood Cliffs, NJ: Prentice-Hall, 1981.

11
Systems Analysis

Transaction Design

Selecting Hardware and Software

System Configuration

Case Study

This chapter discusses aspects of data communications analysis and design that are not covered in previous chapters. At the conclusion of this chapter you should have a fundamental knowledge of transaction design considerations, why some designs are better than others, how to select equipment, and how to calculate the configuration of a system.

TRANSACTION DESIGN

A *transaction* is defined as a user-specified group of processing activities that are either entirely completed or, if not completed, that leave the database and processing system in the same state as before the transaction started. In other words, a transaction always leaves the database and the system in a consistent state. A transaction is also a unit of recovery, an entity that the recovery system manages. Recovery and contention have a great influence on transaction design. From the perspective of an application, it makes little difference as to how or when the transaction begins, ends, or is recovered. But from a systems design and system recovery perspective, good transaction design is very important.

Review of Transaction Activities

Prior to discussing transaction design, it is useful to discuss the activities needed to start, end, and process a transaction. As in Chapter 10, a generic recovery system is assumed; details vary with implementations.

Beginning and ending a transaction requires a certain amount of work, and additional audit processing is required when processing a transaction. Starting a transaction demands that a unique transaction identifier be generated. A beginning transaction record is then written to the transaction log. Each record updated by the transaction must be locked to avoid concurrent update problems. Some records that are read but not updated may also have to be locked. All updates must be posted to the before-and-after image audit trail before being written to the database. At the end of the transaction all audit buffers must be flushed to disk and end-of-transaction marker written to the audit trail.

Grouping Activities in a Single Transaction

Transaction design covers two areas, the grouping of activities into one transaction and the manner in which that transaction is implemented within the system.

In many cases the fact that a transaction must leave the system in a consistent state dictates the transaction's composition. In other cases the composition is not quite so obvious. In transferring funds from one bank account to another, for instance, it is clear that the deposit and withdrawal must be placed together in one transaction, for to do otherwise would make the database inconsistent. A trial balance would not balance if funds are taken from one place but not deposited in another.

An example of a transaction with less obvious boundaries is when a new employee is added to a company database. This assumes that the transaction activities required are selection and assignment of an employee number, addition of an employee record, and addition of zero to several associated records—employment history, payroll, dependents, and benefits. Although the employee will not be fully entered into the system until all these activities have been completed, it may be unnecessary to group all activities in a single transaction. The selection and assignment of an employee number and the creation of an employee record are tightly coupled events, so if an employee number has previously been removed from the sequence, then there should be an employee record by that number, which number should be available for reuse if adding the new employee to the file fails. However, adding a dependent record, which requires only that an employee record exist, is not so tightly linked with the process of creating the employee record. Indeed, dependent records are frequently added long after an employee has been hired. The same could be said for payroll records, benefits, and work history. In this example there could be one or several transactions.

Advantages and Disadvantages of Single vs. Multiple Transactions

What would be the advantages and disadvantages of making the employee transaction a single or multiple transaction?

Brief vs. Long Transactions.   A single transaction requires only one be-gin-and-end transaction activity. Although not an overriding considera-tion, there is an overhead to starting and ending a transaction that a careful designer will attempt to minimize. On the other hand, a long transaction has a greater risk—albeit very slight—of a failure that would involve a recovery. Long transactions also require that records be locked for a longer period of time, which both increases the likelihood of deadlock and re-moves records from available access for longer periods of time. When record locking is used to resolve the multiple update problems of conten-tion (which arise when two or more users attempt to access the same records), deadlock can occur. As discussed earlier, deadlock results when two different users (in this case transactions) have controls over records and attempt to access records the other already locked, as illustrated in Figure 11-1.

	Transaction 1	Transaction 2	
T	Read and lock record A.		**Figure 11-1**
		Read and lock record B.	Deadlock Situation
I	Attempt to read record B.		
		Attempt to read record A.	
M			
	Wait.	Wait.	
E			

Multiple Sessions with One Operator.   The major consideration in whether to group multiple updates into one transaction is none of the above, however. Because the weakest link in a transaction is perhaps the operator, good transaction design avoids multiple sessions with the ter-minal operator whenever possible. If in adding the new employee it is decided to treat all activities as one transaction, then complications could arise, as follows: The terminal operator begins the transaction by entering the employee data, triggering updates to the employee number assign-ment file, the employee file, and perhaps a number of access method files, all accomplished by one interaction with the terminal. Having been up-dated, the employee number assignment record and the new employee record are locked. The operator next enters job history information. If the operator takes a lunch break at this point, putting the transaction on hold, with its records locked, then because the employee number assignment record must be used every time a new employee is added, no new em-ployees can be added during this interval.

The problem with having a transaction span sessions with one operator is not just the operator's potential absence; it is the amount of time that a transaction must be held in limbo while the operator enters more infor-mation. Compared to the milliseconds required to update databases and process transactions, the minutes required to enter the data is rather long. This situation is further complicated when records are locked across sessions with the operator. Fortunately, techniques exist for avoiding such delays.

How to Avoid Multiple Sessions.   If system design requires all of the activities described for adding a new employee to be a single transaction, then the transaction should be planned to avoid multiple sessions with the operator once the transaction begins. Essentially the solution is to gather all necessary information *before* beginning the transaction. One way in which this could be accomplished is as follows.

The operator enters the information for the new employee. The data are edited, and if there are no inconsistencies the record is safe stored. The operator is then prompted for job history data. Again, edit checks are performed and the record is safe stored. The same is done for dependent, payroll, and benefits data. If a failure occurs during this process, the data already input will be available, so the operator will not need to enter them again. Once all of the data have been entered, the transaction is initiated. The database locks are kept for the minimum required time, since no additional sessions with the operator are required. Upon completion, the result is returned to the operator. Should the operator leave the terminal for a period of time in the midst of the transaction, then no records are left locked during the period. At most, some buffer space is held for that period, and even that could be eliminated by proper design.

To summarize, transactions should generally be designed to be as brief as possible and to avoid multiple interactions with one operator. The overriding consideration is to design transactions so the database is always left in a consistent state and so recovery can be assured. The participation of a terminal operator in the recovery process should be kept to a minimum. Operators should be notified of the last activity completed on their behalf so they can continue from the correct place.

SELECTING HARDWARE AND SOFTWARE

When implementing a new on-line application it is sometimes necessary to acquire additional hardware and software to support the application, especially if the on-line application is the first break from the more traditional batch operating environment. In addition to the hardware and software, new services such as communications media, support personnel, and education may be needed. If the new application fits the existing equipment as is or with minor enhancements, then selection of hardware and software is a relatively simple task. In those situations where major acquisitions are necessary, the prudent systems group should evaluate the offerings of several vendors. The remainder of this section assumes that support of the new application requires a major upgrade of hardware and software.

Selecting a hardware or software system involves selecting more than just a system; a vendor is also being selected. The vendor's ability to maintain, enhance, and expand the components may well determine the selection's overall success. Therefore, both the components and the vendor must be evaluated with equal care.

Request for Proposal (RFP)

In general, smaller companies and private companies can take a rather informal approach to system selection. In larger corporations and in most government implementations, selection must be based on fair appraisal. This is accomplished when the user creates and issues a *request for proposal (RFP)*, sometimes referred to as a *request for quotation (RFQ)*. In some countries this is called a *request for a tender offering*. Regardless of the name, the process yields a document describing the problem to be resolved and requesting qualified vendors to submit plans and costs for solving the problem. Henceforth, the term *RFP* refers to the document describing the problem to be solved.

An RFP, which has no well-defined format, is used to procure a broad range of equipment from relatively low-cost items, such as terminals and multiplexers, to large-scale processing systems and software. The RFP for the first category of equipment might consist of less than 20 pages, whereas the latter might require several hundred pages of description. It is up to the user to determine what is pertinent to the proposal.

Format and Content of the RFP

The arrangement of the following topics in an RFP is not set, except that within a document the ordering should be logical (for example, descriptions of how responses are to be delivered should not be placed between descriptions of the hardware and software components).

Table of Contents.   A table of contents should be included for any lengthy RFP document and for some of the shorter ones. Because the RFP is usually aimed at a team of specialists from several disciplines, a table of contents gives the responders a quick reference to specific topics.

Introduction.   The first section of the RFP should be a *brief* introduction. It can include overviews of the company, the problem to be solved, and the anticipated schedule for completion of the proposal, evaluation, selection, installation, and live operation.

Response Ground Rules.   The ground rules for responding to a proposal are ordinarily placed at the beginning or end of the RFP. This establishes the schedule for the selection process, the manner in which responders interact with the user during the process, the format for a proposal, the manner in which proposals are evaluated, and how multiple vendor responses are to be treated. The schedule should include the date proposals are to be made available; the place, date and time for submission of all proposals; the dates during which presentations can be made; when the winning proposal will be selected; the anticipated delivery dates of the equipment being procured, and the anticipated date the system will be operational.

Scheduling.   The **time and place of proposal submission** are quite important. Most RFPs specify a specific date and time after which proposals will no longer be accepted.

RFP responders often are allowed to make a presentation to the selection committee. The presentation enables the vendor to provide additional technical information and to answer any questions the selection committee may have. Since such presentations tend to be time consuming, it is usually a good practice to narrow the field of candidates to a relatively small number of final presenters, perhaps five.

The **date of selection** tells vendors when they will be notified of success or failure. All responders to the RFP should receive a minimum of two notifications, the first an acknowledgment of proposal receipt, and the second notification of proposal acceptance or rejection. Although the **equipment delivery date** applies only to the winning proposals, it is important to all responders, because companies frequently need considerable lead time to manufacture or obtain equipment. If the specified delivery date is too soon for a particular vendor, the vendor can set a more realistic date in the proposal. The anticipated **date to commence operations** is important in helping the vendor to determine the number of employees needed for development and installation and to evaluate the costs and risks involved. Some vendors may have the needed equipment in stock, whereas others might require a significant development investment. As with delivery date, responders might wish to propose their own operational date.

Fair Appraisal.   If the appraisal process is to be conducted fairly, all responders should be treated equally. This can be difficult if one of the responders is the incumbent vendor and because personal associations frequently exist between vendor personnel and the selection committee. Furthermore, vendors' sales representatives like to use the selection period to practice their salesmanship—with lunches, dinners, entertainment, and an increased presence. One common practice during submission and evaluation is to require all communications between a vendor and the selection committee to be made through a small group of user personnel, thus providing each vendor with consistent intermediaries and response.

While evaluating the RFP, vendors frequently need to ask questions of the user. The user can distribute to all vendors a list of relevant questions and answers which is especially helpful to clarify points in the RFP. However, distribution of questions that disclose information regarding a particular vendor's solution should be avoided.

Response Format.   The format of the response is a user option. It is customary to have the response submitted in two volumes, one consisting of technical responses and the other for the financial and contractual response. Each of these sections might be evaluated by a different group, thereby preventing the technical evaluation from being biased by price. In the final analysis it is a combination of the two reports that will determine the winner. Providing an outline for responders to follow in their proposals makes for a consistency in content and format that decreases the work of evaluation. Question sheets and checklists also provide a quick means of obtaining information.

Evaluation Criteria.   The RFP should contain information regarding how the proposal is to be evaluated. Otherwise it is like giving an examination without saying how it will be graded or giving the relative point values for each question. A complete description is usually impossible, but as a minimum, features should be defined as "mandatory," "highly desirable," or "optional but influential." The more influential features should be pointed out so the responder can more completely describe these critical aspects of the system. This also assists the vendors to determine whether their solution is viable and describes the key points to make in the response. In the final analysis, a grading of key requirements plus a weighting applied to each requirement usually makes the overall evaluation easier. For example, 5 points could be assigned for meeting a requirement completely, 3 for meeting it partially, and zero for deficiencies. Weights that reflect relative importance can then be assigned to each requirement. For a communications system, being able to interface with IBM's SNA network might carry a weight of 10, and an interactive screen design feature might carry a weight of 2, which implies that an SNA interface is 5 times as important as interactive screen design aids. The technical winner would be the responder with the highest number of points. If a point value is given to the pricing as well, the technical and financial evaluations can be combined to make the overall best response even more obvious.

Multiple Vendor Bids.   Several vendors can cooperate in proposing a solution for very large projects, one vendor providing the hardware and system-level software while another contracts for custom application software. In other instances, one vendor might supply the processors, another the terminal subsystems, and a third the software. Users should specify any special rules regarding multiple vendor bids. As a minimum, users generally prefer to have one vendor as prime contractor with overall responsibility for the entire proposal. Of course, as long as the implementation goes smoothly, multiple independent vendors pose no problems. But when delays occur, it is much easier for the user to contact one responsible vendor for resolution. Having one vendor as the primary contractor simplifies problem resolution for the user and eliminates finger pointing between vendors.

User Characteristics.   It often helps a vendor to be provided with a description of the user's company, personnel, and current processing environment. This perspective enables the responder to address the proposal more appropriately. For instance, since there are a multitude of payroll and accounts receivables applications, a section describing the user's company would give insight into how the company works and how the payroll or accounts receivable applications differ from those of other companies.

Problem Description.   The major portion of the RFP is devoted to a description of the problem to be solved. This should *not* include any perceived solutions because such solutions are usually biased by a particular hardware and software environment. For instance, an RFP that states that a processor is "capable of executing 2 million instructions per second (MIPS) and supports line speeds in excess of 56 Kbps" is presenting the vendor with a perceived solution to the problem. What is preferable is a problem described in sufficient detail to allow responders to configure a system based on their own hardware and software capabilities.

In actuality, many RFPs are released with the anticipation of only one or a few viable contenders. In some instances the RFP is written in such a way that only one or two vendors even stand a chance of successfully competing. In these cases it is up to the vendors to determine their chances of success and weigh the risk of losing their investment in preparing a response.

Case Study Revisited

For specifics, consider again the Syncrasy Corporation. They have been successful and are again expanding. The company has decided to become a developer of software and an original equipment manufacturer for minicomputer systems as well as personal computers. Their target market is office automation systems. The software development department is to be located in Austin, Texas, and sales offices with computer equipment will be located in 13 large cities throughout the United States and international offices in Montreal, Toronto, London, Paris, Rome, Frankfurt, Oslo, Tokyo, Hong Kong, Sydney, and Mexico City. The objective is to network all of these systems to allow software to be quickly distributed to all sales sites, provide problem communication on a timely basis, manage corporate inventory and accounting, and provide interoffice communication of letters and graphics. To secure the network equipment an RFP will be prepared. A proposal committee consisting of data processing personnel and several key users of the system has been formed. A synopsis of the first draft of the RFP as submitted to Link Editor, the vice president for data processing, follows:

Syncrasy Corp's Draft 1 RFP.   Each of the 18 offices must have processors capable of executing the same object modules. The speed of the processors will vary between 1 million instructions per second (MIPS) and 5 MIPS. The processors must be capable of communicating with each other using HDLC protocol as well as an interface to X.25 networks. A database management system compatible with the CODASYL specifications must be provided. IBM 3270 or compatible terminals must be supported.

Draft 1 Rejected.   This first draft was rejected because it contained too many solutions and not enough problem definition. The object code compatibility is only one solution to the problem of developing software at one location for execution at another; cross compilers might also work. A better problem definition would state that it must be possible for system and application software to be generated at one node and transported to another node for execution. Within a particular vendor's product line, then, the solution might differ from object code compatibility.

MIP Rates.   The quoted MIP rates represent the perceived processing power, most likely based on the amount of work accomplished by one or several processors with which the committee has experience. MIP rates are a measure of instructions executed per unit of time, but not necessarily of throughput. Operating systems, database systems, and data communications systems all consume processing resources while providing varying levels of function. For instance, a system that provides complete recovery of database and data communications networks can be expected to execute more instructions than one without those capabilities. Furthermore, the application software can vary significantly in the number of instructions required, depending on the efficiency of the written code as well as the efficiency of the code generated by the compilers. Higher-level languages such as database query languages and interpreters can also consume more machine cycles.

More on Problem Description.   The statement of the problem should be a description of the applications to be run, together with the type of transactions expected to be executed. For instance, a transaction might be described as being local to one node or requiring communication between nodes and might also define the number of input and output characters, transaction frequency, peak transaction rate, and work performed by the transaction. This type of definition is covered in more detail in the later section on "sizing." The amount of work necessary to provide such information appears to be more than that required in the rejected solution stated above. However, it is impossible to derive the solution without doing the same analysis internally. There are benefits to be derived from this type of problem statement as well: The vendor's response might possibly come up with a novel and economical solution, or it might provide some preliminary design solutions. Regardless, the vendor is allowed to configure the system in a manner fitting their hardware and software rather than some preconceived solution.

Subrequirements.   If the system to be procured is large, the requirements can be broken into subsections dealing with data communications, terminals, hardware, and software. Sufficient transaction and batch processing detail should be provided to enable the vendor to size and then price the system.

Benchmarks.   *Benchmark* testing is sometimes useful in assuring that the proposed configuration will actually solve the problems. Benchmarks are also a measure of how well a group of experts can run benchmark programs. A far better measure of performance is the analysis of an already operational system that supports a processing load similar to that of the anticipated system. If benchmark programs are necessary, they should not be required of all responders. Instead, the field of candidates should be narrowed to a small number, say five, and these finalists should run the tests. This does not preclude other responders from eventually running the benchmark as well. For instance, the five finalists might fail to perform the benchmark as expected on the proposed configuration, thereby elevating the response of other vendors. The rationale behind having only a selected group run the benchmark test is that such tests are expensive for both vendor and user. Equipment must be allocated and configured, tests written, system tuned to maximum performance, results evaluated, and reports written. The user should be involved in the testing as a monitor at least and ideally as a participant. A great deal of information can be gained by such participation.

Other Points in the RFP.   Other factors that should be addressed in the RFP include education offered, including cost and location; maintenance costs and hours; extended maintenance coverage; software license; microcode; maintenance and user fees for the software; location of maintenance offices, escalation procedures for maintenance; locations of spare parts and the time required for delivery; number, location, and type of available support personnel; national and international support policies where applicable; and the availability of backup systems in the event of a prolonged failure for whatever reason.

References.   Every vendor should be asked to submit at least three reference accounts for contact; those unable to supply three good reference accounts should be scrutinized very carefully. The requester should also attempt to contact three additional accounts not listed as references; this can prove very informative. Sometimes the references themselves can point one to other accounts. If the vendor's customer base is large, references in a similar business or with a similar transaction load should be contacted.

Final Selection Considerations.   Once the responses to the RFP have been evaluated, the field should be narrowed to three to five finalists. These are the vendors who can be expected to run a benchmark. These vendors' references should also be contacted at this time. This is also the point at which contract negotiations begin. The vendor's standard contract should be reviewed by the user's attorneys. If nonstandard components are to be used, the user should attempt to make contractual agreements about when the components are to be delivered, what constitutes acceptance of the components, and what penalties, if any, will apply for nonconformance. Support and maintenance issues should be resolved. The user should know from which office their support is coming, what the expected response time will be, what charges are involved, what the escalation procedures are, and whether the vendor is willing to provide backup systems should the purchased system malfunction for any significant length of time.

The user should ascertain how frequently new releases are made, what the policy is for fixing bugs of various levels of severity, distributing the solutions, and what this service costs. The user should determine if enhancements to the product are planned, how frequently they will be made, and the costs involved in receiving them.

Unfortunately, the history of user–vendor relationships is full of well-intentioned but unfulfilled promises of things to be delivered and services to be provided. There is also a history of hidden costs and of support problems. For a sizable purchase, the purchaser should make every attempt to protect their investment. Standard contracts provided by a vendor are designed to protect the vendor. In many instances this does not adequately protect the purchaser. For any significant purchase, attorneys representing the purchaser should review and modify the standard vendor contracts.

A thorough analysis of a number of vendors' solutions to a processing problem provides a user with a higher probability of success in selecting the equipment best suited to an application. And the time invested in this activity is frequently regained several times over in project implementation.

SYSTEM CONFIGURATION

Sizing and configuring a system is an on-going activity. Over time the manner in which an on-line system is used tends to vary. New transactions may be introduced and existing ones changed or discontinued, or the frequency with which they are invoked might change. In addition to changes in on-line activity, changes in batch processing requirements and hardware can alter the response characteristics of a system. For example, in a virtual memory system, memory pages are swapped to disk. So long as sufficient real memory is available, paging does not seriously affect response times. As more applications are added to the system, the paging rate increases and performance decreases. Eventually a point will be reached where the system spends more time satisfying memory management requests than it does processing data. This is just one of a number of potential system bottlenecks.

Sizing and configuring a network requires a comprehensive knowledge of the application, system, and performance objectives. In this section the focus is on the information that must be collected to make an educated estimate of the resources required to meet the response time requirements of the on-line system. Batch processing and the transfer of large amounts of data are not considered.

Response Time

Response time consists of two components, data communications and processing. The data communications component consists of the time required to transmit a message from source to destination and receive any necessary response. The processing component consists of the activity required by one or more processors in satisfying the request, including field editing, message routing, message formatting, data manipulation and calculation, recovery overhead, and database access. All of these factors must be known to properly size and configure a system.

One can start to analyze response time either at the processing or data communications component. It is usually easier to begin with the processing component and then determine the required line speeds needed to meet the data communications component.

Processing Time Requirements.   Processing time requirements start with a detailed definition of the transaction. Because input-output access time is almost always the most time-consuming factor in a transaction, the number and type of accesses must be determined. For example, a banking transaction in which the account record must be retrieved using the customer's name may have a higher overhead than the same transaction using the account number. This would occur if the account number were the primary key of retrieval and the customer name were a secondary key. Furthermore, account numbers are unique, whereas the name may not be. Thus, the transaction using customer name requires the retrieval and search of an index and multiple accesses to the account file if duplicate names exist. The transaction using account number requires only one access to the account file.

Disk Access Time.   For each transaction the number of database or file accesses must be counted, including in the count auxiliary accesses for indices. If optimization features such as cache memory, which reduces disk accesses or storage of indices on the same cylinder as related data, are available, they should be considered in determining the required access times. Being able to complete this step requires a knowledge of the database design, the manner in which records are accessed, and how the transaction requests records from the database management system.

CPU Time.   Another component of transaction processing is the amount of CPU time required. This is difficult to approximate unless the transaction has been measured by a performance monitor. In most cases a very rough estimate based on the number of instructions or processing time is sufficient. For the majority of transactions the amount of time spent executing instructions is minor compared to the amount of time waiting for I/O completions. CPU time becomes a concern only when transactions are CPU-intensive or when CPU time is in short supply. Thus, CPU times become a critical element in a statistical transaction where the solution requires iterative techniques and little or no I/O. In the banking situation mentioned above, CPU time is negligible when compared to the I/O time.

Data Communications Time Requirements.   A transaction's I/O time and processing time (which is assumed to include interprocess communication time if appropriate) make up the processing component of response time. The data communications component consists of line time plus time to handle the message at any intermediate nodes. *Line time* is a function of the type of line used, the transmission speed of the line, and the total number of characters transmitted.

The preceding considerations will result in the minimum expected response time. A number of other factors—all dealing with contention for system resources—will potentially add to the minimum response time. If the communications links are shared by a number of devices through multidrop, multiplexing, or similar techniques, the links may not be immediately available or the terminal's apparent line speed may be less than that of the link. In such cases the average time spent waiting in the transmit queue must be included in the total response time. In most instances it is also beneficial to determine the worst case response time as well. Queuing at the TCP, the application, and the disk are other places where delays can occur. The TCP ordinarily handles multiple terminals, but only one terminal receives the attention of a TCP at a given time. The same is true of the application and disk processes. The service times for these potential delays are derived by calculating the expected transaction arrival rates and mean service times.

Example Computation of Transaction Response Time

This example assumes that disk access time has three components—seek time, latency, and transfer time. *Seek time* is the time it takes to move the read/write heads to the proper cylinder. A seek time of 33 milliseconds (ms), which is typical of a number of disk drives, is used in this example. *Latency* is the average time required for the data to be read to revolve under the read/write heads. After the seek, the data may have just passed under the heads, thus requiring a full revolution of the disk, or they could be just arriving at the heads, thus requiring no latency. Some disks revolve at 3600 rpm, resulting in a full latency of 16.6 ms and an average latency of 8.3 ms. *Transfer time*, usually negligible compared to the other two components, is the amount of time required for the data to be sent over the channel to the CPU's memory. If the channel speed is 5 million characters per second and the block size being transferred is 500 characters, then the transfer time is approximately 0.1 ms (*approximately* because a small amount of processing time is also required). These figures represent the amount of time required for random access to the disk.

Consider the following library transaction. A patron wants to renew two books but does not have a library card available. The transaction requires the following processing:

> Read the patron record using the name as a key. This requires an index record. On the average three names will qualify. These three records, with address and library card number, are displayed on the operator's terminal. This requires reading one index record and three data records.

> Select the proper patron and retrieve the *books checked out* records, one for each book borrowed. In this instance two records are retrieved using the library card number and requiring an index record search of one index record and two data records.

> Update both book records to reflect the new due date. This requires two writes to the book file and no updates to the index file.

Processing Time.   Total disk activity for this transaction involves seven reads and two writes. Furthermore, the system uses transaction auditing, which requires writes to the before-and-after image audit files and two writes to the audit trail for the beginning and ending of the transaction. An efficient audit system is assumed, so the two before images and two after images are written with one disk write each. Thus, there is a total of 13 disk accesses, nine for the transaction and four for the audits. Disk time is therefore

13 seeks @ 33 ms each	429.0 ms
13 latencies @ 8.3 ms each	107.9
Total disk time	536.9 ms

There is approximately 20 ms of processing or CPU time, and approximately 100 ms of queuing time within the system (waiting for disk and application). Total processing time, then, is

Disk access time	536.9 ms
Processing time	20.0
Queue wait time	100.0
Total processing time	656.9 ms

Data Communications Time.   The number of characters transmitted to the terminal are

Input last name	10
Output 3 records	150
Input selected record	10
Output two records	100
Input updated data	100
Output completion status	10
Protocol, formatting	190
Total no. of transmitted characters	570

If the expected response time is 2 seconds, then approximately 4560 bits must be transferred in 1.343 seconds, requiring a transmission speed in excess of 3395 bps. This equates to a standard speed of 4800 bps and represents the minimum line speed. With a multi-point line, polling overhead and possible modem turnaround times must be factored in. This example, however, assumes a point-to-point line.

Sizing exercises almost always make numerous assumptions. For instance, the previous example assumed an average number of disk accesses and average queue times and processing time. With a multi-point line, assumptions would have to be made regarding the number and size of messages transmitted before a particular terminal's poll was received. Prediction of performance becomes easier once the system has been installed and is operational, when variables such as queue time can be more readily determined. Sizing in the case of an already operational system helps determine the impact of changing the transaction load, adding new transactions, or changing the batch component of the processing load. Even though sizing analysis is partly an imprecise estimate, it is still valuable in predicting initial system sizing and components, as well as in anticipating the growth of an established system.

CASE STUDY

Having installed their network, the Syncrasy Corporation has begun development of a distributed order-processing system. A number of transactions have been identified for the system, one of the most complex of which is the order entry transaction. The analysis that went into the design of this transaction follows.

Order Entry Design Requirements

The order entry transaction is to serve the customers in North America. Orders will be filled from the closest warehouses in New York, Chicago, Kansas City, or Los Angeles. Each warehouse location maintains its own computer system and inventory. The network configuration is depicted in Figure 11-2. Placing an order involves the following activities:

1. **Customer Identification.** The operator enters the customer's name. If the name is already in the database, then order entry commences; if the name is not on file, then a customer entry screen is presented and the required information, such as billing and shipping address, entered. A credit limit is established for the customer. When the customer records have been set up, the order can be entered.

2. **Order Entry.** Order line items are entered, consisting of part numbers together with the quantity for each part. Any number of line items can make up an order. It has been determined that the average Syncrasy order has eight line items, and that 10% of all orders have more than 20 line items and 2% more than 30 line items.

Figure 11-2
The Syncrasy Order
Entry Network

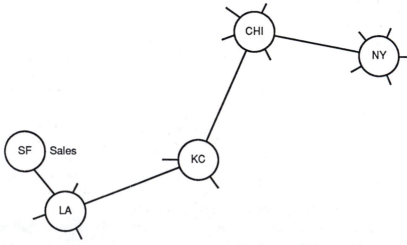

San Francisco searches Los Angeles, then Kansas City, then Chicago, then New York City.

3. **Total Order Value/Credit Limit Check.** The total value of the order is computed by summing the products of price and quantity. This value is then compared with the customer credit limit: If the limit is exceeded, the customer is so advised and credit can be extended by manual authorization procedures if necessary.

4. **Inventory Check.** Inventory is checked to determine which ordered parts are in stock, with the closest warehouse checked first. If the entire order cannot be filled from the nearest warehouse, the others are checked. The operator is notified of any line items unavailable from inventory. The customer then has the options of canceling all or part of the order or entering the entire order and backordering the out-of-stock items. It has been determined that 5% of all transactions encounter the out-of-stock condition and that in only 10% of these situations (0.5% of all situations) are ordered items canceled as a result of insufficient stock.

5. **Inventory/Credit Update.** If an order is placed, the inventory in each shipping warehouse is updated, and if it is not a cash transaction, the customer's credit limit is adjusted.

6. **Receipt and Order Confirmation.** A receipt and order confirmation are printed at the order entry location.

7. **Packing Lists/Shipping Labels.** Packing lists and shipping labels are printed at each of the affected warehouses.

8. **Billing.** Billing information is generated and accounts receivable files updated. If the customer pays cash, no invoice is generated, but the general ledger files are updated.

Syncrasy wants the transaction designed so records can be locked for update as briefly as possible and remain unlocked while awaiting operator inputs. If the entire logical transaction is to be decomposed into multiple database transactions, the subtransactions must be individual elements; that is, for recovery to be consistent, it would be improper to debit the accounting files without a corresponding credit entry. However, the primary design consideration is to provide the best possible response for the customer, meaning that customer identification and order verification must be performed in the minimum possible time. Page mode terminals were selected for this application. They have no local processing capabilities.

Transaction Design Selected

A number of transaction designs can meet the above criteria. The design selected by the Syncrasy analysts and the rationale behind their decisions are described below.

Customer ID/Credit Check.   The operator first enters the customer identification, either customer number or name. This information is transmitted to the local host and the database searched to determine whether the customer has already been defined. If the customer is on file, then their billing and shipping address are displayed on the operator's terminal. If the customer is not on file, then a customer definition form is displayed on the operator's terminal. When the customer data has been entered, they are edited for consistency; if the edit checks are successful, a credit check is performed. If the credit check is successful, then the transaction to add a new customer record is started, the customer data are added to the database, the transaction is completed, and the information is displayed on the operator's terminal together with the order entry line item screen. The new customer who fails to pass the credit check is asked to pay cash or is referred to the credit department for approval.

Customer Order.   Once the customer has been properly identified, the operator enters order line items. This part of order entry can be quite complex, since orders can be open-ended—that is, a virtually unlimited number of line items are allowed and the customer can cancel any or all of the order on an out-of-stock condition or insufficient credit condition.

Ten line items can be entered on the first screen; subsequent screens allow 20 line items. Since orders are open-ended, a design decision must be made regarding long orders. The first design alternative basically consists of limiting the number of items per order, and the second allows any number of items and makes a special case of extremely long orders. The problem with long orders is essentially that the transaction control process (TCP) buffers line items as they are received; however, a maximum buffer size is set. If more items are ordered than can fit in the buffer, then either a buffer overflow algorithm must be employed or the transaction must be limited to a specific number of line items.

In Syncrasy's case, optimization is meant to favor the customer, not the programmer. Because a customer may decide to cancel all or part of an order if a line item is unavailable, dividing a logical transaction into two or more separate recovery transactions was considered impractical. Thus, for instance, if an order for 40 items was divided into two transactions of 20 items each, the customer could find a line item unavailable in the second transaction and cancel the entire order, in which case a completed transaction would need to be backed out, requiring an interface with the audit logs or necessitating that the application keep track of all line items. The first case is usually too difficult in vendor-supplied recovery systems, which are designed to back out a particular uncompleted transaction or to roll all or a group of transactions forward. Very seldom is the recovery system able to back out one particular transaction that has already been completed.

Backing Out a Transaction.   Indeed, backing out one completed transaction could affect other already-completed transactions. If, for example, a part were ordered in both transactions A and B, with B starting after A, then to back out A, it would be insufficient to replace A's before images in the file because that would erase B's update. All transactions completing after A would have to be examined to determine if they affected A's records, or A's order quantity would have to be added back into the inventory. Even this could create problems if automatic reordering is used. B's transaction could have precipitated a reorder, and adding A's quantity back in could place the quantity back over the reorder point. Subsequent orders could again trigger a reorder. In either case, if the item is expensive, then an overstock condition could be reached, which might adversely affect profits. Syncrasy has decided that for transactions in excess of 30 line items (the first two screens), those items over 30 will be written to an overflow disk file. Experience has indicated that only 2% of all transactions fall into this category.

Thus, the operator enters line items until all have been completed. All line items are held in the TCP, with some records possibly in the overflow disk file. The number of line items is maintained in the data entry record, so it is known whether overflow has been used.

Inventory Check.   The next stage of the transaction is to determine whether there is sufficient inventory to fill the order. Since there are four warehouse locations in North America from which the goods can be shipped, the application uses a search priority, with the first search being at the closest warehouse. Two alternatives were considered in doing the database searches. The first involves locking records as the search progresses and the second involves scanning all items without locking them and then rereading the records for update. In the first case, when out-of-stock conditions are encountered, locks must either be released or held across the operator sessions. In the second case, extra reads are required, and the record could be changed by other transactions in the interval between the initial read and the subsequent update read, which could create an out-of-stock condition that was not identified in the initial read.

Inventory Check/Update Alternatives.   Analysis of orders indicates that in only 5% of the transactions is there insufficient stock in all warehouse locations and that in only 10% of those situations are one or more line items canceled as a result. The first of these numbers is the more significant, for in 5% of all transactions the operator must be prompted to determine whether any line items should be canceled. This portion of the overall transaction presented the most significant dilemma for the analysts. The five basic approaches considered follow. In each of them, the customer record is read and locked unless it is a cash transaction, thus prohibiting the same customer from placing orders concurrently and exceeding their credit limit.

1. **Read records without locking them.** If all stock levels could be met then the records would have to be reread, locked, and up-

dated. In 5% of the cases, the operator would be consulted before proceeding. In 95% of the circumstances the records would be read twice and updated once. In some (rare) situations, the stock levels could be decremented by other transactions. In this situation, an insufficient stock level would be recognized, thus defeating the intent of deferring the updates.

2. **Lock records as they are read and defer updates until the entire order can be completed.** If an item is out of stock, the records can be unlocked and the operator informed of the out-of-stock items and the transaction started again if the order is placed.

3. **Same as transaction 2 except do not unlock the records** during the operator session. This ensures that other transactions will not decrement stock levels already checked.

4. **Read the records with lock, update them as read, and back out all updated records when an insufficient stock level is encountered.** The database management system being used can support this situation. A transaction can be started and if an insufficient stock level is encountered, the transaction can be aborted, which automatically reverses all updates.

5. **Lock records and update them as read.** If an out-of-stock condition is encountered, all locks can be maintained across the session with the operator. This option has the problem of potentially locking a large number of records and keeping them locked over a session with the operator. It is possible that the customer will take a long time to decide about canceling line items.

The design team considered options 2 and 4 as the best approaches. Option 4 was selected because the number of exceptions is low and because transaction backout creates less overhead than locking and releasing locks, rereading records, or spanning sessions with an operator. Option 4 optimizes the transaction for the typical situation; the atypical situation results in more overhead. (If the number of exceptions increases, however, then one of the other approaches might be preferable.) As an integral part of the transaction, an order record is written to a log file. This record is important with respect to completing the rest of the transaction. Rather than having the customer wait while picking list algorithms are processed, picking lists written, shipping labels created, accounting records updated, and so on, the order confirmation is returned to the order location as promptly as possible. The log entry is used to activate the rest of the transaction after customer notification. In all of the above scenarios, the transaction would be defined for the updating of the inventory records and the entering of the log file record.

Customer Order Confirmation.   Once the inventory has been updated, the order is confirmed with the customer. The order, together with shipping information, is printed at the order point. A background process used to complete the order reads the transaction log record and produces the packing lists, shipping labels, and accounting entries. While this background activity is occurring, other order entry transactions can be started. Since this design separates the noncustomer portions of order processing from those directly affecting customer wait time, the customer is delayed for the minimum amount of time, the order is divided into recoverable, indivisible components: customer identification, order entry and verification, and background processing.

SUMMARY

The acquisition of hardware, software, and services is a time-consuming process. For potential vendors to adequately size and price a system, a significant amount of information must be collected, organized, and presented to them. The information should be in the form of a statement of a problem to be solved rather than a response to a solution. This request for proposal (RFP) allows the vendors to configure their systems in the way in which they work best. The evaluation of responses is also time-consuming. Careful preparation of the RFP can simplify the evaluation process. The field of viable vendors should be narrowed down to a small number who can best solve the problem. This select group can then be evaluated in depth and be required to make presentations and run benchmarks.

System configuration and sizing is an on-going process. It also requires a good knowledge of the equipment and application involved. By modeling a developing system or monitoring an existing system, performance problems can be anticipated and avoided.

Key Terms

Benchmark	Seek time
Latency	Sizing
Request for proposal (RFP)	Transaction
Request for quotation (RFQ)	

Questions and Exercises

1. What are the implications of having transactions involve multiple sessions with a terminal operator? Are there any benefits to having multiple sessions with an operator?

2. What impact will long transactions have on a system? Are there any applications where long transactions are necessary? If so, what are some examples?

3. Why is transfer time considered insignificant in sizing a system?

4. When a request for proposal (RFP) is released to vendors, why should a single contact point for questions be established?

References

Bronner, L. "Overview of the Capacity Planning Process for Production Data Processing." *IBM Systems Journal* vol. 19, no. 1, 1980.

Cooper, J. C. "A Capacity Planning Methodology." *IBM Systems Journal* vol. 19, no. 1, 1980.

Martin, James. *Systems Analysis for Data Transmission.* Englewood Cliffs, NJ: Prentice-Hall, 1972.

Nguyen, H. C., et al. "The Role of Detailed Simulation in Capacity Planning." *IBM Systems Journal* vol. 19, no. 1, 1980.

Schiller, D. C. "System Capacity and Performance Evaluation." *IBM Systems Journal* vol. 19, no. 1, 1980.

Seaman, P. H. "Modeling Considerations for Predicting Performance of CICS/VS Systems." *IBM Systems Journal* vol. 19, no. 1, 1980.

Yuvall, A. "System Contention Analysis—An Alternate Approach of System Tuning." *IBM Systems Journal* vol. 19, no. 2, 1980.

12
Managing
the Network

INTRODUCTION

This chapter describes the objectives and functions of network management. There is, however, one critical function—staffing and personnel management—that is better left to texts on management. This chapter only touches on this issue when describing the functions of the network management team.

BRIEF HISTORY OF NETWORK MANAGEMENT

The network management team has historically been responsible for the selection, implementation, testing, expansion, operation, and maintenance of the data communications portion of the data processing environment. With the introduction of computerized branch exchanges, digital branch exchanges, and the associated integration of voice, data, and video transmissions on a common medium, this role is expanding to include management of the entire telecommunications needs of an organization. In the past, voice, video, and data communications were usually separate, being managed by different groups. In today's communications environment, sharing media and hardware components and integrating these functions can produce significant savings for a company.

The role of network manager, like that of database administrator, is a relatively new position within the data processing industry. Both positions were created by the technological expansion of the 1970s and the recognition of the increasing importance of these technologies to the storage, retrieval, and maintenance of business data. These positions are similar in several respects: Both have high visibility among system users. The database administrator is called when the required data are unavailable, and if terminals do not work or response time is unsatisfactory, then the network manager is notified. Both roles are responsible for configurations, planning, tuning, and establishing standards and procedures in their respective areas. Both positions require personnel with a strong technical background, good leadership qualities, and an ability to work well with people having a wide range of technical expertise. In the remainder of this chapter, the term *network manager* refers to the function of network management, a team of people, rather than to a single individual holding that title.

OBJECTIVES OF NETWORK MANAGEMENT

There are two primary objectives of network management: to satisfy system users and to provide cost-effective solutions to an organization's telecommunications requirements. Each objective could give rise to a number of subobjectives, but if these two objectives are met, the network management team will be successful.

User Satisfaction

User satisfaction implies a host of requirements, the three most obvious of which are performance, availability, and reliability. User satisfaction can also be enhanced by keeping users informed of system changes and through formal and informal training.

Good Performance.   Good performance means a predictable transaction response time. What makes for good response time depends on the transaction and the users. Transactions differ in the amount of work to be accomplished and the number of characters to be transmitted. For every transaction in the system, a realistic response time objective should be established. Predictable response times require that most transactions be completed within a small range around the established response time goal. For example, for an expected transaction response time of 10 seconds, it is realistic to expect 95% of all transactions of that type to be completed within 9–11 seconds, and that all such transactions would be completed within 20 seconds. Erratic response times are generally perceived by users to be worse than slower but predictable responses.

Of the two response time components—processing time and communications time—the network manager ordinarily has little or no control over the application processing and database access components, but does have control over configuration and line speed. The configurational aspects include the number of terminals on a given line, hardware employed (such as multiplexers, front end processors, and concentrators), types of terminals used, number of intermediate nodes through which the message must travel (hops), networking software (see Chapter 9), and circuit error characteristics. Each of these affect the performance of the system.

Availability.   *Availability* means that all necessary components are operable when a user requires them, which for a terminal operator are the terminal, cables, connectors, modems, medium or media, controllers, processors, and software. Three factors influence availability: mean time between failures (MTBF), mean time to repair (MTTR), and operational considerations.

Operational considerations may require that portions of the system be taken out of service. Some portions of the on-line system may be available only during standard working hours. Thus, the payroll system may be unavailable at night, when payroll transactions are not anticipated. In some installations the on-line system is given priority during the day, whereas batch operations have priority on night shifts, when all or portions of the on-line system can be stopped. Other operational requirements such as preventive maintenance and installation of new hardware or software can remove all or parts of the system from use. Generally, operational considerations can be planned in advance so on-line users are able to work around them.

Mean time between failures (MTBF) is the average period of time that a component will operate before failing. For example, a CRT terminal with MTBF of 2000 hours that operates an average of 8 hours a day, 23 days a month, would be expected to fail once every $2000 \div (8 \times 23) = 10.86$ months. *Mean time to repair (MTTR)* is the average amount of time required to place a failed component back into service. For certain components, repair time is relatively constant—for example, replacing a failed modem with a spare (unless travel time is required). For a CPU, however, there may be considerable variation in repair time, for problems are seldom solved by replacing the CPU (although board replacement is quite common). Often they require the repair person to travel, and usually require a varying number of diagnostic routines and testing procedures.

Availability can be defined by the following probability function [Nickel, 1978]:

$$A(t) = \frac{a}{a + b} + \frac{b}{a + b} e^{-(a + b)t}$$

where $a = 1/MTTR$, $b = 1/MTBF$, e is the natural logarithm, and t is a time interval. The equation gives the probability that a component will be available when required by a user. For example, for a terminal with an MTBF of 2000 hours and an MTTR of 0.5 hours (typical of replacement with an on-site spare),

$$a = \frac{1}{0.5} = 2 \qquad b = \frac{1}{2,000} = 0.0005$$

Availability for an 8-hour period, then, is,

$$
\begin{aligned}
A(8) &= \frac{2}{2 + 0.0005} + \frac{0.0005e^{-(2 + 0.0005)8}}{2 + 0.0005} \\
&= \frac{2}{2.0005} + \frac{(0.0005)(0.0000001121)}{2.0005} \\
&= 0.99975 + 2.8 \times 10^{-11} \\
&\cong 0.9997
\end{aligned}
$$

So on the average, an operator can expect the terminal to be unavailable three times in every 10,000 tries. And since the exponential term approaches zero and becomes insignificant as the time interval increases, availability in such cases becomes

$$A = \frac{MTBF}{MTBF + MTTR}$$

For the terminal with an availability of 0.9997, if the operator used it 20 times an hour, it would take 500 hours for the terminal to be used 10,000 times. At 8 hours a day that equates to 62.5 days. Thus, three failures can be expected every 10,000 uses, which means that on the average, the terminal will be unavailable once every 20.8 days. Superficially this may seem to be too frequent for a terminal that fails only once every 10.86 months (assuming use is based on 8-hour days). With the use pattern described, the operator will be denied approximately 10 access attempts to the system, (since access is attempted every 3 minutes on the average and MTTR is 30 minutes) and thus, being unavailable once every 20.8 days equates to 10 times every 208 days or 9.04 months. A different use pattern would give a different availability profile. For instance, used 10 times an hour, the terminal will be unavailable an average of once every 41.6 days.

Availability with Multiple Components.   If a number of components must be linked together to make the system available to the user—for instance, terminal, modem, medium, and CPU—then system availability is given by the product of the availabilities of the component parts [Nickel,1978]:

$$A_s = A_t \times A_m \times A_l \times A_m \times A_c$$

where *A* represents availability and the subscripts s, t, m, l, m, and c represent the system, terminal, modem, link, modem, and CPU, respectively. Thus, if each component has an availability of 0.999, then the user will see a system availability of

$$A_s = 0.999^5 = 0.995$$

In this situation, statistically the user would find the system unavailable five times every 1000 attempts, or once every 200 attempts.

The availability factor is important in determining how many spare components to stock and how much productive time might be lost when the system is unavailable. System availability as a function of MTBF and MTTR is graphically illustrated in Figure 12-1.

Reliability.	*Reliability* of a system is the probability that the system will continue to function over a given operating time period. For example, if a transaction requires 3 seconds for a response to be received, then the reliability of the system is the probability that the system will not fail during that 3 seconds.

Reliability of the network involves error characteristics of the medium and stability of the hardware and software components. More specifically, network reliability is a function of the MTBF. In some cases the user will see circuit errors in the form of slow response times. Data received in error

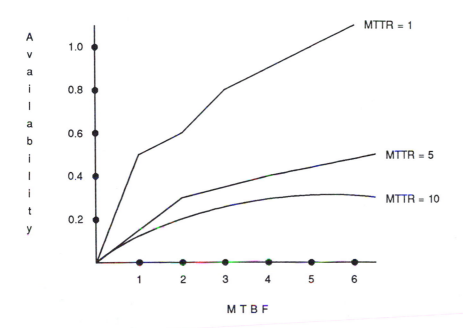

Figure 12-1
Availability, MTBF and MTTR

will cause retransmissions, slower apparent response times, and congestion of the medium. If the errors are persistent, the retry threshold for the
link might be exceeded and the link removed from service. For some modems, a large number of errors will cause the modem to change to a lower
speed to minimize the impact of the errors. Failure of hardware and software components is usually seen by the user as a down system. With
fault-tolerant systems the effect is either negligible or somewhat reduced
response times, depending on the system load. Even though the processor
and all components of the system except one are functioning properly, the
user unable to continue working because of that one failed component
views the system as being down.

The reliability function is the probability that the system will not fail
during a given time period and is given by [Nickel, 1978]

$$R(t) = e^{-bt}$$

where b is the inverse of the MTBF, as described above. For instance, if
the MTBF for a terminal is 2000 hours and a transaction requires 1 minute
to complete, then the reliability is

$$R(1/60) = e^{-(1/2000)(1/60)}$$
$$= e^{-(1/120,000)} = 0.999992$$

All times are expressed in hours. Thus, if the terminal is available at the
beginning of the transaction, the probability is high that it will remain
available throughout a 1-minute transaction.

Reliability with Multiple Components.   Like availability, system reliability is the product of the reliability of its components. Thus, if a system
consists of a terminal, a medium, two modems, and a CPU, then the
reliability of the system from the user's perspective is

$$R_s = R_t \times R_m \times R_l \times R_m \times R_c$$

where s, t, m, l, m, and c represent the reliability of the system, terminal,
modem, medium link, modem, and CPU, respectively. Reliability as a
function of the MTBF is graphed in Figure 12-2.

Overall Effectiveness.   The overall *effectiveness* of a system is a measure
of how well it serves users' needs. Mathematically it is given by the following formula [Nickel, 1978]:

$$E = A \times R$$

where E is the effectiveness, A is the availability, and R is the reliability of
the system. From the formula, it can be seen that, for a given system
effectiveness, when $R>A$ then the amount of time available for repairing
a fault increases, whereas if $A>R$ then the repair time is reduced [Nickel,
1978]. That is, since R is entirely a function of the MTBF, an increase in R

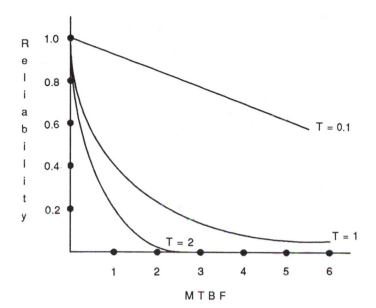

Figure 12-2
Reliability, MTBF

means that more time can be devoted to repairing the system to attain the same overall effectiveness. This is illustrated in Figure 12-3 on page 398.

Reliability of Backup Components.   In many networks, alternate components are available should one component fail. Communication paths frequently have alternate links available, and fault-tolerant systems have available a backup CPU, disk drive, or other component. These backup components decrease the MTBF of the system. A decrease in the MTBF increases reliability, availability, and effectiveness. With backup components available, the reliability of the components operating in parallel is given by [Nickel, 1978]:

$$R_p = 1 - (1 - R_s)^2$$

where R represents reliability, and p represents the components operating in parallel, and s represents a single component. Thus, if the reliability of a communications link is 0.995, then the reliability of the link with a backup is

$$R = 1 - (1 - 0.995)^2 = 0.999975$$

Clearly, backup components significantly increase the reliability and effectiveness of a system.

Repairing Failures in a Network.   When failures occur, the management team must either patch around the failure, replace the failed component, or repair it.

Figure 12-3
Reliability,
Availability, and
Effectiveness

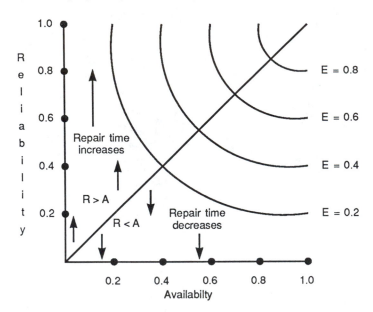

Figure 12-3
Reliability,
Availability, and
Effectiveness

Patching around a problem means maintaining service without repairing the failed component, usually by devising an alternate hardware or software configuration. Take for example, the patch panel configuration in Figure 12-4 (a patch panel is a piece of hardware used by some vendors to interface between a communications line and the controller). Most patch panels have adaptors for several lines, say 4, 8, 16, or 32; if one of the ports on a patch panel malfunctions, the problem can be bypassed by moving the attached line to a spare port. Similarly, common carriers are frequently able to provide alternate paths should a line be disabled for a long time. Satellites usually have spare transponders in case one transponder fails.

Replacement is becoming the most common means of repairing problems in computer systems and networks. If a part fails, a spare is installed to return the system to operation, and the failed part is sent to a repair depot to be fixed. The network manager should make sure that for relatively low-cost components such as modems, terminals, and multiplexers, spares are available on site or can quickly be obtained from the vendor or distributor. For example, suppose a particular university uses statistical multiplexers to link a terminal room housing 30 student terminals to the processor, which is located in another area of campus, and that the university does not stock spare parts. If the power supply in one of the multiplexers fails at the end of the quarter, just when the terminals are in especially high demand, then replacement could take over a week. This is unfortunate because the cost of a spare multiplexer would have been less than the loss incurred by having the terminals unavailable.

Repairing a broken component is usually more time-consuming than replacement; however, simple replacement is not always practicable. For

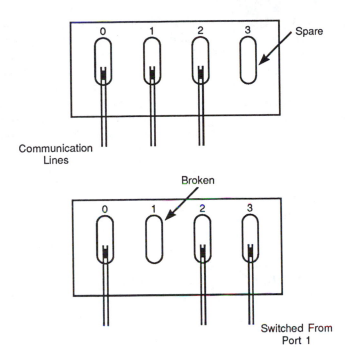

Figure 12-4
A Patch Panel
Reconfiguration

instance, if one of the several circuit boards in a terminal should fail, the user would probably first try to replace it with an in-house spare. If none were available, it is unlikely that the distributor would replace the entire terminal. Instead, a repair person would diagnose the fault and replace the failed board or component. The time required to effect the repair consists of the time for the report to reach the user's network management team, some amount of local diagnosis, travel time for the repair person, time to diagnose the problem, and the time to install the new part. Unless the repair person is on site, it is frequently half a working day or more before the repair is made. And if the failure occurs near the end of the workday, the elapsed time between fault detection and correction might be even longer. Again, the cost of one or more spare terminals usually is less than the cost of the productivity lost when a terminal fails.

Keeping Users Informed. In addition to performance, availability, and reliability, there are a number of less obvious factors that affect user satisfaction. Keeping the user community informed is one of the easiest and most overlooked of these. Users should be informed of scheduled down time, imminent down time, periods when other processing requirements are likely to adversely affect response times, certain changes in hardware or software, and changes in personnel with whom users will be interfacing. This information can be disseminated in several ways, the most direct one being to reserve a portion of the terminal output area for system or network news bulletins. Users ordinarily understand the inconveniences in cases where down time is unanticipated and no prior warning is possible. On the other hand, it can be difficult for users to remain civil when arriving at 4 A.M. to catch up on some work and find the system down for a scheduled but unannounced reason. It is even more disconcerting for a user to prepare a demonstration during normal operational periods and find the same situation. Many systems are able to send notices to users when they log on to the system, and to send notice of system status for short-term, emergency network interruptions.

A second beneficial communication medium is **newsletters**, which can alert users to down times scheduled for preventive maintenance and re-configurations, announce new capabilities, serve as training aid, answer frequently asked questions, solicit comments and suggestions, and generally help people feel they are an integral part of the network team. Newsletters have the advantage of being able to reach all users of a system.

Meetings between users and the network management team should be held at least quarterly. Mature systems not undergoing change require meetings less frequently than those that are new, changing, or experiencing problems. Such forums can serve to air grievances, disseminate information, propose new ideas, educate both users and network managers, resolve problems, and plan for future changes. Again, one important side effect is to get groups communicating with one another and to help users feel they are an important part of the network.

Another form of user communication is **formal and informal training**. Some companies find informal seminars at lunchtime or after hours a very effective way to exchange information. Formal training classes serve not only to educate users, but also to establish contacts within the organization. New users especially usually develop an association with training instructors, giving them an expert to call on should a problem arise.

Cost-Effectiveness

The second objective of network management is to provide cost-effective solutions to the telecommunications needs of an organization. As shown in previous chapters, there are many solutions to communications problems. Network management is charged with selecting those that are feasible and cost efficient. If the network is unable to contribute positively to the financial position of a company, then it should probably not be implemented.

Prior Planning.   Proper prior planning is one way to save money. In configuring a network several basic alternatives exist: install equipment to meet immediate needs and pay the price of upgrading when the time comes—which sometimes leads to lower immediate costs but with a higher cost of expansion—or immediately buy equipment in anticipation of future needs—which creates higher immediate costs, with relatively low-cost, easy expansion. Usually the best alternative is to purchase modular equipment, which can be upgraded in small increments so that overpurchasing is seldom necessary and expansion is relatively easy. A variation of this approach is the planned movement of equipment, whereby lower-capacity equipment is gradually pushed outward and absorbed elsewhere in the network as newer, higher-capacity equipment is acquired.

Modular Expansion.   Modular growth is available for several network components, the most fundamental being the processor. Many computer vendors offer a broad line of systems that allow growth within the product line. Most of these have several different models spanning the distance between small systems and very large systems, and within one model there is also a certain amount of growth potential. The transition from one model to another is not always easy, often requiring a recompilation of programs, as a minimum, and too frequently necessitating significant rewrites. When an organization has finally reached the top of one model line and is ready to move up to the next model, even through the same vendor, the processors, operating systems, and network software are too frequently not the same as those in current use so a conversion is required. At such a time the vendor is almost always very positive regarding the ease of conversion to their new model, because the user is probably examining other vendors' alternatives, which may be no more complex than conversion to the incumbent's next model.

This approach can be contrasted with those vendors' systems that allow modular expansion from a relatively small system to an extremely powerful one by adding more of the same type of processor. There is no need to remove, sell, or return the existing equipment; it is simply augmented to provide the additional processing power. Several computer vendors offer this capability; some of them also have systems designed for the transaction processing market, where expansion is very common, for example, Tandem Computers Inc. and Stratus Computers Inc.

Modular expansion is also possible with front end processors and multiplexers. A number of vendors offer muxes that can be expanded from 4 to 32 or more lines, in increments of 4, 8, or 16 lines, so the user pays for the cost of expansion only when necessary. Many FEPs are able to have increases in memory capacity and number of lines controlled; some allow users to add processors as well.

Planned Equipment Moves.   Planned migration of equipment is useful when modular expansion is not possible. For example, the central site could begin with an 8-port multiplexer, with remote sites having 4-port muxes. As the number of applications in a remote site grows, the central-site 8-port mux could be moved there, a new 16-port mux added to the central site, and the old 4-port mux used in a new location or cascaded off of the 8-port mux. This is illustrated in Figure 12-5 on page 402. Similarly, low-speed modems can be moved to lower-traffic locations as they are

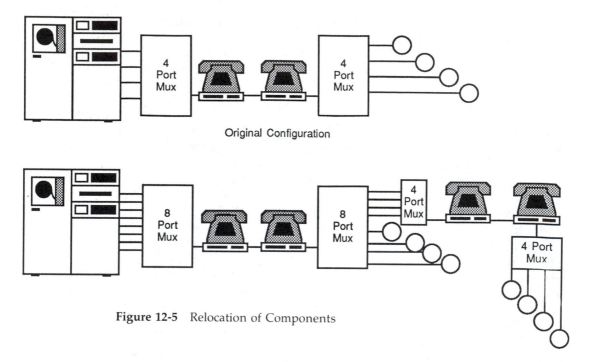

Figure 12-5   Relocation of Components

replaced by high-speed modems. If there is no need for the older equipment, it could be kept in inventory, to be used as replacements for failed equipment. This type of activity requires somewhat longer-range planning than the other options. The financial rewards may make it preferable to the disposal of old equipment—possibly at a significant loss—every time a new piece is acquired.

MEETING THE OBJECTIVES

The objectives of network management are met by a combination of competent staff, hard work, careful planning, good documentation, implementing standards and procedures, and by being able to work with other people to resolve problems. Although every one of these elements may not be present in a successful network, the probability of success is directly proportional to how well they are realized.

Competent Staff

The most important of these elements is creating a competent staff, which can even overcome deficiencies in other areas. While specific staff qualifications depend on the hardware and software employed, some generalizations can be made.

The functions of network management can be grouped into the areas of design and configuration, testing, diagnosis, documentation, repair, and on rare occasion coding. The team must have detailed knowledge of both hardware and software; ideally, every person would know both areas. The staff should be versatile and creative in resolving problems, for many solutions are ad hoc, temporary ones that require some ingenuity.

Design and Configuration.   The staff should be skilled in use of the diagnostic and planning tools described later in this chapter. In design and configuration, they should be knowledgeable of configuration alternatives and their strengths and weaknesses. They must be willing and able to learn in order to keep up with changes in hardware and software of the existing system as well as capabilities continually offered by other vendors, including a multitude of different tariff structures from a growing number of common carriers. Finally, and perhaps most importantly, they should be able to work well with both technical and nontechnical personnel.

Diagnosis.   Skill in diagnosing the cause of problems is essential, and being able to do so under considerable pressure is very valuable. Whenever a problem in a production system is encountered that disables all or a portion of an on-line application, immediate resolution is desirable. A failed system usually means financial loss: Personnel being unable to perform certain of their job functions leads to a loss in productivity. In some situations, direct revenue is also lost, for instance, in an airline reservation system. If a problem is not resolved quickly, management often becomes involved in emphasizing the critical nature of the situation and marshaling resources to effect a correction sooner, a pressure that can become counterproductive, as in the following example.

A business providing service to trucking companies experienced a failed system during a holiday period. The system vendor provided support to return the system to operational status. During the repair period, the service company president consistently reminded the vendor's suport personnel of the amount of money being lost per minute and threatened to remove the system. In this case there was a great deal of emotion and pressure during the diagnostic and corrective process. Under such circumstances it is important to maintain composure and concentration.

Planning.   Planning is another key to success. Because of the dynamic nature of networks, constant planning and replanning is necessary to ensure that objectives are met. Too often, network managers are so caught up in day-to-day activities they ignore longer-range planning. This type of behavior is both common and self-perpetuating. Without good planning, problems occur more frequently and require a greater amount of time to get solved. Planning should include short-term and long-term objectives. Short-term planning includes scheduling of personnel, hiring, training, budgeting, and network maintenance and enhancement activities. Long-term planning involves predicting and resolving expansion issues, integrating new technologies, and budgeting.

Documentation, Standards, and Procedures.   Documentation, standards, and procedures are an outgrowth of good planning. Good documentation increases the productivity of the staff. It includes listings of the software, logic diagrams, internal and external specifications for the system, wiring and connection diagrams, hardware specifications, and users' manuals. These are used in all phases of the management of the network. Standards and procedures together provide consistency in system management. Standards set minimal acceptable levels of performance and implementation. Procedural guidelines aid in operating and maintaining the system, and are especially necessary in resolving problem situations. Procedures are discussed in more detail in the section on "Operations."

In summary, meeting network management objectives requires a group of talented individuals who have the right tools in place, have a well-defined but flexible direction for the short term and the long term, are willing to work unusual hours in sometimes difficult or stressful environments, and can work effectively with people at all levels of capability. The growth in network management has prevented the supply of competent people from meeting the demand. As a result, network management personel are currently among the hardest to find and highest paid in the computer industry.

ANALYSIS

Network analysis is concerned with capacity, performance, reliability, and growth. The network should be under continuous scrutiny to make sure that the objectives of customer satisfaction and cost effectiveness are met.

Statistics

Network managers must keep a constant watch on the capacity of the network so they have all the information needed to plan and implement growth. At the heart of capacity planning are the statistics regarding how the network is functioning and changing. Some of the necessary statistics are easy to obtain, and others require the use of hardware or software monitors that are not always available within a system. The statistics that are easy to gather are response times, number of transactions per unit of time, and transaction mix. All of these statistics are external to the system and can be counted or measured manually; however, it is much easier if this information is captured internally. State-of-the-art software provides the user with sufficient statistical information to tune the system and to alert the management to potential problem areas.

Response Times.   One of the design objectives of on-line applications is a well-defined response time for a given transaction type. The first external sign of network congestion or processing congestion is usually a degradation of response time, often gradual and hence relatively unnoticeable to users. Network managers should continually check response times at different periods of the workday and workmonth. Especially critical are the response times during peak processing hours. A slight variation is to be expected in the times recorded, so managers need to look for trends such as a gradually increasing response time or wide fluctuations in response times.

A gradually increasing response time indicates an increasing workload, which can be attributed to increased utilization of network components, additional load on the processor, changes in how the system is being used, or all of these.

Fluctuations in response times result from peaks in the system or from transient situations. Peaks, which are much easier to diagnose than transient conditions, are usually regular in nature and externally caused—for example, the significant rise in the use of bank ATMs during lunchhour and at the end of the workday. Transient situations are created by abnormalities in the system, such as power fluctuations at various times of the day that disrupt processing and possibly produce errors in the transmission circuits; a faulty communications interface board that intermittently transmits garbage on the circuit and creates congestion; or the infrequent transaction that consumes a large amount of resources, for example, an on-line query that must examine every record in a large data file.

Transaction Mix.   Over time the ratio of transactions can change. When a system is designed, its configuration is usually based on an idea of the type and mix of transactions to be processed. If this mix changes then the design parameters should be reviewed to determine if, when, and where a bottleneck is likely to occur. For instance, Chapter 5's analysis of the Syncrasy Corporation situation was predicated on the fact that there would be only 30 orders per hour from the catalog stores, which transactions placed the heaviest load on the network portion of the system. If the number of such orders begins to increase, then the system must be analyzed to determine how performance will be affected. Plans to ensure an acceptable level of performance for all transactions must be developed.

Circuit Utilization   Transmission media utilization is closely related to transaction mix and the number of transactions processed. Other factors also influence the amount of line use, such as how the terminal operators perform their transactions, polling, screen formatting, system advisory messages, and errors. The only item in this list that may not be obvious is how the operators perform the transactions. To explain: Imagine an installation that employs smart or intelligent terminals where the transactions are selected by menus and there are also help menus with varying levels of detail. Experienced operators will hardly ever need the help screens. Instead they will select their transactions, move to those screens, and perform the transactions. They will move back to a menu screen only when absolutely necessary. Inexperienced or less efficient operators on the other hand, will make more use of the help facilities. In performing transactions they will also move around between screens more frequently than experienced operators. All of this creates a greater load on the communications circuits. Preventing the media from becoming saturated is the motivation behind monitoring their use.

Queue Lengths.   Queues can build up in many parts of the system. Whenever they form, it means that something is waiting and hence taking longer to complete. Terminals may be queued up to send data in a multi-drop configuration; statistical multiplexers may have queues of messages to send; processes may be waiting for CPU availability; messages may be queued up in one network node to transmit to a neighbor node; there may be queues for buffer space; busy application and network software may have queues awaiting attention; and peripherals such as disk, tape, and printers may have queues of pending requests. This is illustrated in Figure 12-6. All of these queues affect the performance and response time of the system.

The application and database queues are not strictly the responsibility of the network management team; however, they can cause a degradation in performance that will likely be reported as a network problem, in which case the network managers and the application and database administrators must cooperate to resolve the problem. For example, a large user of computing equipment was in the process of developing a system on a new

Figure 12-6
Queues Within a
System

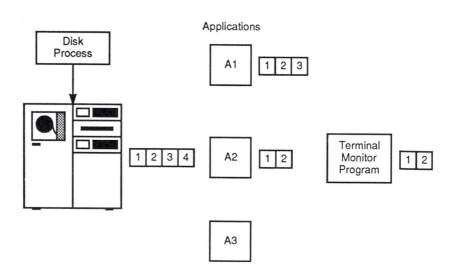

series of hardware. The design called for routing messages between processes using a vendor-supplied facility in which very long messages sometimes created system problems. To work around this, long, infrequent messages were queued and dequeued from a disk file created just for this purpose. As the implementation proceeded, this uncommon event became a common one and performance deteriorated because the disk wait time had become significant. There were a number of other, less costly solutions, but the initial design assumed that such occurrences would be infrequent enough so that the extra overhead would be an insignificant factor.

Routing.   Keeping track of message routing can help decrease the load on the network links and improve the transaction processing times. If node A sends most of its messages to node X through several intermediate nodes, then establishing a direct link between the two nodes will increase performance by reducing the number of hops for those transactions. This would also decrease the workload on the intermediate nodes and links.

Buffers.   On some systems, especially certain minicomputers that are sometimes used as front-end processors, buffer and memory space is restricted and must be used efficiently. Important buffer statistics include buffer allocation failures when buffer memory is unavailable, and whether buffers are being used efficiently. In most cases, users control buffer size either directly through system generation parameters or indirectly via message sizes. If buffer allocation failures occur with any degree of regularity, corrective action should be taken. In some cases this means the acquisition of more memory. On some systems, adding memory does not solve the problem; in these instances, it is the ability to address memory that becomes the problem. For example, on some systems, the amount of memory that can be managed by the operating system is 64K words, which must hold the operating system's working set as well as system buffers. If the entire 64K is used up, then adding memory will not resolve the problem, since the buffer management software would be unable to address additional memory.

Making more efficient use of existing buffer space is one way to resolve the buffer allocation problem. If larger buffers than actually required were allocated when a system was first installed, checking the maximum percentage of buffer utilization over time might help reduce the allocated buffer areas. Buffer size in some systems is determined by a message size specified in the read parameters to a terminal. The buffer is usually allocated when the read is posted. If the terminal is a smart terminal operating in synchronous mode, it need not send the data until the operator is ready, in which case the buffer can be allocated for a long time before being used. Alternatively, a function key can be used to signal that the data are available for reading, which requires only several bytes of buffer space during the waiting period; a larger buffer will be needed only for the short duration while the data are actually being transferred. The savings in buffer space can be appreciable with this method. In a system with 100 terminals each of which has 1000-character reads posted, 100,000 bytes of buffer space must be allocated. Function key reads of four characters each would require only 400 bytes of buffer space.

Errors.   Tracking errors in the system enables system managers to identify circuits and equipment that are not performing as expected. Although, as observed in Chapter 3, it is impossible to eliminate all errors, this does not mean that errors should be ignored. If the incidence of errors is higher than expected from the medium being used, then network managers must isolate the source of the errors and make corrections. The more errors encountered, the greater the utilization of the processor and the circuits. An increase in the number of errors also causes an increase in buffer space (the originator of the message must retain messages until they have been acknowledged).

Processes and Processing Time.   Monitoring processing time allows the network manager to determine which processes are the busiest. A process that uses a lot of processing time is a candidate for tuning or recoding. Another process statistic is queue depth—that is, the number of users waiting to use the process while it is busy servicing other requests. Other things to look for in a process are the number of accesses to disk, tape, and so forth; page faulting; overlay calls; wait conditions; and memory utilization. Network managers usually perform this type of analysis only on the network software, with the applications and database software left to other groups. In smaller installations, such segmentation of duties is usually too expensive, and network managers have a much broader charter than those in larger installations.

Making Changes Based on Statistics

Gathering statistics on system performance is a continuous process. After the statistics have been collected they must be analyzed. This can be done by hand, but preferably the user will have analysis tools that report the data in a number of formats. The objective of gathering and analyzing statistics is to identify potential problem areas before they become catastrophes. The solutions might run from minor tuning of the system to the acquisition of an entirely new system, and their exact nature depends on the system and the circumstances. Although it is impossible to cover all instances, some general comments can be made.

Tuning.   Tuning is essentially changing the system parameters systematically in an attempt to make the system operate more efficiently, such as changing the link parameters so the network routing tables change, adjusting buffer sizes, and adding more copies of a busy process. If analysis indicates four or five areas in which improvement can be made, then the best approach to fixing a problem is to change only one area at a time and observe the effect of the change; if there is improvement, then the next area can be fixed. This approach might seem more time-consuming than making all the changes at once, but the opposite is frequently true, for the shotgun approach of simultaneously fixing multiple problems could actually make system performance worse. Taking a step at a time is the safest way to make improvements. Some consultants claim that most systems can be improved up to 20% with careful tuning.

One of the drawbacks of tuning is that correcting a problem in one area sometimes produces or emphasizes a problem in another area. Consider an application responsible for processing ATM transactions: Statistics showed that during peak processing times the queue of transactions awaiting this process was quite long. Customers had to wait for their transaction to reach the top of the queue for processing, so response times were excessive. The obvious solution was to add more ATM server processes and thus avoid the long queues. But after making the changes, response time was even slower than before. Statistics were again collected; they indicated that the original analysis was not incorrect, but the additional processes required more memory to be allocated, which pushed total memory use over a threshold and created an excessive number of page faults. Only when additional memory was installed were the expected performance gains realized.

Another situation that sometimes arises during tuning is *cascading bottlenecks*. When a system is tuned, resolving what appears to be the major obstruction to good performance may result in little or no gain (or even negative gain as in the case above). This means that either a new bottleneck has been created or a second obstruction closely followed the first. When the factors inhibiting performance are close together, multiple iterations of tuning may be necessary to attain a desirable level of response time and throughput.

Reconfiguration.   Reconfiguration is necessary when an existing piece of equipment or software process becomes saturated. The solution lies in reducing the load on the existing facilities—such as moving terminals from one multi-drop line to another, or changing the transaction mix at a group of terminals—or increasing their performance characteristics—such as adding faster circuits, additional lines, or more memory.

Reevaluation After Changes Are Made

Once changes are made, reevaluation of the network is necessary. Changes in one area of the system sometimes have a negative effect on other portions, such as when increasing the transmission speed of a line raises the number of transactions received by the host and adds to the memory and processing pressure, thereby slowing down the entire system and actually making the situation worse.

Evaluating New and Enhanced Hardware and Software

Another aspect of the analysis process is evaluation of new and enhanced software and hardware components. Even though an organization may not be immediately ready for such capabilities, keeping a library of relevant alternatives and advances prepares the group for the time when major or minor upgrades are necessary. When that time arrives, the network managers are responsible for performing all or part of the feasibility study to determine what solutions are viable. This eventually leads to either direct procurement of equipment or to a *request for proposal (RFP)*, also sometimes called a *request for quotation (RFQ)*. Responses to the RFP must then be studied and graded. This process leads to the selection of equipment, services, and software. RFPs are discussed in more detail in Chapter 11.

INSTALLATION

Users ordinarily assume the responsibility for installing small, common components, such as modems and terminals. For larger components, the vendor or the vendor's representative usually handles installation in conjunction with the user. There is work for both parties.

Installation Schedule and Plan

Installation procedures begin long before equipment is delivered. For major pieces of equipment such as a front-end processor, a schedule and installation plan should be prepared that details what must be accomplished, the responsible party (vendor or user), and the date the task is to be completed.

Lead Time.   Many facets of installation require significant lead times. Training of users, operators, and programmers should usually commence well in advance of the expected operational date. Items such as communications links might also need to be ordered well in advance of anticipated completion.

Placing Equipment.   In determining where the equipment is to be located, network managers should make sure there is a convenient way to get all the components to the site. For instance, the tenth floor of a building with no service elevator is usually considered an unacceptable location for a large-scale computing system.

After site selection, drawings are made showing the equipment in place. Most vendors provide scaled paper and templates for this task. Care must be taken that cabinets are positioned so they can be opened for maintenance and that recommended cable lengths are not exceeded. The vendor should approve the layout before proceeding with installation. Once the space has been allocated, site preparation can begin. Power, cabling, and air conditioning are important considerations. Raised floors may be necessary. Window coverings may be required, to avoid excessive heat from the sun. Again, the vendor should be consulted during this preparation to ensure that the site is acceptable.

Security Features.   If the facility is to be secure, the security features should be installed. Fire suppression systems, uninterruptable power supplies, and power surge protection should be installed if necessary.

Training.   Training should run concurrent with installation, starting as soon as the equipment and vendor are selected. By the time the equipment is installed, operations personnel should be ready to assume their responsibilities. If programmers are involved, they should be ready to use the system effectively by the time of installation.

Acceptance Testing.   Following delivery and installation, acceptance testing begins. There should be a clear understanding of the conditions that constitute acceptance of the system. Depending on the circumstances, this could be as little as passing the vendor's diagnostics or as much as successful implementation of the application.

TESTING

Once a system has been installed, a period of testing begins. (This could be a part of the acceptance process.) The following assumes the worst case of totally untested software and hardware. The emphasis is on software testing, since the hardware has presumably passed all the vendor's diagnostic tests.

Three-Phase Testing

Testing has three separate phases: functional, integrated, and stress. *Functional testing* is done at the program and subprogram levels, with the purpose of assuring that the logic is correct. *Integrated testing*, also referred to as *system testing*, involves the integration of programs into a system to ensure that different modules fit together. Often, the outputs of one process become inputs to another. Integrated testing ensures that the formats of the data being exchanged are correct and that the system meets all processing objectives. *Stress testing* involves testing the system under load conditions so as to be sure that performance parameters are met. This testing step is too often delayed until the system goes live; only then do the designers find that performance expectations are not met.

Initial Implementation

Once testing is completed, the system is brought into production. There are three ways this can be accomplished, one of them is wrong. The wrong way is to abandon the old system completely to move to the new one. Unfortunately, if the new system does not work correctly, there is no fallback position, as in the case of one company that canceled a computer system lease six months prior to having a new system programmed and installed, anticipating that software would be completed on schedule. Like many software projects, the application was not ready on time, the existing system was taken back by the vendor, and the company had neither the new system nor the old.

Phased Implementation.   The acceptable ways to implement a new system are the phased approach, the parallel approach, or both. *Phased implementation* involves implementing the entire system in several steps. For example, the first phase of an order entry application might be the actual entering of orders, the second the inventory management, and the third the accounts receivables.

Parallel Implementation.   In *parallel implementation* the old and new systems are both run concurrently and the results compared to determine if the new system is functioning properly. After some period of successful parallel operation, the old system can be entirely abandoned in favor of the new one.

OPERATIONS

Once a system has been successfully installed, tested, and placed into operation, the day-to-day management of the network begins. From an operations perspective, network management is more than just a function, it is an application. Just as application developers design a system to solve business problems, network managers should design a system—part manual, part automated—that solves the problems of operations. The manual portion of the system is necessary to restoring a down system, a task that cannot be accomplished with software when the hardware is not running.

Operations deals with monitoring, control, diagnostics, and repair. The statistics needed to monitor a system have already been mentioned.

Control

Control functions to be performed include putting failed lines or terminals back in operation, adding new lines or terminals, and taking failed components out of the system. Control of a geographically separated, multiple computer network is somewhat more difficult, since parts of the control function must also be distributed. The distributed case is discussed here, since a subset of it applies also to single-node or colocated-node networks.

Control Center.   A control center is required to manage a network of any size. In a distributed network, it is not uncommon to have more than one control center. For example, an international network with European, North American, and Asian nodes would likely have three control centers, one for each node area. In a network of cooperating, independent users—for example, a network of universities—each node can participate in the management and control functions, each installation being responsible for control of its part of the net. Usually, however, there is a control point—the central control site—that has the ability to resolve any problem. The center is responsible for monitoring the network and taking corrective action where necessary.

For very large nets, the network control center may have a processor dedicated to that function. A number of companies manufacture network control systems centered around a minicomputer for network management, a computer that monitors the network. Typically such a system consists of special microprocessor-based modems that collect network statistics periodically transmitted to the network monitor for storage and analysis. Such systems maintain such current information as error rates, data rates, and retries. Trend analysis of this data can help determine gradual degradation so that faults are immediately reported and corrective measures taken.

Control Monitors.   The control facility must have a minimum of one or more monitors so the management team can probe every node for problems, and gather network parameters and statistics. The monitors also enable managers to make any necessary changes to the system, such as bring lines and terminals into and out of service, bring network applications to an orderly halt and start network applications, alter network parameters such as the process controlling a terminal (discussed in Chapter 9), check for line errors and implement corrections, initiate and evaluate line traces, run diagnostic routines, add and delete users from the system, administer passwords for local and remote nodes, and maintain the control center database.

Maintaining the database is an important function because network management is an application. Thus, a network database should be established that contains the network configuration, the release level of all software and hardware components, the names of contact individuals at remote sites, histories of problems and solutions, outside contact points for vendors, and documentation.

Problem-Reporting System.   Ideally an on-line *problem-reporting system* is also available that can retrieve trouble reports via key words. This capability is especially helpful in managing a distributed network, where problems can be encountered and resolved in multiple locations and where one problem can be worked on simultaneously in multiple locations, thus avoiding having to repeatedly solve the same problem.

Control Messages.   Another part of the control application is a process for sending control messages to the network. Such processes can usually perform many functions for the network managers, such as receive all network messages; log the messages to a printer, tape, or disk; react to messages by sending network control messages; and perform most mechanical control functions, like initiating diagnostic routines and gathering statistics. This programmatic interface is either unavailable or very limited in function in some earlier systems, but most state-of-the-art systems provide it. Usually it is the user's responsibility to write the program, often using an example program provided by the vendor or other users.

Problem Reporting

One of the primary functions of a control center is the acceptance and resolution of problems. In some instances, a solution may lie outside the control center itself; however, the center should still remain active as intermediary between the reporters and solvers of the problem. This section describes a prototype control center's operation with respect to problem reporting and resolution. Although a computerized problem-reporting system is assumed, a manual system with the same functionality could exist.

Problem-Reporting Procedure.   Network managers should publish a problem-reporting procedure that describes the information that users must gather to report a problem, and to whom the report should be made. It is assumed that users have been directed to contact their control center about network problems, and by telephone rather than by any automated problem-reporting system. An end user such as a terminal operator ordinarily should not be expected to interface with an automated problem reporting system.

When the problem report call is received, the network manager captures all relevant information, including: date and time of the call; date and time the problem was first observed; name of the caller and how the caller might be reached; names and contact information for any other personnel involved in the problem; and a brief but detailed description of the problem—its severity as well as consequences expected before a solution is available, whether the problem is reproducible or intermittent, possible contributing external influences such as installation of a new software release, reconfiguration, power glitches, or the equipment being used.

A problem report of all relevant information is generated, and a copy returned to the reporting person. As soon as the problem is resolved, the solution is noted in the trouble report, a final copy sent to the reporting installation, and the trouble report marked closed. If the solution is not immediately known, the control center begins its evaluation, first searching the problem database to determine whether such a problem was ever resolved before. If not, then problem investigation begins. The first objective of such an investigation is to isolate the problem, pinpoint the source of the difficulty, which can involve looking at statistics and system console or log messages, initiating line traces, using line monitors, taking program dumps or traces, debugging, or running hardware diagnostics. If the problem is isolated to an area of vendor responsibility, such as network control programs, then the vendor is contacted and the supporting documentation passed to them for analysis. The degree of vendor involvement varies among vendors, and within one vendor company, the support level can vary among individual customers, depending on the expertise available. Some users provide a vendor with a complete analysis and suggested solution, whereas others simply report the existence of a problem and leave the diagnostics to the vendor.

How a problem is actually resolved varies, but what should not vary is the reporting and tracking function. The responsibility for the problem lies with the network control center, the initial recipient of the problem. The problem may be passed to other groups for resolution, but the responsibility for monitoring the progress, reporting results, and ensuring final resolution resides with the control center. Every time the status of the problem changes, it should be noted in the reporting and tracking system, including assignment to someone for resolution, problem resolution, request for additional information, and changes in the severity of the problem's impact. The control center has an obligation to keep the user informed of problem status, either on a regular basis, say every week, or whenever status changes. A periodic report should be issued by the control center listing open problems, status, elapsed time since first being reported, person assigned to resolution, severity, and anticipated completion time (if available).

Additional Control Center Responsibilities

The control center has additional responsibilities: creating and maintaining documentation, security, establishing procedures, release control, and training of personnel. Documentation, which should be kept currrent, includes operations manuals, procedures for emergency and routine activities, notification lists, contingency plans, inventory, program listings, statistics, and manuals. *Security measures* include creating and assigning passwords, setting user access levels, monitoring and reacting to unsuccessful log-on attempts, ensuring that passwords are changed periodically, and checking physical security where applicable. *Procedures* should cover normal operating guidelines as well as those for handling abnormal situations such as network failures. Escalation policies and contact names and numbers are also included. *Release control* involves the installation, testing, and implementation of new versions of hardware and software, to ensure compatibility of new features with existing software and hardware, and to uncover any new problems (frequently introduced with new releases). Training involves all levels of personnel that use or maintain the network.

TOOLS

The right tools make network management considerably easier. Network management tools can be divided into three categories: diagnosis, monitoring, and management. Diagnostic tools are used for detecting problems; monitoring tools, for checking the state of the system; and management tools, for predictive, performance, and pure management functions.

Diagnostic Tools

Digital Line Monitors and Breakout Boxes.   Two diagnostic tools are discussed elsewhere in the book (Chapter 5), *digital line monitors* and the *breakout boxes* with or without bit sequence generation.

Analog Line Monitors.   Another type of line monitor is also available—the analog line monitor. Where the digital line monitor looks at digital signals on the data terminal side of the modem, and so has the same view of the data as the data terminal equipment, an *analog line monitor* measures and displays the analog signals on the communications circuit or on the data communications side of the modem, enabling the user to check for noise and proper modulation. Analog line monitors are seldom employed in a user's environment; more often they are used by a common carrier to evaluate their circuits.

Emulators.   An *emulator* is a diagnostic tool that enables the user to check for adherence to a specific protocol. For example, a vendor must have their X.25 software certified by a packet distribution network before being allowed to connect to the system, to avoid disrupting other system users, and one way the software can be tested is with an emulator. The emulator acts like an X.25 node, generating both correct and incorrect messages so as to ensure that the system reacts according to the X.25 specifications. Usually, emulators of this type allow the user to specify the types of messages to be transmitted. That is, a scenario or script can be defined on which the emulator acts. Emulators can also be used during the development process to ensure that the interfaces between software levels are correct.

Current Documentation.   One of the best diagnostic tools is current documentation, including software listings that reflect the correct release and patch levels, logic diagrams, internal documentation, maintenance manuals, and any other supporting documents. Although documentation may seem obvious as a diagnostic tool, its importance cannot be understated.

Whereas diagnostic tools help *locate* problems in the network, monitoring and management tools are used to *avoid* problems in the network, including areas such as capacity planning, general project management, performance, and configuration. A number of these tools have been developed for microcomputers and are thus economically feasible for most users.

Capacity planning is an extremely important function of network managers, who must recognize when resources are approaching full utilization and plan for expansion or reconfiguration in order to avoid saturation and potentially degraded service. Three tools are very effective in this area, performance monitors, simulation models, and load generators.

Monitoring Tools

Performance monitors provide snapshots of how a system is actually functioning, typically capturing such information as number of transactions, type of transaction, transaction response times, transaction processing times, queue depths, number of characters per request/response, buffer utilization, number of I/Os, and processing time by process or process subprogram. When collected over time, information of this nature enables the management team to spot trends in the use or misuse of the network—for instance, whether the number of a specific type of transaction is steadily increasing and whether the capacity for handling that transaction type is being reached, or whether an increasing number of users is playing Startrek or Adventure during lunch, which period may also coincide with the day's peak processing load.

Simulation Models.   *Simulation models* allow the user to describe network and system activities and receive an analysis of how the system can be expected to perform under the described conditions, which is useful during the development stage to predict response times, processor utilization, and potential bottlenecks. During operational situations, simulation models help determine what size of transaction load will reach or exceed full capacity and the affect of adding new transactions, applications, and terminals to the existing system. A good simulation model in the development stage can avert performance issues during the design stage.

Simulation models vary significantly with respect to the amount of information provided and the manner in which the user defines the workload. A simple model for line utilization and polling overhead might interactively prompt the user for the speed of the line, data link protocol, number of polling characters, modem turnaround time, and number of stations on the line, resulting in a report indicating the processing and line overheads of the polling and the maximum and average wait times a device might expect between polls. A comprehensive model, on the other hand, uses a network configuration file and a transaction file as input (both user-supplied). The configuration file will contain the complete hardware configuration, including disk drives, disk drive performance characteristics, line types, data link protocols, terminal types, database files and their locations, and access methods. The transaction file will contain a list of transaction types and the activities each transaction type performs, such as number of inputs/outputs to which disk using what type of access method, number of instructions executed, and number of characters input from and output to a terminal.

In addition to the two user-supplied files, the simulation model is driven by software performance characteristics, such as polling overhead, instruction execution times, and disk access times. Such a model outputs information similar to that provided by a performance monitor—that is, expected response times, line utilization, processor utilization, disk utilization, and so forth. In essence, the model enables the user to see, without ever writing it, how an application will run. For example, if the model predicts that a particular communications line will have 300% utilization and a response time of 10 minutes, then either a faster circuit or more circuits will be needed to support the workload.

The time required to set up a simulation run varies with the amount of detail needed. The comprehensive model just described requires a considerable amount of information regarding the application. Usually it is unnecessary to have the correct initial configuration, as the model will indicate areas of over- and underutilization. If the processor is 150% busy, then either a larger or an additional processor is needed. The benefit that can be realized from a simulation model is considerable.

Workload Generators.   Another helpful tool, a *workload generator,* is analogous to the simulation model. But where the simulation model predicts system utilization and can be run on a system much smaller than that required for the actual application, a workload generator actually generates the transaction loads and pseudo-application processes for execution on the proposed configuration. If the model and the workload generator were perfect, the results would be identical; in actual practice, however, some variation between the two is likely. A workload generator together with a performance monitor can illustrate how the system will actually function in the proposed configuration. It can also be used for stress testing.

As with any model, the above models are only as good as the inputs, the people who use and interpret them, and the closeness of the models to real life. Their value decreases with the amount of time required to utilize them and their ability to accurately portray an application. This means that they should be used carefully and the results interpreted sensibly.

Log Files.   Log files are another tool valuable in monitoring a system. Certain logs—such as logs of system messages *(system log)* or network messages—should be maintained continually, whereas others can be used only when necessary—for example, a line trace, which is a log of the activity on a particular line that is normally used only when a problem has been detected. Some software has been designed to log their activities on demand; the network manager would enable or disable the logging, depending on what information is required. Log files are used both for diagnostic functions and predictive or management functions.

Network Configuration Tools.   Network configuration tools are used to plan the optimum network configuration with respect to sources and types of circuits. In the past these have been relatively expensive to purchase or use, and some were limited to one common carrier's facilities or geographical locations. These systems are now available on microcomputers and at more affordable prices.

Management Tools

Project Planning Tools.   Project planning tools are beneficial in the administration of the network, and they can help in planning the activities of the team members, the installation of new equipment and software, and numerous other management activities. Many of these tools are now available on microcomputers, bringing them to more users at a relatively low cost.

Database Management Systems and Report Generators.   Database management systems and report generators are also useful management tools. The database can be used to store statistical and operational information, and a good query/report writer is capable of selecting, synthesizing, and summarizing this collected information. These systems can schedule members of the network management team, store and retrieve error and *trouble report* information, and produce reports on modeling, amongst a multitude of other uses. Database management systems are available on most systems today and can be very useful in storing, modifying, and retrieving data relating to the network management function. State-of-the-art systems enable users to define a database; enter, modify, and delete information; and generate reports without writing any or much code. Many of the microcomputer-relational model database systems provide all these features, and are oriented toward users with little expertise in programming or systems.

CASE STUDY

The Syncrasy Corporation has received bids on terminals and modems from two different vendors. The prices and functions of the equipment are the same, but MTBF and MTTR figures differ. Syncrasy wishes to minimize the number of vendors involved in the network, intending to select the terminals and modems from one vendor only. The company that can provide the greatest effectiveness will be awarded the contract. The MTBF and MTTR figures for both vendors' products are provided in Figure 12-7.

Figure 12-7
MTFB and MTTR
Figures (in hours)

	Vendor A		Vendor B	
Device	MTBF	MTTR	MTBF	MTTR
Terminal	2600	3	3000	2
Modem	6500	1	6000	2

Reliability

Vendor A's Equipment.　Using the formula for reliability, with a time of 1 hour, gives

$$R(\text{terminal}) = e^{-(1/2600)} = 0.9996$$

$$R(\text{modem}) = e^{-(1/6500)} = 0.9998$$

The reliability of both components in serial, then, is

$$R(\text{system}) = 0.9996 \times 0.9998 = 0.9994$$

Vendor B's Equipment.

$$R(\text{terminal}) = e^{-(1/3000)} = 0.9997$$

$$R(\text{modem}) = e^{-(1/6000)} = 0.9998$$

$$R(\text{system}) = 0.9997 \times 0.9998 = 0.9995$$

Thus, Vendor B's components are slightly more reliable.

Availability

To determine the availability of the components, the simplified formula is used:

$$A = \frac{\text{MTBF}}{\text{MTBF} + \text{MTTR}}$$

Vendor A.　Availability is given by

$$A(\text{terminal}) = \frac{2600}{2600 + 3} = 0.9988$$

$$A(\text{modem}) = \frac{6500}{6500 + 1} = 0.9998$$

$$A(\text{system}) = 0.9988 \times 0.9998 = 0.9986$$

Vendor B.   The corresponding figures for vendor B's equipment are

$$A(\text{terminal}) = \frac{3000}{3000 + 2} = 0.9993$$

$$A(\text{modem}) = \frac{6000}{6000 + 2} = 0.9997$$

$$A(\text{system}) = 0.9993 \times 0.9997 = 0.9990$$

Thus, the availability of vendor A's equipment is slightly higher than that for vendor B.

Effectiveness

The effectiveness for each system (the product of the reliability and availability) is

$$E(A) = 0.9994 \times 0.9986 = 0.9980$$

$$E(B) = 0.9995 \times 0.9990 = 0.9985$$

Thus, vendor B has the more effective system, and Syncrasy should buy their terminals and modems.

SUMMARY

As the use of data communications expands, so will the role and importance of network management. The keys to effective network management are personnel who are competent and knowledgeable, and who can work well with a broad spectrum of users, planning, and the effective use of network management tools. Network management is involved in the design, testing, and operations of a system. In some installations a certain amount of implementation or development is also required.

Network management is both a function and an application. The application portion should be designed and implemented like any other business application. The primary functions for computerized implementation are problem-reporting systems, tools, network management software that reacts automatically to problems in the network, and diagnostic systems.

With careful management, the network can be a valuable asset to a company; with poor or no management, even the best-designed application system can fail. If the network is incorrectly designed, not modified to meet changing demands, or frequently inoperable, and if problems are not readily resolved, users will lose confidence in the system, and the network's effectiveness will be diminished.

Key Terms

Analog line monitor
Availability
Breakout box
Capacity planning
Digital line monitor
Effectiveness
Emulator
Mean time between failures
  (MTBF)
Mean time to repair (MTTR)
Network management
Parallel implementation

Performance monitor
Phased implementation
Problem-reporting systems
Reliability
Request for proposal
  (RFP)
Request for quotation
  (RFQ)
Simulation model
Stress testing
System log
Trouble reports

Questions and Exercises

1. What functions are performed by the network management team?

2. How do problems get reported and resolved? What documents are generated as a result of the problem-reporting system? Who receives copies of these documents?

3. How are project management tools used in network management?

4. Why is stress testing an important part of the testing process?

5. What are the advantages and disadvantages of parallel operations?

6. What are the advantages and disadvantages of a phased implementation?

7. Why is performance analysis necessary in network systems?

8. What should be considered when selecting a vendor?

9. How are statistics used in network management?

References

Armstrong, Thomas R. "An Automated Network Management System." *Mini-Micro Systems* 12 (March 1979).

_____ "Managing the Communications Menagerie." *Computerworld on Communications* 17 (September 26, 1983).

Chu, Van. "Monitoring Network Performance." *Computerworld on Communications* 17 (May 18, 1983).

Deal, Richard L. and Wood, P. C. "Data Communications: Putting It All Together." *Datamation* 18 (December 1972).

Doll, Dixon R. "Strategic Planning." *Computerworld Office Automation* 18 (April 11, 1984).

FitzGerald, Jerry. *Business Data Communications, Basic Concepts, Security, and Design.* New York: Wiley, 1984.

Harper, William L., and Pollard, Robert C. *Data Communications Desk Book: A Systems Analysis Approach.* Englewood Cliffs, NJ: Prentice-Hall, 1982.

IEEE Computer Society. *Computer Networks: A Tutorial.* Long Beach, CA: IEEE Computer Society. Catalog no. 297, Document EH0162-8.

Kanupke, William C. "Network Management." *Computerworld on Communications* 17 (May 18, 1983).

Kaufman, Bob. "Cost-Effective Telecommunications Management." *Computerworld on Communications* 17 (May 18, 1983).

Levin, David P. "Needs Assessment in Data Communications Networking." *Journal of Information Systems Management* 1 (Summer 1984).

Mandell, Steven L. *Computers, Data Processing and the Law—Text and Cases.* St. Paul, MN: West Publishing Co., 1984.

McCormick, J. H. "Controlling the Data Exchange." *Infosystems* 30 (March 1983).

Miehe, William H. "Remote Diagnostics." *Mini-Micro Systems* 10 (October 1977).

Nickel, Wallace E. "Determining Network Effectiveness." *Mini-Micro Systems* 11 (November 1978).

Ryan, Jerry. "Considering Network Management Software." Computerworld on Communications 17 (May 18, 1983).

Soudant, Robert. "Managing the Remote Computing Function." *Data Management* 12 (April 1974).

Stiefel, Malcolm L. "Network Diagnostic Tools." *Mini-Micro Systems* 12 (March 1979).

13

Managing
the Data

Evolution of Distributed Systems

Distributed System Example

Advantages and Disadvantages of Distributed Systems

Database Management in Distributed Systems

INTRODUCTION

The establishment of local and long-distance computer networks is changing how data are stored and processed. One of these changes is distributed
processing. At the conclusion of this chapter you should have a good
understanding of applications in which distributed processing can be beneficial, and of different configurations for establishing a distributed system.

As used in this text, *distributed processing* refers to the geographical
distribution of hardware, software, processing, data, and control. A data
communications system, then, is the glue that holds the distributed system
together and makes it workable. More than a data communications topic,
distributed processing is also a subject in database management. In fact,
many of its open issues are database issues. Thus, this chapter is more
about databases than about data communications, because designers of
data communications networks for distributed systems need to be aware
of the issues faced by such systems.

Geographical distribution does not necessarily mean great distances. A
local area network with multiple processors, for instance, is a typical distributed processing system. Although several processors in one room and
sharing a processing load could be considered a distributed system, such
loosely or tightly coupled processors are not so considered.

One objective of distributed processing is to move data and processing
functions closer to the users that need those services, thereby to improve
the system's responsiveness and reliability. A second objective when data
or processing are to be accomplished by another node is to make transparent to the system user the fact that remote access is required. That is,
the user should have little or nothing to do to access the other nodes of
the system. How these objectives are met is explained below.

EVOLUTION OF DISTRIBUTED SYSTEMS

At the dawn of the computer age, computers were big and expensive, and operating systems were either nonexistent or incapable of supporting multiple job streams. As a result, for the organizations that could afford it, computer systems were acquired for every department needing computational power. Thus, in a manufacturing organization, one computer would be dedicated to inventory, one to accounting, one to manufacturing control, and so on. These were distributed processing systems, but considerably different from the current concept of distributed systems in one important respect, the sharing of resources.

Duplicated Database and Inconsistent Data

Processors in those early systems were usually not connected via communications links. As a result each maintained its own database, often with duplicated data. Thus, both the warehouse database and the accounting department database contained the same customer information, the former for shipping and the latter for invoicing. When a customer moved, the address change was quite unlikely to be reflected in both databases at the same time, and in some instances not before a considerable amount of time had elapsed. Thus, redundant storage of data, with the attendant update problems, created report inconsistencies. Perhaps more important, shipments or invoices could be sent to the incorrect address and lost. And because each department was essentially the proprietor of its own system, there was little sharing of computer resources. Thus, one system might be completely bogged down with work while another was relatively idle. One possible early distributed processing system is depicted in Figure 13-1.

Centralization

These early distributed systems were far from ideal. In addition to the inconsistencies of the data, there were extra costs for operations, maintenance, and programming. Therefore, as systems grew larger and operating systems more comprehensive, there was a movement to large, centralized systems, as illustrated in Figure 13-2 which had the benefits of a single operations center, control, and—according to some—economies of scale, since one single, large system was likely to cost less than a number of smaller systems. A single programming department was established for all application development and maintenance. To reduce redundancy of storage, and promote sharing of data among users, centralized databases were established.

Disadvantages of Centralization

Large, centralized systems also have their problems. First, if the large, central system fails, the entire system fails. In the distributed approach,

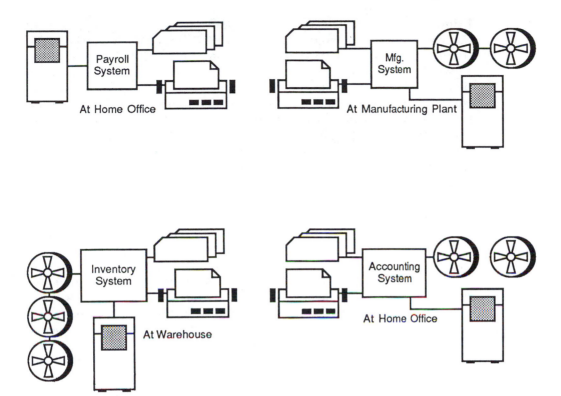

Figure 13-1 Early Distributed Processing System

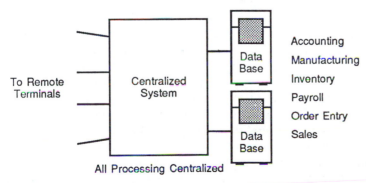

Figure 13-2 A Centralized System

failure of one node results in part of the system being lost, but many processing functions would be allowed to continue. In this respect, distributed systems are more reliable than the single, centralized system.

Many of the end users—that is, the accounting department, warehouse, and so forth—found their needs inadequately met by the centralized system. Because the system was shared, users often found it unresponsive, not only in terms of when and how long jobs would be run, but also in terms of getting resources dedicated for new development. With a dedicated system in the distributed situation, a user would have to contend only with other programs in the user's own department, so it was relatively easy to establish satisfactory group priorities. Establishing interdepartmental priorities, however, was usually not quite so easy. The same held true for programming: A programming team may have been assigned to develop an application or a new report, but being not under the control of the user's department made it more difficult to change priorities and directions.

Expansion and growth of the large, centralized system posed another problem for some. Too often growth was not in small, manageable increments, but in giant steps, such as conversion to a larger processor with a different operating system. This conversion meant down-time while the new system was being installed, potential recoding, finding and fixing a new set of bugs, and disrupting all users in the process. In contrast, when distributed systems needed to upgrade processors and operating systems on occasion, growth was generally in smaller, more manageable increments. If a new processor became necessary, only the using department was affected, not the entire user community.

Networking

Networking has provided some of the benefits of both centralized and distributed environments—more localized processing and control with a shared database and the additional attraction of sharing of processing power. Thus, in a local area network in which every worker has a work station capable of performing text editing, spreadsheet, and similar processing functions, each work station would be able to call on the processing power and database capabilities of a larger system in order to accomplish more complex and time-consuming processing tasks. By the same token, some of the processing that an ordinary terminal would require of a larger host—such as field editing, screen formatting, and code conversion—could be processed by the work station. Some of the data required frequently by the work station could be resident on its disks, including documents in process and budget data for spreadsheets. Data that are either not used or infrequently used or required in too great a volume for the work station would be maintained at a larger host. Despite its being maintained by another node, the work station would be able to access it as though it were a local database.

DISTRIBUTED SYSTEM EXAMPLE

A bank has decided to regionalize its bank card authorization system. The area served by the bank has been divided into five regions, each with a data center for authorizing credit card purchases, including a database of its customers' transactions. Merchants within a region have a toll-free number for the authorization center within their region. A picture of the network is given in Figure 13-3.

In the usual situation, customers make charges within their own region. In a smaller percentage of transactions, credit card customers make charges in a region outside their home region, in which case the merchant still telephones the local region for authorization: The credit card number is identified as being that of another region and the authorization system sends a message to the remote node for authorization information. Suppose that a customer from region A makes a charge in region B. The merchant telephones the authorization center in region B. The authorization clerk enters the credit card number and charge amount. The software, recognizing a card number from region A, sends a message to the processing center in region A, upon which the region A software authorizes the charge and updates the customer's record. The authorization message is routed back to the node B terminal and the transaction is completed.

Negative File

In the event of a communications failure, it may be impossible to reach a remote node for authorization, in which instance a negative file is used

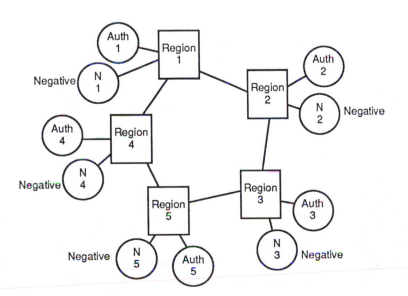

Figure 13–3
A Distributed Bank
Card Authorization
Network

for authorization. The negative file, replicated at each node, contains a list of all bad credit risks from all regions. The negative file is maintained centrally and updated periodically.

Local Node Failure

If a local node fails, authorizations can still be made. Suppose, for instance, that the region A system is unavailable. Authorizations from the other nodes would be made by using the negative files at those nodes. Calls to the region A authorization center could still be processed, in which case the bank uses a packet distribution network to access another region's system. Authorization for region A's customers would be made using the negative files, and foreign authorizations would be made in the usual manner.

Distributed Database

The fact that the credit card is from another region is transparent to both the merchant and the authorization clerk. Neither had to do anything different in that situation. With their *distributed database*, the data were distributed so as to be located where used most often. On occasion it was necessary for one node to access and update the database at another node. One file, the negative file, was replicated on all nodes, since each node would have occasion to use it. These files were kept up-to-date from a centralized location.

Distributed Processing

In the credit card authorization system it was primarily the data that were distributed, and one center used very little processing resources of another. In other distributed systems the opposite is true. In a number of university networks, for instance, it is primarily the processing that is distributed. Large computational jobs would be routed to a processor more or less dedicated to that purpose, and if one node became saturated with student programs, the messages might be routed to another, less congested node for processing. In this academic situation it is not the data that are shared among the different nodes as much as it is the processing power.

Combination Distributed Database and Distributed Processing

Between these two situations is a continuum of sharing of data and processing. For example, consider a computer manufacturer with manufacturing and marketing facilities in a number of locations. Each manufacturing location maintains its own inventory database, each warehouse has its inventory maintained locally, and marketing offices have local databases describing their customers, prospects, and installed systems. The home office contains information on personnel, accounts receivable and payable, and so on. The distributed software makes the distributed data accessible to all authorized users. Some of the distributed uses of the system follow.

If inventory shortages occur in one manufacturing area, the other manufacturing plants' databases are checked to determine if the parts are available.

Marketing offices can check the inventory at any warehouse to determine if a piece of equipment is available for shipment to a customer. Salespeople ordinarily have equipment shipped from the nearest warehouse. They have the added flexibility of being able to determine the stock levels at any warehouse and have one composite order shipped from several locations. The system provides this capability automatically.

Home office managers can initiate reports at remote nodes for forecasting and planning. For example, suppose the vice president of manufacturing is interested in a summary report on the inventories at all of the plants. She can initiate a process on each of the manufacturing nodes to access and summarize the information there, the summaries to be transmitted to the corporate node, where they would be consolidated and printed. In this instance, it is less time-consuming to access the large volume of data at multiple local nodes, summarize it, and transmit the results. Both remote data and processing facilities are used.

Because of time zone differences, one area of the country is able to use the processors in another area when they might otherwise be idle. For instance, if the system in a West Coast office is busy at 4 P.M., a user could initiate a job at an East Coast node, which at 7 P.M. eastern time would be relatively uncongested.

The network provides instant access to documents and personnel files within the corporation. Documents and graphic images can be made immediately available to those who need them.

ADVANTAGES AND DISADVANTAGES OF DISTRIBUTED SYSTEMS

Advantages

Each of the distributed systems just described has numerous advantages. For one, storing data close to the location that uses them most in a network situation minimizes the amount of data that must be transmitted between nodes, and provides better response times. And since maintenance of the data is a local responsibility, there is more of a vested interest in keeping the data current. Third, nonlocal transactions are still possible, as are transactions that must span several nodes, the only penalty being slower response times due to relatively slow transmission speeds on the communications links.

Distributed systems also give local users more control over their data processing system, providing them with the flexibility to tailor changes to their own particular needs without disrupting other network nodes. In addition, reliability is higher than with a centralized system, for the failure of one node does not mean the entire system is down. Each node has most of the data it needs to continue most functions, so processing can continue with only a slight degradation in service.

Disadvantages

There are also disadvantages to the distributed approach.

Multiple-Node Transactions Are Slower.   To begin with, whenever a transaction must span more than one node, response time is longer. If, for instance, a salesperson for a computer vendor enters an order for a new system consisting of processors, disks, and terminals, the response time for placing the order will be faster if all the equipment is available in the local warehouse than if each component must come from a different location, in which latter case a message would have to be sent to the other warehouses in sequence until the order was filled.

Contention and Deadlock.   Second, update transactions on multiple nodes increase the risk of contention and *deadlock*. As discussed in previous chapters, a record being updated is locked until the end of the transaction, to avoid the problems of concurrent updates. (Deadlock is defined in Chapter 8.) And since a transaction that spans several nodes is slower than one on a single node, because of line time, the records locked by the transaction remain locked longer, the probability increases that the records will be needed by another transaction, and hence the amount of contention and the potential for deadlock increase.

Potential for Failure.   The longer response time for transactions that span multiple nodes also increases the probability of a failure that will produce an unsuccessful transaction. In fact, because more components are involved, the probability of equipment failure also increases, though this is becoming less of a concern as the reliability of systems increases and with the use of fault-tolerant computing systems and networks.

Determining Participating Nodes

Most of the database management systems available today were not designed for distributed databases. With a transaction that accesses and updates records on multiple nodes, the first problem is to determine which other nodes must participate. It is unthinkable to require the user to do this, because one of the objectives is to make the distributed nature of the system transparent to the user, and because it is desirable to reserve the ability to redistribute data and processes without disrupting users.

A second approach to identifying the location of resources is to programmatically define the nodes that are to participate, which requires the programming staff to know the location of all nodes. And as additional nodes are added it is likely that program changes will be required, also true if redistribution is required. This approach is preferable to relying on the user to decide, but presents considerable problems with respect to maintaining the system, extending the system, and redistributing its resources.

Network Dictionary of Locations.   A better way to identify resource locations is to have a network dictionary that describes the locations of all data and processing entities referenced in the system. The database manager or transaction control process can access the dictionary to learn where the required resources are located. Redistribution requires a simple update to the dictionary.

Central vs. Distributed Dictionary.   The dictionary can be either centrally located and maintained or replicated at all nodes, like a negative file. The centralized approach, with several weaknesses, is the less desirable of the two. First, when the central node becomes unavailable, the distributed system is inoperable. Local operations could continue, but finding remote resources would be impossible. The centralized dictionary approach could be augmented by establishing one or more alternate nodes with backup dictionary capability.

A second problem with a centralized dictionary is that additional access time is required to obtain the information. Although in a local area network with high-speed links this might not be significant, accessing the information via a slow communications link with several hops through intermediate nodes can significantly slow the application response time, especially if the dictionary must be consulted several times—or even once—for each transaction. A time-saving alternative is to have the application software remember resource location from prior access, information that could be refreshed periodically based on time intervals, number of transactions, or some other algorithm. Replicating the network dictionary on each node eliminates the access problems of the centralized approach.

Routing, Transmission, and Processing

Once the locations of the distributed resources have been determined, a message must be transmitted to the node for servicing. The network software is responsible for routing and transmission of the message. The designers of distributed systems have several options in determining how the remote processing/accesses will be handled, depending on the type of transaction.

Remote Access for Local Processing.   One method for processing with a distributed database is remote access. In this transaction, a process in one node requests database service from another node. There is no application processing required in the remote node other than the data access. This type of distributed access is typical of transactions that require a specific set of directly retrievable data. For instance, in a police transaction to determine all outstanding traffic citations for a given driver's license number, the database management system can directly access these records, and will not have to perform an extensive search of multiple records to select the few that qualify. In such a case, the local application process would send a database request to the remote node. Depending on the implementation, the message could be sent directly to the database management system or to an application that invokes the database management calls. The important distinction is that no application-type processing is performed at the remote node. The transaction is simple data retrieval.

Partial Remote Processing.   A second method for handling distributed processing requires that the remote node perform some amount of application processing at the remote node. Consider a transaction to determine how many of a company's employees have over 10 years of service and a salary below $20,000: With 5000 employees, all 5000 records might need to be accessed to satisfy the query. To pass each of the 5000 records to the requesting node for selection would obviously place a large load on the communications subsystem and take considerable extra time. The better alternative is to have a server process on the remote node access the records, perform the selection, and then transmit only the results to the requesting node.

Total Remote Processing.   A similar situation holds with transactions that update records at a remote node. When the record is required locally, the remote record is transmitted to the local node, an update made, and the record sent back to the remote node and updated in the database. In some instances the entire update is performed remotely, as in cashing a check for a banking customer: Before the check can be cashed, the balance record must be sent to the local node to determine whether the check is covered. The account balance is decremented and the record returned and written to the database. A transfer from a local account into a remote account could be effected without transferring the remote record to the local node.

Many other examples could be cited of the division of activity between nodes. But in essence there are the two basic methods just discussed, plus a third combination method: (1) Access remote records, pass them to the local node, process the records locally, and then return them to the remote node(s) for updating as necessary. (2) Send messages to remote application servers that accept and process them and then return only the required information to the requesting node. (3) A combination of the two approaches is sometimes the best alternative. The design objective is always to make the transaction as efficient as possible, which means minimizing the transmission of large numbers of records between nodes.

DATABASE MANAGEMENT IN DISTRIBUTED SYSTEMS

Most current database management systems were designed to operate on only one node, meaning there was no need to keep track of files or databases on another node or to manage transactions that span multiple nodes. To operate in the distributed mode, users were left much to their own devices. In some instances the problem was compounded by having two different database management systems involved, for example, where one node employed one vendor's hardware and software and the other used a different vendor and database management system. In such a case, one database system is unlikely to cooperate with the other except through user-written programs.

Relational Model and Network Model

Only in the last several years have computer vendors addressed the issues of distributed databases and their management. The *relational model* database system, which uses the content of data records or relations to form associations between files, has been a positive factor in establishing distributed database systems. This model allows data to be distributed and relocated without altering record pointers. The other major database model is the *network model*. In it, association is frequently created by storing the absolute disk address on one record to point to another record, and moving the related record either updates the pointer or renders it invalid.

Figure 13-4 on page 436 illustrates the relational approach and Figure 13-5 on page 437 the network approach, using two files, an employee file and a dependent file. Note that in the relational system the employee identification number is on each record in the dependent file as well as on the employee record. To find all dependents of a particular employee, the employee ID column of the dependent file is searched for the matching ID. Ordinarily it is not necessary to examine every record to satisfy the search. Indices or other search strategies make the search more efficient.

In the network model, a list of pointers or a chain of records implements the same logical relationship. In the *list approach* shown in Figure 13-6 on page 437, a list of pointers maintained on the employee record or an associated record contains the disk addresses of the related dependent records. The *chain approach* is illustrated in Figure 13-7 on page 438. The employee record contains a disk pointer to the first and possibly the last dependent record. Each dependent record in turn contains a pointer to the next and possibly the prior related record. In some implementations the dependent record also may have a pointer back to the employee record.

Figure 13-4
A Relational Model

Employee Relation (File)

Employee ID	Employee Name	Employee Address	
01743	Smith	1748 Pine Rd.	
01924	Johnson	203 Madison Ave.	
02155	Mackey	12873 Grand Blvd.	
03881	Adams	1288 17th St.	
04774	Stephenson	12222 N. Fremont	
04937	Hicks	142 Sydney Pl.	
05011	Dickson	32A Rembrandt Dr.	
⋮		⋮	
10877	Stanley	1743 Melbourne Dr.	

Dependent Relation

Employee ID	Dependent Name	Relation	Age	
01743	Alice	Spouse	30	
01743	John	Son	9	
01743	Mary	Daughter	7	
02155	Jerry	Spouse	28	
03881	Mike	Son	10	
03881	Sharon	Daughter	12	
04937	Karen	Spouse	48	
⋮	⋮	⋮	⋮	

↑ Association
made via
this field

With the network approach, moving a dependent file from one location to another will likely invalidate all record pointers, making it necessary that the records be reloaded and the relationships reestablished, a time-consuming process. In contrast, the relational model is location-independent. Thus, the related files could be moved and the association would be maintained as long as the ability to find the new node and file exists. A locations dictionary would resolve this problem. Implementation of distributed databases using network model systems is not impossible; it is just more difficult, especially if relational techniques are not utilized.

File Distribution

A second obstacle that the database management systems must overcome is the manner in which files are distributed. In the warehouse application mentioned above, it should be transparent to the user that the records are

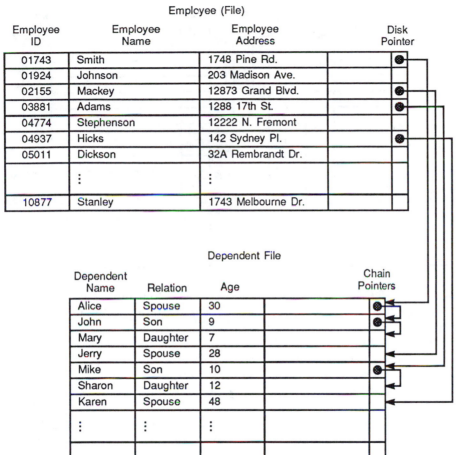

Figure 13-5
Network Model

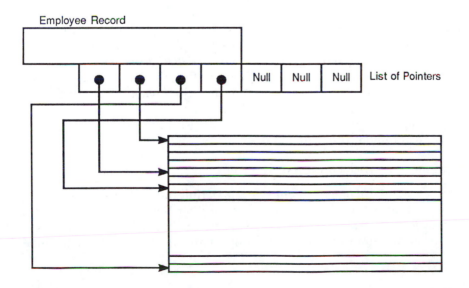

Figure 13-6
A Relationship Using
a List of Pointers

Figure 13-7
A Relationship Using
Chain Pointers

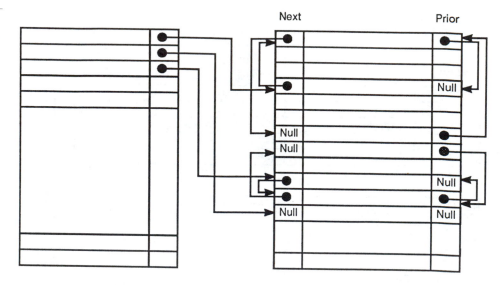

actually stored in multiple locations. Almost all current systems require that data in multiple locations be on separate files, and running under separate database managers. Thus, for five warehouses, the application software must open five database files and access each separately. Rather than having a view of one logically consolidated file, the application must access and merge records from each of the individual files. It becomes the user's responsibility to make the five separate files look like one logical file.

An ideal solution to the five warehouse files would have the database management system present them to the application as one file with partitions or subdivisions in five separate locations. The application would then have only one file to open and one access path to the entire set of data; thus shifting responsibility for creating one logical file from files in five separate locations from the user or application to the database management system, which is where it belongs. This type of file partitioning would enable the user to specify rules regarding the node on which a record would be stored and would allow restriction of access to the local node or to all nodes. It would also require that the loss of one node not prohibit any other node from accessing the other available partitions. The techniques for realizing this type of distributed file exist, but the capability has yet to be implemented. Expansion of distributed systems will make this a requirement of future database management systems.

Transaction and Database Recovery

Very few database management systems permit transactions to span nodes or allow transaction and database recovery between two or more nodes. However, one system does—the ENCOMPASS database management system from Tandem Computers. It is important for a database management system operating in a distributed environment to maintain the integrity and consistency of the database by providing node-spanning transactions and transaction recovery. Without this ability, transactions such as a transfer from one account on one node to another account on a different node would be treated as two separate transactions, allowing one but not the other to complete successfully, and leaving the database in an inconsistent state. For those of today's systems that do handle transfers between accounts as separate transactions, it is up to the application to recognize the failure of any transaction and to effect recovery. Again this capability should be provided by the database management system. An abbreviated explanation of how this is accomplished follows.

Example. A transaction is started to transfer funds from account X on node A to account Y on node B. A network-wide unique transaction ID is created, its uniqueness guaranteed by appending a node identification number to a date-time stamp. Every application that works on the transaction receives this unique transaction ID and performs work on behalf of that transaction.

Account record X is retrieved on node A and the transfer amount subtracted from the balance. In order to update the record to reflect the new balance, the record is locked, and will remain locked until the end of the transaction, thus preventing any other transaction from interfering with the balance until the transfer is completed. A message is sent to node B requesting that the transfer amount be added to the account Y record, which is retrieved, locked, and updated. A message is returned to the application at node A indicating that the update was successfully completed. With the updates successfully completed, the transaction is in a position to end successfully. The database manager at the initiating node sends a message to all participating nodes that the transaction is ready to end. After each node has ensured that its audit buffers are flushed to the audit medium and that the transaction's integrity at that node has been maintained, it sends a completion message to the originating node. When all involved nodes have successfully responded, the transaction is completed by writing the end-of-transaction record to the log. This *two-phase commit procedure* guarantees that the transaction is fully recoverable.

The ENCOMPASS system does all of this through the database and recovery managers. The application is responsible only for identifying the records to be updated. If for any reason a part of the transaction is uncompletable, a *transaction abort* message requesting that the transaction be backed out is transmitted to all participating nodes.

Deadlock. When updates involve several nodes, records are locked for longer periods of time due to the relatively low speed of the communications medium. Furthermore, since the lock managers on one node are almost always independent, they are unaware of locks on remote nodes, thus increasing the probability of deadlock. This situation is further complicated by the fact that the deadlock could result from locks on more than one node. For example, a double transfer between accounts X and Y could proceed as follows:

Transaction 1 locks account X on node A.

Transaction 2 locks account Y on node B.

Transaction 1 attempts to access account Y on node B.

Transaction 2 attempts to access account X on node A.

These conditions lead to a deadlock for the two transactions, but recognition of this fact is made difficult because two nodes are involved and the lock managers are unaware of each other's activities. Deadlock detection algorithms to resolve this problem have been proposed, but as yet, none have been implemented commercially.

Archiving.   Archiving of database files, also known as *backup and restore*, also presents unique problems in the distributed environment. *Archiving* means to keep a historical copy of a database as it existed at a specific point in time. Such copies can be used to recover the database in the event of catastrophic failure such as fire, program logic errors, or head crashes on disk. The recovery procedure requires the historical copies to be restored to disk and the after-images from the audit trails to be posted to the database to bring it forward to a consistent point in time.

Synchronizing Files.   Files in a distributed database must be kept in synchronization to ensure consistency. In the account transfer example, it would be unsatisfactory to have yesterday's files reloaded onto node B and today's files loaded onto node A, for node A's files would then reflect the transfer that had just occurred, whereas node B's files would reflect the previous day's balance. Keeping the files synchronized following a major failure is an operations problem, one made more difficult when the archival copies have been created at different times on different nodes. The recovery system will reestablish the database on individual nodes, but there is currently little or no help from the database management system software to ensure that files on different nodes are at the same level of update.

Data Placement

One of the most critical factors affecting performance in the distributed system is placement of the data. In most on-line applications, accessing data is the most time-consuming function, even more so when accessing data from a node with several intervening nodes.

Centralized Database.   The simplest approach for the database management system is to centralize the data. All or most of the database is made resident on one or several nodes, a situation that eliminates many of the database problems described earlier, since a transaction spanning several nodes is quite rare. The disadvantage of such an implementation is that almost all accesses must span a data communications link and will thus be somewhat slower. With a star network, having the central node as the database node provides reasonable performance. In an interconnected configuration with many nodes, a centralized database approach may be impractical. This is illustrated in Figure 13-8. This approach is viable for a LAN but usually not for a long distance network. In Figure 13-8 node K's request must pass through three intermediate nodes, resulting in increased response time and network congestion.

Replicated Files. Files common to applications on several nodes can be replicated to reduce or eliminate accessing those records across the network. In the bank card authorization application discussed earlier, a negative file was replicated at each node. This type of file is ideal for *replicated files*. The negative file was potentially required by every node, its use was required whenever the communications link to another node was severed, and the file was not volatile—that is, not updated frequently—which is quite a significant factor.

To illustrate the significance of volatility and file replication, consider again the credit card authorizaion system. An alternative to the negative file is to replicate the customer file on all nodes, whereby each node in each of the five regional authorization centers would contain the entire customer database, meaning that all authorizations would be run very efficiently because the needed data would always be available locally. The bank's risk of loss from improper authorizations would decrease somewhat because a negative file would no longer be necessary. (The only purpose

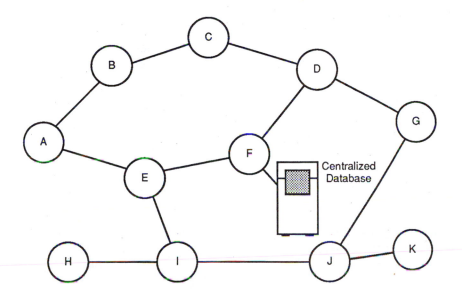

Figure 13-8
A Centralized
Database

of the negative file was to allow an authorization when the path between the authorizing node and the customer's home node was unavailable.) These are the advantages of full replication.

Unlike the negative file, however, the customer file is very volatile. Every time an authorization is made, the customer credit limit must be adjusted. For an authorization in the fully replicated configuration, then, a message must be sent to every other node to update their copy of the customer record. Instead of only a small percentage of the transactions requiring network transmission, every transaction would result in four update messages being transmitted, an unsatisfactory solution for many applications.

Updating replicated files in real time is further complicated by disruption of network communications. In the above example, if the link between two nodes is severed, there are three alternatives: disallow further transactions until the link is repaired, batch the updates for the unavailable nodes and send them along when the link is restored, or continue processing and restore consistency in a batch-type operation as soon as possible. Disallowing transactions until the link is repaired is hardly ever viable. Saving the transactions until the link is reinstated is the best alternative in most cases because the replicated files are inconsistent for the shortest period of time. When the link is restored this solution creates a high level of network traffic and impedes the speed of the current transactions. Even if the batch transactions are paced to the remote nodes, the additional traffic and workload will affect system performance. Restoring file consistency in batch mode is satisfactory for certain types of files, for instance, the negative file. For the customer files, however, the risk of inconsistent data would be too great.

Variations of the alternatives just described can be effective for certain types of data files. One such variation is to update the replicated file in one location only. Periodically the entire file or changed portions thereof are distributed to the rest of the nodes. This restoration would normally be effected at off-peak times. The types of files that generally qualify for this type of update are those that are freqently referenced and for which absolute currency of data is not required. In an inventory application, a parts description file might qualify for such treatment. If the part number changes or a description of the part changes, a day's delay in changing the description at every node is unlikely to present a problem. The negative file update in the banking application might also qualify for such treatment.

SUMMARY

Distributed systems are becoming viable processing systems. They are currently at the frontier of database management systems and data communications systems. Many of the problems that impede their widespread use are in the area of database rather than data communications. Distributed data and distributed transactions may have a significant impact on the utilization of network resources. Specifically, data transfers, message transfers, and recovery messages can cause increased media traffic. Development in the problem areas should be spurred by potential advantages of distributing data to where they are most often used, sharing of processing and data resources, and more control by end users.

Key Terms

Deadlock   Network model
Distributed database   Relational model
Distributed processing   Replicated files

Questions and Exercises

1. What are the disadvantages of replicating data on multiple nodes?
2. What types of files are candidates for replication?
3. Describe three methods for keeping replicated files current.
4. What benefits do relational model database management systems provide in distributed database applications?
5. List four current problems in distributed processing.
6. List four applications that are good candidates for distributed processing.

References

Bernstein, Philip A.; Rothnie, James B., and Shipman, David W., *Tutorial: Distributed Data Base Management*. IEEE Catalog no. EHO 141-2. Copyright New York, NY IEEE Computer Society, 1978.

Champine, G. A. "Six Approaches to Distributed Data Bases." *Datamation*, May 1977.

Date, C. J. *An Introduction to Database Systems*, vol. II. Reading, MA: Addison-Wesley, 1983.

Kallis, Stephen A., Jr. "Networks and Distributed Processing." *Mini-Micro Systems*, March 1977.

Moore, William G., Jr. "Going Distributed." *Mini-Micro Systems*, March 1977.

Q.E.D. Information Sciences. *Distributed Processing: Current Practice* and *Future Developments*, vols. 1 and 2. Wellesley, MA: Q.E.D. Information Sciences and On-line Expertise Limited, 1978.

14

Industry
Trends

The preceding chapters provide an overview of the data communications industry, including its history, the hardware and software components used, and techniques for transmitting information from one location to another. Data communications is perhaps the most dynamic area of data processing in the last decade. From 1970 on, the industry has seen significant changes in costs, competition, hardware, and software, changes that have provided the impetus for more systems to be implemented with on-line applications. The future promises additional growth.

TRANSMISSION MEDIA

The second half of the 1980s should see continued expansion of certain technologies, while others perhaps begin to disappear. As more communications satellites are placed in orbit, the availability and utilization of this medium will increase. With its high-speed transmission and attractive expansion capabilities, the satellite medium appears to be a natural for some of the expanding technologies—specifically, image processing, voice synthesis, and perhaps video, all candidates for digital storage and transmission. Each of these technologies requires a large number of bits for storage and data transmission. The approximately 0.5-second response delay due to the distance the signal must travel is unlikely to affect the growth of this type of transmission.

The use of fiber optics should continue to expand, especially for relatively static local area networks. If methods can be found to tap the fiber optic cable to easily add or remove stations, then fiber optics could replace coaxial cable as the favored medium for many local networks.

Development in the PBX field should continue to enhance office telephone systems by allowing voice, data, and video images to exist on the same network. IBM's apparent intentions in this area have been indicated by planning building wiring for a local area network. IBM's acquisition of Rolm Incorporated, a leading manufacturer of PBX systems, may indicate the future importance of corporate telephone systems.

NETWORKS AND SOFTWARE

Expansion in the use of local and wide area networks should continue at a rapid pace. Some existing network systems can be expected to fall into disuse as new systems emerge to replace them. It is unlikely that the industry will be able to support the current number of local area network implementations (in excess of 100). When IBM introduces its LAN, a number of current system providers are likely to discontinue their offerings.

Instead of developing new network systems, software vendors may turn to the development of bridges and gateway systems to allow the large number of existing systems to interface with each other. The current need for such facilities is already recognized and is beginning to be met.

VENDORS AND PROVIDERS

The mid-1980s is likely to see a settling among the providers of communications facilities. The AT&T divestiture of 1984 will no doubt bring gradual and sometimes dynamic changes over a period of years. AT&T will probably attempt to expand further into the computer marketplace, with a gradual expansion of models and capacity. Computer vendors will likely begin to provide communications services. IBM has already made its entry into this area. The rationale behind computer firms acquiring communications facilities and communications companies offering computers is in part due to the fact that users of computing equipment are so frequently looking for solutions to problems. A firm that is able to supply a complete processing and communications package may be able to gain an edge on competitors who specialize in only one or the other.

TECHNOLOGICAL ADVANCES

Digtal data transmission will continue to expand, providing users with higher data transmission rates and lower error rates. This will have a positive influence on all aspects of data communications, particularly distributed processing systems, where transactions must span multiple nodes and where bulk data transfer is sometimes necessary. This trend coupled with anticipated improvements in database management systems to provide recovery, contention resolution, deadlock resolution, and transaction management over networks should remove some of the current barriers to the technology. In addition, knowledge of distributed systems will expand as a result of current implementations. Thus, the expected and unexpected problems of technology and performance are likely to be solved.

The low price of communications equipment such as modems and processors will probably make computers and data communications an integral part of both private and professional life. Satellite transmission to automobiles is in its development stages and could become an operational option in the late 1980s for such uses as display of maps and route determination. The location of specially equipped automobiles could be pinpointed and the driver or navigator could request the display of maps with varying degrees of detail. A route could be programmed into the system and warnings given should an improper turn be taken. More sinister uses of such technology are also possible, for example, monitoring the location of vehicles and occupants.

PERSONAL COMPUTERS

The personal computer as home appliance is fast becoming a reality. In addition to its use for games, education, and budget and household tasks, the PC will begin to function as an integral part of individual finances. Many banks are currently investigating, testing, or operating networks for clients with home computers. The services already available include on-line banking, bill paying, information on a variety of subjects, and catalog purchasing. It is not unrealistic to expect additional services to include investments in stocks, bonds, and commodities; electronic mail delivery; security sytems on-line to police or private agencies; and educational and cultural programs. The coupling of data transmission with video and voice will provide options limited only by the imagination.

OFFICE AUTOMATION

Computers and data communications have already had an impact on the work environment. The office of today is vastly different from that of only 20 years ago, and industry is only beginning to tap the resources available. Interoffice correspondence, image, voice, and video transfer, and portable devices should all play a significant role in shaping how companies communicate.

FIFTH-GENERATION COMPUTERS

The most significant changes yet are likely to come from the fifth generation of computer systems currently being developed in a number of countries, thus far led by Japan. When completed, these knowledge-based systems will be able to assist in quickly solving many problems that require days, months, or years with current technology. Application of current technology to problems in medicine, geology, and law have already demonstrated the principles and effectiveness of knowledge-based problem solving systems or limited artificial intelligence. Faster processors, improved problem statement and problem solving languages, together with data communications, have the potential of altering the world's current business and educational processes.

DRAWBACKS

Computers and communications networks also have their drawbacks. Criminals of the future may well need advanced degrees in computer science. As more and more of corporate and national finances are controlled and transferred via computers and data communications, the opportunities to illegally divert funds increase. Computer crime is often subtle and difficult to detect, at least by today's standards. The number of computer-related crimes appears to be increasing. Several large-scale crimes have already been detected and reported. An even larger number may have been detected but not reported, and others may have been committed without being detected. Without a significant increase in the implementation and enhancement of security systems, this trend can only be expected to continue.

Another negative potential of computers and data communications is the monitoring and possible control of individuals. As more of our cash or financial transactions are converted to on-line systems, the potential exists to more closely monitor the movements and activities of people—shades of science fiction.

EXPANDING JOB OPPORTUNITIES

Almost all industry forecasters predict continued growth in service industries, led by the computer industry. New and changing jobs will be available, and data communications should continue to lead this expansion. In the decade between 1974 and 1984, computer personnel with a knowledge of data communications systems were in demand and were among industry salary leaders. This trend is likely to continue into the 1990s.

DATA COMMUNICATIONS AND THE FUTURE

Computers and data communications bring a potential for social change equivalent to that wrought by the telephone and the automobile.

In the early 1900s, when the telephone industry was expanding and the switching of telephone calls was still largely manual, it was predicted that everybody would be working for the telephone company by the end of the century. This prediction has come true insofar as self-dialing of telephone numbers has made everyone a telephone operator. In the same way, everyone is likely to become an operator of computer equipment and a user of data communications equipment. Already there are many nations of bank tellers who use ATMs for deposits, withdrawals, and inquiries.

Telecommuting

Experiments with telecommuting have already begun, with people performing their jobs in the comfort of their own homes. The reviews on this experiment have been somewhat mixed, but the possibilities are immense. One Chicago company allows employees in certain job categories to work at home several days a week. Thus, a word processing operator could have a word processing system at home, with assignments transmitted by electronic mail or courier, and the operator able to structure the workday for convenience, the only objective being to get the work finished on time.

A valued programmer for a major computer company prefers the wilderness to the congestion of the city. Her employer provides her with a terminal and a communications link to the corporate system. She is able to make a contribution to the company, perform work that challenges her, and still maintain her preferred living environment. Of course, there is still a need for periodic personal discussions, so this programmer makes regular trips to the development center for project reviews and updates. Much routine dialogue, such as memos and messages, are delivered to the programmer via an electronic mail system.

This type of telecommuting is probably on the increase. Not only does it allow employees to more or less set their own pace and hours, it also enables additional qualified individuals to enter the job market. Parents who wish to continue working and also be at home with their children may be able to do both. There are also benefits for the employer. Potentially less office space would be required if some percentage of the staff were engaged in working in their homes. The possibility of remote work centers, close to the workers' homes, is also created. This would not only decrease commute time and expense, but it would also probably reduce the overall cost of office space, since urban offices tend to command higher prices than those in more remote settings.

There are disadvantages as well as advantages to telecommuting. Not all jobs lend themselves to this situation, and not all employees are suited to it. Some employees who had started telecommuting have reverted to a standard office work schedule because they missed getting out of the house, dressing in office attire, and socializing with other employees.

These are but a few of the possibilities that may reshape work and play. The potential is there, and most of the tools are in place. It is up to society and governments to see that these tools are used for the benefit of humankind and not to its detriment.

Index